A
Daily Routine for
Intellectual and Spiritual Hygiene

Fitness Training
For The Mind and Spirit

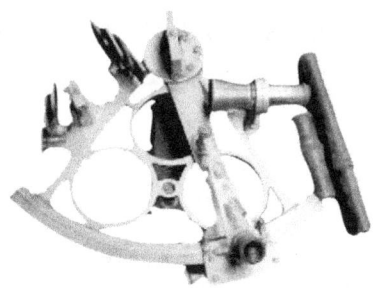

Volume Six

Philip M. Hudson

"Throw off the bowlines. Sail away from safe harbor.
Catch the wind in your sails. Explore. Dream. Discover."
(Mark Twain).

Copyright 2017 by Philip M. Hudson.
The book author retains sole copyright to his contributions to this book.

Published 2017.
Printed in the United States of America.

All rights reserved.

No portion of this book may be reproduced, stored in a retrieval system, or transmitted in any form or by any means – electronic, mechanical, photocopy, recording, scanning, or other – except for brief quotations in critical reviews or articles, without the prior written permission of the author.

ISBN 978-1-943650-42-2

Library of Congress Control Number 2017930768

This book was published by BookCrafters
Parker, Colorado.
www.bookcrafters.net

This book may be ordered from
www.bookcrafters.net
and other online bookstores.

Table of Contents

Acknowledgements……………………………………………………………………………1

Preface…………………………………………………………………………………………3

Introduction……………………………………………………………………………………9

Alphabetical List of Essays…………………………………………………………………15

Essays…………………………………………………………………………………………19

Author's Note………………………………………………………………………………427

Appendix One (List of Essays: Volumes 1 - 6)……………………………………………429

Appendix Two (Topical List of Essays: Volume 1- 6)……………………………………443

About the Author……………………………………………………………………………471

Also by the Author…………………………………………………………………………473

Acknowledgements

In these essays, I have attributed quotations to original authors whenever possible, as well as when I have editorialized their ideas. In many cases, however, my language will naturally reflect the teachings of leaders and members of The Church of Jesus Christ of Latter-day Saints.

The list of those who have contributed their ideas to these essays is endless. As I have collected my own thoughts, I have realized how heavily I have borrowed from the towering examples of those who, over the years, have been my mystical mentors, my sensible chaperones, my spiritual guides, my surrogate saviors, my compassionate critics, and everything in between. They are my avatars, the manifestations of deity in bodily forms, and my divine teachers incarnate. They have stretched my mind as they have shown me the way, reinforced my faith, strengthened my testimony, lifted my spirits, helped me to spread my wings, provided of their means, given immaterial support, emboldened me with words of encouragement, offered listening ears, cheered me on with wise counsel, taught me humility, been there to steady me, soothed my troubled soul, stepped in to nurture me, applied the balm of Gilead, wet my parched lips from fountains of living water, bound up my wounds, and extended open arms.

Every family member, teacher, student, classmate, business associate, mentor, friend, priesthood brother, relief society sister, ordinance worker, and temple patron with whom I have come in contact has influenced me. Every author, poet, journalist, essayist, thespian, satirist, and lyricist, has moved me in some positive way. They have taught me to find the silk purse in every sow's ear and the silver lining in every cloud. When I have been given a lemon, they have shown me how to find a recipe for lemonade.

From their positive influence, I have learned that there is so much good in the worst of us, and so much bad in the best of us, that it hardly behooves any of us to talk about the rest of us. I have done my best to keep tempests confined to the teapots where they belong, and to put the confusion of the world in perspective. I have tried to retain the joyful anticipation of the optimistic little boy, who, when faced with the daunting task of shoveling up an enormous pile of manure in a horse stall near his home, enthusiastically set about his task with the exclamation: "There's got to be a pony in there, somewhere!"

Long ago, well did the poet teach: "No man is an island, entire of itself. Every man is a piece of the continent, a part of the main. If a clod be washed away by the sea, Europe is the less, as well as if a promontory were, as well as if a manor of thy friends or of thine own were. Any man's death diminishes me, because I am involved in mankind, and therefore never send to know for whom the bell tolls. It tolls for thee." (John Donne).

When I think of the influence of a multitude of angels thinly disguised as my family, friends, and peers, I remember the words of Sir Isaac Newton, who, when pressed to reveal the great secret behind his accomplishments, simply replied: "I stood on the shoulders of giants." Of course, at the end of the day, I alone am responsible for the contents of this volume. But I hope my interpretations of doctrine will cultivate your interest to dig deeper into the themes woven into the tapestry of these essays by turning to the scriptures and seeking inspiration from the Spirit. My only goal is to help you to expand your insights into the telestial tips, the terrestrial truths, and the celestial certainties that I have attempted to embed within these essays.

Preface

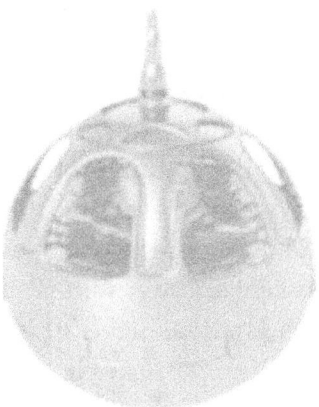

There may have been a selfish motivation for writing these essays, for whenever an intriguing idea strikes me, the wheels begin turning as my thinking revolves around it. I go to my conceptual wardrobe closet to see if my coat of many colors might brighten up the thoughts that do not seem to want to leave.

The coat to which I refer has been sewn by the Master Tailor Himself, and is an allegory for the fabric of my life, with each fiber individually selected and personalized to suit my circumstances. Taken as a whole, these yard goods represent, not the drab monochromatic, unimaginative, and featureless machinations of the world, but a true Technicolor Dream Coat that epitomizes the glories and riches of eternity awaiting those with inquiring minds. As my impressions begin to coalesce into a pattern, the polychromatic backdrop of the design that God has created for me begins to take shape, until it reaches a point where it stand out in sharp contrast to the grey-toned obstacles to my progression.

When I think about the inherent power of my coat of many colors to influence my grasp of the topography of the temporal terrain that stretches out before me, I remember something that Q said about the delights that await us, as we consider the cosmos of God's creations: "It's wondrous, with treasures to satiate desires both subtle and gross. But it's not for the timid." Then, he invited Jean Luc Picard to become something more than an armchair explorer, to move away from his comfort zone, and to embark upon a real journey of mind and spirit that would ultimately lead him to the edge of forever: "Con permiso, Capitan. The hall is rented, and the orchestra is engaged. It's now time to see if you can dance." ("Star Trek: The Next Generation," Episode 16, "Q Who").

Sometimes, it seems that we are fettered by a one-dimensional temporal reality and the parameters of a three-dimensional spatial world whose bounds and conditions are deterministic. If we are fortunate, however, the spirit nudges us away from the narrow confines of that telestial scale, and pushes us in the direction of our dreams. It is at these times, during my negotiation of treacherous terrain, that my coat becomes a cloak of comfort as well as a robe of responsibility. As the poet sagaciously observed: "My life is but a weaving between my God and me. I cannot choose the colors. He weaveth steadily. Oft' times He weaveth sorrow, and I in foolish pride, forget He sees the upper, and I, the underside. Not 'til the loom is silent and the shuttles cease to fly, will God unroll the canvas and reveal the reason why. The dark threads are as needful in the weaver's skillful hand, as the threads of gold and silver in the pattern He has planned." (B.M. Franklin).

We have received our coats of many colors as gifts from our Heavenly Father, and I invite you to discover their magic as you walk with me, through these essays, down the runway of life. Perhaps they will help us to appreciate His latest fall collection of ready-to-wear fashions. Inquiry was designed to be a memorable experience, precisely because God's carefully selected bolts of cloth have been cut to meet the palpable and esthetic needs of every exigency in our lives. The pattern of His Plan makes a sweeping sartorial statement, with enough room for growth to accommodate the full stature of our spirits.

The wide range of topics covered by these essays suggests that, although my coat fits me perfectly, it is not necessarily the one that would be best suited for you. But all have several things in common. They exhibit the same unmistakable evidence of impeccable tailoring, and when we wear them, we feel comfortably motivated, subtly inspired, gently refined, and spiritually satisfied. Our coats provide us with a shield of protection from both the winds of adversity and the wiles of the adversary. Their comfortable form and fit inspires us to honor our Father with obedience to correct principles. These essays reflect my appreciation for the endowment of opportunity that He has given us.

I hope that your coat will keep you snug and safe during your journeys, and that it may bless and keep you. I trust that His countenance will shine upon you, and bring you peace; "that your heart may be full, your life long, and your days as sweet as an Irish song." (Anonymous). May the topics addressed in these essays help you to appreciate the insulating quality of the materials utilized in the construction of your coat of many colors. If there are other outfits in your closet whose designs are after the similitude of the world, may you resolve to choose instead this modestly uplifting and complementary ensemble that projects a more realistic representation of your noble character. If you neglect your coat, you may find yourself no better off than the poor soul described by Sir Walter Scott, who, despite his "titles, power, and pelf, the wretch, concentered all in self, forfeit fair renown, and, doubly dying," went "down to the vile dust from whence he sprang, unwept, unhonored, and unsung." ("Lay of The Last Minstrel").

On the other hand, if you wear your coat with dignity, it will make a statement exceeding that of the cape worn by Superman, for its fabric has come, not from Krypton, but from Kolob. Its power thereby derived will be more than otherworldly, for its megastar status of the supernal is well-deserved. Its vibrant colors will infuse you with the strength of the Lord, and it will transform you. It will allow you to move faster than a speeding bullet, be more powerful than a locomotive, and empower you to leap tall buildings in a single bound. Your coat will endow you with a heavenly power to give strength to the poor and to the needy in distress, and to be "a refuge from the storm, (and) a shadow from the heat, when the blast of the terrible ones" rages against the solid sanctuary of your spiritual security and stability. (Isaiah 25:4). Make no mistake; it is your coat that will have kindled within you the fire for these noble deeds, and if these essays are consumed in the process, within that cauldron of conviction, commitment, and creation, they will have been consenting casualties.

If you desire attention, adrenaline, or the adoration of the world; if you are embarrassed by your coat, or if you are tempted to leave it hanging in the back of your wardrobe closet behind your more contemporary outfits, then attune your ear to our Father, Who quietly encourages you: "Be still, and know that I am God" (D&C 101:16). From the Book of Exodus, Aaron's example teaches us how to maximize the protection afforded by our coat of many colors. "And thou shalt bring Aaron and his sons unto the door of the tabernacle of the congregation, and wash them with water. And thou shalt put upon Aaron the holy garments, and anoint him, and sanctify him." (Exodus 42:12-13). From time immemorial, there has always been a coat of many colors provided by Heavenly Father that has been intended to shield each of His children from the power of the destroyer. The Prime Directive is embodied within its design and purpose, and that is to protect each of us from his evil influence, that we might finish our work on the earth to reach our potential without oppressive external influence or constraint.

These essays are intended to make it easier for you to charge your coat with enthusiasm, for the fire of God will be manifest to you by holy angels whose own garments have become pure and clean as the result of their comprehensive understanding of the power of the Atonement. This transformative process promises to likewise endow you with countenances that have become as lightning, and with glory beyond description. (See D&C 20:6 & J.S.H. 1:32).

Until we reach that exalted plane, however, we need all the help we can get, and I offer these essays as figurative fabric softeners. But, ultimately, it is the special handling and gentle touch of our Heavenly Father that will condition your coat with magical qualities. It is He who will provide spiritual swaddling clothing that resonates with an intrinsic light whose source is more than the pigment and dye that only superficially gives telestial tailoring its vibrancy. It is the guidance of God that permeates every element of the fabric of your being. That direction will be evident to even the most hardened skeptics, such as worldly Belshazzar, whose greeting to Daniel in his royal court betrayed his wonder and awe: "I have even heard of thee, that the spirit of the gods is in thee, and that light and understanding and excellent wisdom is found in thee." (Daniel 5:14). The king did not consciously realize it, but the power that he intuitively sensed in Daniel came from the prophet's coat of many colors that had been calibrated to a celestial scale by the hand of God. A gospel-centered lifestyle can transform us in the same way. These essays are only small pieces of the larger puzzles that permeate our lives, whose successful construction contributes to our religious recognition that "trailing clouds of glory do we come, from God, Who is our Home." (Wordsworth, "Ode: Intimations of Immortality").

The light of the Spirit gives vitality and vivacity to each individual thread in our coats. It provides the vim and vigor that are unique to holy vestments whose colors are fast and can only fade if we neglect to properly maintain them. Inasmuch as we do not defile them, but are true and faithful to the care instructions that are clearly printed on their labels, they will be shields of protection to us. But if we inadvertently or carelessly mingle our coats with profane clothing that has been soiled with the stain of sin, their powers of enchantment will be in jeopardy of being neutralized. They have been permanently pressed, so that even if we wear them throughout the day and well into the evening hours, they will never appear unkempt, but will always give the appearance of virtue, even as silk and purple. (See Proverbs 31:22).

Each of our individual coats has many colors that, like the images in a kaleidoscope, are continually evolving into even more intricate, delicate, and interconnected schematics. Just as a caterpillar miraculously emerges from its chrysalis as a butterfly, our coats become the very evidence of our awe-inspiring metamorphosis. Though we may have wandered forty years in the wilderness, our clothes are not waxen old upon us. (See Deuteronomy 29:5)

When that amazingly complex neural mechanism, our eye, is "single to the glory of God," our coat of many colors will be a delight to behold. (D&C 82:19). But the spiritual design of our vision is even more astounding. Psycho-physicists tell us that the human eye can distinguish around 10 million different colors, which is really quite remarkable, since there are only the three primary colors of red, green, and blue, in the visible light spectrum. Sir Isaac Newton, who was the first to use a prism to separate white light (at wavelengths between 390 and 700 nm) into its individual colors, divided the spectrum into red, orange, yellow, green, blue, indigo, and violet. The presence of myriad colors in our coats represents a wide range of latitude that makes them uniquely suited to meet our individual needs. For example, I am certain that for every twelve persons who read a particular essay within this volume, each of the color values that are described below will be weighted by subtle differences, causing them to be perceived from a dozen slightly dissimilar perspectives.

As you engage in your own subjective evaluations, I invite you to discover prevailing colors that touch you in personal and particular ways. Red might call you to action, and remind you that the Savior trod the winepress alone. Orange could be a warning to take care to conform your life to the Lord's design. Yellow will encourage you to seek the light that is gathering in the east. Green may bring to mind the power of envy, and your invitation to keep the 10th commandment. Perhaps blue will remind you to mourn with those that mourn, and to comfort those that stand in need. Indigo is a color that has such depth and brightness that it will surely represent the profundity of the gospel, and its ability to illuminate truth wherever it may be found. Violet is the color of amethyst, lavender and beauty-berries, and will certainly touch your spirit with a remembrance of the stunningly landscaped and impressively attended celestial garden of God.

Grey (black and white) is associated with neutrality, conformity, uncertainty, and indifference. It will prompt you to choose whom you will serve, and encourage you to stand on the Lord's side. Purple (red and blue) will urge you to remember the royal robes of Christ, our King. Black (blue, red, and yellow) will underscore the necessity of the opposition that stands out in sharp contrast to the pathway of your progression. White (red, orange, yellow, green, blue, indigo and violet) will solemnly suggest the ordinances of the priesthood, temple covenants, and the purity of the Spirit.

From ultraviolet to infrared, the 55 essays in this volume represent just a few of the colorful threads in my own coat that remind me of every nuance of visible light. It is my hope that the influence of the Spirit will help my thoughts to resonate with radiation, recognition, and revelation from within a much wider spectrum that encompasses the flush of faith, the tint of timelessness, and the blush of heaven. These are the qualities that can only be seen with eyes that have been attuned to Gods' magnificent palette.

I began this preface by suggesting that perhaps I had been motivated by selfishness when writing these essays. But I would prefer to believe that, in some small way, this anthology might provide a way to polish to an even higher luster the spiritual prism that enables each of us to sharpen our visual acuity, that we might comprehend the individual tracings of God's Plan for us. I have tried to touch on its design that has been stitched into the fabric of our coats of many colors, that every one of us might experience the visions of eternity for ourselves.

The real objective of these essays, then, is to help each of us, "by the power of the Spirit" to have eyes that might "see and understand the things of God." (D&C 76:12). That may seem ambitious, coming from one whose literary efforts have accomplished so little; nothing more, really, than hastily throwing together a few words between the covers of a book. But "with God all things are possible." (Mark 10:27). He works in mysterious ways, and these essays may remind you of His penchant to labor with the weakest of vessels. But I would willingly accept that characterization if it would help to strengthen your faith and testimony. "I had rather be a doorkeeper in the house of my God" than to receive the accolades or adoration of the world, although a Pulitzer Prize would be nice. (Psalms 84:10). At the very least, may these essays help to push open the portal that leads to your awareness of the seeds of greatness that lie within you.

Introduction

2009 was a banner year for huckleberries in the North Idaho Panhandle. My family picked dozens of gallons, and we enjoyed endless servings of huckleberry ice cream, pancakes, muffins, pies, brownies, and lemon bars, and put berries over fish, steak and poultry and even in peanut butter sandwiches and mashed potatoes. We froze enough berries to last through the fall, winter, and spring, and hoped that 2010 would produce another bumper crop.

Picking was a challenge, however, because the bushes were so heavily laden the supporting branches drooped almost to the ground, which made it difficult to see through the leaves. But lifting a branch would reveal twenty or thirty berries in each of several clusters. We sometimes plucked them one-by-one, but more often we just raked them in, as we have seen grizzly bears do many times in the Trapper Creek drainage, north of Upper Priest Lake.

Interspersed with the huckleberries, however, were a fair number of chokeberry bushes, equally endowed with fat berries of a slightly lighter hue, with a whitish powder on their surface, and a telltale "flare" on the underside, opposite the stem. To a casual observer, or to someone in a hurry to quickly pick as many berries as possible, it would be easy to mistake a chokeberry for a huckleberry. Sometimes, in the excitement of the moment, in our eagerness, or maybe because of overzealousness, a fair number of chokeberries inadvertently made it into our collection buckets.

Those who have salivated over the prospect of gobbling up handfuls of delicious huckleberries, but have instead crunched down on nasty chokeberries, know the feeling well. The difference in taste and texture is jolting, to say the least. Whereas a mouthful of plump huckleberries pops open between the teeth, releasing savory juices to wash over eager taste buds, a chokeberry is a completely different experience. It is bitter, astringent, and quite granular. To put it mildly, anyone who has inadvertently eaten a chokeberry when anticipating a huckleberry will understand the scripture that warns: "I will spue thee out of my mouth." (Revelation 3:26). They will recognize why the Spirit impressed upon Lehi, in a sweeping, panoramic vision of eternal life, the metaphor of fruit that was delicious to the taste, and very desirable. "And it came to pass," said Lehi, "that I did go forth and partake of the fruit thereof; and I beheld that it was most sweet, above all that I ever before tasted." (1 Nephi 8:11).

Learning about gospel doctrine can be like harvesting and enjoying huckleberries, because it is delicious to the taste and very desirable. We nurture and protect our developing comprehension that comes with personal illumination from the Spirit as zealously as we would our treasure troves of coveted berries. However, in our eagerness, we might inadvertently pick a few chokeberries that look very similar to huckleberries. Hopefully, our palate will be discriminating enough to be able to tell the difference between the two.

Sometimes, as we gather the ripe berries of gospel doctrine, a particularly appealing bush consumes an inordinate amount of our time, causing us to push aside other, equally productive plants. We ignore other easily accessible and appealing berries, as we concentrate solely on the find that had initially caught our attention. We are like the "merchant man, seeking" a tasty crop, "who, when he had found one" huckleberry "of great price, went and sold all that he had, and bought it." (Matthew 13:45-46). Sometimes, we prize our study of doctrine in the same way. A topic may be interesting because others have touched on its multifaceted applications, and because their perspective adds flavor to our daily routines of personal improvement that may have become tedious. Their fresh and exciting new approach induces us to make inordinate expenditures of energy to learn more, as we follow one particular path, to the exclusion of other equally productive avenues that would have also led to satisfying harvests.

That innocent tactic may be satisfying, but it can also be distracting. We need to remember to seek promised blessings that come from focusing on proven pathways of personal progress. We must rely on the Spirit for our primary source of inspiration. We certainly cannot allow an occasional chokeberry to deflect our concentration. Certainly, this book of essays will never take the place of dipping our cupped hands directly into the providently provided cool and refreshing fountain of living water in which the doctrinal huckleberries of the gospel are bobbing about.

At the end of the day, the way we spend our time in study is related to how we feel about huckleberries. A bucket full of just-picked berries speaks volumes to others; our harvest becomes the tangible expression of our efforts, and reveals our priorities. Those of us who have found a good patch of berries knows how difficult psychologically it can be to leave, especially when we have stumbled upon heavily laden bushes just as we were making our way back to the trailhead.

As we go about the business of finding the "Huckleberry Heaven" that is represented by our understanding by the Spirit of the principles of the gospel, we must never forget that this person's, or that person's, perspective is just another form of distraction. Doctrine is found in the scriptures and in the teachings of the prophets, who alone speak the will of the Lord, the mind of the Lord, the word of the Lord, the voice of the Lord, and the power of God unto salvation. (See D&C 68:4).

Those of us who pick huckleberries with a passion have made the activity a family tradition, and each season brings loved ones together for fellowship and an appreciation of the out-of-doors. Upon arrival at the patch whose location is a carefully guarded secret, we first allow fond memories from prior years' picking to wash over us, and then we get down to the business of adding new chapters to the book of our life experiences. I hope we can remember to bring these essays along on our outings, but that we will never confuse the journey for the destination.

We always want to make decisions that lead us to huckleberries, rather than to chokeberries. But sometimes, we are deceived into thinking that we are choosing wisely, when, in fact, we are not. Before even thinking about gorging ourselves on handfuls of berries, we need to make sure that the bush from which the bounty has come is what we believe it to be. If the deceptive allure of chokeberries overshadows our natural attraction to huckleberries, we might spend our time barking up the wrong bush. It goes without saying that I have zealously tried to make sure that no chokeberries have found their way into these essays. I have made every effort to keep my focus on the spiritual equivalents of huckleberries.

If you find that a few scattered chokeberries have been squashed within these pages, please do not allow their stain to undermine your overall trust in what I have written. I hope you will always be able to find spiritual sustenance as you read these essays. In them, I hope you will find enough huckleberries to garnish your daily fare of ice cream, pancakes, muffins, pies, brownies, lemon bars, fish, steak, poultry, peanut butter sandwiches, and mashed potatoes. I hope they will enliven your palate with the variety that is the spice of life.

I am well aware of Aesops' fable of "a wolf in sheep's clothing." Had he lived today in the North Idaho Panhandle, he might have entitled it: "Huckleberries and

Chokeberries." I hope these essays encourage you be about your Father' business on a strait and narrow path that leads directly to vast patches of huckleberries. I remember how Alice in Wonderland implored the Cheshire Cat: "Would you please tell me which way I ought to go from here?" "That depends a good deal on where you want to go," answered the cat. Alice acknowledged: " I admit, I don't much care where." To which the cat responded: "Then it doesn't matter which way you go." Alice begged: "Just so I go somewhere!" The cat purred: "Oh, you are sure to do that, if you only walk far enough." If we are careless in our study of principles and doctrines, we are likely to wander to and fro in our journey through life, and wind up with nothing more than a bucket full of chokeberries for our efforts, instead of the huckleberries that could have been our reward. I hope these essays can help you to stay on track, amid the distraction of chokeberry bushes that always seem to be in our peripheral vision, and jostling for our attention.

It is sometimes our inclination to settle for chokeberries even though we are well aware that they are only poor substitutes for the real thing. If we allow ourselves to fall into the rut of bad habits, we may become conditioned to the taste of bitter produce. We may even forget what it had been like to savor the fruit that is sweeter than anything we have ever experienced. It is that telestial desensitization to counterfeit substitutes that gets us in trouble, by accustomizing us to the bitterness of chokeberries. Of such a phenomenon, Alexander Pope wrote: Chokeberries "are of such a frightful mien, as to be hated, need but be seen. But seen too oft, familiar with her face, we first pity, then endure, and then embrace."

Too often, long after the picking season has ended, we may go to the freezer and pull out a bag full of berries, only vaguely aware that the harvest that we have carelessly preserved is nothing more than chokeberries. We expect that time will have somehow tempered their terrible taste and texture. I hope that those who read these essays are aware of the considerable effort that has gone into their creation to make sure that they faithfully reflect the doctrine of the kingdom; that each time this book is taken down from the shelf, a huckleberry experience cannot be far off.

When we content ourselves with chokeberries, we deny ourselves the unique and wonderful experience of enjoying a genuine Huckleberry Delight that has been carefully prepared by a celestial confectioner whose attention to every detail has been rigorously maintained. We satisfy ourselves with the bitter gall of its negative opposite. We may even become enthusiastically ignorant and invent elaborate fairy tales to justify our support of the chokeberry subdivision that is built on the outskirts of our cultural tradition. If we are always careful to nurture and build upon the fertile fields in which huckleberry bushes flourish, these essays will have fulfilled their purpose. That is to provide a solid foundation for our righteous application of principles and doctrine.

Isaiah prophesied that in the Last Days the branch of the Lord would "be beautiful and glorious (and) the fruit of the earth excellent and comely." (Isaiah 4:1). He foresaw that the Lord would provide us with every needful thing, with "every fruit in the season thereof." (D&C 89:11). He promises us gallons of ripe, plump, juicy, tart, visually appealing and tastefully satisfying huckleberries. In turn, I pledge to provide you with essays that are free of sticks, stems, leaves, and green berries, and of obnoxious, physically damaging, and spiritually compromising chokeberries. But I do not pretend to be the source of the huckleberries that I hope have been blended into these essays. They can only be provided by the Creator of heaven and earth and all that lies therein.

I believe that it was from the vantage point of Five Mile Ridge, high above Priest Lake, that Joshua declared: "Choose you this day whom ye will serve, but as for me and my house," we will brush aside the noxious chokeberries, and instead "serve the Lord" as we pick from the abundance of delightful huckleberries that have been scattered by our loving Father throughout the forest of life. (Joshua 24:15). For we know that we have been "planted in a goodly land, by a pure stream, that yieldeth much precious fruit." (D&C 97:9).

These essays are not the flourishing native plants that are descended from those that were cultivated by God on the third day of creation. (See Genesis 1:12-13). They are only my poor hybrid imitations of the organic non-GMO huckleberries that are the pure principles and unadulterated doctrines of the kingdom. I only hope to provide the motivation for you to grab your own picker, head into the woods, discover treasure troves of berries, and come to know for yourself how Lehi must have felt when he put forth his hand and partook of the mouth watering fruit of the Tree of Life.

Enjoy these essays, and receive them in the spirit in which they have been written. zI hope they will provide a small measure of assistance as you make your own journey to Christ along proven pathways that are well marked by inviting purple berries.

List of Essays

Reflections on Her Mission..19
Sealed For Time and For All Eternity...23
Service: Mission Reflections..29
Serving in The Temple...33
Sharing the gospel..39
Similitudes in Hosea...43
Snowbiking Through Life..47
Strengths and Weaknesses..59
Swiss Chocolate...65
Take My Yoke Upon You...67
Teachings of The Minor Prophets..71
Temple Blessings for All Mankind...77
The Bestowal of Spiritual Gifts...83
The Church Has Been Restored..101
The Creation..109
The Fall...113
The Germination of Our Faith..117
The Highways and Byways of Life..121
The Holy Ghost: Getting to Know Him..151
The Holy Grail of Religious Doctrine..163
The Hourglass of Life...165
The Light of The World...169
The Lord's Patient Protection and Affordable Health Care Act......................173

The Lord's Touchstone	177
The Mantle of The Prophet	183
The Martyr's Mirror	189
The New American Bible: Uninspired Version	193
The Number of The Disciples Was Multiplied	197
The Parable of The Hiawatha Trail	203
The Plan of Salvation: 15 Names	217
The Political Spotlight	223
The Power of Proverbs	235
The Priests of Baal in Our Lives	241
The Principle of Agency	247
The Prophet Joseph Smith: The Third of The Three Pillars of Testimony	251
The Sacrament	257
The Second Mile	267
The Seven Deadly Sins	275
The Strait and Narrow Path to Discipleship	287
The Tools of The Trade	295
The Twelve Tribes of Israel	307
The Unknown Possibilities of Existence	325
The Year Without Summer	329
Thoughts of Kolob	337
Thou Hast Done Wonderful Things	343
Tithing	347
Travel at The Speed of Thought	353
True Discipleship	359
Walk in The Light	363
We Ask Thee in Humility	369
What Think Ye of Christ?	379
William Tyndale: An Appreciation	389
Woe Unto You Hypocrites	409
Words of Mormon	413
Work and Personal Responsibility	423

The Savior is real. He loves
us. We must trust in Him, and have
faith in Him. Sadness, pain, discomfort, and
disappointment are so temporary in
this life. Yet, through Jesus
Christ, we can have
eternal joy.

Reflections on Her Mission:
Sister Joanna Hudson

Last night the moon was beautiful. I went out on the balcony to look at it, and just stared in awe. There is something about a full moon. Ralph Waldo Emerson said: "The man who has seen the rising moon break out of the clouds at midnight has been present like an archangel at the creation of light and of the world." I've always had a fascination with the heavens. From Albert Peak in British Columbia, to the rocky summit of Sinai, from under the delicate arches at Moab, to my M.T.C. window, I have learned much, spiritually, as I have stared into the cosmos and pondered life's mysteries.

On especially starry nights, I like to think of another Emerson observation: "If the stars should appear but one night in a thousand years, how would men believe and adore and preserve for many generations the remembrance of the city of God which had been shown." It has been a while since the weather has permitted me to gaze up into the heavens, but every now and then I catch a glimpse of the moon, and take a moment to appreciate it. Just by coincidence, earlier in the week I noticed on my calendar that last night there was to be a full moon.

After my bath, when I went to sit outside, I looked up and the sky was grey. No moon. I knew it was there, behind the clouds, but I couldn't see it! "Where is the moon?" I whispered out loud, almost as if talking to somebody. "Where is the moon?" That was a very symbolic moment for me, and as I continued to think about it, the Spirit taught me a lesson. I knew the moon was there, but it was hidden from my view. It was only my faith that assured me it was there.

I thought about my mission, and the message of hope that we carry to the world. I feel like I have been running around trying to get people to look up, to see not only the moon and its beauty, but also to "gaze into the heavens" and to learn more about our Father's Plan for them. But they just don't want to believe it's there. And besides, when they finally do look up, sometimes all they see is a gray covering of clouds.

We have to walk by faith in this life. Clouds do come, and then we have to simply trust in the Lord. We are here on earth to be tried, to prove ourselves worthy of our Heavenly Father's blessings. When we show Him that we believe, and that we have trust in Him, He will send the wind to blow away the clouds that have obscured our vision. It is only after the trial of our faith that the witness comes. I am trying to understand that better, and at the same time trying to help those whom I teach to understand it, as well.

The important thing is to remember that the Savior is there. He is real. He loves us. We must trust in Him, and have faith in Him. Sadness, pain, discomfort, and disappointment are so temporary in this life. Yet through Jesus Christ we can have eternal joy.

"Look death in the face with joyful hope, and consider this a lasting truth: The righteous man has nothing to fear, neither in life nor in death, and the gods will not forsake him."
(Socrates).

Sealed for Time
and For All Eternity

Hugh Nibley described the temple as the place where we go to get our bearings on eternity. He also said, on one occasion, that if he didn't learn something new every time he attended the temple, he'd stop going, and he continued to go once a week throughout his life. He went, because "the temple becomes a school of instruction in the sweet and sacred things of God. Here we have outlined the plan of a loving Father in behalf of His sons and daughters of all generations. Here we have sketched before us the odyssey of man's eternal journey from premortal existence through this life to the life beyond. Great fundamental and basic truths are taught with clarity and simplicity well within the understanding of all who hear." (Gordon B. Hinckley, "Ensign," 3/1993).

Initially, Brother Nibley went to receive his endowment, just as we all do, "to receive all those ordinances in the house of the Lord, which are necessary for you, after you have departed this life, to enable you to walk back to the presence of the Father." (Brigham Young, D.B.Y., p. 416, see D&C 124:39). He went, because the Lord has arranged in His church that we learn about Him and our Father in Heaven through the commandments and ordinances. He went to make covenants relating to morality, charity, discipline, stewardship, sacrifice and consecration. Most importantly, he went to make covenants relating to marriage that is ordained of God.

Eternal marriage is essential to Heavenly Father's Plan. There are at least 14 descriptions of the Plan in The Book of Mormon, including The Merciful Plan of the Great Creator (2 Nephi 9:6), The Plan of our God (2 Nephi 9:13), The Great and Eternal Plan of Deliverance from Death (2 Nephi 11:5), The Plan of Redemption (Alma 12:25), The Plan of Salvation (Alma 24:14), The Great Plan of the Eternal God (Alma 34:9), The Great and Eternal Plan of Redemption (Alma 34:16), The Great Plan of Redemption (Alma 34:31), The Plan of Restoration (Alma 41:1), The Great Plan of Salvation (Alma 42:5), The Great Plan of Happiness (Alma 42:8), The Plan of Mercy (Alma 42:15), The Plan of Happiness (Alma 42:16), and The Great Plan of Mercy (Alma 42:31).

All of these relate to our happiness, which "is the object and design of our existence, and will be the end thereof, if we pursue the path that leads to it, and this path is virtue, uprightness, faithfulness, holiness, and keeping all the commandments of

God." (Joseph Smith, "Teachings," p. 255). Our temple covenants address each of these virtues.

We learn about the covenant of eternal marriage in D&C Sections 131 & 132. Parley P. Pratt, one of the original members of the Quorum of the Twelve in this dispensation, recalled his feelings when he first heard the Prophet Joseph teach these doctrines. "I had loved before, but I knew not why. But now I love with a pureness, an intensity of elevated, exalted feeling, which would lift my soul. I felt that God was my Heavenly Father indeed; that Jesus was my Brother, and that the wife of my bosom was an immortal, eternal companion. In short, I could now love with the spirit and with understanding also." ("Autobiography of Parley P. Pratt," p. 298).

Marriage is an essential part of God's eternal plan because "in the celestial glory there are three heavens or degrees; And in order to obtain the highest, a man must enter into this order of the priesthood (meaning the new and everlasting covenant of marriage); And if he does not, he cannot obtain it. He may enter into the other, but that is the end of his kingdom; he cannot have an increase." (D&C 131:1-4). As Paul taught: "Neither is the man without the woman, neither the woman without the man, in the Lord." (1 Corinthians 11:11).

The Plan of Salvation cannot succeed without marriage ordained of God. Joseph B. Wirthlin said: "The sweet companionship of eternal marriage is one of the greatest blessings God has granted to His children. Certainly, the many years I have shared with my beautiful companion have brought me the deepest joys of my life. From the beginning of time, marital companionship of husband and wife has been fundamental to our Heavenly Father's great plan of happiness. Our lives are touched for good, and we are both edified and ennobled as we savor the sweet blessings of association with dear members of the family." (C.R., 10/1997).

Boyd K. Packer taught: "The ultimate purpose of all we teach is to unite parents and children in faith in the Lord Jesus Christ, that they are happy at home, sealed in an eternal marriage, linked to their generations, and assured of exaltation in the presence of our Heavenly Father." ("Ensign," 5/1995). Joseph Fielding Smith said: "Marriage is the foundation for eternal exaltation, for without it there could be no eternal progress in the kingdom of God." ("Doctrines of Salvation," 2:58).

According to the doctrine of the church, if a husband and wife are not married in the temple, the status of their marriage when one of them dies is in grave jeopardy. "The conditions of God's law are these: All covenants, contracts, bonds, obligations, oaths, vows, performances, connections, associations, or expectations, that are not made and entered into and sealed by the Holy Spirit of Promise…are of no efficacy, virtue, or force in and after the resurrection from the dead; for all contracts that are not made unto this end have an end when men are dead." (D&C 132:7).

"Therefore, if a man marry him a wife in the world, and he marry her not by me nor by my word, and he covenant with her so long as he is in the world and she with him…they are not bound by any law when they are out of the world. …They cannot, therefore, inherit my glory; for my house is a house of order, saith the Lord God." (D&C 132:15 & 18).

Temple marriage and our eternal progress involve making covenants with the Lord. Promised blessings include being together "in time, and through all eternity" (D&C 132:19), being exalted in the highest degree of glory in the Celestial Kingdom with Heavenly Father and Jesus Christ (D&C 131:1-3, & 132:23-24), inheriting "thrones, kingdoms, principalities…powers, (and) dominions" (D&C 132:19), having children in the eternities (D&C 132:19, & 30-31), and "enjoying divine attributes, (and) becoming as "gods, because (we) have all power." (D&C 132:20-21).

God is our Father, and He is perfect in every way. He could give us everything He has, but what He is, we must earn for ourselves, as we struggle to overcome adversity and gain self-mastery. Ordinances that focus on covenants help us in our efforts to become as He is. This is their purpose. If it were not possible to become as God is, covenants would be unnecessary.

Temple marriage is strikingly different from its worldly counterparts. Perhaps, this is why Gordon B. Hinckley counseled: "Choose a companion of your own faith. You are much more likely to be happy. Choose a companion you can always honor, you can always respect, one who will complement you in your own life, one to whom you can give your entire heart, your entire love, your entire allegiance, your entire loyalty." ("Ensign," 2/1999).

Richard G. Scott said: "There is more to a foundation of eternal marriage than a pretty face or an attractive figure. There is more to consider than popularity or charisma. As you seek an eternal companion, look for someone who is developing the essential attributes that bring happiness: a deep love of the Lord and of His commandments, a determination to live them, one that is kindly understanding, forgiving of others, and willing to give of self, with the desire to have a family crowned with beautiful children and a commitment to teach them the principles of truth in the home.

An essential priority of a prospective wife is the desire to be a wife and mother.

She should be developing the sacred qualities that God has given His daughters to excel in their ordained character traits: patience, kindliness, a love of children, and a desire to care for them rather than seeking professional pursuits. She should be acquiring a good education to prepare for the demands of motherhood.

A prospective husband should also honor his priesthood and use it in service to others. He should accept his role as a provider of the necessities of life, be one with the capacity to do it, while making concerted efforts to prepare himself to fulfill those responsibilities." (C.R., 4/1999).

When a man and woman are sealed in the temple, they will receive the promised blessings only if they "abide in (the) covenant." (D&C 132:19). "I was just sure the first ten years would be bliss. But during our first year together I discovered…there were a lot of adjustments. Of course, they weren't the kind of thing you ran home to mother about. But I cried into my pillow now and again. The problems were almost always related to learning to live on someone else's schedule and to do things someone else's way. We loved each other; there was no doubt about that. But we also had to get used to each other. I think every couple has to get used to each other." (Marjorie P. Hinckley, "The Biography of Gordon B. Hinckley," p. 118).

It takes love, work, and dedication to have a successful marriage. As a husband and wife abide in the covenant, they are fiercely loyal to each other. My wife Jan, for example, is the rudder of my ship, guiding me past unseen rocks and reefs. She is my helm, holding steady when winds of adversity blow. She is my telltale, alerting me to impending storms. She is my keel, helping me to move against the current and the wind. She is my mainsheet, holding firmly with just enough pressure to prevent me from capsizing when I am recklessly heeled over. She is my safety-line, providing security when my footing is unsure and the foaming sea is streaming across my deck. She is my compass, showing me the way, especially when the course is unclear. She is my chart, warning me of hidden dangers. She is my barometer, alerting me to impending storms. She is my lookout, standing as my sentinel when I am distracted by trivial concerns. She holds the line that trails in my wake, to rescue me should I fall overboard. She is the wind that fills my sails. We may be partners, but she is my better half.

We look up to a God
Who loves us so much, Whose
outstretched hands are there to bring
us into the warmth of His bosom,
and to turn us into instruments
that can bless the lives of
our fellow travelers.

Service:
Mission Reflections
of Sister Joanna Hudson

This is a world of constant extraction and absorption; a spiritual blood draw and a transfusion all rolled into one. I'm learning that the only way we can increase our strength is to give away that which we have received. I have realized that at the end of the days when I expend the least amount of energy serving others I am the most tired, and it is on the days when I serve my heart out that I feel so rejuvenated.

I have loved working with the people in Belgium. As I have served them, my desire to be better has been strengthened. Service is not the price we pay to get to the Celestial Kingdom. It is the very fabric of which it is made.

More than ever before, on my mission I have looked to Christ as my example. Unselfishness marked His every action. Personal pleasures and comfort came last, if at all. He spent His ministry serving others. As great as was His suffering on the cross and in Gethsemane, I am touched by His example just hours before His appointed time. As He explained to one disciple who wanted to join Him, "Foxes have holes, and birds of the air have nests; but the Son of man hath no where to lay his head." (Luke 9:58).

Prior to His birth, during His mortal ministry, and in the eternities, the Savior has continued to give. His love for us is infinite. To feel that love is one of our greatest blessings. To feel that same quality of love for Him, to begin to have just a hint of that capacity, is yet another blessing. To feel that love for all of our brothers and sisters is the ultimate goal. Until we have the pure love of Christ, our love of the Savior is incomplete. We gain this love in small increments that are directly related to giving service to others.

The Savior is not looking forward to retirement and relaxation. He is, and will be throughout eternity, looking for new opportunities to serve. We see this philosophy in action, as He came to the earth to live in much less comfortable circumstances than those to which we are accustomed. During His ministry, He thought only of others. While here, He experienced all that we experience and more.

I love my mission because it allows me to join the Savior in His work to bring to pass our immortality and eternal life. I am grateful for it all; not only for the joy and the incredible happiness, but even for the heartache and frustration. Through it all, I have come to know my Savior. As we seek to become purified and sanctified as we move along the pathway that leads to exaltation, we must all pass through our own Gethsemane, the refiner's fire, so that our spirits will be malleable and ductile in the hands of the Lord. I know this holds true especially during a mission. We are asked to follow the road less traveled. Sometimes it hurts. But we look up to a God who loves us so much, whose outstretched hands are there to bring us into the warmth of His bosom, and Who turns us into instruments that can bless the lives of our fellow travelers.

"I have received the holy anointing, and I
can never rest until the last enemy is
conquered, death destroyed, and
truth reigns triumphant."
(Parley P. Pratt).

Serving
in The Temple

Many of us have served in teaching capacities or in administrative positions that are oriented toward redemptive practices that encourage and provide support to members of the church who are struggling with the trials and temptations of life. These can be emotionally exhausting, and satisfactory solutions can be elusive.

In the temple, however, we deal with members of the church who grapple with these same challenges, but who have somehow made the transition from hesitancy to conviction, from instability to commitment, from timidity to confidence, from indecision to resolution, from doubt to certainty, from struggle to celebration, from vacillation to purpose, and from spiritual itinerancy to moral discipline.

Temple patrons take commitment to a new level. They redefine dedication. They exercise their duties and responsibilities in ways that are truly selfless. The gospel has transformed their lives. They are as the people of Zarahemla, who declared to King Benjamin: "The Spirit of the Lord Omnipotent…has wrought a mighty change in us, or in our hearts, that we have no more disposition to do evil, but to do good continually." (Mosiah 5:2).

King Benjamin could have been speaking of temple patrons, when he said: "Because of the covenant which (they) have made (they) shall be called the children of Christ, his sons, and his daughters; for behold, this day he hath spiritually begotten (them); for (they) say that (their) hearts are changed through faith on his name; therefore, (they) are born of him and have become his sons and his daughters." (Mosiah 5:7).

Nothing that takes place in the temple directly benefits its patrons. Their service is wholly, completely, and unequivocally in behalf of those who have passed beyond the veil, and it is through their efforts that those who might have otherwise been forgotten are clothed in the robes of the holy priesthood and are ushered through the veil into the presence of the Lord. In the process of a holy anointing, they are endowed with the power to come forth in the Morning of the First Resurrection, as kings and priests, queens and priestesses, destined to rule and rein in the House of Israel forever. The ordinances of the temple commemorate and celebrate lives that would have otherwise remained everlastingly incomplete. These ordinances impart dignity, nobility, and worth to every one of Heavenly Father's children, and insure that their memory will not be trivialized, and that none of them will be neglected, overlooked, or forgotten. These ordinances reassure us that when the process of securing their eternal legacy has been completed, there will be no gaps in their family history, and that no names will be missing from the book of life that has been carefully compiled by the angels in heaven. It is because of the temple that we can take God at His word, when He declares: "This is my work and my glory, to bring to pass the immortality and eternal life of man." (Moses 1:39).

This may be why Alma's descriptions of the Plan of Salvation were so expansive. Like so many of us, he had seen life from both sides of the fence, and was effusive in his desire to share his joy with others. He envisioned the Merciful Plan of The Great Creator as His vehicle to generate a celestial spark with a capacity for combustion, that our souls might be saved. (See 2 Nephi 9:6). The Plan of our God testifies that Heavenly Father is the Author of our eternal life and exaltation. (See 2 Nephi 9:13). The Great and Eternal Plan of Deliverance from Death speaks to the doctrine that it was clearly explained before we came here, that the death of our mortal bodies would propel our spirits forward toward unimagined opportunities. It testifies that when Adam was sent into the Garden of Eden, it was with the understanding that he would violate or transgress God's law in order to bring to pass our mortality, our immortality, and our eternal life. (See 2 Nephi 11:5). The Plan of Salvation would become a Plan of Redemption, a Plan of Mercy, and a Plan of Happiness, paving the way for the resurrection of otherwise imperfect mortals to an eternal life of glory. (See Alma 24:14). It would allow God to be both just and merciful at the same time. We see this in the symbolism of the cherubim and a flaming sword that guarded the way to the tree of life. (See Moses 4:31). They satisfied an eternal purpose, and were only the first of many gifts that our Heavenly Father promised our mortal parents.

None of us can hope to find meaning in our lives if we treat these integral elements of the Plan superficially, or if we regard the ordinances of the temple carelessly. Their conscious appreciation must be earned. If we take them for granted or if we abandon the core principles they represent, their power to bless our lives may slip away and be lost forever. While the Plan guarantees free will, it also gives us wide latitude to use our agency inappropriately to make poor choices. The temple provides us with currency sufficient for our needs, but the Plan of which it is an integral part also allows us to substitute for legal tender wads of counterfeit cash with which late payments may be made with interest tacked on for bad behavior. If we attempt to subvert the Plan by turning our backs on the blessings that could have been ours through the ordinances of the temple, our futile and destabilizing efforts to obtain and retain opportunities that we do not deserve, will reward us with a pyrrhic victory at best.

The "great and eternal purposes of God," Whose Plan is dramatically articulated in the temple, "were prepared from the foundation of the world." (Alma 42:26). The Great Plan of Redemption, (Alma 34:31), that is beautifully illustrated in the ordinance of the temple endowment, required that "an Atonement should be made; therefore, God Himself atoneth for the sins of the world, to bring about the Plan of Mercy, to appease the demands of justice, that God might be a perfect, just God, and a merciful God also." (Alma 42:15). The Atonement allowed God to satisfy justice and still mercifully reclaim us from physical and spiritual death. The Savior thus became the Master of the situation. In His sacrifice, the debt would be paid, redemption made, the covenant fulfilled, justice satisfied, the will of God done, and all power, including the keys of resurrection, would be given to the Son.

The Plan of Restoration (Alma 41:2), clearly teaches that the purpose of the Fall was to give us the opportunity to experience mortality in order to prepare for a resurrection. "And we see that death comes upon mankind, yea, the death which has been spoken of by Amulek, which is the temporal death; nevertheless there was a space granted unto man in which he might repent; therefore, this life became a probationary state; a time to prepare to meet God; a time to prepare for that endless state which has been spoken of by us, which is after the resurrection of the dead." (Alma 12:24). Through the Atonement, we would be raised in the resurrection, impeccably clothed in exactly the kinds of bodies needed to dwell in the degree of glory in which we would feel most comfortable.

Into every ordinance of the temple are woven the principles of the Great Plan of Salvation. (Alma 42:5). Without their light, we are doomed to suffer in shadows where we experience only the indistinct flicker of illusions and caricatures of reality. The discrepancy between marginalized behavior and the ideals of the temple are readily apparent to its patrons, and are addressed by the covenants they make at sacred altars. These covenants stand in contrast to the short-lived pleasure in worldly ways that must evaporate as the morning dew in the full light of day. Obedience to our covenants mitigates the unfortunate consequences that would otherwise inevitably occur when disobedience to correct principles reaches "critical mass." In the experience of every individual whose life is not in harmony with the Plan, there comes a point when a requisite readjustment must tear down the façade of corruption and hypocrisy. As painful as the process may be, it is necessary to allow the cultivation of a more nurturing lifestyle made possible by embracing special promises made with God. To have this assurance is one of the great blessings of temple worship.

The principles of The Great Plan of Happiness (Alma 42:8), are the threads in the coat of many colors that temple patrons wear as their daily vestments. Alma taught that in the absence of repentance for our sins, and without the benefit of the gospel Plan of Salvation, we must ultimately remain in a wretched state. "And now behold, if it were possible that our first parents could have gone forth and partaken of the tree of life they would have been forever miserable, having no preparatory state; and thus the Plan of Redemption would have been frustrated, and the word of God would have been void, taking none effect." (Alma 12:26). Without a Redeemer to atone for their sins, if Adam and Eve were to have partaken of the fruit of the tree of life, which is eternal life, it would have been impossible for them to sustain a celestial existence. Left in their fallen state with no avenue of escape, they would have been incapable of obedience to celestial principles, and would have lived forever in their sins. Thus, the Plan of Salvation, and the purpose of temples, would have been frustrated.

We learn in the temple that we came into this world to die, but at the same time we also learn about the Plan of Mercy. (Alma 42:25). Alma explained: "If it had been possible for Adam to have partaken of the fruit of the tree of life at that time, there would have been no death, and the word would have been void, making God a liar, for he said: If thou eat thou shalt surely die." (Alma 12:23).

The cherubim that God placed before the Tree of Life to guard the way guaranteed that the Plan of Salvation would not be frustrated. In fact, it would instead become The Plan of Happiness. (Alma 42:16). "For behold, if Adam had put forth his hand immediately, and partaken of the tree of life, he would have lived forever, according to the word of God, having no space for repentance." (Alma 42:5). This would have posed an immediate problem. Because of his transgression in the Garden, the flaming sword of justice demanded that "man became lost forever, yea, they became fallen man. And now, ye see by this that our first parents were cut off both temporally and spiritually from the presence of the Lord." (Alma 42:6-7). So it was, that "they became subject to follow after their own will." The crowning principle of agency was to be honored, even if it meant that justice must be served. Therefore, "it was appointed unto man to die" (Alma 42:6), rather than to reclaim him "from this temporal death, for that would destroy the Great Plan of Happiness." (Alma 42:8).

As it turns out, the Great Plan of Mercy (Alma 42:31), symbolized by cherubim, confronts Justice with an equal and opposing force, giving us the opportunity to live our lives, push the envelope, and take justifiable risks. When we fail to measure up to the requirements of eternal laws, and Justice demands that we suffer the consequences, Jesus Christ stands ready to intervene in our behalf, as He promised to do at the Council. If we Recognize our mistakes, if we experience Remorse for having made them, if we attempt to make Restitution if our behavior has wronged others, if we learn from our mistakes and Reform our ways, and Resolve to Refrain from Repeating them, His Atonement will allow us to continue along the path of progress, with a complete Resolution of what would have otherwise been incapacitating shortcomings.

Possibly reflecting on his temple experiences, and recognizing the power of its ordinances, Parley P. Pratt exclaimed: "I have received the holy anointing, and I can never rest until the last enemy is conquered, death destroyed, and truth reigns triumphant." (J.D., 1:15). Elder Pratt's joy was full, because he had complete confidence in the capacity of the Great Plan of Mercy to redeem him from his sins, and propel him toward his celestial destiny.

Those who have been set apart to perform temple ordinances regularly enjoy sacred experiences, including singing the hymns of the Restoration and bearing testimony to each other in the ordinance rooms prior to the opening of the temple to its patrons. They receive recurring instruction from the temple presidency. They have the privilege of pronouncing initiatory ordinances, of officiating in the endowment, of kneeling at sacred altars, of lending their voices to the expressions of thanksgiving in the order of prayer, and of assisting patrons at the veil. They regularly enjoy the quiet serenity of the celestial room, of the sealing rooms, and of the baptistry.

When, with temple patrons, they bring their right arm to the square to make sacred covenants with God, the Spirit quietly confirms that "happiness is the object and design of our existence, and will be the end thereof, if we pursue the path that leads to it, and this path is virtue, uprightness, faithfulness, holiness, and keeping all the commandments of God." (Joseph Smith, "Teachings," p. 255).

The Lord has created
a wonderful program designed
to bring family exaltation within reach
of all of His children. It is called "Sharing the
gospel." But missionary work is not easy,
because as it turns out, "salvation
is not a cheap experience."
(Dallin Oaks).

Sharing The Gospel

Our reluctance to share the gospel also has something to do with timidity, which is ironic, because the powerful exhortation of Paul resonates within us. While a prisoner for the truth's sake in Rome, he declared: "I am not ashamed of the gospel of Christ: for it is the power of God unto salvation to every one that believeth." (Romans 1:16). At one time or another, many of us have had similar missionary zeal. But we may have lost that fire in our belly. Parley P. Pratt never did. He exclaimed: "I have received the holy anointing and I can never rest, till the last enemy is conquered, death destroyed, and truth reigns triumphant." (J.D., 1:15).

Perhaps we could re-acquire that fervor if we would adjust our attitudes a bit. Maybe we could be missionaries by simply teaching correct principles and by being more aware of the example we are setting. If we could be undeviatingly true to ourselves, we could be false to no man. (Shakespeare, "Hamlet," Act 1, Scene 3). Perhaps missionary work is nothing more complicated than loving others as ourselves. (See Mark 12:31). After all, we do missionary work because God loves his children. If we just learn to love as He does, and if we live to learn, we'll love to live, and our charity will become infectious.

Perhaps we need to pay more attention to our own testimonies, and do a better job of nurturing them. On a daily basis, we might need to find a thermometer with which to take our own testimony temperature. Perhaps, if we put our hand to our forehead, we might detect its feverish pitch. As Alma asked: "Have ye spiritually been born of God? Have ye received his image in your countenances? Have ye experienced this mighty change in your hearts?" (Alma 5:14). "I say unto you, my brethren, if ye have experienced a change of heart, and if ye have felt to sing the song of redeeming love, I would ask, can ye feel so now?" (Alma 5:26).

We might need to step back, inhale deeply, take time, and prioritize the items on our busy agendas. Missionaries typically tithe their time. What if we were to dedicate 10% of our waking hours to the service of the Lord? What if we were to serve more energetically, and pray with greater specificity. Ninety five percent of the members of the church do not pray for missionary opportunities. Five percent of the members of the church do. That five percent has ninety five percent of the missionary opportunities. Do you think the Lord is trying to tell us something?

We need to take the time to invite our neighbors to church activities or meetings, and to welcome them into our homes. We need to have real gospel conversations with them. Of course, we need to strive to obtain the Spirit, acquire humility, love the people, and work diligently. If we are waiting for spectacular results, we may need to ratchet down our expectations, and pay closer attention to the constant flow of revealed communication that comes from the Holy Ghost, that guides us into the warm embrace of daily spiritual experiences, and introduces our friends and neighbors to that same undiscovered country.

We need to act upon our spiritual promptings, for proper prior planning will prevent poor priesthood performance. As Spencer W. Kimball taught: "We have paused on some plateaus long enough. Let us resume our journey forward and upward, and quietly put an end to our reluctance to reach out to others, whether in our own families, wards, or neighborhoods. We have been diverted at times from fundamentals on which we must now focus, in order to move forward as a person or as a people."(C.R., 4/1979). Gordon B. Hinckley re-affirmed: "The church cannot hope to save a man on Sunday, if during the week it is a complacent witness to the destruction of his soul." ("Helping Others to Help Themselves: The Story of The Mormon Church Welfare Program," p. 4). Rather than only taking the glowing embers of a gospel centered life out into the world, we need to bring others into the crackling fire of a church that resonates with the eternal burnings of the Kingdom of God.

Most of us have enjoyed the delicious texture and flavor of Swiss chocolate. If we hold up a poster of an assortment of Lindt chocolates and show it to our friends, they may or may not be inclined to try a piece for themselves. If we actually show them a real piece of chocolate, we might catch their interest, and they might begin to salivate with the stirrings of hopeful anticipation. But, in our enthusiasm, if we unwrap a piece before their eyes, and pop it into our own mouths, and then try to describe how wonderful it tastes, they might be disappointed and be underwhelmed by our gesture. They might even think it insincere or disingenuous. However, what if we were to take a piece of chocolate that had their name written upon it, and we unwrapped it with them, and on our open palms presented it to them, and then allowed them to savor it for themselves, encouraging them to roll it over and over on their tongues while it slowly and deliciously melted in their mouths? Better yet, what if we were to share in their gustatory delight, and enjoy a similar piece of chocolate with them? How much easier and more fluid would be our expressions relating to a life that was enriched by Swiss chocolate. If we further augmented their sensory delight with words of encouragement, their experience might expand to new proportions, and they would almost certainly forevermore enthusiastically endorse and desire, and perhaps even crave, Swiss chocolate. They might even be willing to pay a premium, just to relive the experience. From that day on, they might be hooked on Swiss chocolate.

Nearly everyone has a "sweet tooth," something that really hits their hot button and gets their juices flowing. For the two disciples on the Road to Emmaus, it was the Spirit. After their personal encounter with the resurrected Lord, one said to the other: "Did not our heart burn within us, while he talked with us by the way, and while he opened to us the scriptures?" (Luke 24:32). We do not know what happened to these travelers, but we can be sure that their lives were thereafter never the same. When we allow the Spirit to guide us with tailor-made messages to our friends and neighbors, sooner or later they will be moved upon to wash their flesh in water and put on holy garments, that they might be prepared to enjoy the delight of the Swiss Chocolate that is the gospel. (See Leviticus 16:4).

Many of the prophets, including Hosea,
have used similitudes, literary devices that involve
comparing complicated or unfamiliar ideas with those
that are simpler, making them more understandable to the
people who are being taught. These comparisons help
provide detail in a few words, just as similes and
metaphors do in contemporary writing.

Similitudes in Hosea

Hosea wrote: "The children of Israel shall be as the sand of the sea." (Hosea 1:10). "I will pour out my wrath upon them like water." (Hosea 5:10). "The Lord ... shall come unto us as the rain." (Hosea 6:3). "He shall come as an eagle." (Hosea 8:1). "Israel is an empty vine." (Hosea 10:1). "Judgment springeth up as hemlock in the furrows of the field." (Hosea 10:4). "They shall be...as the smoke out of the chimney." (Hosea 3:3). "I will meet them as a bear that is bereaved of her whelps." Hosea 13:8). "I am like a green fir tree." (Hosea 14:8).

One of the most frequently used scriptural similitudes describes the Lord as a bridegroom (or husband) and his covenant people as his bride (or wife). In the book of Hosea, the Lord's relationship with Israel, and by extension, with the church today, is compared to the relationship between a husband and wife. The prophet's comparisons teach us about the level of commitment and devotion the Lord expects from us.

Hosea powerfully used a similitude when he compared Israel's idol worship to adultery. In his writings, the prophet represented the Lord as the husband, and Israel as Gomer, the wife. Gomer is described as "a wife of whoredoms" who had left her husband for her lovers. In other words, Israel had forgotten the Lord and had become wicked. (Hosea 1:2-3).

Israel's "lovers," or the things that caused the people to turn away from the Lord, were other gods, material goods, and the practices of the world. For example, the adulterous wife gave credit for her food and clothing to her lovers who had given her bread, water, wool, flax, mine oil, and drink. (See Hosea 2:5).

In Hosea's similitude, the husband reminded his wife that it was he, and not her lovers, who had supplied her with all of her material goods. Did she "not know that I gave her corn and wine, and oil, and multiplied her silver and gold?" he asked. (Hosea 2:8-9).

The attitude of the husband toward his unfaithful wife was clear: "Therefore, behold, I will hedge up thy way with thorns, and make a wall, that she shall not find her paths. And she shall follow after her lovers, but she shall not overtake them; and she shall seek them, but shall not find them: then shall she say, I will go and return to my first husband, for then was it better with me than now." (Hosea 2:6-7).

Even though his wife had been unfaithful, the husband still loved her and wanted her to come back to him. Likewise, the Lord still loves His people who have gone astray, and wants them to turn again to Him. "I will have mercy upon her that had not obtained mercy; and I will say to them which were not my people, Thou art my people; and they shall say, Thou art my God." (Hosea 2:23).

Henry B. Eyring explained: "This was a story (about) a marriage covenant bound by steadfast love. The Lord, with whom I am blessed to have made covenants, loves me, and you, with a steadfastness about which I continually marvel, and which I want with all my heart to emulate." (B.Y.U. Address, 8/15/1995).

If his wife would return to him, the husband promised: "I will betroth thee unto me for ever; yea, I will betroth thee unto me in righteousness, and in judgment, and in loving kindness, and in mercies." (Hosea 2:19). If they would repent and return to him, the Lord promised: "I will even betroth thee unto me in faithfulness: and thou shalt know the Lord." (Hosea 2:20).

In Old Testament cultures, women were often considered property, and could be bought or sold. Hosea 3:1-2 describes how the husband does just this; he purchased his wife from her lover. Afterward, he promised her: "Thou shalt abide for me many days; thou shalt not play the harlot, and thou shalt not be for another man: so will I also be for thee." (Hosea 3:3). In the same way, Jesus Christ has "bought" each of us. Peter declared: "Ye were not redeemed with corruptible things, as silver and gold, from your vain conversation received by tradition from your fathers; but with the precious blood of Christ, as of a lamb without blemish and without spot." (1 Peter 1:18-19). Because of his love for his people, the Lord continued to invite Israel to repent and return to him. "I will ransom them from the power of the grave; I will redeem them from death." (Hosea 13:14). In order to return to and be delivered by the Lord, Israel needed only to turn to God, to "keep mercy and judgment, and wait on (Him) continually." (Hosea 12:6).

If they would repent, the Lord promised to heal Israel's backsliding. "I will love them freely, for mine anger is turned away from him. I will be as the dew unto Israel: he shall grow as the lily, and cast forth his roots as Lebanon. His branches shall spread, and his beauty shall be as the olive tree, and his smell as Lebanon. They that dwell under his shadow shall return; they shall revive as the corn, and grow as the vine: the scent thereof shall be as the wine of Lebanon." (Hosea 14:4-7).

Hosea's similitudes help us to understand how the Savior feels about us. Even when we turn away from Him through sin, the Lord loves us and provides a way for us to repent, so that we may return to Him.

"Preparation must precede inspiration. There must be effort before there is excellence."
(Spencer W. Kimball).

Snowbiking Through Life

In 2012 there were 1.4 million snowmobiles in the U.S. and over 500,000 in our neighbor to the north. At the same time, there were only 600 Timbersled Snowbikes worldwide. I was fortunate enough to be able to take up this sport in 2010. Today, when I am asked "Which is better, snowmobiling or snowbiking?" I respond by making the comparison between snowboarding and skiing. They are different sports, and their merits can never be reconciled in the minds of their respective aficionados. One might as well try to compare apples and oranges. In any event, snowbiking is catching on fast, and deserves our attention.

As I think about it, I wonder why I enjoy snowbiking so much. I marvel at how often I get high on endorphins and ask myself if the same principles that make me enthusiastic about life also apply to snowbiking. I'd like to think that it is a positive experience with intrinsic value, and that participation in the sport generates a significant butterfly effect that influences every aspect of my life's journey. So, I have to ask myself if I am anxiously engaged when I am snowbiking. (See D&C 58:27). Do I consciously prepare for it with the same level of preparation that I give to life? (See D&C 78:13). Could a more thoughtful engagement with its vertical challenges help me to more fully connect with my horizontal dry-land experiences?

If, with patience, I run the race that is set before me, I will recognize snowbikings' physical, mental, emotional, and spiritual counterparts to life. When I consciously apply my core values to snowbiking, it becomes a vitalizing experience allowing me to more fully embrace life itself so that it becomes richer and more satisfying. (See Hebrews 12:1). Snowbiking blesses me with positive learning opportunities. (See D&C 122:7).

As I explore these possibilities and enlarge my perspectives, I will need to make sure that I am equipped for the terrain that is likely to be encountered during a journey that takes me not only over well-marked trails, but also transports me into boondocking adventures in big mountains. I will need to determine if my loins are girt about as they should be, if I have donned the appropriate chest protection, if my feet are shod properly, and if I have prepared myself in the armory of thought with the helmets, shields, and other protective clothing that will be critical to the success of my venture. (See Ephesians 6:14-17).

After I have unloaded the snowbike in the parking lot and before the day's ride begins, I will need to go over the game plan with my buddies. As I do this, I will be comforted by the 23rd Psalm: "Though I walk through the valley of the shadow of death, I will fear no evil: for thou art with me." (Psalms 23:4). Gear will be checked to make sure there is no loose clothing, that pockets and ditty bags are zipped up, the Go-Pro is properly adjusted, radios and beacons are on, the oxygen bottle of the avi-vest has been charged with 3,000 p.s.i. of compressed air, and that its rip cord is easily accessible. I will make sure that my food and water supplies are secured, and the gas tank and extra fuel container have been topped-off. I will confirm that the gasoline has the additives that will optimize the bike's performance in the variety of conditions that will be encountered throughout the day. I will meditate upon these things, and give myself wholly to them, paying attention to every detail. (See 1 Timothy 4:15).

I will start the engine to warm up my bike for several minutes before I swing my leg over the seat and plant both feet on the dependable platform of oversize swivel foot-pegs. As I do so, I'll remember the counsel of Paul: "Now, therefore, perform the doing of it; that as there was a readiness to will, so there may be a performance also out of that which ye have." (2 Corinthians 8:11). As I evenly twist the throttle and apply power to ease the bike forward, my balance will be delicately maintained. I realize that leaning too far to the right or to the left will negatively influence my equilibrium. I will need to be able to stand and not be moved, as it were. (See D&C 87:8).

I know that I can always put my foot out, much as a tightrope walker would do, to stabilize myself, but I also realize that it is generally better if I keep my feet firmly fixed on the pegs. I will be careful to avoid crooked paths, neither will I turn to the right hand nor to the left, neither will I vary from my proven route. Therefore, my path will be straight. (See D&C 3:2).

I can expect the snow that I initially encounter to be hard packed and rutted near the parking lot, but as I venture off the beaten track, I anticipate that it will be consistent and undulating and even forgiving in its pristine glory. I remember the Groomer of whom it was said: "He can cause the rough places to be made smooth." (1 Nephi 17:46). Still, I must be prepared for unanticipated icy and windblown conditions, and will rely on my consistent forward momentum to carry me through these encounters. The secret to my success will be my reliance on the power of inertia, or my resistance to external influences that might change my state of motion. When in doubt, I will power out, and remember the cautions given as inspired counsel, as I rely on the Lord for my strength. (See D&C 3:20). I will take fresh courage, and put my shoulder to the wheel, as it were.

My ride will be enhanced by a Rekluse clutch that automatically disengages when the engine is at idle. Isaiah wrote of this innovative mechanical feature: "This is the rest wherewith ye may cause the weary to rest; and this is the refreshing." (Isaiah 28:12). This innovation decreases the likelihood that I will "stumble and fall, and be broken, and be snared, and be taken." (2 Nephi 18:15). When I apply the throttle and the engine speed increases, the clutch will engage automatically. This won't change the way I shift gears, but will simply prevent the engine from stalling. (If Solomon had been able to employ this device, he might not have suffered the embarrassment of "forty thousand stalls," that is recorded in 1 Kings 4:26).

My bike also has a rev-limiter that prevents damage to the engine should I get carried away at the peak of its power band and forget to shift to a higher gear. It is not requisite that the crankshaft turn faster than it has strength, and my bike needs to rest from its labors from time to time. (See D&C 59:10). I will try to see that this is done in wisdom and order, and to be diligent, that thereby I might win the prize of returning to the parking lot at the end of the day with the bike in the same condition as when I departed in the morning. (See Mosiah 4:27).

When I purchased it, my bike was "Ready to Race" right out of the box, so I have not done any off-label after-market engine modifications that could potentially have an adverse effect on its performance. I need to simply twist the throttle smoothly and stay on the gas to help me get out of awkward situations. In its stock set-up, "there is no variableness, neither shadow of changing" that I need to worry about. (Mormon 9:9). As I gain more experience with its capabilities, my bike's performance will be characterized by smoother acceleration without lurching. The improvement in my riding skills will be indirectly measured by a close look at my track in the snow that will have fewer holes, smoother transitions, and less evidence of foot-drag. I will constantly ponder the path of my feet, and let all my ways be established. (See Proverbs 4:26).

I have learned by sad experience that it is the nature and disposition of almost all snowbikers, as soon as they are in command of 50 horsepower, to exercise unrighteous dominion, as it were, over their machines. (See D&C 121:39). I will try to avoid the snare described by Lord Acton, who said: "Power corrupts, and absolute power corrupts absolutely."

Before starting out, I will go over my preventive maintenance checklist to insure a trouble-free ride. These include adjusting the chain tension, checking the ski and track balance, fine tuning the handlebar control adjustments, changing the oil, topping off the radiator coolant, and replenishing the fluid, when necessary, in the clutch and brake reservoirs. I have learned by sad experience that these measures are only possible if I make frequent use of the owner's manual and carefully follow its instructions. (See John 5:39). I must ask myself if I am organized, if I have prepared every needful thing, and if I have put in place well-established protocols. (See D&C 88:119).

Using high octane gasoline that is uncontaminated by water or ethanol is necessary to support the muscle of the bike's big bore engine and to create enough torque to turn the track in deep snow to get me where I want to go. At the same time, I will take advantage of the motorcycle's innovative features, recognize their capabilities, appreciate their potential, and understand their value. I will feast upon these qualities until my hunger and thirst have been satisfied. (See Alma 32:42).

I must be properly clothed before embarking on my backcountry adventure. This repertoire includes waterproof gloves and boots, layered undergarments, bib overalls, and a windbreaker and parka to provide protection against the raw elements. In pleasant 20 degree riding weather, a 10 mph breeze drops the wind chill factor to 3 degrees above zero. In a storm's 35 miles per hour winds, the wind chill plummets to 20 degrees below zero. While this temperature generally presents little danger to well-prepared winter travelers, higher wind chill may cause exposed flesh to freeze within minutes. In any event, cold muscles do not respond well to the demands of sustained strenuous physical activity. We have all seen the train wreck of those who "stumble and fall when the storms descend, and the winds blow, and the rains descend, and beat upon their house." (D&C 90:5).

A good pair of goggles is essential, because poor visibility significantly diminishes performance. We are not always blessed with brilliant sunshine, as we journey through life. In flat light, we cannot see prominent terrain features that are right before our eyes. A functioning headlight on the bike is essential as well, because delays in our travel plans may keep us on the trail after darkness has fallen. We do not want to be as those of whom it was recorded: "There arose a mist of darkness; yea, even an exceedingly great mist of darkness, insomuch that they who had commenced in the path did lose their way, that they wandered off and were lost." (1 Nephi 8:23). We need our eyes to be open and our understanding to be enlightened, so as to see and clearly understand the landscape that is stretched out before us. (See D&C 76:12).

In the scriptures, we are admonished hundreds of times to "prepare for that which is to come." (D&C 1:12). I hope I never have to use my safety kit, but it's a comfort to know that I have packed enough gear for an unexpected overnight stay in the mountains. I wear a helmet with the chin strap secured, not to mention the previously referenced avalanche vest with a canister of air that has been charged and checked. My beacon makes it easier to both find others and to be found myself, should a slide occur. My shovel and probe will help me to locate a buried companion within its debris, and to quickly create a breathing space for him during the rescue.

A well-equipped toolbox ensures that minor repairs can be made if my bike breaks down miles from civilization. A fully charged two-way radio that is locked on the correct channel keeps me in touch with my companions, and a SPOT GPS device pinpoints and sends my location to both loved ones and potential rescuers. These aids to navigation relate to the counsel of Isaiah, who wrote: "Seek ye the Lord while he may be found, call ye upon him while he is near." (Isaiah 55:6).

A saw is handy for cutting away entanglements and to create a path for travel should thick trees or brush prove to be obstacles to my progression. I remember the experience of the Prophet Nahum, who recalled "the day of his preparation, (when) the fir trees (in his path were) terribly shaken." (Nahum 2:3). Sometimes, it is necessary to "prune the vineyard," as it were. (Jacob 5:11). If I need to tow another rider's bike, a sturdy strap is mandatory. As the scriptures teach: "Which of you shall have an ass or an ox (or a snowbike) fallen into a pit, and will not straightway pull him out." (Luke 14:5). A strobe light and flashlight will help me to both see and be seen. (See D&C 50:24). Highway flares from my pack can be used as signal devices, or to quickly start fires, even if scavenged wood fuel is green or wet. I take comfort in Psalms 83:14 that reassures me "the fire burneth a wood, and…the flame setteth the mountains on fire." If the sun goes down and the air temperature plummets, I will be grateful for "a fire which cannot be consumed, even an unquenchable fire." (Alma 5:52). Preparing a cup of hot cocoa from my supply of stores, I will enjoy a "fire (that) causeth the waters to boil." (Isaiah 64:2).

A smoke flare can be used to quickly identify my position to others who might be searching for my location. As Job asked: "Where is the way where light dwelleth? and as for darkness, where is the place thereof." (Job 38:19). No matter in what circumstances I might find myself if I am disabled, my training and preparation will allow me to fashion a sanctuary and tabernacle for my edification, even if it is only a rudimentary snow cave. (See D&C 88:137).

I will pick good lines when boondocking and will habitually steer to the right when a choice is placed before me. (See: "Choose The Right," lyrics by Joseph Townsend). I welcome steep slopes that are within my skill level, and when side-hilling, I do not hesitate to first loop down if it is necessary to gain momentum in order to then continue going up. I am constantly aware of my surroundings, particularly in regard to the danger of avalanche. I look for its red flag warning signs, and for changing weather patterns manifested by wonders in the heavens above and in the earth beneath. (See D&C 45:40).

Evidence of recent slides or unstable snow makes me feel as Belshazzar of old, whose "countenance was changed, and (whose) thoughts troubled him, so that the joints of his loins were loosed, and his knees smote one against another." (Daniel 5:6). If the snowpack is cracking or collapsing, I am careful to open my ears to hear it; and to cast my eyes towards the sound thereof; and to look steadfastly towards heaven, from whence the sound comes. (See 3 Nephi 11:5). A whumping or hollow drum-like sound on hard pack is dreadful in my ears. (See Job 15:21). Recent significant snowfall may cause me to "sink in deep mire, where there is no standing." (Psalms 69:2). I look for wind-blown snow, especially on leeward or north-facing slopes, as well as for signs of significant warming, as if summer were nigh at hand. (See Luke 21:30).

In particular, I am wary of exposed slopes that are steeper than 30 degrees. I look for anchors on the slope, "both sure and steadfast," that provide a measure of stability. (Hebrews 6:19). If the contour of the snow is dangerously and unpredictably convex, or if there are terrain traps at the run-out of a potential slide, unless I am careful, I realize that I might "stumble and fall, and be broken, and be snared, and be taken." (2 Nephi 18:15). Cornices that indicate prevailing wind direction could be signs that the snow beneath is unstable. In particular, a storm associated with an east wind could hurl me out of my place. (See Job 27:21). On my radio, I listen for weather forecasts that warn: "When it is evening, ye say, it will be fair weather, for the sky is red. And in the morning, it will be foul weather today, for the sky is red and lowring." (Matthew 16:2-3). If I do not take all of these things into consideration, I risk being as "a double minded man (who) is unstable in all his ways." (James 1:8).

I have rehearsed ahead of time what to do if I am caught in a slide. I will first attempt to outrun it, but if it engulfs me, I will power off and try to angle to its edge. I will wait for the best moment to bail off and get away from my bike before pulling the rip cord of my avi-vest. I will hang on to the downhill side of trees, but if the snow pulls me away, I will try to roll onto my back with my feet facing downhill obstacles. I will swim hard, fight, grab at trees, and try to self-arrest as my heels search for a bed of stable snow beneath the slide. As the avalanche slows, I will attempt to thrust some part of my body above its surface, and to create an air space around my mouth. In the panic of the moment, I hope that I will retain enough composure to realize that I have been reconciled unto God, and that it is only in and through His grace that I may be saved. (See 2 Nephi 10:24). In any event, I hope that I "shall escape, and shall be on the mountains" to ride yet another day. (Ezekiel 7:16).

If my buddy is caught, I will watch to determine his "last-seen" position. I will begin my search as soon as it is safe to do so, after the slide has stopped. Our party will establish a leader and make a plan. We will look for surface clues such as gloves, boots, and equipment. We will listen. Then, we will conduct a beacon search, get close to our companion, and use our probes to locate his position before we dig him out with our shovels. If fortune smiles upon us, we will exult: "This my (companion) was dead, and is alive again. He was lost, and is found." (Luke 15:11). If necessary, we will conduct an emergency medical evaluation before readying him for evacuation. We will use our radios and GPS locators to coordinate his transport with emergency search and rescue personnel. As I exhaust my energies, I hope that I will find hidden reserves in the promise: "If it so be that you should labor all your days and…save it be one soul…how great shall be your joy." (D&C 18:15).

I will be ready for any unforeseen and unlikely emergency situation. I anticipate having an epic day, and my confidence will be enhanced because of my preparation. I'll stop frequently to savor my adventures, and I'll take lots of photos and video to share later with my companions and loved ones. I'll anticipate becoming famous on You Tube. (See: "Snowbike Boondocker Priest Lake"). Nevertheless, I'll try to remember that it is the meek who "shall inherit the earth," even as they "delight themselves in the abundance" of snow. (Psalms 37:11).

My experience will be heightened as I evaluate where others have gone before in order to avoid the trenches they've made in the snow. I'll pre-play before I re-play, and remember the admonition: Prepare ye, prepare ye for that which is to come." (D&C 1:12). Sometimes, a deep cleansing breath will be required before I attack a particularly challenging line. I will first identify hidden obstacles, such as tree wells and wind ridges, rocks, stumps, cliffs, gullies, and running water, not to mention impenetrable walls of thick trees on the downhill borders of clear cuts. I'll survey the terrain, and remember with sobriety that "whoso diggeth a pit shall fall therein, and he that rolleth a stone (or causeth an avalanche), it will return upon him." (Proverbs 26:27).

I'll try not to stop on uphill sections, but will power through these to get to plateaus, or at least to terrain where the track of the bike is on an even keel. When I am on level ground, it will be easier to organize my thoughts to plan my next course of action. I'll avoid the unstable edges of cornices that might unexpectedly break away, and I will stay on snow that is "firm and steadfast, and immovable." (1 Nephi 2:10). My proper prior planning will prevent poor performance. Above all, I'll maintain my equilibrium, even if the snow is deep and I can't put my foot down for stability, because "a false balance is not good." (Proverbs 20:23). I'll remember Joseph Smith's exhortation to snowbikers everywhere: "Go forward and not backward. Courage, brethren; and on, on to the victory! Let your hearts rejoice, and be exceedingly glad. Let the earth break forth into singing." (D&C 128:22).

If I do crash, I'll need to find the reserves of strength to reorient my bike and lift it into an upright position. As long as it remains upside down, I know I won't be going anywhere. The bike weighs in at 300 pounds, and one would think it would be "too heavy for me." (Numbers 11:14). So, if I am going to pick up the bike without assistance, I know that I will need to put my shoulder to the wheel. I'm going to have to get it right the first time, because repetitively trying to lift the bike is just going to wear me out. If I do not allow myself to become "weary in well doing," I will soon be on my way again. (Galatians 6:9).

I am reminded of an experience my grandson, Parker Edwards, had when he was 10 years old. His interest in dirt bikes had reached an almost feverish pitch. For a time, his excitement exceeded his skill, and he consequently took his fair share of spills. Motorcycling, like snowbiking or life itself, can be a lot of work, and for a ten year old it can be exhausting, especially in the aftermath of a yard-sale crash. Fortunately, his motorcycling experiences had been (for the most part) free of serious injury, 1) because of his ability to carefully follow instructions, 2) because of attentive parental control, and 3) because of a serious investment in protective equipment.

Nevertheless, after an especially grueling morning at the O.R.V. Park in the Coast Range west of Portland, Oregon, Parker was ready to hang it up right there on the trail, and just walk away from his (upside-down) bike. The only problem was that we were miles from the parking lot, and slinking away to lick his wounds was not a viable option. I was impressed with the simple wisdom and broad application of the counsel given by his father, when he gently urged Parker: "Just get back on the bike."

I think dirt biking is similar to our life experiences. Maybe that's why I enjoy it so much. I can be zooming along standing on my foot-pegs without a care in the world, with the wind in my face and relishing the freedom of the trail. Then, almost without warning, I might hit a rock that jerks the handlebars sideways, causing me to lose my sure grip, so that I suddenly find myself one with Mother Earth. (Maybe that's why they call it "dirt-biking!").

I just need to remember that when life throws me a curve, and I go south when the trail goes north, I must "get back on the bike." When I do, and I think of Parker when I say this, I will find that in no time, I'll have forgotten the spill as I twist the throttle to get back up to speed, looking with eager anticipation for the next opportunity to get serious air. Then, when the next rock in the road looms before me, I'll be so much the wiser for having had the experience, I'll be less intimidated, and will be better prepared to avoid another close encounter of the dirt kind.

Parker needed the mental discipline to refocus, just as I do when I find myself facing a difficult challenge while snowbiking. Each time I concentrate on the task at hand, I first put the engine in gear. I have learned by sad experience that inadvertently revving the engine while in neutral is not a productive exercise, but can instead be a recipe for disaster. I try to wrap my mind around my emotions, to get a grip and avoid the panic that causes me to lose focus. I force myself to have a positive mental attitude, and say to myself: "I can do this!" At this critical juncture, peace speaks to my soul, as a voice reassuring me that my adversity and afflictions will be but for a moment. (See D&C 121:7).

If I get tired, I try to be self-aware in order to identify the telltale signs of fatigue. I must not allow drowsiness to overpower me because of overexertion, or because of the weariness that is the natural consequence of my labors during the heat of the day. (See Alma 51:33). If I experience mental lapses, I try to notice their telltale signs and deal with them before they cause my performance level to plummet. When I find myself getting tired, or am "in a state of thoughtless stupor," I immediately stop for nourishment and to rehydrate. (Alma 60:7). I take a few deep, cleansing breaths, because I know that running on empty isn't good for me or for my snowbike.

Why would anyone want to snowbike?" I think of the adage: "No one said it would be easy. They only said it would be worth it!" There are many rewards related to snowbiking. It puts me in the wilderness where new vistas constantly open up before me. It blesses me with a larger view of life. It challenges me to push myself to new levels of performance that I had believed to be beyond my reach. It's a good winter pursuit to keep myself active during a time of year when many experience cabin fever and "hole up" with a fortress mentality while waiting for spring to come. It's good to be "anxiously engaged" and to do many things of my own free will. It confirms for me that a bad day in the mountains is better than a good day in town. It teaches me that life is truly beautiful.

It puts me close to God. While snowbiking, I often think of the poem "High Flight," by John Magee. "Oh, I have slipped the surly bonds of (flat) earth and danced the (mountain tops) on laughter-silvered wings. Sunward I've climbed, and joined the tumbling mirth of sun-split clouds, and done a hundred things you have not dreamed of; Wheeled and soared and swung high in the sunlit silence. Hovering there, I've chased the shouting wind along, and flung my eager craft through footless halls of (powder). Up, up the long, delirious, burning blue I've topped the windswept heights with easy grace, where never lark, or even eagle flew. And, while with silent lifting mind I've trod the high untrespassed sanctity of (the wilderness), I put out my hand, and touched the face of God."

When I snowbike, I get a sense of accomplishment to know that I have probed the limits of my potential, have mastered a skill through vigorous participation, have received the adrenaline rush of adventure, felt the flush of endorphins, and enjoyed the quiet satisfaction to know that I can really do it. Nerve endings that seldom fire on their own are repetitively stimulated. Snowbiking allows me to fail, sometimes spectacularly, and then to try again, to ultimately experience the exhilaration of success. It permits me to do all these things in the company of friends.

While steep hills challenge me, they also allow me to put down lines that will stand as a testament to others, at least until the next snowfall, when I get to do it all over again. My tracks shout out: "Phil Hudson was here." Snowbiking exercises my mind as much as it does my body, and it's way more fun than a Stairmaster, rowing machine, or a treadmill.

Snowbiking puts me in touch with The Plan of Happiness. Those who master the fundamentals of the sport realize that full participation in the Plan is within their reach, no matter what their cultural, social, political, or economic circumstances might be. The portals to the Plan are supported by scriptures and buttressed by gospel principles that relate to snowbiking. As much as I would like to think that I am in control when snowbiking, I realize that, in a larger context, I can do pitifully little to influence my circumstances. It is only through the miracle of continuing, enduring, immeasurable, infinite, uncorrupted, unfathomable uninterrupted, and unspoiled grace embodied within the Plan that I am permitted to enjoy a sport that swallows me up in the joy of my God, even to the exhausting of my strength. (See Alma 27:17). Each time I reach that epiphany, my heart brims with joy. (See Alma 26:11).

At the end of a day of snowbiking, I feel like the man who has been in the arena, "whose face is marred by dust and sweat and blood; who strives valiantly; who errs and comes short again and again; who knows the great enthusiasms, the great devotions, and spends himself in a worthy cause; Who, at the best, knows in the end the triumph of high achievement; and who, at the worst, at least fails while daring greatly, so that his place shall never be with those cold and timid souls who know neither victory nor defeat." (President Theodore Roosevelt, Speech at the Sorbonne, 4/23/1910).

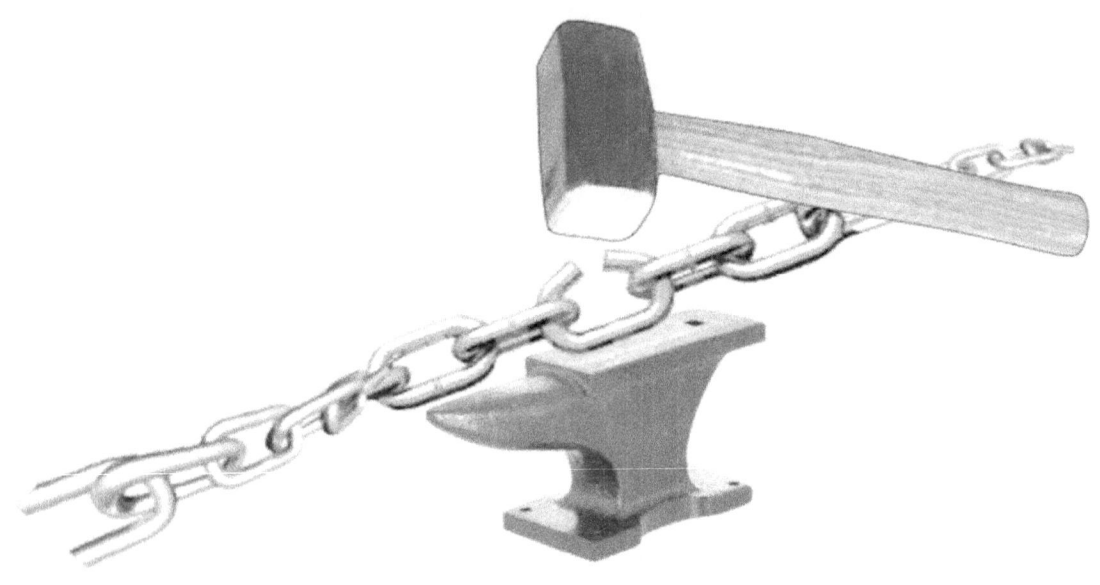

We need to give proper
attention to the mental, physical, and
spiritual dimensions of our existence, so that they
remain in proper balance and help us to maintain our
equilibrium as we move along the strait and
narrow path leading to eternal life.

Strengths and Weaknesses

"We generally think of Satan attacking us at our weakest spot. But weakness is not our only vulnerability. Satan can also attack us where we think we are strong, in the very areas where we are proud of our strengths. He will approach us through the greatest talents and spiritual gifts we possess. If we are not wary, Satan can cause our spiritual downfall by corrupting us through our strengths, as well as by exploiting our weaknesses." (Dallin Oaks, "Ensign," 10/1994).

Just before King David died, Zadok the priest and Nathan the prophet anointed Solomon as the new king of Israel. Solomon, who was a son of David and Bathsheba, received the following counsel from his father: "Be thou strong…and shew thyself a man; and keep the charge of the Lord thy God, to walk in his ways, to keep his statutes, and his commandments, and his judgments, and his testimonies…that thou mayest prosper in all that thou doest" (1 Kings 2:2-3).

Soon after Solomon became king, the Lord appeared to him in a dream and said: "Ask what I shall give thee." (1 Kings 3:5). Solomon replied: "Give, therefore, thy servant an understanding heart to judge thy people, that I may discern between good and bad." (1 Kings 3:9). The Lord granted his request, "and all Israel heard of the judgment which the king had judged; and they feared the king: for they saw that the wisdom of God was in him, to do judgment." (1 Kings 3:28). "And God gave Solomon wisdom and understanding exceeding much." (1 Kings 4:29).

Solomon must have felt he had a special need for that blessing, because the scriptures record his heartfelt prayer: "And now, O Lord my God, thou hast made thy servant king instead of David my father: and I am but a little child: I know not how to go out or come in." (1 Kings 3:7-8). The Lord was pleased with Solomon's request for an understanding heart, and "said unto him, because thou hast asked this thing, and hast not asked for thyself long life; neither hast asked riches for thyself, nor hast asked the life of thine enemies; but hast asked for thyself understanding to discern judgment; Behold, I have done according to thy words: lo, I have given thee a wise and an understanding heart; so that there was none like thee before thee, neither after thee shall any arise like unto thee." (1 Kings 3:11-12).

Today, the Lord grants similar spiritual gifts to His unselfish servants. "To some it is given by the Holy Ghost to know that Jesus Christ is the Son of God, and that he was crucified for the sins of the world. To others it is given to believe on their words, that they also might have eternal life if they continue faithful. And again, to some it is given by the Holy Ghost to know the differences of administration, as it will be pleasing unto the same Lord, according as the Lord will, suiting his mercies according to the conditions of the children of men. And again, it is given by the Holy Ghost to some to know the diversities of operations, whether they be of God, that the manifestations of the Spirit may be given to every man to profit withal. And again, verily I say unto you, to some is given, by the Spirit of God, the word of wisdom. To another is given the word of knowledge, that all may be taught to be wise and to have knowledge. And again, to some it is given to have faith to be healed; And to others it is given to have faith to heal. And again, to some is given the working of miracles; And to others it is given to prophesy; And to others the discerning of spirits. And again, it is given to some to speak with tongues; And to another is given the interpretation of tongues. And all these gifts come from God, for the benefit of the children of God." (D&C 46:13-26).

The Lord told Solomon He would grant him these gifts of the Spirit, with conditions: "If thou wilt walk in my ways, to keep my statutes and my commandments, as thy father David did walk, then I will lengthen thy days." (1 Kings 3:14).

The first situation requiring King Solomon's judgment concerned a child custody dispute. "And the king said, Bring me a sword. And they brought a sword before the king. And the king said, divide the living child in two, and give half to the one, and half to the other. Then spake the woman whose the living child was unto the king, for her bowels yearned upon her son, and she said, O my Lord, give her the living child, and in no wise slay it. But the other said, Let it be neither mine nor thine, but divide it. Then the king answered and said, Give her the living child, and in no wise slay it: she is the mother thereof." (1 Kings 3:24-27).

During his reign, King Solomon oversaw the construction of a temple. He said: "I purpose to build an house unto the name of the Lord my God, as the Lord spake unto David my father, saying, Thy son, whom I will set upon thy throne in thy room, he shall build an house unto my name." (1 Kings 5:5). Regarding the temple, the Lord promised Solomon: "Concerning this house which thou art in building, if thou wilt walk in my statutes, and execute my judgments, and keep all my commandments to walk in them; then will I perform my word with thee, which I spake unto David thy father: And I will dwell among the children of Israel, and will not forsake my people Israel." (1 Kings 6:11-13).

Today, the Lord has similarly promised: "And inasmuch as my people build a house unto me in the name of the Lord, and do not suffer any unclean thing to come into it, that it be not defiled, my glory shall rest upon it; Yea, and my presence shall be there, for I will come into it, and all the pure in heart that shall come into it shall see God. But if it be defiled I will not come into it, and my glory shall not be there; for I will not come into unholy temples." (D&C 97:15-17).

Following seven years of construction, in the temple dedicatory prayer, Solomon asked for answers to prayers, forgiveness, rain, help during famine and sickness, and help in battle. (1 Kings 8). Ezra Taft Benson said of the latter-day House of the Lord: "In the peace of these lovely temples, sometimes we find solutions to the serious problems of life. Under the influence of the Spirit, sometimes pure knowledge flows to us there. Temples are places of personal revelation. When I have been weighed down by a problem or a difficulty, I have gone to the House of the Lord with a prayer in my heart for answers. These answers have come in clear and unmistakable ways." ("Liahona," 6/1992).

Solomon prayed that the temple would help lead unbelievers to the Lord. (1 Kings 8:41-43). "Moreover concerning a stranger that is not of thy people Israel, but cometh out of a far country for thy name's sake; (For they shall hear of thy great name, and of thy strong hand, and of thy stretched out arm;) when he shall come and pray toward this house; Hear thou in heaven thy dwelling place, and do according to all that the stranger calleth to thee for: that all people of the earth may know thy name, to fear thee, as do thy people Israel; and that they may know that this house, which I have builded, is called by thy name." (1 Kings 8:41-43).

After he offered the dedicatory prayer, Solomon counseled his people: "Let your heart…be perfect with the Lord our God." (1 Kings 8:61). He directed that "two and twenty thousand oxen, and an hundred and twenty thousand sheep" be sacrificed as an offering to the Lord during the dedication. (1 Kings 8:63). Then, "on the eighth day he sent the people away: and they blessed the king, and went unto their tents joyful and glad of heart for all the goodness that the Lord had done for David his servant, and for Israel his people." (1 Kings 8:66).

Following the dedication of the temple, the Lord cautioned Solomon, saying: "I have heard thy prayer and thy supplication, that thou hast made before me: I have hallowed this house, which thou hast built, to put my name there for ever; and mine eyes and mine heart shall be there perpetually. And if thou wilt walk before me, as David thy father walked, in integrity of heart, and in uprightness, to do according to all that I have commanded thee, and wilt keep my statutes and my judgments: Then I will establish the throne of thy kingdom upon Israel for ever, as I promised to David thy father, saying, There shall not fail thee a man upon the throne of Israel.

But if ye shall at all turn from following me, ye or your children, and will not keep my commandments and my statutes which I have set before you, but go and serve other gods, and worship them. Then will I cut off Israel out of the land which I have given them; and this house, which I have hallowed for my name, will I cast out of my sight; and Israel shall be a proverb and a byword among all people: And at this house, which is high, every one that passeth by it shall be astonished, and shall hiss; and they shall say, Why hath the Lord done thus unto this land, and to this house? And they shall answer, Because they forsook the Lord their God, who brought forth their fathers out of the land of Egypt, and have taken hold upon other gods, and have worshipped them, and served them: therefore, hath the Lord brought upon them all this evil." (1 Kings 9:3-9).

As time passed, Solomon became obnoxiously wealthy and married non-Israelite women out of the covenant, who persuaded him to worship idols. He "exceeded all the kings of the earth for riches and for wisdom." (1 Kings 10:23). But he "loved many strange women, together with the daughter of Pharaoh, women of the Moabites, Ammonites, Edomites, Zidonians, and Hittites; Of the nations concerning which the Lord said unto the children of Israel, Ye shall not go in to them, neither shall they come in unto you: for surely they will turn away your heart after their gods: Solomon clave unto these in love." (1 Kings 11:1-2).

"And he had seven hundred wives, princesses, and three hundred concubines: and his wives turned away his heart…after other gods: and his heart was not perfect with the Lord his God." (1 Kings 11:3-4). Note that J.S.T. 1 Kings 11:4 adds the following: "and it became as the heart of David his father." Then the order of expressions in verse 6 is significantly changed in the J.S.T. from: "And Solomon did evil in the sight of the Lord, and went not fully after the Lord, as did David his father," to read: "And Solomon did evil in the sight of the Lord, as David his father, and went not fully after the Lord."

In his dedicatory prayer at the temple, Solomon encouraged Israel: "Let your heart, therefore, be perfect with the Lord our God, to walk in his statutes, and to keep his commandments, as at this day." (1 Kings 8:61). Nevertheless, Solomon's blessings of wisdom, riches, and honor ultimately contributed to his downfall, and he lost his kingdom. "And the time that Solomon reigned in Jerusalem over all Israel was forty years. And Solomon slept with his fathers, and was buried in the city of David his father: and Rehoboam his son reigned in his stead." (1 Kings 11:42-43).

The Lord has similarly warned Latter-day Israel to be true and faithful to her covenants, promising: "If your eye be single to my glory, your whole bodies shall be filled with light, and there shall be no darkness in you; and that body which is filled with light comprehendeth all things." (D&C 88:67).

To prevent our strengths from becoming our downfall, humility can be the catalyst for all learning, and the greatest antidote against pride. Through the prophet Moroni, the Lord gave us insight into the role of humility: "I give unto men weakness that they may be humble; and my grace is sufficient for all men that humble themselves before me; for if they humble themselves before me, and have faith in me, then will I make weak things become strong unto them." (Ether 12:27).

We can prevent the adversary from exploiting our spiritual gifts if we are humble and teachable, and listen to the promptings of the Spirit. We can rely on the Lord's direction and promise: "Be thou humble; and the Lord thy God shall lead thee by the hand, and give thee answer to thy prayers." (D&C 112:10).

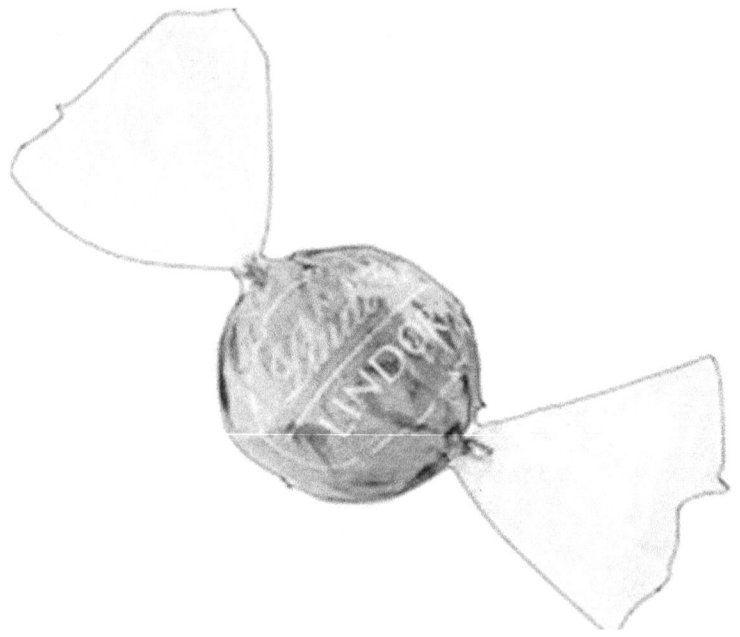

"We are the music makers, and we are the dreamers of the dreams. There is no life I know to compare with pure imagination. Living there, you'll be free if you truly wish to be."
(Willie Wonka).

Swiss Chocolate

Most of us have enjoyed the delicious texture and flavor of Swiss chocolate.

If we hold up a poster of an assortment of Lindt, Cailler, Suchard, or Toblerone chocolates and show it to our friends, they may or may not be inclined to try a piece for themselves. If we actually show them a real piece of chocolate, we might catch their interest, and they might begin to salivate with the stirrings of hopeful anticipation.

But, in our enthusiasm, if we unwrap a piece before their eyes, and pop it into our own mouths, and then try to describe how wonderful it tastes, they might be disappointed and be underwhelmed by our gesture. They might even think it insincere or disingenuous.

However, what if we were to take a piece of chocolate that had their name written upon it, and we unwrapped it with them, and on our open palms presented it to them, and then allowed them to savor it for themselves, encouraging them to roll it over and over on their tongues while it slowly and deliciously melted in their mouths?

Better yet, what if we were to share in their gustatory delight, and enjoy a similar piece of chocolate with them? How much easier and more fluid would be our expressions relating to the enrichment of life because of Swiss chocolate.

If we further augmented their sensory delight with words of encouragement, their experience might expand to new proportions, and they would almost certainly forevermore enthusiastically endorse and desire, and perhaps even crave, Swiss chocolate. They might even be willing to pay a premium, just to relive the experience.

From that day on, they might be hooked on it.

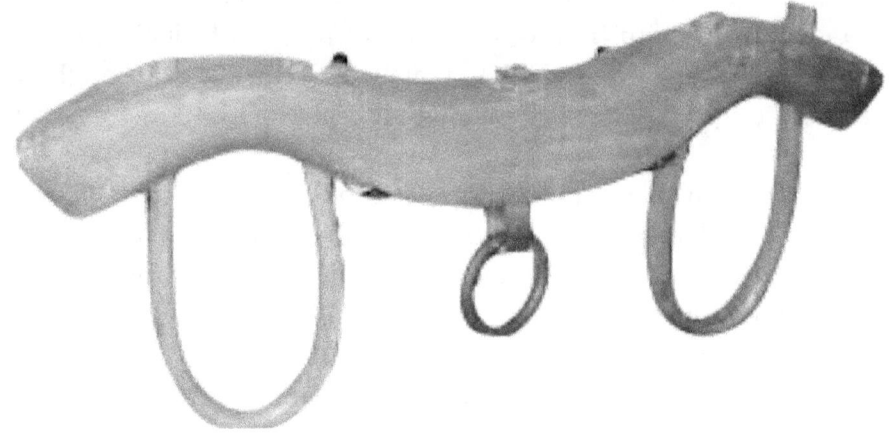

"The second mile is a gift of spiritual independence that removes the veil of insensitivity to a destiny."
(Richard L. Gunn).

Take My Yoke Upon You

"Come unto me, all ye that labour and are heavy laden, and I will give you rest. Take my yoke upon you, and learn of me; for I am meek and lowly in heart: and ye shall find rest unto your souls. For my yoke is easy, and my burden is light." (Matthew 11:28-30).

We all carry burdens, whether they be health, educational or emotional concerns, anxieties about our safety, our security, our future, our relationships, or our temporal well-being. Sometimes our concerns relate to our standing before the Lord, or to the burdens we carry that are related to unresolved sin.

Some of these worries we can address successfully, by ourselves and without outside intervention or assistance. However, "anyone who imagines that bliss is normal, is going to waste a lot of time running around shouting that he's been robbed. The fact is that most putts don't drop, most beef is tough, most children just grow up to be people, most successful marriages require a high degree of mutual toleration, and most jobs are more often dull than otherwise. Life is like an old-time rail journey, with delays, sidetracks, smoke, dust, cinders and jolts, interspersed only occasionally by beautiful vistas and thrilling bursts of speed. The trick is to simply be thankful to the Lord for letting you have the ride." (Jenkin Jones, Editor of "The Tulsa Tribune").

Jesus Christ can provide significant relief from the exigencies of life by allowing us to take upon ourselves His yoke. A yoke is a frame or bar that balances a heavy load, making it easier to manage. The Lord eases our burdens by effectively putting us in the traces with Him. This casts "working out our salvation with fear and trembling" in a whole new perspective. As we learn to do the Lord's will and allow Him to guide us and direct our lives, we are released from bondage to sin, and from servitude to the adversary.

David put it well, in the 23rd Psalm: "The Lord is my shepherd, I shall not want. He maketh me to lie down in green pastures. He leadeth me beside still waters. He restoreth my soul. He leadeth me in the paths of righteousness for his name's sake. Yea, though I walk through the valley of the shadow of death I will fear no evil, for though art with me. Thou preparest a table before me in the presence of mine enemies. Thou anointest my head with oil; my cup runneth over. Surely goodness and mercy shall follow me all the days of my life and I will dwell in the house of the Lord forever."

In order to dwell in the house of the Lord and experience the exhilarating feeling of freedom from bondage and from being yoked to sin, rather than to the Savior, we must first pass through a portal. In the beginning, we accepted mortality as a lifestyle choice, with the double-edged sword of agency as its lynchpin. We knew there would be telestial traffic jams, religious round-abouts, and conceptual cul-de-sacs to negotiate, and that bad habits might even lead to our forfeiture of agency. But we also knew that sooner or later, our innate sense of morality would propel us along the strait and narrow way, through the portal of personal preparedness, accountability, and responsibility, toward expanding circles of opportunity, the perfect law of liberty, and celestial sureties. That gateway would be akin to being born again, and on the other side would be the Lord's Rest and eternal life.

The example of the Savior illustrates how we can facilitate His power to remove the yoke of sin from our shoulders. "And, behold, a woman in the city, which was a sinner, when she knew that Jesus sat at meat in the Pharisee's house, brought an alabaster box of ointment." (Luke 7:37). The woman who entered the house of Simon the Pharisee carried the weight of sin, but her actions allowed Jesus to take away that heavy burden. She "stood at his feet behind him weeping, and began to wash his feet with tears, and did wipe them with the hairs of her head, and kissed his feet, and anointed them with the ointment." (Luke 7:38). The woman exhibited profound repentance, respect, humility, and love for the Savior. "And he said unto her, Thy sins are forgiven." (Luke 7:48).

We must do likewise in order to benefit from the ability of the Savior to take upon Himself our burdens, that He might grant us the gift of peace. We can either choose to bear these burdens ourselves, or accept the yoke of Jesus Christ. It comes down to us, but remember this: His teachings are true and we will only find rest when we follow Him.

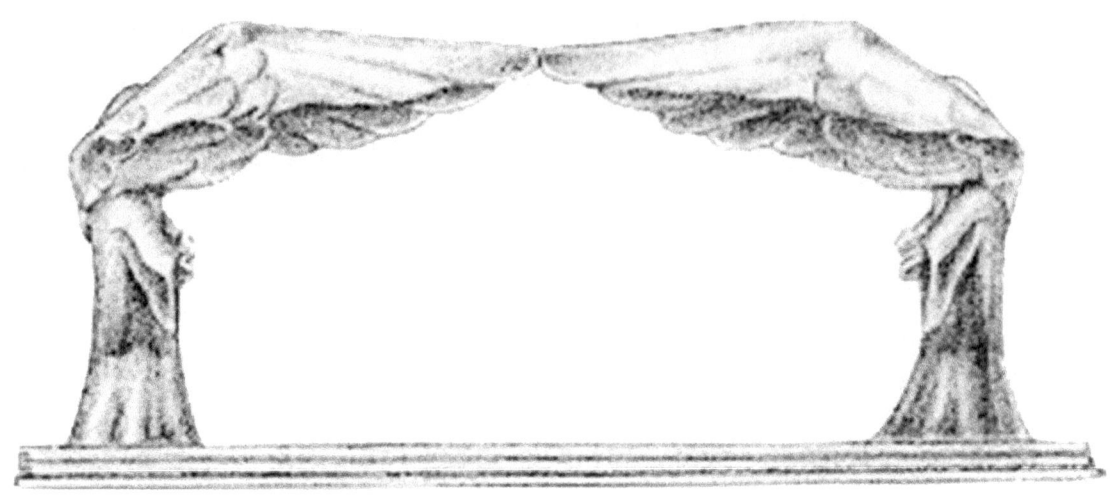

"And I will have mercy
upon her that had not obtained
mercy; and I will say to them which
were not my people, Thou art my
people; and they shall say,
Thou art my God."
(Hosea 2:23).

Teachings of The Minor Prophets

"The role of Israel as the depositary of true religion and the freeing of mankind from the idolatry which obstructs its salvation is almost self-evident. As Isaiah envisioned, there can be no hope for our redemption unless we conquer self-deification. We must abandon the worship of our own creations, and liberate ourselves from our lust for power, avarice, domination, and the cult of the state. There can be no redemption until we recognize our moral obligations as transcendent and divine. No form of government, no level of material well-being, will save us. We will be redeemed only when towers fall, and Jerusalem triumphs over Babylon. What is at stake, finally, is not only intelligence, but also feeling. We have to change our hearts. Salvation, the prophets tell us, is preconditioned by repentance. The redeeming act of God waits upon our initiative." (Abba Eban, "My People: The Story of The Jews,"p. 59-60). The teachings of the Minor Prophets can help us to develop the resolve to act upon our promptings.

One of those prophets, named Amos, was from a small town south of Jerusalem named Tekoa (a city of tents). He ministered to the inhabitants of the Northern Kingdom from about 800 to 750 B.C., and famously wrote: "Behold, the days come, saith the Lord God, that I will send a famine in the land, not a famine of bread, nor a thirst for water, but of hearing the words of the Lord." (Amos 8:11).

That famine symbolically addressed the phenomenon of societal spiritual starvation in the Last Days. We live in a time when multitudes are dying because their obstinate spiritual illiteracy prevents them from comprehending the voice of gladness of modern-day prophets. Of our day, Nephi wrote: "It must needs be that the Gentiles be convinced also that Jesus is the Christ, the Eternal God." (2 Nephi 26:12). As Thomas Jefferson exclaimed: "The religion builders have so distorted and deformed the doctrines of Jesus, so muffled them in mysticisms, fancies and falsehoods, have caricatured them into forms so inconceivable, as to shock reasonable thinkers. Happy in the prospect of a restoration of primitive Christianity, I must leave to younger persons to encounter and lop off the false branches which have been engrafted into it by the mythologists of the middle and modern ages." ("Jefferson's Complete Works," 7:210 & 257).

In order to address the scarcity of spiritual supply in the land, the Lord revealed to Nephi: "The time cometh, saith the Lamb of God, that I will work a great and a marvelous work among the children of men; a work which shall be everlasting, either on the one hand or on the other - either to the convincing of them unto peace and life eternal, or unto the deliverance of them to the hardness of their hearts and the blindness of their minds unto their being brought down into captivity, and also into destruction, both temporally and spiritually, according to the captivity of the devil." (1 Nephi 14:7).

Famine in the land occurs whenever prophets have been taken from the earth, or whenever there is a prophet, but the people reject his message. Today, we too often look for answers in the wrong places, and the solutions to our problems in the wrong way, or we simply ask the wrong questions. If we want to survive the famine, we must find the Lord. "Seek ye me, and ye shall live." (Amos 5:4). We cannot simply seek out the status quo, the lowest common denominator of existence, and then sit with our engines idling while we languish in our comfort zones, for "Wo unto them that are at ease in Zion," cautioned Amos. (Amos 6:1).

Amos taught that the Lord is actively concerned about our welfare. He wrote: "Surely the Lord God will do nothing, but he revealeth his secret unto his servants the prophets." (Amos 3:7). But He waits upon our initiative. As the Joseph Smith Translation renders this verse: "Surely the Lord God will do nothing, until he revealeth his secret unto his servants the prophets." (J.S.T. Amos 3:7).

Jonah lived about the same time as Amos, just a few years before Lehi was born. He was called by Jehovah to cry repentance to the people of Nineveh. Jonah's message is that Heavenly Father is the God of all people, and not only of Israel. The story of Jonah is an unusual example of God extending His mercy to those who were not His chosen people.

Although Jehovah was bonded to Israel in a covenant relationship reminiscent of marriage, He desired all to come unto Him through repentance. "Now the word of the Lord came unto Jonah the son of Amittai, saying, Arise, go to Nineveh, that great city (of 120,000 people), and cry against it; for their wickedness is come up before me." (Jonah 1:1-2). Sometimes, we view the church as an exclusive theological country club situated on a narrow ecclesiastical terrace, and we fall into the trap that ensnared the Israelites of old, developing the attitude that we are somehow better than those around us who do not enjoy the blessings of the gospel. "But, behold," declared Nephi, at a time when the Jews felt strongly that they alone were the chosen people, "all nations, kindreds, tongues, and people shall dwell safely in the Holy One of Israel, if it so be that they will repent." (1 Nephi 22:28). The great equalizing power is repentance, no matter who the sinner might be, for we are all sinners.

Following Jonah's cry to repentance, "the people of Nineveh believed God, and proclaimed a fast, and put on sackcloth." (Jonah 3:5) "And God saw their works, that they turned from their evil way, and repented; and God turned away the evil that he had said he would bring upon them." (J.S.T. Jonah 3:10). In truth, "as many of the Gentiles as will repent are the covenant people of the Lord; and as many of the Jews (or the Latter-day Saints) as will not repent shall be cast off; for the Lord covenanteth with none save it be with them that repent and believe in his Son." (2 Nephi 30:2).

The story of Jonah teaches us that the Lord is no respecter of persons, and He "esteemeth all flesh in one; (for) he that is righteous is favored of God." (1 Nephi 17:35). "He inviteth them all to come unto him and partake of his goodness; and he denieth none that come unto him, black and white, bond and free, male and female; and he remembereth the heathen; and all are alike unto God, both Jew and Gentile." (2 Nephi 26:33).

Hosea and Micah were additional prophets, who were contemporaries of Isaiah, and ministered in both the Northern Kingdom, and then in Judah after the Assyrian conquest of the Northern Kingdom. As did many of the other prophets, Hosea used marriage as a symbol of the Lord's relationship with His Chosen People. When we depart from Him, he wrote, we commit "great whoredom." (Hosea 1:2). This prompted Him to exclaim: "Turn, O backsliding Israel, for I am married unto you." (Jeremiah 3:14). "Surely as a wife treacherously departeth from her husband, so have ye dealt treacherously with me, O house of Israel, saith the Lord." (Jeremiah 3:20).

The portrayal by John of this marriage relationship was gladsome: "Let us…rejoice, and give honour to him: for the marriage of the Lamb is come, and his wife hath made herself ready. And to her was granted that she should be arrayed in fine linen, clean and white: for the fine linen is the righteousness of saints." (Revelation 19:7-8). The New & Everlasting Covenant of Marriage is the culminating ordinance into which one may enter in the temple, and in consequence of the restoration of all things in the Dispensation of the Fulness of Times, today it is necessary to enter into the New & Everlasting Covenant of Marriage in order to be saved in the highest level of the Celestial Kingdom.

Hosea continued: "My people are destroyed for lack of knowledge: because thou hast rejected knowledge, I will also reject thee, that thou shalt be no priest to me: seeing thou hast forgotten the law of thy God, I will also forget thy children." (Hosea 4:6). Today, the Lord teaches: "It is impossible for a man to be saved in ignorance." (D&C 131:6). Knowledge, we learn, is a spiritual gift: "The word of knowledge (is given) that all may be taught to be wise." (D&C 46:18).

Nephi mourned: "Because of the unbelief, and the wickedness, and the ignorance, and the stiffneckedness of men…they will not search knowledge, nor understand great knowledge, when it is given unto them in plainness, even as plain as word can be." (2 Nephi 32:7). We cannot allow ourselves to be pacified and lulled away into a false sense of security, that we will ignorantly exclaim: "All is well in Zion; yea, Zion prospereth, all is well; (for) thus the devil cheateth (our) souls, and leadeth (us) away carefully down to hell." (2 Nephi 28:21).

Micah taught that the Lord only requires of us that we "do justly, and…love mercy, and…walk humbly." (Micah 6:8). Micah was in awe of the power of our Father in Heaven, and asked: "Who is a god like unto thee, that pardoneth iniquity, and passeth by the transgression of the remnant of his heritage? He retaineth not his anger for ever, because he delighteth in mercy." (Micah 7:18).

Spencer W. Kimball taught: "Revelations come to prophets as deep, unassailable impressions settling down on the prophet's mind and heart as dew from heaven, or as the dawn dissipates the darkness of night. The great volume of revelation comes to today's prophets in this less spectacular way - in deep impressions, without spectacle or glamour or dramatic events. In Thursday meetings in the temple, to hear (the prophet) conclude important new developments with such solemn expressions as 'The Lord is pleased,' or 'Our Heavenly Father has spoken' is to know it positively. The voice of the Lord is a continuous, pleasant sound, a sweet peaceful melody, and a thundering appeal." As the Lord taught Job: "For God speaketh once, yea twice, yet man perceiveth it not. In a dream, in a vision of the night, when deep sleep falleth upon men, in slumberings upon the bed. Then he openeth the ears of men, and sealeth their instruction." (Job 33:14-16). When changes come through the prophet, there is certainty and calm, tranquil assurance; and the peace of heaven that settles over the hearts of true believers with sureness. Great and good men rise to new stature under the mantle of prime authority, and when keys of heaven are closed in their palms, the voice of authority comes from their lips." (Munich Area Conference, 1973).

In chapels, we
organize stakes, wards,
quorums, etc., but the purpose
of the temple is to organize
families for eternity.

Temple Blessings
for All Mankind

Before offering the dedicatory prayer in the Ogden Utah temple, Joseph Fielding Smith said: "When we dedicate a house to the Lord, what we really do is dedicate ourselves to the Lord's service, with a covenant that we shall use the house in the way he intends that it shall be used." ("Ensign," 3/1972). We thereby avoid the curse spoken of by Malachi, the last of the prophets of the Old Testament, who closed his ministry with these words: "Behold, I will send you Elijah the prophet, before the coming of the great and dreadful day of the Lord. And he shall turn the heart of the fathers to the children, and the heart of the children to their fathers, lest I come and smite the earth." (Malachi 4:5-6).

We might better understand the meaning of Malachi's prophecy if we turn to the words of the Angel Moroni, who appeared to Joseph Smith on September 21, 1823. "Behold, I will reveal unto you the Priesthood, by the hand of Elijah the prophet, before the coming of the great and dreadful day of the Lord. And he shall plant in the hearts of the children the promises made to the fathers, and the hearts of the children shall turn to their fathers. If it were not so, the whole earth would be utterly wasted at his coming." (D&C 2:1-3).

The message of Malachi is so important that it has been repeated, with only slight variations, in each of the four standard works. The Bible variant (Malachi 4:5-6) is quoted above, and is identical to the Doctrine & Covenants variant. (See D&C 128:17). In The Book of Mormon, Nephi 25:5-6 reads: "Behold, I will send you Elijah the prophet before the coming of the great and dreadful day of the Lord. And he shall turn the heart of the fathers to the children, and the heart of the children to their fathers, lest I come and smite the earth with a curse." J.S.H. 1:37-39 in The Pearl of Great Price reads the same as D&C 2:1-3, quoted above.

The earth would be wasted simply because if there is no welding link between parents and children, then the work of God, the Plan of Salvation, provided by the purposeful presence of a powerful priesthood, would fail and be utterly wasted.

We learn from latter-day revelation that Elijah held the sealing power of the Melchizedek Priesthood and was the last prophet on earth to do so before the time of Jesus Christ. ("Bible Dictionary"). He appeared with Moses and others, on April

3, 1836, in the Kirtland temple and conferred his keys of authority upon Joseph Smith and Oliver Cowdery. (D&C 110:13-16). Joseph Fielding Smith, Jr. explained: "This Priesthood holds the keys of binding and sealing on earth and in heaven of all the ordinances and principles pertaining to the salvation of man, that they may thus become valid in the Celestial Kingdom of God. It is by virtue of this authority that ordinances are performed in the temples for both the living and the dead. It is the power that unites for eternity husbands and wives when they enter into marriage according to the Eternal Plan. It is the authority by which parents obtain the claim of parenthood concerning their children through all eternity and not only for time, which makes eternal the family in the Kingdom of God." ("Doctrines of Salvation," 2:117).

The fullness of the power of the priesthood is "the opportunity of entering into covenants, accepting ordinances that pertain to our salvation beyond what is preached in the world, beyond the principles of faith in the Lord Jesus Christ, repentance from sin and baptism for the remission of sins and the laying on of hands for the gift of the Holy Ghost. These principles and covenants are received nowhere else but in the temple of God." (Joseph Fielding Smith, Jr., "Doctrines of Salvation," 2:40).

The sealing power of the priesthood is "the leaven that saves the earth from being utterly wasted at the coming of Jesus Christ. It is "so interwoven with the Plan of Salvation, that one cannot exist without the other. In other words, there can be no salvation where there (are) no temple ordinances." (Joseph Fielding Smith, Jr., "Liahona: The Elders' Journal," 4/15/1930).

In fact, the sealing power is irrevocably integrated with exaltation in the kingdom of God. Where there is one, there is the other. Where the one is not present, neither can be the other. This is why chosen servants of the Lord have today been given this sealing power, to perform the saving ordinances of the gospel for both the living and the dead. (See D&C 128:8).

The ordinances performed in the temple on behalf of those who have passed beyond the veil establish a covenant relationship with our Father and are cornerstones of the Plan of Salvation. When you stop and think about it, "the entire work of salvation (for ourselves and for our kindred dead) is a vicarious work, Jesus Christ standing as the propitiator, redeeming us from death, for which we were not responsible, and also redeeming us from the responsibility of our own sins, on condition of our repentance and acceptance of the gospel. In the Last Days, He has delegated authority to the members of His church to act for the dead who are helpless to perform the saving ordinances for themselves." (Joseph Fielding Smith, Jr., "The Restoration of All Things," p. 174–175).

Our unselfish work for our dead in the House of the Lord harmonizes perfectly with the doctrine that God is no respecter of persons. (See Acts 10:34). He esteems all flesh as one. (See 1 Nephi 17:35). He views all of His children as living. (See Genesis 2:76, & Job 33:4). The dead are undoubtedly as concerned about our welfare, as we are of theirs. They may very well view family history research as our mutual avenue of protection from the adversary, as an opportunity to receive divine assistance in the conduct of our lives, and as an inspired program to bring our eternal families closer together, as conversions are deepened and light and knowledge are received through the Holy Ghost on both sides of the veil.

Joseph Fielding Smith, Jr. taught: "The Lord has decreed that all of his spirit children, every soul who has lived or shall live on earth, shall have a fair and just opportunity to believe and obey the laws of his everlasting gospel." This creates a minor problem with family research as it is currently being performed. As President Smith continued: "It is obvious that only a small portion of mankind has so far heard the word of revealed truth from the voice of one of the Lord's true servants. In the wisdom and justice of the Lord, all must do so." ("B.Y.U. Speeches of the Year," 1/12/1971).

How can that be possible, if it is true that "humanity has produced an astonishing 108 billion individual people over the past 50 millennia?" ("Population Reference Bureau"). How could we ever do the work for 108 billion people? To help to answer this question, Joseph Smith explained that "immortal beings will frequently visit the earth" during the Millennium. "These resurrected beings will help with the government and other work." ("Teachings," p. 268).

Brigham Young added: "We will have revelations to know our forefathers clear back to Father Adam and Mother Eve, and we will enter into the temples of God and officiate for them. Then, man will be sealed to man until the chain is made perfect back to Adam, so that there will be a perfect chain of priesthood from Adam to the winding-up scene." (J.D., 15:137-138).

Joseph Fielding Smith, Jr. taught: "There is too much work to finish before the Millennium begins, so it will be completed during that time. Resurrected beings will help us correct the mistakes we have made in doing research concerning our dead ancestors. They will also help us find the information we need to complete our records." ("Doctrines of Salvation," 2:167, & 251-252).

This might help to explain why there is to be a thousand years of peace on the earth following the Second Coming of the Lord. During the Millennium, "Christ will reign personally upon the earth. (10th Article of Faith). This will allow members of the church unimpeded access to the temples, where they will perform vicarious work for the dead. "Guided by revelation, they will prepare records of their ancestors all the way back to Adam and Eve." (LDS.org: "Millennium").

Temples are going to be humming with activity during the Millennium. The Church News reported on August 27, 1988: "The 100 millionth endowment for the dead was performed sometime in August. The first endowments for the dead were performed about 111 years ago, but, in keeping with an accelerating rate of temple (construction) and temple work, more than half have been performed in the last 11 years." That's about 50 million endowments in just 11 years, from 1977 to 1988, which is all the more remarkable, because at the time this article was published, there were only 41 temples in operation.

If we do the math, if we were to continue performing work for the dead in all of those 41 temples at the same pace, about a billion endowments could be performed in 1,000 years (+/- one million endowments per year x 1000 years = 1 billion endowments). But if there were not 41, but 1,000 temples in operation, all performing endowments at the same pace as those initial 41 temples, almost 25 billion endowments could be performed in a thousand years.

The real question is: Is it necessary to perform the work for all 108 billion people envisioned by the Population Reference Bureau to have lived on earth? After all, priesthood ordinances are only important for those who are willing to accept the gospel in the Spirit World. In fact, "Wilford Woodruff taught that almost all in the spirit world will accept the vicarious ordinances when they are performed for them." ("The Improvement Era," 11/1941). So the answer may very well be "Yes."

Joseph Fielding Smith, Jr. said: "Those who did not have the opportunity to hear the message of salvation in this life but who would have accepted it with all their hearts if such an opportunity had come to them - they are the ones who will accept it in the spirit world; they are the ones for whom we shall perform the ordinances in the temples; and they are the ones who shall, in this way, become heirs with us of salvation and eternal life." ("B.Y.U. Speeches of the Year," 1/12/1971).

In 1856, Brigham Young famously proclaimed" "To accomplish this work there will have to be not only one temple but thousands of them, and thousands and tens of thousands of men and women will go into those temples and officiate for people who have lived as far back as the Lord shall reveal." (J.D., 3:372).

President Young could have been speaking figuratively (thousands being a very big number), hyperbolically (sometimes, he got carried away), analytically (he was the Great Colonizer, after all), or prophetically (he knew the numbers, by revelation).

Or it could have been all of the above. Perhaps he was recalling his own experience, back in Nauvoo, when about 5,200 individuals had received the endowment in just 42 working days. At the Nauvoo Temple pace, it would take 4,320 such temples to reach the magical number of 108 billion endowments during the Millennium.

Here is the Nauvoo math: In one temple, 123.8 endowments were performed per day (5,200 / 42 days), equaling 45,187 projected endowments per year, (123.8 x 365), or 45,187,000 in a thousand years (45,187 x 1,000). If 2,400 such temples were in operation, 108 billion endowments could be performed (108,000,000 x 1,000). However, things could change dramatically; for example, if the logistics of providing endowments were modified; for example, if the 21,000-seat Conference Center were converted into one large endowment room, or if endowments were broadcast to the chapels in which any of the 29,000 congregations of the church meet, or, if the endowment itself were streamlined in some way.

In any event, temple work is "one of the grand principles of truth revealed through the Prophet Joseph Smith. Obedience to this principle will allow us to "rejoice in the kingdom of God with our relatives and friends in the grand reunion and assemblage of the saints of the Church of the First Born." (Joseph Fielding Smith, Jr., C.R., 10/1911).

The greatest miracle is not the raising of the dead, but the healing of the spiritually sick.

The Bestowal
of Spiritual Gifts

"Now there are diversities of gifts, but the same Spirit. ...But the manifestation of the Spirit is given to every man to profit withal. For to one is given by the Spirit the word of wisdom; to another the word of knowledge by the same Spirit; to another faith by the same Spirit; to another the gifts of healing by the same Spirit; to another the working of miracles; to another prophecy; to another discerning of spirits; to another divers kinds of tongues; to another the interpretation of tongues." (1 Corinthians 12:4, & 7-10).

"All things must be done in the name of Christ, whatsoever you do in the Spirit." (D&C 46:31). The baptism of water qualifies us for membership in the church but does not guarantee the total spiritual transformation necessary to regain the presence of God. This comes through the baptism of fire and the Holy Ghost, which is the receipt of the Spirit unto sanctification: "For by the water ye keep the commandment; by the Spirit ye are justified, and by the blood ye are sanctified." (Moses 6:60).

Alma asked his brethren, "Have ye spiritually been born of God?" (Alma 5:14). He wanted to know if these baptized members of the church had experienced the pure and unconditional love of Christ, and if they had charity for all men. He already knew they had been converted to the church; what he really wanted to find out was if they had also been converted to the gospel. Mahatma Gandhi once said" "If a single man achieves the highest kind of love, it will be enough to neutralize the hatred of millions." Alma knew that the pure love of Christ in the hearts of his people would be a dynamic influence for good. With this kind of dedication, they would perform mighty miracles in His name, through the workings of the Spirit.

The Spirit is ready to guide us unerringly, that we may know the truthfulness of all things. (See Moroni 10:5). Even more importantly, it molds and shapes us into new creatures in Christ. As Joseph Smith said: "By the power of the Spirit our eyes were opened and our understandings were enlightened, so as to see and understand the things of God." (D&C 76:10).

As our powers expand, we experience the glittering facets of the life of the Spirit, and we are cast off into a stream of revelation that brings us into direct experience with God. "To use the careful preparation and training we receive as a springboard, to be capable of disciplined, controlled procedure and to be receptive to flashes of insight, is what a solid Latter-day Saint should have going for him in his inner life. The gospel sets us free to be creative, and sets us creative to become more free," as we learn to respond to the guidance of the Spirit and enjoy spiritual gifts. It is the perfect law of liberty." ("My Religion & Me," Lesson #9).

Every member of the church "is given a gift by the Spirit of God." (D&C 46:11). These gifts can be positive, motivational, and uplifting, by allowing us to vividly pre-play, role-play, and re-play our life's experiences. They provide us with a safety net circumscribing the healthy expression of our agency.

When we have the image of God engraved upon our countenances, we will recognize our spiritual gifts, and give thanks to Him Who has bestowed them. "Who shall ascend into the hill of the Lord," asked the Psalmist, "or who shall stand in his holy place" to partake of the Divine Nature? "He that hath clean hands and a pure heart; who hath not lifted up his soul unto vanity, nor sworn deceitfully." (Psalms 24:4-5).

"To some is given one, and to some is given another, that all may be profited thereby." (D&C 46:12). Sometimes, it is necessary to fast and pray to gain a witness of the Spirit and receive a strong, independent testimony of the gospel. Only when we have paid the price, can we comprehend the language of the Spirit. Otherwise, it is foreign to us. If we have never made the journey to Christ, if we have not traveled the path leading to the tree of life, if we have not partaken of the delicious fruit of that tree, if we disregard the essentials, we are tongue-tied, and cannot receive "the things of the Spirit of God, for they are foolishness unto (us), neither can (we) know them, because they are spiritually discerned." (1 Corinthians 2:14-15). Faith precedes the miracle of the receipt of spiritual gifts.

Regarding our comprehension of the different manifestations of the Spirit, Marion G. Romney said: "Having a testimony and being converted are not necessarily the same thing. A testimony comes when the Holy Ghost gives the earnest seeker a witness of the truth. A moving testimony vitalizes faith, that is, it induces repentance and obedience to the commandments. Conversion, on the other hand, is the fruit or the reward for repentance and obedience." (C.R., 10/1963). Spiritual gifts follow conversion that is built on the foundation of testimony.

The Gifts of the Spirit are given to the members of the church in priesthood ordinances. Our Heavenly Father is anxious to bless us with these gifts. Without interfering with our agency, they are sufficient to guide us in the direction of behavioral lifestyle choices that are in harmony with celestial principles. God wants each of us to succeed, to pass our individual tests of mortality, and then to move on toward our celestial home, having satisfied the entrance requirements for admittance to His kingdom. With what greater gifts could our Heavenly Father bless us than those that help us to reach this goal?

"And it shall come to pass that he that asketh in Spirit shall receive in Spirit." (D&C 46:28). It is appropriate to ask for spiritual gifts, that we might grow in the grace of God. As we do so, we become more and more like Him, developing His divine attributes and spiritual stature. We follow the path of His Only Begotten Son, Who commanded: "I would that ye should be perfect, even as I, or your Father who is in heaven is perfect." (3 Nephi 12:48, see Matthew 5:48). God glories in the possibility that we might become like Him, as we endure to the end in righteousness.

"It is a serious thing to live in a society of possible Gods and Goddesses," wrote C.S. Lewis, "to remember that the dullest and most uninteresting person you talk to may one day be a creature which if you saw it now you would be strongly tempted to worship. It is in the light of these overwhelming possibilities, it is with the awe and the circumspection proper to them, that we should conduct all our dealings with one another...all friendships, all loves, all play, all politics. There are no ordinary people. You have never talked to a mere mortal. It is immortals with whom we joke, work, marry, snub and exploit. Our charity must be a real and costly love. Next to the blessed Sacrament itself, your neighbor is the holiest object presented to your senses. If he is your Christian neighbor, he is holy in almost the same way, for in him also Christ is truly hidden and glorified." ("The Weight of Glory," p. 14-15).

"If ye by the grace of God are perfect in Christ, and deny not his power, then are ye sanctified in Christ by the grace of God, through the shedding of the blood of Christ, which is in the covenant of the Father unto the remission of your sins, that ye become holy, without spot." (Moroni 10:33). It would be difficult to put more succinctly, or to state more powerfully, the essence of the gospel of Jesus Christ, than in this verse. If we open our hearts, we can become holy, without spot. "Holy," Peter taught, is one of the name-titles of God Himself. As Paul described Him, He was as a lamb without spot or blemish. (See 1 Peter 1:19, & Hebrews 9:14).

Spiritual gifts cannot be purchased with the treasures of the earth. Perhaps this is why in their efforts to obtain the sacred records in Laban's treasury, Lehi's sons were stripped of all their gold, silver, and precious things. The task was to be accomplished in the Lord's way, by the power of His mighty arm that is great in the sight of the faithful, but that has a terrible effect upon the wicked. As Alma asked: "Can ye dispute the power of God?" (Mosiah 27:16). Certainly not, for the arm of flesh is weak in comparison to the power of the Spirit.

The gift of faith motivates us to action. The miracles from the scriptures with which we are familiar were only made possible by the exercise of faith that may be active, or may lie dormant, within each of us. When we read in the sacred records of these experiences, a way is prepared that we, too, might be "partakers of the heavenly gift." (Ether 12:8). It becomes possible for us to share the intensity of feeling experienced by the two disciples on the Road to Emmaus, who, after communing with the Resurrected Lord, declared: "Did not our heart burn within us, while he talked with us by the way, and while he opened to us the scriptures?" (Luke 24:32).

The gift of discernment stands in sharp contrast to the cold, harsh rationality of those in the world, who, as long as they have visible proof, grudgingly acknowledge the hand of the Lord in their affairs. These individuals can discern neither good nor evil; their only reality is that which may be defined by their five physical senses.

Heavenly Father, on the other hand, has provided a way to discern truth through the operation of the Spirit. For example, He does not offer up holy writ to be scrutinized, analyzed, criticized, and rationalized by pompous doctors and professors of religion clothed in the robes of the false priesthood and cloistered in the ivory towers of academia. "You cannot prove the genuineness of any document to one who has decided not to accept it," declared Hugh Nibley. "When a man asks for proof we can be pretty sure that proof is the last thing in the world he really wants. His request is thrown out as a challenge, and the chances are that he has no intention of being shown up. After all these years, the Bible itself is still not proven to those who do not choose to accept it. So The Book of Mormon as an 'unproven' book finds itself in good company." ("An Approach to The Book of Mormon," p. 2).

Nor will the Lord indulge the prurient interest of men who only want theological titillation to satisfy their adulterous curiosity. Again, The Book of Mormon provides a classic example. Critics of that book "often remark sarcastically that it is a great pity that the golden plates have disappeared, since they would conveniently prove Joseph Smith's story. They would do nothing of the sort. The presence of the plates would only prove that there were plates, no more. It would not prove that Nephites wrote them, or that an angel brought them, or that they had been translated by the gift and power of God, and we can be sure that scholars would quarrel about the writing on them for generations without coming to any agreement, exactly as they have done about parts of the Bible. The possession of the plates would have a very disruptive effect and it would prove nothing.

On the other hand, a far more impressive claim is put forth when the whole work is given to the world in what is claimed to be a divinely inspired translation. In such a text, any cause or pretext for disagreement and speculation is reduced to an absolute minimum. It is a text which all the world can read and understand, and it is a far more miraculous object than any gold plates would be." (High Nibley, "An Approach to The Book of Mormon," p. 17-18). The only thing that a spiritual witness does not do is pander to the base instinct of the world's fallen and depraved nature.

The gift of wisdom is given to those who press forward with complete dedication, feasting upon the words of Christ, receiving physical and spiritual strength and nourishment, and enduring to the end with continuing responsibility and accountability. These are they who have been promised the spiritual gift of hidden treasures of knowledge.

Moroni wrote: "To one is given by the Spirit of God, that he may teach the word of wisdom." (Moroni 10:9). The Lord instructed Joseph Smith to "teach one another the doctrine of the kingdom," to the end that all might be edified in Christ. (D&C 88:77). Perhaps the most dramatic spiritual manifestation that was the result of one seeking wisdom from God, was that received by Joseph Smith in The Sacred Grove. He had read in James 1:5-6: "If any of you lack wisdom, let him ask God, that giveth to all men liberally, and upbraideth not; and it shall be given him. But let him ask in faith, nothing wavering." This promise was powerfully fulfilled when he learned that wisdom leading to salvation comes from God by personal revelation.

The Lord said that we should not seek not for riches, but for wisdom. To understand spiritual things, we must have discernment or guidance from the Holy Ghost. For example, those who are sincerely investigating the church are taught by the Spirit, and receive its witness. When they are confirmed as members of the church they are endowed by ordinance with the special gift of the companionship of the Holy Ghost. One of His purposes is to guide the faithful from the covenant waters of baptism, along the strait and narrow path leading past the second mile marker to the other covenants of the priesthood that are necessary for us to obtain eternal life. This is one reason why members of the church are given the Holy Ghost in an initial priesthood ordinance beside the waters of baptism, or shortly thereafter.

The mysteries of God are those truths that can only be known by revelation from the Holy Ghost. When we "hunger and thirst after righteousness," the doctrine of the priesthood, or words of wisdom, will distill upon our souls as the dews from heaven, and the Holy Ghost will be our constant companion. (See D&C 121:45-46). Then, to him that will not harden his heart "is given the greater portion of the word (of wisdom), until it is given unto him to know the mysteries of God until he know them in full." (Alma 12:10). We gain access to the spiritual gift of knowledge of the mysteries of God, that are the saving principles of the gospel of Jesus Christ.

To those who harden their hearts to the truth, however, "is given the lesser portion of the word until they know nothing concerning his mysteries, and then they are taken captive by the devil, and led by his will down to destruction. Now this is what is meant by the chains of hell." (Alma 12:11). The terrible thing about hardening our hearts is that our understanding of the word is withheld, leaving us vulnerable to the devil's influence. The scriptures identify the consequences of sin in very plain language. Its effect on those who sin after having been taught the principles of the gospel in plainness is that the guidance of the Spirit is withdrawn, and they are left alone to grope in darkness. Guilt causes them to shrink from church activity, and in the absence of the Spirit, they have no claim on the blessings of prosperity or preservation. Having eyes, they see not, and having ears, they hear not.

Tragically, these individuals, feeling uncomfortable in proximity to spiritual experiences, withdraw to lifestyles that are devoid of such associations. Thus begins a downward spiral that can only gain momentum as sinful practices, more easily committed, become entrenched. Even worse, "the man that doeth this, the same cometh out in open rebellion against God." (Mosiah 2:37). "Thus saith the Lord concerning all those who know my power, and have been made partakers thereof, and suffered themselves through the power of the devil to be overcome, and to deny the truth and defy my power. They are they who are the sons of perdition." (D&C 76:31-32). They suffer a spiritual death that is devoid of light and truth.

When the word and the will of the Lord came to the Saints through Brigham Young, it was: "Let him that is ignorant learn wisdom by humbling himself and calling upon the Lord his God, that his eyes may be opened that he may see, and his ears opened that he may hear. For my Spirit is sent forth into the world to enlighten the humble and contrite." (D&C 136:32-33).

The gift of knowledge is given to those who seek "line upon line, precept upon precept." (D&C 98:12). Personal revelation is the ultimate source of our understanding of God's will. "These currents and many more are part of the flowing fountain of the church. If we do not drink, if we die of thirst while only inches from the fountain, the fault comes down to us. For the free, full, flowing, living water is there." (Truman Madsen, "Christ & The Inner Life," p. 31).

Mormon wrote of Alma's teaching style: "And now, as the preaching of the word had a great tendency to lead the people to do that which was just - yea, it had had more powerful effect upon the minds of the people than the sword, or anything else, which had happened unto them – therefore, Alma thought it was expedient that they should try the virtue of the word of God." (Alma 31:5).

Joseph Smith similarly taught: "A person can get nearer to God by reading The Book of Mormon than by reading any other book." (H.C., 4:461). There is great motivating and sanctifying power in the words of The Book of Mormon, precisely because as a companion to the Bible it is Another Testament of Jesus Christ.

"Young men," counseled Ezra Taft Benson, "The Book of Mormon will change your life. It will fortify you against the evils of our day. It will bring spirituality into your life that no other book will. It will be the most important book you will read in preparation for a mission and for life. A young man who knows and loves The Book of Mormon, who has read it several times, who has an abiding testimony of its truthfulness, and who applies its teachings, will be able to stand against the wiles of the devil and will be a mighty tool in the hands of the Lord.

Oh, my brethren," he continued, "let us not treat lightly the great things we have received from the hand of the Lord. His word is one of the most valuable gifts He has given us. I urge you to recommit yourselves to a study of the scriptures. Read them in your families, and teach your children to love and treasure them. Then, prayerfully and in counsel with others, seek every way possible to encourage the members of the church to follow your example." (C.R., 4/1986).

Moroni wrote: "To another (it is given) that he may teach the word of knowledge." (Moroni 10:10). Joseph Smith taught: "It is impossible for a man to be saved in ignorance" of the saving principles of the gospel." (D&C 131:6). We must have knowledge of them, and of our Heavenly Father, for as Jesus taught: "This is life eternal, that they might know thee the only true God, and Jesus Christ, whom thou hast sent." (John 17:3). Our knowledge of Them is a gift of the Spirit.

The gift of administration is given to those who discern correctly the services and agencies through which the Lord operates His church. "These ordinances are not empty, passive rituals; rather, they bind individuals to receive the promises and blessings of the gospel by means of a covenant of action between themselves and the Lord." ("Doctrinal Commentary on The Book of Mormon," 4:319). These ordinances bridge the gulf between earth and heaven, attest to the nature of God, confirm that His church is founded on unchanging principles, and illustrate that the requirements for obtaining salvation are the same for all.

Churches that operate on borrowed light are sometimes quite popular with people who seek the form without the substance, the sizzle without the steak, and who enjoy the relative ease of putting forth minimal effort in an organization that makes few demands for personal sacrifice. But the Church of Christ is powered by the Spirit, and there is a performance requirement associated with every blessing received.

When we think of the gift of speaking in tongues, the missionaries who serve throughout the world come to mind. We also remember the Nephite children whom Jesus blessed. These received an endowment of spiritual power, for the Savior "did loose their tongues, and they did speak unto their fathers great and marvelous things, even greater than he had revealed unto the people." (3 Nephi 26:14). The multitude "both saw and heard these children; yea, even babes did open their mouths and utter marvelous things; and the things which they did utter were forbidden that there should not any man write them." (3 Nephi 26:16).

The gift of the interpretation of tongues may include the ability to comprehend the words of the scriptures. As the Lord told Joseph Smith: "These words are not of men nor of man, but of me; wherefore, you shall testify they are of me and not of man. For it is my voice which speaketh them unto you; for they are given by my Spirit unto you, and by my power you can read them one to another; and save it were by my power you could not have them." (D&C 18:34-35).

The gift of faith to be healed was illustrated most dramatically during the Savior's post-mortal ministry among the Nephites. He manifested His power, and His disciples exhibited their faith, when He "healed all their sick, and their lame, and opened the eyes of their blind and unstopped the ears of the deaf." (3 Nephi 26:15). Certainly, His efforts to bless the people were enhanced by their great faith in Him. The Savior does not want lukewarm converts; He desires those whose commitment is profound. Then, He can truly bless their lives. After entering the fold, such devoted disciples may see and hear "unspeakable things, which are not lawful to be written." (3 Nephi 26:18). They will remember the counsel of the Master, Who said: "Ye know the things that ye must do in my church; for the works which ye have seen me do that shall ye also do." (3 Nephi 27:21). Without realizing it, the children of Christ are transformed into a Zion society, "for this is Zion – the pure in heart." (D&C 97:21). Collectively, they are the Church of Christ.

Malachi was speaking of the gift of faith to heal when he declared in the name of the Lord: "Unto you that fear my name shall the Sun of righteousness arise with healing in his wings." (Malachi 4:2). There is also another dimension of faith to heal. Only six generations after Adam, "Enoch looked upon the earth; and he heard a voice from the bowels thereof, saying: Wo, wo is me, the mother of men; I am pained, I am weary, because of the wickedness of my children. When shall I rest, and be cleansed from the filthiness which is gone forth out of me? When will my Creator sanctify me, that I may rest, and righteousness for a season abide upon my face?" (Moses 7:48). When one comprehends the significance of the terrible pollutions on the face of the earth, and the physical and spiritual cleansing that will be required of it before the Kingdom of God can return, the concept of "healing" moves to a more comprehensive, all-encompassing, level.

At the millennial day, all shall lift up their voice and sing, declaring that "the earth hath travailed and brought forth her strength," as a mother who has borne a new child, "and the heavens have smiled upon her," for she is pure and delightsome. "And she is clothed with the glory of her God," adorned in the strength of His priesthood. "For he stands in the midst of his people (with) glory, and honor, and power, and might. For he is full of mercy, justice, grace and truth, and peace." (D&C 84:101-102). Peter indicated that true Saints "have obtained like precious faith with us through the righteousness of God and our Saviour Jesus Christ. According as his divine power hath given unto us all things that pertain unto life and godliness, through the knowledge of him that hath called us to glory and virtue; whereby are given unto us exceeding great and precious promises: That by these ye might be partakers of the divine nature." (2 Peter 1:1, 3 & 4). These are they who know the power of God, understand His nature, and experience the whisperings of the Spirit.

The gift of prophesy is "the testimony of Jesus." (Revelation 19:10). It follows that those who have received this spiritual gift are prophets, since a testimony can only be received by revelation from the Holy Ghost, and since prophecy consists of the words we speak when we are moved upon by the Spirit.

"Wo unto him that shall deny the revelations of the Lord, and that shall say the Lord no longer worketh by revelation, or by prophecy, or by gifts, or by tongues, or by healings, or by the power of the Holy Ghost!" (3 Nephi 29:6). In contrast, the church testifies "to the world that revelation continues, and that the vaults and files of the church contain these revelations which come month to month, and day to day." (Spencer W. Kimball, C.R., 4/1977).

The gift of the working of miracles is a manifestation of the power of God that is incomprehensible to the world. For "the natural man receiveth not the things of the Spirit of God: for they are foolishness unto him: neither can he know them, because they are spiritually discerned." (1 Corinthians 2:14).

"Wo unto him," in the Last Days, "that shall say that there can be no miracle wrought by Jesus Christ; for he that doeth this shall become like unto the son of perdition, for whom there was no mercy, according to the word of Christ!" (3 Nephi 29:7). Those who deny the divinity of Christ cannot be saved on His merits, because they have not generated saving faith in his power. They are like the hypothermic individual whose core temperature cannot be raised without an external source of warmth. Unless they experience a profound attitude adjustment that allows the Holy Ghost to quicken their own spirits with vitality, their progression will come to a grinding halt, and they will be damned.

Those who enjoy the gift of a testimony of Jesus Christ unflinchingly declare that He was "the Son, the Only Begotten of the Father, full of grace, and mercy, and truth." (Alma 5:48). "Either this man was, and is, the Son of God, or else a madman or something worse," declared C.S. Lewis. "But don't let us come with any patronizing nonsense about His (only) being a great human teacher" as the secular apologists would have us believe. ("Mere Christianity," p. 55).

The gift to believe the testimony of others may be enjoyed by investigators, little children, and church members in general, who listen to the authorities of the church bear testimony. "And by doing so, the Lord God prepareth the way that the residue of men may have faith in Christ, that the Holy Ghost may have place in their hearts." (Moroni 7:32).

Alma said that preaching the gospel with power and authority is the responsibility of those who bear the priesthood of God. "This is the order after which I am called," he said, "yea, to preach unto my beloved brethren, yea, and every one that dwelleth in the land." (Alma 5:49). The objects of his attention were members and non-members alike. He felt that it was his duty to bring the gift of the gospel to all, and his message was the same, that all must repent and be born again.

Some have all the spiritual gifts. "Unto some it may be given to have all those gifts, that there may be a head, in order that every member may be profited thereby." (D&C 46:29). When members of the church have faith in the atoning power of Christ, and if they furthermore possess the resolve to do whatever is necessary to activate that energy in their own lives, they will profit by the administration of the gifts of the Spirit. Those who have faith in the power of Christ to save them from their sins will have a profound motivation to live in accordance with His will. They will see with an eye of faith, or with an eternal perspective. They will not only believe in Christ, but they will believe Christ, when He says that they are celestial raw material. The manifestation of spiritual gifts will dramatically validate their continuing efforts to be transformed. On the other hand, those who are not valiant in the testimony of Jesus, who do not stand for something, will fall for anything. If they don't know where they are going, they will end up somewhere else, and probably won't even care if they made the trip.

Beginning in 1830, an unbroken line of prophets has led the restored church. Since 1847, these have administered its affairs "from Salt Lake City, Utah. They have dedicated themselves to their appointed mission of helping the people of the world prepare for eternal life, and for the second coming of Jesus Christ. They have provided leadership for the international missionary program of the Church and for the building of temples. The living prophet continues to receive revelations, select and ordain leaders by the spirit of prophecy, and serve as the principal teacher of the church, instructing its members in doctrine and in righteous living." (L.D.S. Infobase). The prophet is supported in these efforts by all of the gifts of the Spirit.

Spiritual gifts were created "for the benefit of the children of God." (D&C 46:26). It will be difficult for those who have lived a telestial existence to justify their actions before God, in light of the many signs and wonders He has provided as both warnings and blessings. "Any man who hath seen any or the least of these hath seen God moving in his majesty and power." (D&C 88:47). "Earth is crammed with heaven, and every common bush with fire of God. But only those who see take off their shoes. The rest stand around picking blackberries." (Elizabeth Barrett Browning).

Ours is the Age of Inspiration and of the gifts of the Spirit, when the Holy Ghost is being poured out in rich abundance. With prophetic foresight, Joseph Smith promised: "God shall give unto you knowledge by His Holy Spirit, yea, by the unspeakable gift of the Holy Ghost, that has not been revealed since the world was until now." This is a time when "nothing shall be withheld. All thrones and dominions, principalities and powers, shall be revealed. And also, if there be bounds set to the heavens or to the seas, or to the dry land, or to the sun, moon, or stars," all this "shall be revealed in the days of the dispensation of the fulness of times." (D&C 121:26-31).

Those to whom the gospel has been dispensed "receive the gifts of sensory delight, of fragrance, sound, and form and color." Theirs "is the realm of human associations, of gratitude, loyalty, and appreciation, of selflessness, helpfulness and forgiveness, of friendship, love, and compassion. It is the realm of human growth and transcendence and of truth discovered and accepted, of beauty created and enjoyed, of goodness deepened and made manifest in life.

None of us are strangers to these realms of spirit. We have sensed the world about us, smelled its fragrance, heard its sounds, and glimpsed its form and colors. We have warmed our souls in the glow of human associations; have had our moments of selflessness and gratitude, love and forgiveness. We have felt an upward reach within us when made suddenly aware of a truth, a beauty, a goodness above and beyond our own attainment." (P.A. Christensen, "B.Y.U. Studies," Autumn, 1975).

These whisperings confirm to our hearts that there is more to the gospel than outward observances, obedience, and covenants. Spiritual enlightenment is the key to the discovery of undreamed of vistas of otherwise inaccessible experience.

The Apostle Paul testified that "eye hath not seen, nor ear heard, neither have entered into the heart of man, the things which God hath prepared for them that love him." (1 Corinthians 2:9). Nephi declared: "No tongue can speak, neither can there be written by any man, neither can the hearts of men conceive so great and marvelous things as we both saw and heard Jesus speak." (3 Nephi 17:7). Joseph Fielding Smith, Jr., described the spiritual "impressions on the soul that come from the Holy Ghost (as) far more significant than a vision. It is where spirit speaks to spirit, and the imprint upon the soul is far more difficult to erase." ("Seek Ye Earnestly," p. 213–214).

The scriptures allude to the thin line between the material world and the world of spiritual matters: "And when the servant of the man of God was risen early, and gone forth, behold, an host compassed the city both with horses and chariots. And his servant said unto him, Alas, my master, how shall we do? And he answered, Fear not: for they that be with us are more than they that be with them. And Elisha prayed, and said, Lord, I pray thee, open his eyes, that he may see. And the Lord opened the eyes of the young man; and he saw: and, behold, the mountain was full of horses and chariots of fire round about Elisha." (2 Kings 6:15-17).

"When you lay down this tabernacle, where are you going?" asked Brigham Young. "Into the spirit world," he replied. "Where is the spirit world? It is right here. Do the spirits go beyond the boundaries of this organized earth? No, they do not. They can see us, but we cannot see them, unless our eyes were opened." ("The Vision," p. 55-56).

A reminiscence by a friend and associate of Joseph Smith reflects the gossamer fabric of the veil separating the world we know from the world of spirits. "I am getting tired and would like to go to my rest, said Joseph. His words and tone (both) thrilled and shocked me, and like an arrow, pierced my hopes that he would long remain with us, and I said, as with a heart full of tears: Oh Joseph, what could we, as a people, do without you and what would become of the great Latter-day work, if you should leave us? He saw and was touched by my emotions, and in reply he said, Benjamin, I would not be far away from you, and if on the other side of the veil, I would still be working with you, and with a power greatly increased, to roll on this kingdom." ("The Vision," p. 140-141).

It is the challenge of every member of the church to learn to understand the language of the Spirit with perfect fluency, because twenty-first century Americans especially, "tend to fill space, as if what they have, what they are, is not enough. Being affluent, they strangle themselves with what they can buy, things whose opacity obstructs their ability to see what is really there." (Gretel Erlich, "The Atlantic Magazine"). The bestowal of spiritual gifts is the antidote for poisonous telestial tendencies that can choke the expression of celestial sureties.

"And ye must give thanks unto God in the Spirit for whatsoever blessing ye are blessed with. And ye must practice virtue and holiness before me continually." (D&C 46:32-33). The gifts of the Spirit cause our breasts to swell with joy. Spirituality, the kind of life where we may enjoy these gifts, "is the consciousness of victory over self, and of communion with the infinite." (David O. McKay, "Teachings of Presidents of the Church," p. 10-19). The gifts of the Spirit help us to be richer today than we were yesterday, to laugh often, to give something, to forgive even more, to make new friends, to change stumbling blocks into stepping stones, to think more in terms of "thyself" than "ourselves," to be cheerful even when we are weary, and to bless the lives of others. The gifts of the Spirit help us to receive the image of Christ in our countenances, and to experience a mighty change in our hearts that is real. "Happy is the person who has truly sensed the uplifting, transforming power that comes from this nearness to the Savior, this kinship to the Living Christ." (David O. McKay, C.R., 4/1944).

We must "always remember and always retain in (our) minds what those gifts are, that are given unto the church." (D&C 46:10). For "whatsoever good cometh from God." (Alma 5:40). The gifts of the Spirit are given so that we may have the fortifying influence necessary to combat evil in the world. "We have no excuse to err in our knowledge and understanding of right and wrong. By inquiring of the Lord and listening to the voice of His Spirit, and having a willingness to be guided thereby, we will always find ourselves on the Lord's side of every issue, and be strengthened to hold fast to that which is good." (Delbert Stapley, C.R., 4/1965).

As we do this, the windows of heaven will be opened unto us, and the blessings of the Lord will be poured out upon our heads, to the end "that (we) may not be seduced by evil spirits, or doctrines of devils, or the commandments of men." D&C 46:7). The mission statement of all who have ever labored in our behalf is summarized in the last verses of The Book of Mormon. It is to "come unto Christ, and lay hold upon every good gift, and touch not the evil gift, nor the unclean thing." It is to "come unto Christ, and be perfected in him, and deny (ourselves) of all ungodliness." (Moroni 10:30 & 32).

That we may not be deceived, we must seek "earnestly the best gifts, always remembering for what they are given." (D&C 46:8). God will continue the ministry and work miracles among the children of men as "long as time shall last, or the earth shall stand, or there shall be one man upon the face thereof to be saved." But "if these things have ceased, wo be unto the children of men, for it is because of unbelief, and all is vain." (Words of Mormon 1:36-37). The Last Days are a reflection of the final days of the Nephites, when "there were sorceries, and witchcrafts, and magics, and the power of the evil one was wrought upon all the face of the land" because of the lack of faith of the people. (Mormon 1:19).

When the gifts of the Spirit are absent, we must declare, as did Mormon, that "faith (has) ceased also; and awful is the state of man, for they are as though there had been no redemption made." (Words of Mormon 1:38). Alma warned: "For behold, if ye have procrastinated the day of your repentance even until death," or if you have waited to develop saving faith until you were spiritually dead to the Light of Christ, "behold, ye have become subjected to the spirit of the devil, and he doth seal you his," because you can no longer make the vital distinction between good and evil, or light and darkness. "Therefore, the Spirit of the Lord hath withdrawn from you, and hath no place in you, and the devil hath all power over you," for you have voluntarily surrendered your agency to act independently, "and this is the final state of the wicked," for there is no recovery, and it will be as if there had been no redemption made for such individuals who refuse to repent. (Alma 34:35).

Mormon exhorted his brethren to rise to the occasion. He said: "I judge better things of you, for I judge that ye have faith in Christ because of your meekness; for if ye have not faith in him then ye are not fit to be numbered among the people of his church." (Moroni 7:39). He was like wise old Tevya, in "The Fiddler on The Roof," who told his daughters: "In Anatevka, God knows who you are, and what you may become." (Sheldon Harnick).

Those who ask "for a sign that they may consume it upon their lusts," only want theological titillation. (D&C 46:9). Those whose spiritual sensitivities have been dulled, desire only the thrill of the moment. While signs and wonders, and gifts of the spirit, may be exhilarating and spine-tingling, they are completely misunderstood and wasted on such individuals.

But the wicked may still receive spiritual manifestations for a variety of reasons. Sometimes they demand and receive signs as proof of the authority of servants of the Lord. (See John 2:18 & 6:30). Those who have adulterous hearts seek signs to satisfy their carnal desires that require greater and greater intensities of validation for the same level of gratification. (See Matthew 12:39). Signs are sometimes given for no reason other than to vindicate the prophets. (See Mosiah 20:21). Signs thus given leave the wicked with responsibility for what happens. Because consequence follows action, signs establish accountability. (See D&C 63:7 & 11).

Mormon recorded that the people who lived in Zarahemla just before the birth of the Savior attributed the signs that had been given them to "the power of the devil, to lead away and deceive the hearts of the people." (3 Nephi 2:2). In reality, it was the devil himself who was the source of their rationalizations: "And thus did Satan get possession of the hearts of the people again, insomuch that he did blind their eyes, and lead them away to believe that the doctrine of Christ was a foolish and a vain thing." (3 Nephi 2:2).

When Mormon observed that "the people began to wax strong in wickedness and abominations," he might have been drawing particular attention to those who had made covenants with God, and who should have known better when they consciously chose to conspicuously compromise their conduct. (3 Nephi 2:3). It is one thing for an ignorant people to live in opposition to the laws of God, but it is quite another for those who have had the light, and who have enjoyed spiritual gifts, to turn from them, willfully rebel, and intentionally seek out darkness. That circumstance is an abomination, because it represents unfaithfulness to God. It is not easy for those who refuse to accept the gifts of God to obtain forgiveness. Those who have not allowed Christ into their lives "die in their sins, and they cannot be saved in the kingdom of God." (Moroni 10:26).

Professors of religion have made a business of teaching "for doctrines the commandments of men. Having a form of godliness…they deny the power thereof." (J.S.H. 1:19). Creeds are an abomination in the sight of God and are corrupt when they lead people away from the truth. Insult is added to injury when hypocrisy further perverts and transforms doctrine into humanized, spiritually impotent dogma; when it is only a caricature of its former self; when people do not really believe, but are only "professors" of religion.

The Saints are entitled to the unspeakable gifts of the Spirit. Melvin J. Ballard related an experience that might be shared by all those who have received the covenants and hope to enjoy the witness of the Second Comforter. He said: "I found myself one evening in the dreams of the night in the sacred building, the temple. After a season of prayer and rejoicing, I was informed that I should have the privilege of entering into one of those rooms, to meet a glorious Personage, and, as I entered the door, I saw, seated on a raised platform, the most glorious Being my eyes have ever beheld or that I ever conceived existed in all the eternal worlds. As I approached to be introduced, he arose and stepped towards me with extended arms and he smiled as he softly spoke my name. If I shall live to be a million years old, I shall never forget that smile. He took me in his arms and kissed me, pressed me to his bosom and blessed me, until the marrow of my bones seemed to melt. When he had finished, I fell at his feet, and as I bathed them with my tears and kisses, I saw the prints of the nails in the feet of the Redeemer of the world. The feeling that I had in the presence of Him who hath all things in his hands, to have his love, his affection and his blessing was such that if I ever can receive that of which I had but a foretaste, I would give all I am, all that I ever hope to be, to feel what I then felt." ("Sermons and Missionary Experiences of Melvin Joseph Ballard," p. 156).

"We are concerned to restore to the
church that ideal of perfection and beauty that
corresponds to its original image, and we have
the desire of renewing its whole structure."
(Pope Paul VI, 8/6/1964).

The Church Has Been Restored

"We believe in the same organization that existed in the primitive church, namely, apostles, prophets, pastors, teachers, evangelists, and so forth." (6th Article of Faith). When the Lord instructed the Nephite saints regarding His church, He said: "If it be called in my name then it is my church, if it so be that they are built upon my gospel," which is the critical point upon which hangs the credibility of any church proclaiming to be the Lord's. (3 Nephi 27:8). Today, many churches have the name of Christ or a derivative in their titles, and so the essential element that becomes the substance of the issue is obedience to revealed gospel principles that are taught by the Savior's earthly representatives who solemnly bear His priesthood authority.

Interestingly, of all the churches in the world, when the Lord restored His church in this dispensation there was not a single one that bore the name of Jesus Christ. To Joseph Smith, He declared: "For thus shall my church be called in the last days, even The Church of Jesus Christ of Latter-day Saints." (D&C 115:4, recorded April 26, 1838). Before this revelation was received, the church was variously called The Church of Christ, The Church of Jesus Christ, The Church of God, and The Church of The Latter-day Saints. Even today, it is sometimes inaccurately called The Mormon Church, or The L.D.S. Church.

There are a lot of churches in Spokane. Some include the name of Christ, while others do not. Among them are the following: Jehovah's Witness, The Church of The Resurrection, The Cornerstone Pentecostal Church, Jesus is The Answer, The Living Truth Tabernacle, Amazing Grace Fellowship, The Assembly of God, The Crosswind Church, The Glad Tidings Church, The Trinity Lighthouse, The Baptist Church, The Living Water Community Church, The Shiloh Hills Fellowship, Christ Our Hope Bible Church, The Church of The Nazarene, The Catholic Church, The Christian Life Church, The Calvary Chapel, The Presbyterian Church, The Methodist Church, The Holy Temple Church of God in Christ, The Slavic Christian Church, The Refreshing Soaring Church of God in Christ, The Unity Church of Truth, The Life River Fellowship, The Cornerstone Pentecostal Church, The Northview Bible Church, The Lutheran Church, The New Beginnings Church, The Pentecostal Evangelical Church, The River of Life Open Bible Church, The Spokane Dream Center Women's Discipleship, The Unity Church of Truth, The New Hope Christian Reformed Church, The First Church of Christ Scientist, The Church of Christ, The Jesus Lord Church of the Living

God International, The Holy Temple Church of God in Christ, The Church of Jesus Christ of Latter-day Saints, The Heritage Congregational Church, The First Covenant Church, The All Nations Christians Center, The Christ our Hope Bible Church, The Christ the Savior Orthodox Church, The First Church of The Open Bible, The Shalom Church, The Fellowship of The Messiah, A Fresh Start Ministries, Christ The Savior Orthodox Church, and The Unitarian Universalist Church of Spokane

"There is no valid reason why Latter-day Saints should speak of themselves as 'Mormons,' or of the church as 'The Mormon Church.' Missionaries should teach people to believe in Christ, the Son of God, and encourage them to become members of His church - The Church of Jesus Christ. We should all emphasize that we belong to The Church of Jesus Christ of Latter-day Saints, the name the Lord has given by which we are to be known and called." (Joseph Fielding Smith, Jr., "Answers to gospel Questions," 4:174-175).

Anciently, the disciples of Christ called themselves "saints," a title that identifies members of His true church today. "The word 'saint' is a translation of a Greek word also rendered 'holy,' the fundamental idea being that of consecration or separation for a sacred purpose; but since what was set apart for God must be without imperfection, the word came to mean 'free from blemish,' whether physical or moral. In the New Testament, the saints are all those who by baptism have entered into the Christian covenant." ("Bible Dictionary," p. 768).

The King James Version of The New Testament freely uses the term "saint" in exactly this context: "To all that be in Rome, beloved of God, called to be saints." (Romans 1:7). "Unto the church of God which is at Corinth, to them that are sanctified in Christ Jesus, called to be saints." (1 Corinthians 1:2). "Paul and Timotheus, the servants of Jesus Christ, to all the saints in Christ Jesus which are at Philippi." (Philippians 1:1).

If anything, The Book of Mormon expands upon the use of the term: "But, behold, the righteous, the saints of the Holy One of Israel, they who have believed in the Holy One of Israel, they who have endured the crosses of the world, and despised the shame of it, they shall inherit the kingdom of God, which was prepared for them from the foundation of the world, and their joy shall be full forever." (2 Nephi 9:18). "For the natural man is an enemy to God, and has been from the fall of Adam, and will be, forever and ever, unless he yields to the enticings of the Holy Spirit, and putteth off the natural man, and becometh a saint through the Atonement of Christ the Lord, and becometh as a child, submissive, meek, humble, patient, full of love, willing to submit to all things which the Lord seeth fit to inflict upon him, even as a child doth submit to his father." (Mosiah 3:19). "And the remission of sins bringeth meekness, and lowliness of heart; and because of meekness and lowliness of heart cometh the visitation of the Holy Ghost, which Comforter filleth with hope and perfect love, which love endureth by diligence unto prayer, until the end shall come, when all the saints shall dwell with God." (Moroni 8:26).

Another feature of the gospel that identifies The Church of Christ is that of robust and vigorous ongoing revelation. Paul believed in a "God, who at sundry times and in divers manners spake in time past unto the fathers by the prophets, (who also) hath in these last days spoken unto us by his Son." (Hebrews 1:1-2). "Whom say ye that I am?" asked the Savior. "And Simon Peter answered and said, Thou art the Christ, the Son of the living God. And Jesus answered and said unto him, Blessed art thou, Simon Bar-jona, for flesh and blood hath not revealed it unto thee, but my Father which is in heaven. And I say also unto thee, that thou art Peter, and upon this rock" of revelation "I will build my church." (Matthew 16:15-18).

Revelation can come by the gift of the Holy Ghost, embraced by church members through a priesthood-administered ordinance. Jesus taught: "The Comforter, which is the Holy Ghost, whom the Father will send in my name, he shall teach you all things, and bring all things to your remembrance, whatsoever I have said unto you." (John 14:26).

Another principle that identifies The Church of Jesus Christ is that of priesthood. Of this authority, Paul wrote: "No man taketh this honour unto himself, but he that is called of God, as was Aaron." (Hebrews 5:4). The Savior referred to His investiture of priesthood authority in a parable: "For the Son man is as a man taking a far journey, who left his house, and gave authority to his servants, and to every man his work, and commanded the porter to watch." (Mark 13:34). "Ye have not chosen me," He taught, "but I have chosen you, and ordained you, that ye should go and bring forth fruit." (John 15:16). After the close of His mortal ministry, the Apostles continued His example of the delegation of priesthood authority, and "ordained them elders in every church." (Acts 14:23).

The church is also identified by its organization, "built upon the foundation of the apostles and prophets, Jesus Christ himself being the chief corner stone." (Ephesians 2:20). "And he gave some, apostles; and some, prophets and some, evangelists; and some, pastors and teachers; For the perfecting of the saints, for the work of the ministry, for the edifying of the body of Christ: Till we all come in the unity of the faith, and of the knowledge of the Son of God, unto a perfect man, unto the measure of the stature of the fulness of Christ." (Ephesians 4:11-13).

The Lord explained that priesthood ordinances are a necessary part of the Restoration: "In the ordinances (of the Melchizedek Priesthood) the power of godliness is manifest.

And without the ordinances thereof, and the authority of the priesthood, the power of godliness is not manifest unto men in the flesh. For without this no man can see the face of God, even the Father, and live." (D&C 84:20-22).

Guiding principles and ordinances that are basic to the gospel of Jesus Christ have come to be known as the First Principles & Ordinances of the gospel, that have been codified in The Articles of Faith. They guide us unerringly to the true church. Priesthood powered teaching is driven by the basic principles of faith and repentance, that in turn lead to the foundation ordinances of baptism and the bestowal of the Holy Ghost. "Except a man be born of water and of the Spirit," explained the Savior, "he cannot enter into the kingdom of God." (John 3:5).

On the Day of Pentecost, Peter and others who had been empowered with priesthood authority to preach the gospel taught over three thousand people. "Now when they heard this, they were pricked in their heart, and said unto Peter and to the rest of the apostles, Men and brethren, what shall we do?" Their faith had convicted them of their sins, and they wanted to know what their next step should be. "Then Peter said unto them, repent, and be baptized every one of you in the name of Jesus Christ for the remission of sins, and ye shall receive the gift of the Holy Ghost." (Acts 2:37-38). "And they continued steadfastly in the apostles' doctrine and fellowship, and in breaking of bread, and in prayers." (Acts 2:42).

Since God is no respecter of persons, (Acts 10:34), the true gospel of Jesus Christ must circumscribe those who have died without having had the opportunity to join the Lord's church, participate in the ordinances of the gospel, and receive the covenants of exaltation. The doctrine of Christ encompasses all who have ever lived on the earth, and explains that He preached to the dead, between His death and resurrection. "For Christ also hath once suffered for sins, the just for the unjust, that he might bring us to God, being put to death in the flesh, but quickened by the Spirit: By which also he went and preached unto the spirits in prison. Which sometime were disobedient, when once the longsuffering of God waited in the days of Noah, while the ark was a preparing, wherein few, that is, eight souls were saved by water." (1 Peter 3:18-20).

It was for the specific reason that the dead might also participate in the First Principles and Ordinances of the gospel, that the word was "preached also to them that are dead, that they might be judged according to men in the flesh, but live according to God in the spirit." (1 Peter 4:6). "Else what shall they do which are baptized for the dead, if the dead rise not at all?" asked Paul. "Why are they then baptized for the dead?" (1 Corinthians 15:29).

The manifestation of spiritual gifts is also a hallmark of the true church. "There are diversities of gifts," explained Paul. (1 Corinthians 12:4). Those who have the image of God engraven upon their countenances use spiritual gifts that are retained through righteousness to benefit the Saints. "Who shall ascend into the hill of the Lord," asked the Psalmist, "or who shall stand in his holy place" to partake of the Divine Nature? "He that hath clean hands and a pure heart; who hath not lifted up his soul unto vanity, nor sworn deceitfully." (Psalms 24:4-5).

Regarding our comprehension of the manifestations of the Spirit, Marion G. Romney said that "having a testimony and being converted are not necessarily the same thing. A testimony comes when the Holy Ghost gives the earnest seeker a witness of the truth. A moving testimony vitalizes faith, that is, it induces repentance and obedience to the commandments. Conversion, on the other hand, is the fruit or the reward for repentance and obedience." (C.R., 10/1963). In the Lord's true church, spiritual gifts follow conversion, which is built on the foundation of testimony.

Another powerful evidence of the latter-day work is the historical reality of an apostasy from the truth. The Great Apostasy, as it has come to be called, is not so much evidence of the Restoration, as the Restoration is of the Great Apostasy. Isaiah foresaw that the earth would be "defiled under the inhabitants thereof; because they have transgressed the laws, changed the ordinance, (and) broken the everlasting covenant." (Isaiah 24:5). Luke clearly understood the necessity of a latter-day restoration, and wrote of Jesus Christ, "whom the heavens must receive until the times of restitution of all things, which God hath spoken by the mouth of all his holy prophets since the world began." (Acts 3:20-21).

Paul also predicted the apostasy, reassuring the Thessalonian saints: "Be not soon shaken in mind, or be troubled, neither by spirit, nor byword, nor by letter as from us, as that the day of Christ is at hand. Let no man deceive you by any means: for that day shall not come, except there come a falling away first." (2 Thessalonians 2:2-3).

Nephi also foresaw our day of apostasy from the truth, and wrote of illiterate copyists: "They have taken away from the gospel of the Lamb many parts which are plain and most precious; and also many covenants of the Lord have they taken away." (1 Nephi 13:21-29).

The Reformers of the Middle Ages also recognized that there had been an apostasy. "I have sought nothing beyond reforming the church in conformity with the Holy Scriptures," declared Martin Luther. "I simply say that Christianity has ceased to exist among those who should have preserved it." (Reinhold Seeberg, "Text-Book of the History of Doctrines," 3:290). Later, Roger Williams emphasized: "There is no regularly constituted church on earth, nor any person authorized to administer any church ordinance; nor can there be until new apostles are sent by the Great Head of the Church for Whose coming am seeking." (This has been cited to a quotation in "Picturesque America" by William Cullen Bryant, p. 502, first published in 1872, but such a statement has not been located in the 1874 or 1894 editions.)

Finally, John "saw another angel fly in the midst of heaven, having the everlasting gospel to preach unto them that dwell on the earth, and to every nation, and kindred, and tongue, and people." (Revelation 14:6). That angel was Moroni, who appeared to Joseph Smith and helped to usher in a new dispensation of gospel truth, a time when "God shall give unto (us) knowledge by his Holy Spirit, yea, by the unspeakable gift of the Holy Ghost, that has not been revealed since the world was until now; Which our forefathers have awaited with anxious expectation to be revealed in the last times, which their minds were pointed to by the angels, as held in reserve for the fulness of their glory; A time to come in the which nothing shall be withheld, whether there be one God or many gods, they shall be manifest. All thrones and dominions, principalities and powers, shall be revealed and set forth upon all who have endured valiantly for the gospel of Jesus Christ. And also, if there be bounds set to the heavens or to the seas, or to the dry land, or to the sun, moon, or stars - All the times of their revolutions, all the and all their glories, laws, and set times, shall be revealed in the days of the dispensation of the fulness of times - According to that which was ordained in the midst of the Council of the Eternal God of all other gods before this world was, that should be reserved unto the finishing and the end thereof, when every man shall enter into his eternal presence and into his immortal rest. (D&C 121:26-32).

This takes us full circle, back to Pope Paul VI, who declared: "We are concerned to restore to the Church that ideal of perfection and beauty that corresponds to its original image, and that is at the same time consistent with its necessary, normal and legitimate growth from its original, embryonic form into its present structure." ("Encyclical of Pope Paul VI on The Church," 8/6/1964).

Physics tell us that every
heavy element in our bodies, the calcium
in our bones, and the iron in the hemoglobin
of our blood, was created during the explosion of a
supernova somewhere in the vast universe. So, in
our attempts to understand the cosmos, we are
just trying to understand ourselves. When
we ask, what is its origin, or what is its
ultimate destiny, we are really asking
where did we come from, and
where are we going.

The Creation

As our circle of knowledge grows, so does the border of darkness that surrounds the kernel of wisdom that we have so carefully nurtured. The more we know, the more we need to learn. Maybe this is why the Lord used the illustration of grains of sand, when He was describing for Moses His vast creations. Moses "beheld also the inhabitants thereof, and there was not a soul which he beheld not; and he discerned them by the Spirit of God; and their numbers were great, even numberless as the sand upon the sea shore." (Moses 1:28).

If you hold a single grain of sand at arm's length, the area of the sky that is blocked behind that grain holds about 2,000 galaxies. We know this is so, because the Hubble telescope is able to "see" them. That optical instrument is so powerful that, were it on the earth in New York City, and were able to focus on two fireflies in Tokyo, it could distinguish between them if there were only 10 feet of separation. Expanding that scale exponentially, if each of those 2,000 galaxies hiding behind the grain of sand contains 100 billion stars, the number of stars within that restricted field of view would be over 200 trillion. That is the number 2, followed by fourteen zeroes, or 200,000,000,000,000, which is, for all practical purposes, "numberless." (If you counted stars at a rate of 1 per second, it would take about 1.26 million years to get to 200 trillion).

Physics tell us that every heavy element in our bodies, the calcium in our bones, and the iron in the hemoglobin of our blood, was created during the explosion of a supernova somewhere in those vast creations. So, in our attempts to understand the universe, we are just trying to understand ourselves. When we ask, what is its origin, or what is its ultimate destiny, what we are really asking is where did we come from, and where are we going.

Before we even attempt to understand revealed truth relating to the creation, we might ask ourselves how much information we would give to a preschool child if we were trying to answer their questions about how an airplane stays in the air, or how a television works, or how plants grow? Most of us would consider the intellectual capacity of the child, and consequently provide only vague and general concepts, only later filling in details that would correspond to their increasing intellectual maturity.

The Lord has given us only that portion of eternal truth that our mortal minds can understand and that we need to know in order to gain salvation. We have yet to design the scientific tools that might provide a working understanding of the Creation. Even with the world's most powerful microscopes and telescopes, we have only taken a peek at what Moses beheld while under the influence of the Spirit. In the meantime, wisdom and knowledge are seamlessly acquired through the Spirit of God. As Moses was blessed with this discerning spirit, he was able to behold the earth in its most minute fashion and to begin to comprehend the greatness of the Creation. Speaking of spiritual knowledge, Joseph Smith said: "Could you gaze into heaven five minutes, you would know more than you would by reading all that ever was written on the subject." ("Teachings," p. 156). Thus, if we wish to fully understand the Creation, we must prepare ourselves as did Moses. Academic study, though worthwhile, can only give us a hint of the knowledge that is available from the Source of all truth.

Moses beheld a vision of God's creations but was told: "Only an account of this earth, and the inhabitants thereof, give I unto you." (Moses 1:35). It would be fascinating to know more about the universe and how its physical structure harmonizes with the gospel Plan. Apparently, it is unnecessary for us to have that knowledge in order for us to fulfill the measure of our creation, because the scriptures remain virtually silent on the subject. In order to work out our salvation, it seems clear that our focus should be on the scriptures and revelations the Lord has given us, and not on mysteries that have not yet been revealed, and that may pertain only obliquely to the Plan of Salvation.

We can be sure that the account of the Creation written by Moses provided only the details that relate to the Fall of Adam and to the Atonement of Christ, that we must understand in order to become heirs of salvation. We know that the purpose of the Creation was to provide a place where we could come to obtain physical bodies and be tested, or proven, to see if we would obey God when we were no longer in His presence. Interestingly, although an account of the Creation is included in the book of Genesis, its purposes and importance are explained only in latter-day revelation. For example, the Book of Abraham expands upon the Genesis account by clearly revealing that the Gods declared: "We will go down, for there is space there, and we will take of these materials, and we will make an earth whereon these may dwell. And we will prove them herewith, to see if they will do all things whatsoever the Lord their God shall command them." (Abraham 3:24-25).

We were to be proven "herewith," or "with this earth." In other words, the Lord created the earth as an institution of higher education, a testing center, a learning laboratory, and as place where we could be tried, and our trustworthiness could be proven. "For behold," He declared, "this is my work and my glory—to bring to pass the immortality and eternal life of man." (Moses 1:39).

Wilford Woodruff taught: "The Lord Almighty created the earth that we might come here and exercise our agency. The probation we are called upon to pass through is intended to elevate us," and refine us, so that we can comfortably "dwell in the presence of God our Father." (J.D., 25:2). The earth provides an environment where we receive physical bodies, learn to use our agency, gain knowledge, have families, receive ordinances, and make covenants.

No less than eight times in the brief account of the process of Creation, God declared that his work was good. So we know, without a doubt, not only that He knew what He was doing, but that He also envisioned the successful implementation of the Plan. Among His numberless creations, our own experiences were not a dry-run. Everything had already been played out countless times, not as tedious dress rehearsals, but as flawless parts of the Great and Merciful Plan of our Eternal Creator.

The home that we call "earth" was created with us in mind. (See Abraham 3:24 & Abraham 4:1). Joseph Smith said: "The word create came from the (Hebrew) word baurau which…means to organize; the same as a man would organize materials and build a ship. Hence, we infer that God had materials to organize the world out of… chaotic matter." ("Teachings" p. 350-351). This has a nice ring to it, because it fits in neatly with the star-child concept of supernova "creation" that was mentioned near the beginning of this essay. It may be no coincidence that our blood runs hot, reminiscent of the microwave background radiation from the Big Bang that likely occurred 14 billion years ago. Only time will tell, or, then again, maybe not.

After the Fall,
the door to Eden may
have swung shut, but there
was opened unto us another portal
leading to the knowledge of both good
and evil, in the learning laboratory
that we know as "life."

The Fall

The world misinterprets the account of the Fall because there have been "taken away from the gospel of the Lamb many parts which are plain and most precious; and also many covenants of the Lord have they taken away. And all this have they done that they might pervert the right ways of the Lord, that they might blind the eyes and harden the hearts of the children of men." (1 Nephi 13:26-27). The account in Genesis treats the Fall as an event, rather than as a process that unfolded over time, without delving into its related doctrine. Fortunately, the account in the Pearl of Great Price, the temple endowment, and the inspired commentary by Book of Mormon prophets, help to fill in the gaps.

We know that Satan "sought to beguile Eve, for he knew not the mind of God, wherefore he sought to destroy the world." (Moses 4:6). He took advantage of Eve, for she was pure and without guile. In such situations, the sin lies with the deceiver. Satan told both a truth and a lie. He said that Adam and Eve would have knowledge, but he also said that they should not die. (Genesis 3:4-5). Satan came to Eve with the intent to deceive. He was full of treachery, and he sought to mislead her. He was deceptive, and his offer was a forgery. He was, after all, a liar from the beginning. (D&C 93:15). After God made Adam, he was given the commandment to dress and keep the Garden and to abstain from partaking of the fruit of the tree of knowledge of good and evil. (Moses 3:15 & 17). It is also possible that Eve, having been created at a later time, did not receive the same instructions that had earlier been given to Adam.

After the Fall, God put enmity between Satan and the family of Adam and Eve, for He recognized the danger that would lie in their familiarity with sin. (Genesis 3:15). As Alexander Pope observed: "Vice is a monster of such frightful mien, as to be hated needs but to be seen. Yet seen too oft, familiar with her face, we first pity, then endure, then embrace."

Genesis tells us that Eve would have "sorrow" in her conception. But as Spencer W. Kimball observed: "I wonder if those who translated the Bible might have used the term distress instead of sorrow. It would mean much the same, except I think there is great gladness in most Latter-day Saint homes when there is to be a child there." ("Ensign," 3/1976).

When Adam and Eve were driven from the Garden, they were "punished" with the very things that would later prove to bring them the greatest happiness. A Savior would be provided for them, but in the meantime, cherubim and a flaming sword were placed to keep the way of the tree of life, to preserve the principle of moral agency that was now in the possession of Adam and Eve. (See Genesis 3:24). Both justice and mercy would allow them and their posterity to experience all of the wonders of mortality, without mutating their eternal identity. "For behold, if Adam had put forth his hand immediately, and partaken of the tree of life, he would have lived forever, according to the word of God, having no space for repentance; yea, and also the word of God would have been void, and the Great Plan of Salvation would have been frustrated." (Alma 42:5).

The door to Eden may have swung shut after the expulsion of Adam and Eve from the Garden, but there was opened unto us another portal leading to a knowledge of both good and evil, in the wonderful learning laboratory of life.

Just as
the living kernels
of wheat from Pharaoh's
tomb were destined to whither
and die without the sustaining influence
of light, water, and fertile soil, so our divine
potential cannot germinate without the
similar influence of the gospel,
the priesthood, and the
nurturing influence
of Jesus Christ.

The Germination of Our Faith

Garden and flower seeds are good illustrations of our potential for salvation. At first glance, they may appear to be "lifeless," but all they typically need to sprout is sunlight, fertile soil, and water. If we want to germinate the god in embryo within us, we similarly need: 1) the light of the gospel, 2) the fertile soil of the priesthood, and 3) the living water that is found in the teachings of Jesus Christ.

The first of these three ingredients is personified by the Savior, Who "hath brought life and immortality to light through the gospel." (2 Timothy 1:10). The second recalls Ezekiel, who spoke in a parable about a great vine that, in the Last Days "was planted in a good soil by great waters, that it might bring forth branches, and that it might bear fruit, that it might be a goodly vine." (Ezekiel 17:8). The third is reminiscent of the woman of Samaria, who came to a well "to draw water: Jesus saith unto her, Give me to drink. (For his disciples were gone away unto the city to buy meat). Then saith the woman of Samaria unto him, How is it that thou, being a Jew, askest drink of me, which am a woman of Samaria? for the Jews have no dealings with the Samaritans. Jesus answered and said unto her, If thou knewest the gift of God, and who it is that saith to thee, Give me to drink; thou wouldest have asked of him, and he would have given thee living water. The woman saith unto him, Sir, thou hast nothing to draw with, and the well is deep: from whence then hast thou that living water? Art thou greater than our father Jacob, which gave us the well, and drank thereof himself, and his children, and his cattle? Jesus answered and said unto her, Whosoever drinketh of this water shall thirst again: But whosoever drinketh of the water that I shall give him shall never thirst; but the water that I shall give him shall be in him a well of water springing up into everlasting life." (John 4:7-14).

Only under these essential conditions, can we be spiritually reborn. "Now I say unto you that ye must repent, and be born again; for the Spirit saith if ye are not born again ye cannot inherit the kingdom of heaven; therefore, come and be baptized unto repentance, that ye may be washed from your sins, that ye may have faith on the Lamb of God, who taketh away the sins of the world, who is mighty to save and to cleanse from all unrighteousness." (Alma 7:14).

"And the Lord said unto me: Marvel not that all mankind, yea, men and women, all nations, kindreds, tongues and people, must be born again; yea, born of God, changed from their carnal and fallen state, to a state of righteousness, being redeemed of God, becoming his sons and daughters." (Mosiah 27:25).

Because of His covenant relationship with the faithful, they may be born again. As Mosiah 5:7 teaches, those who enter into the Covenant become "Born Again Christians." It is not a question of their development or maturation, but rather of generation. One of the most emotional, miraculous, and awe-inspiring events of mortality is birth, and it would be difficult to more dramatically conceptualize in metaphor the process of kindling our divine spark, of awakening our eternal potential, or of igniting the spirit lying dormant within each of us as a God in embryo, than to say that we must be born again in order to inherit eternal life.

Latter-day Saints are quintessential Born Again Christians, for only members of Christ's true church can reach that epiphany through the ministration of His priesthood. (See Mosiah 27:25, Alma 5:14, & 7:14, then Mosiah 15:10-11, and Alma 22:15, & 36:24). As the Lord revealed to Joseph Smith, the "greater priesthood administereth the gospel and holdeth the key of the mysteries of the kingdom, even the key of the knowledge of God. Therefore, in the ordinances thereof, the power of godliness is manifest. And without the ordinances thereof, and the authority of the priesthood, the power of godliness is not manifest unto men in the flesh." (D&C 84:19-21).

Without these ordinances, and without the authority of the priesthood, gospel seeds cannot properly germinate. We cannot procrastinate the day of our repentance, and defer our spiritual rebirth until later on when it is more convenient. The example of kernels of grain discovered in Pharaoh's tomb helps to illustrate why this is so.

Thanks to scores of scientific studies, we now have a pretty good idea of how long most seeds are able to germinate. Under normal dry and cool conditions, most seeds will remain viable for only a few years, and anything over 50 to 100 years is quite remarkable. The reason is, of course, that during this time the seed is using up its food supply, albeit very slowly.

In nineteenth century England, a mummy was unrolled in London, and in its hand was a small bag of wheat. "Some grains of it were sown and vegetated. Its produce has again been sown and has produced an average of 38 ears or spikes for each grain sown. To be sold in packets of 10 grains each at £1 per packet." In 1843, when "The Gardeners' Chronicle" ran this ad, the public was already infatuated with ancient Egypt. And nothing was more fascinating than the notion that "mummy wheat," grain discovered in the tombs of kings, would spring to life after thousands of years. At £1 a packet, worth $86.00 U.S. today, people were paying for something more than a few stalks of wheat.

From the start, botanists dismissed the claims of "The Gardeners' Chronicle" as romantic nonsense. Yet the belief in the astonishing powers of ancient seeds lingered on. "You can blame it on Napoleon. When he invaded Egypt in 1798, he took along 175 scholars. Although his army failed to conquer Egypt, his troop of intellectuals were triumphant. They "discovered" ancient Egypt and so triggered a craze that swept the whole of Europe. Fashionable society was soon in the grip of mummy fever. By the 1840s, the English papers carried regular reports of the amazing regenerative powers of "mummy wheat" - grain discovered in tombs up to 6000 years old." (Source: BrightSurf.com "Pharaoh's Ear," 1/23/2002).

But, alas, just as the living kernels of wheat from Pharaoh's tomb were destined to whither and die without the sustaining influence of light, water, and fertile soil, so our divine potential cannot germinate without the similar influence of the gospel, the priesthood, and the nurturing influence of Jesus Christ.

THE ROAD LESS TRAVELED

When negotiating the highways and
byways of life, we are likely to encounter a variety
of road signs that are designed to help us to smoothly
regulate the conduct of our journey, as well as to warn us
of impending danger. We are familiar with more than sixty
of these signs, although we may not have previously thought
of them in the way described in this essay. After reading
about the hidden meaning behind these sign posts,
you may forever look at them differently.

The Highways and Byways of Life

1. "Headlight safety zone." We need to keep our headlights on at all times, so that hidden obstacles to our progression may be clearly illuminated, and thereby avoided.

Joseph Smith, when asked how he could govern so many people, simply said: "I teach people correct principles, and they govern themselves." If we listen to our file leaders and follow their counsel, we can act independently within our sphere of influence, and we will live life abundantly. This course entails risk, but it is God's ordained way. He declared to Adam while he was yet in the Garden: "Nevertheless, thou mayest choose for thyself, for it is given unto thee." (Moses 3:17). However, if we choose unwisely, carelessly, or thoughtlessly, we may forfeit our agency, and lose our freedom.

2. "Follow detour signs." The roadmap of life will present many seeming detours. Some may actually turn out to be the most direct route to our envisioned destination, while others will need to be recognized as dead-ends, and avoided.

In a very real sense, each of us is confined to a world of our own making, and many of us are trapped within the narrowly defined perceptual prisons we have created for ourselves. Its walls are reinforced with the razor-wire of limiting beliefs, those stories we tell ourselves that cause us to sabotage our own best efforts. They can damage and even cripple our lives, diminish our abilities, compromise our progress, and prevent us from attaining our goals. Although all of us have limiting beliefs, everyone has the power to change them. Most people, however, don't realize it's possible, and for that matter, aren't even aware that they have made conscious decisions about what they choose to believe and not to believe.

3. "Rough road ahead." Heavenly Father never said it would be easy, but He has assured us that it will be worth it.

It is a marvelous thing to see how the gospel helps us to handle the challenges of life. We can see the growth occurring almost on a daily basis. We must never think that our weaknesses are imperfections; rather, they are as steppingstones that have been strategically placed so that we can cross safely over the rapids of life. When God "made" us, He pronounced us good! As the bumper sticker suggests, "God don't make junk." He created us with an extra measure of resolve to see things through to their successful conclusion, or in the case of challenges, to their resolution based on gospel principles.

4. "Heavy loads." When our burdens seem too heavy for us to bear, the Savior will always be there to carry them for us.

He said: "And if men come unto me, I will show unto them their weakness. I give unto men weakness that they may be humble; and my grace is sufficient for all men that humble themselves before me; for if they humble themselves before me, and have faith in me, then will I make weak things strong unto them." (Ether 12:27).

5. "Speedometer check ahead." We have been counseled that we should not try to run faster than we have strength. Nor should we rely upon the arm of flesh to give us a boost of telestial horsepower. When God measures a person, He does not put the tape around the head, or the biceps, or the quadriceps, but around the heart.

"Great and marvelous are the works of the Lord," Jacob exclaimed. "How unsearchable are the depths of the mysteries of him; and it is impossible that man should find out all his ways. And no man knoweth of his ways save it be revealed unto him." (Jacob 4:8). "O the vainness, and the frailties, and the foolishness of men!" wrote Lehi. For "when the are learned, they think they are wise" and they suppose "they know of themselves, wherefore, their wisdom is foolishness and it profiteth them not." (2 Nephi 9:28-29). As Paul cautioned the Colossian saints: "Beware lest any man spoil you through philosophy and vain deceit, after the tradition of men, after the rudiments of the world." (Colossians 2:8).

6. "Frost heaves." We can expect obstacles to be thrown up before us, to obstruct our path of progress. To be forewarned is to be forearmed.

Heber J. Grant said: "I do not believe that any man lives up to his ideals, but if we are striving, if we are working, if we are trying, to the best of our ability, to improve day by day, then we are in the line of our duty. If we are seeking to remedy our own defects, if we are so living that we can ask for light, for knowledge, for intelligence, and above all, for His Spirit that we may overcome weakness, then, I can tell you, we are in the straight and narrow path that leads to life eternal." ("gospel Standards," p. 184-185).

7. "Stop, look, and listen." Sometimes, we just need to be still, in order to know that God is there.

During mortality, there are probably many questions we will never be able to answer. The reassurance, "In time, you will understand." may not be entirely valid, for mortality impels us to see through a glass darkly. At some point, when time no longer exists, we will be able to "go forth from our dwelling place and discarding the poor lenses of the body, peer through the telescope of truth into the infinite reaches of immortality." (Helen Keller "My Religion," p. 76).

8. "Reduced visibility." Sometimes, we simply need to raise our eyes beyond the limited horizon of our sight, in order to see the visions of eternity.

"I wish I could remember the days before my birth, and if I knew the Father before I came to earth. In quiet moments when I'm all alone, I close my eyes and try to see my Heavenly home. Although I can't remember and cannot clearly see, I listen to the spirit and so I must believe. But still I wonder, and I hope to find the answer to the question that is on my mind. Where is Heaven? Is it very far? I would like to know if it's beyond the brightest star." (Janice Kapp Perry, "Where is Heaven?").

9. "Rest area ahead." Every man and every woman has a compelling, innate need to know to what source they may look in order to receive a remission of their sins.

If we lack faith, there will be no sanctuary when the winds blow and the rains beat down. We will find no safe harbor to which we may flee. When the ocean of life is in turmoil and we are tossed about as flotsam and jetsam, never coming to a knowledge of what is real, our faithlessness will cloud the path back to the source to which we would, in other circumstances, have been able to look for the stability we so desperately need. It is a lack of faith that conceals the answers to life's greatest questions that continually trouble our spirits.

10. "Do not drive in left lane." We need to choose the right, in all the labors we're pursuing.

There is a direct relationship between weakness and sin, although not all weakness or limitation is sin. A lot depends upon how we handle weakness, and on what weakness does to us. We may allow it to impede our own or another's progress; on the other hand, we may use weakness as a stepping-stone to higher achievement. Adversity can be the diamond dust that polishes us to a high luster, or it can be the abrasive that wears us down and grinds us up.

11. "Obey flagman." Our Savior is the Great Exemplar, and He has ordained His authorized servants to minister among the children of men, through the ordinances of the priesthood.

Only with ordinances and covenants, does the Plan of Salvation shift into high gear and can the Atonement become fully effective in our lives. The unique source of peace can be traced to our complete and all-encompassing repentance through the power of the Savior's Atonement, and our Heavenly Father's consequent forgiveness of our sins. As Parley P. Pratt declared: "I have received the holy anointing, and I can never rest until the last enemy (that is unresolved sin) is conquered, (spiritual) death destroyed, and truth reigns triumphant." (J.D., 1:15). From our perspective, this is accomplished when we conquer those self-defeating behaviors and character flaws that limit our progression. Joseph Smith said: "Salvation consists in a man's being placed beyond the power of his enemies, meaning the enemies of his progression, such as dishonesty, greediness, lying, immorality, and other vices."

12. "Slow – construction zone." Each of our lives is a work in progress. The Savior is much more interested in building our character than He is in anything else. That undertaking will be a long and slow process of growth. The attainment of our spiritual maturity will be a progressive development, until "we all come in the unity of the faith, and of the knowledge of the Son of God, unto a perfect man, unto the measure of the stature of the fulness of Christ." (Ephesians 4:13).

The Atonement stacks the deck in our favor, in terms of achieving that goal. "The first condition of happiness," taught David O. McKay, "is a clear conscience." In medical terms, before an abrasion can heal, it has to be clean. Anyone who has had a physician vigorously scrub out an ugly wound knows how carefully and thoroughly the task must be accomplished before sterile dressings may be applied, allowing the healing process to begin. The same principle applies to repentance. There is no room for dry rot and there can be no skeletons lurking in the closet. We cannot superficially whitewash our sins to cover them up. The Savior called the scribes and Pharisees hypocrites, for they were "like unto whited sepulchres, which indeed appear beautiful outward, but are within full of dead men's bones, and of all uncleanliness." (Matthew 23:27).

The purpose of earth life is to grow and progress in stature, until we have developed both the image and likeness of our Heavenly Father. During the process, we will fail again and again in our efforts. This creates a problem because "no unclean thing can dwell with God," and yet it is human nature to repeatedly violate the commandments. Unfortunately, sin does stop our progress. God, however, provided the principle of repentance, together with the Atonement of our Savior, so that we may yet become holy. Therefore, we are commanded, "All men, everywhere, must repent." (Moses 6:57).

13. "No services for 100 miles." When we have spiritually been born again, and have internalized the principles of the gospel, we must resolve to go the second mile, for that is exactly what is required of the dedicated disciples of Christ.

Spencer W. Kimball told those who urged him to slow down: "I am like an old shoe, to be worn out in the service of the Lord." His successor prophet, Gordon B. Hinckley, observed: "Too many of us die with wasted capacity." He was a self-effacing, humble man, who unconsciously worked harder than many retirees thirty years younger than he. We should all follow his tireless example, to defend the faith, follow the Plan of Salvation, express our thanks in prayer, reconcile ourselves to negative responses to our petitions, lay our lives on the altar of sacrifice, consistently repent, pattern our lives after the Savior, gain spiritual fluency, focus on the positive, forgive others, keep the commandments, endure to the end in righteousness, recognize the merits of the principles of righteousness, righteously exercise what power or authority we do possess, acknowledge Him as the sole source of our protection, determine to serve Him, recognize His majesty and power and that of His servants, see His presence in the earth around us, use our agency wisely to validate the wisdom of our self-government, indicate by our actions that we understand the true value of things and do not covet the profane things of the world, understand the relationship between commandments and blessings, and multiply our talents and turn weaknesses into strengths.

14. "Fines double in work zone." If we are to be counted among the saints, we must obey the greatest of the commandments, to love God and our neighbors.

When we are in the service of others, we are in God's service, but without love it is insincere and is often unappreciated or even resented. So we need to make sure our prayers, repentance, and love of our fellowmen translate into affirmative action. Gordon B. Hinckley said: "My plea is that we stop seeking out the storms and enjoy more fully the sunlight. I am suggesting that as we go through life, we accentuate the positive. I am asking that we look a little deeper for the good, that we still our voices of insult and sarcasm, that we more generously compliment and endorse virtue and effort." ("New Era," 7/2001).

"God does notice us, and He watches over us. But it is usually through another person that He meets our needs. Therefore, it is vital that we serve each other. The abundant life is achieved as we magnify our view of life, expand our appreciation of others, and recognize our own possibilities." (Spencer W. Kimball, "Ensign," 12/1974).

The more we follow the teachings of the Master, the more enlarged will our perspective become. We will see more possibilities for service that we would have otherwise seen without the magnifying lens of eternal perspective. We will find that "there is great security in spirituality, and we cannot have spirituality without service." (Spencer W. Kimball, "Ensign," 12/1974).

15. "Congestion ahead." Bad things happen to good people, and even the righteous suffer. But they do not need to suffer the consequences of poor choices, or of unresolved sin.

Some people grumble that roses have thorns. Others are thankful that thorns have roses. The poet wrote: "Why is it, whenever I reach for the sky to climb aboard cloud nine, it evaporates and rains upon my dreams? Is it a matter of science, or simply a matter of fact, that not even a cloud with a silver lining can hold the weight of our dreams without some precipitation. I think I've found the answer to this dilemma. Keep on reaching for the sky, but don't forget your umbrella." (Susan Stephenson).

16. "Roundabout ahead." There is no confusion or uncertainty in the minds of the faithful regarding where they are going or the route they should follow, because they know that they are children of God, and that He knows each of them personally. They know what it means to be about their Father's business.

When Alice was in Wonderland, she asked the Cheshire Cat: "Would you please tell me which way I ought to go from here?" The Cat responded: "That depends a good deal on where you want to go." Alice acknowledged: "I admit, I don't much care where." To which the cat retorted: "Then it doesn't matter which way you go." Alice implored: "Just so I go somewhere!" The cat observed: "Oh, you are sure to do that, if you only walk far enough." (Lewis Carroll, "Alice's Adventures in Wonderland").

17. "No unsecured loads." The righteous are confident that the burdens placed upon their shoulders will not shift, because they have been secured with the strong cords of commitment, covenants, and consecration.

The drags of uncertainty and lack of conviction will slow down the unrighteous. The friction of sin grating against the strait and narrow way will unnecessarily heat up its smooth cobblestones, making it uncomfortable for them to continue along that path. The righteous, on the other hand, do not want to find themselves gliding smoothly and effortlessly through life, because when they do that, they have discovered that they are generally going downhill. Instead, they want to be steadily improving, and moving upward as they encounter and conquer opposition.

The righteous dream big. They have developed spirituality. They are known as persons of character, with clearly defined and realistic goals. They do not procrastinate, but accept responsibility. They do what they love to do, and establish priorities and stick with them. They are understanding, and consciously choose habit patterns that are based on correct choices. They have single-minded concentration, but remain flexible in their approach to problem-solving. They never consider the possibility of failure. They are honest, and dedicated to service. They are leaders and not just managers, and recognize and act upon the switch-points in their lives. They love to work and are dependable. They have a clear vision of who they are, and they persist at tasks until they succeed. They seize the moment. They are unified, and are teachers and mentors.

18. "Look both ways before proceeding." The faithful do not hesitate to venture into the unknown, but they have learned to rely upon the presence of the Spirit to guide them as they do so.

In life, we take a couple of steps into the darkness, and then faith, the spiritual strong searchlight, shows us the way. Helen Keller recorded a moving expression of her faith, writing: "I believe that no good shall be lost, and that all man has willed or hoped or dreamed of good shall exist forever. I believe in the immortality of the soul because I have within me immortal longings. I believe that the state we enter after death is wrought of our own motives, thoughts, and deeds. I believe that my home there will be beautiful with colour, music, and speech of flowers and faces I love. Without this faith, there would be little meaning in my life. I should be a mere pillar of darkness in the dark. Observers in the full enjoyment of their bodily senses pity me, but it is because they do not see the golden chamber in my life where I dwell delighted; for dark as my path may seem to them, I carry a magic light in my heart. Faith, the spiritual strong searchlight, illuminates the way, and although sinister doubts lurk in the shadow, I walk unafraid towards the Enchanted Wood where the foliage is always green, where joy abides, where nightingales nest and sing, and where life and death are one in the presence of the Lord." ("Midstream").

19. "Obey the speed limit." For now, we live by faith, but then, we shall be bathed in a celestial fire that lights the kingdom of God..

Of our relationship to His realm, William W. Phelps wrote: "No man has found pure space, nor seen the outside curtains, where nothing has a place." Perhaps in His kingdom, "there is no end to matter, space, spirit, or race, virtue, might, wisdom, or light, union, youth, priesthood, or truth, glory, love, or being," because these things are defined by different bounds and conditions in the infinite reaches of immortality and eternal life, where He and His exalted sons and daughters live. ("If You Could Hie to Kolob").

20. "Reduced visibility." When the cares and concerns of the world get in the way, our vision is obstructed. There are 2,165 references in the scriptures to "seeing," 402 to "understanding," and 154 to "repentance." Clearly, when the scales of sin fall from our eyes, we are in a better position to identify the path leading to the portals of heaven.

Because there is very little room for error in skydiving, jumpers have an Automatic Activation Device that deploys the chute if consciousness is lost, or if the jumper falls too far without deploying the main chute. It will also deploy a reserve chute, if it is needed. In life, if we lose our way, the Spirit will "deploy our chute," as well. "I will go before you and be your rearward," promised the Lord, "and I will be in your midst, and you shall not be confounded." (D&C 49:27). The Savior is our Jumpmaster and our Flight Instructor. He is the Canopy over our head, and the Reserve Chute in our pack. With trust in Him, and "with a little bit of pixie dust, we can fly!" as Peter Pan urged. That magical formula allows us to "be like a bird, that pausing in her flight a while on boughs to light, feels them give way beneath her, and yet sings, knowing that she hath wings." (Victor Hugo). Then we will "fly away as an eagle toward heaven." (Proverbs 23:5).

21. "Construction zone." Each of us is a work in progress, an unfinished masterpiece, a grand ouvre, and a magnum opus. We cannot start over and make a new beginning. But we can begin right now, and make a new ending.

In life, the list of the things that can and do go wrong is long. In fact, it is probably endless. Fortunately, the Atonement of Christ makes it possible for us to enjoy mortality without making mistakes that are ultimately and irreversibly spiritually fatal. Boyd K. Packer once told the story of a World War II naval aviator, who left the security of his aircraft carrier for a dangerous mission. True to the predictions of his superior officers, he endured enemy anti-aircraft fire and engaged in lethal dogfights. His plane was hit numerous times by flack that tore away parts of his wings. His Plexiglas canopy was shattered and he could hardly see through blood-splattered goggles to navigate back to his ship. As he came in for a landing on the pitching deck of the carrier, his controls were nearly useless, his descent too steep and his angle wrong. He was frantically waved off by the crewman on deck who was guiding him in, but he figured he had only one chance and this was it, and he would take it. With a sickening thump he pancaked on the deck, the fuel tank burst into flame, and the tail hook failed to engage the cables that would have brought him to a halt. As he careened into the safety net at the end of the deck, what was left of his plane crumpled into twisted metal. A rescue crew in asbestos suits rushed to his aid, smothered the wreckage in fire-retardant foam, clamored up to the cockpit, unsnapped his safety harness, grabbed him by the shoulders, and dragged him to safety. Doctors and nurses attended to his wounds even before he arrived at sickbay. Due to their skill and attention, as well as to his unconquerable spirit, he made a remarkable and full recovery. This, Elder Packer suggested, is how most of us will return from our mortal mission to the presence of our Father.

22. "Blasting area – turn off radio." Often, in life, we will need to eliminate all of the distractions competing for our attention, so that we can focus on what is really important.

Satan wears many hats. He is an honorary member of the Screen Actor's Guild, and has been enthusiastically awarded its Life Achievement Award. He is a much sought-after image consultant. He methodically cruises the Internet, and is a permanent resident of chat-rooms. He has a twitter account: (@Sataninhell). He is the great deceiver who bombards us with spam emails. He is a prize-winning author of books and periodicals. He is a talented composer, lyricist, and scriptwriter. He is the creative influence behind television programs, video games and other diversions too numerous to mention. He is a fashion designer, travel agent, vintner and beer distributor, an actor, newscaster, politician, scientist and power broker. He may even be a teacher or wear clerical robes.

23. "No stopping or standing." We have to keep moving along the path of eternal progression. We cannot afford to set up camp on that path, because by doing so, we will lose our forward momentum.

That the thief and robber from the unseen world is actively seeking our destruction is certain, evidenced by the fact that because of his influence we are often "in perils of waters, in perils of robbers, in perils by (our) own countrymen, in perils by the heathen, in perils in the city, in perils in the wilderness, in perils in the sea, in perils among false brethren, in weariness and painfulness, in watchings often, in hunger and thirst, in fastings often, in cold and nakedness." (2 Corinthians 11:26-27).

24. "Two way traffic." There are always two ways that lie before you. Which one you choose is up to you.

"Young women of Scotland, life is before you," exhorted Helen Keller. "Two voices are calling you. One comes from the marsh of selfishness and force where success is won at any cost, and the other from the hilltops of justice and progress where even failure may ennoble. Two lights are on your horizon for you to choose. One is the fast-fading, will-o-the-wisp of power and materialism, the other the slowly rising sun of human brotherhood. Two laws stand today opposed, each demanding your allegiance. One is the law of death which daily invents new means of combat; this law obliges the nations to be ever at war. The other is the law of peace, of labour, of salvation, which strives to deliver man from the scourges which assail him. One looks only for violent conquest, the other for the relief of suffering humanity. Two ways lie open before you, one leading to a lower and yet lower plane of life, where are heard the weeping of the poor, the cries of little children, and the moans of pain, where manhood and womanhood shrivel, and possessions destroy the possessor; and the other leading to the highlands of the mind where are heard the glad shouts of humanity, and honest effort is rewarded with immortality." (Commencement Address to Queen Margaret College, Glasgow, Scotland, June 15, 1932, in "Helen Keller: Sightless but Seen; Deaf but Heard," p. 113).

Those who are on Satan's payroll falsely represent themselves. They write checks they cannot cash. Their tanks are running on empty and there is no reserve. They are deceitful because they are spiritually and morally bankrupt. "Who shall ascend into the hill of the Lord," asked the Psalmist, "or who shall stand in his holy place? He that hath clean hands, and a pure heart, who hath not lifted up his soul unto vanity, nor sworn deceitfully." (Psalms 24:3-4).

Paul hoped that, in the Last Days, we would "henceforth be no more children, tossed to and fro, and carried about with every wind of doctrine, by the sleight of men, and cunning craftiness, whereby they lie in wait to deceive." (Ephesians 4:14). Elsewhere, he cautioned: "Beware lest any man spoil you through philosophy and vain deceit, after the tradition of men, after the rudiments of the world." (Colossians 2:8). We must be on our guard, "for many deceivers are entered into the world." (2 John 1:7). "For there shall arise false Christs, and false prophets, and shall shew great signs and wonders, insomuch that, if it were possible, they shall deceive the very elect." (Matthew 24:24).

25. "Do not follow too closely." Choose very carefully the path you will follow. The story is told of a deep track in a meadow that led to a fork, before which was a sign that read: "Choose very carefully which rut you will follow. You will be in it for the next twenty miles."

Satan has a Ph.D. (Philosophy of the Devil) in computer science, and is preoccupied with hacking into and compromising our integrity. The Pentagon's computer systems, by comparison, are under cyber-attack over 2 million times a day. Shawn Henry, assistant director of the F.B.I.s cyber division, declared: "Other than a nuclear device or some other type of destructive weapon, the threat to our infrastructure, the threat to our intelligence, the threat to our computer network is the most critical threat we face." (1/7/2009). The righteous face even greater challenges. If Satan can succeed in inserting a virus into our software that reduces our distinctive personality signatures to the lowest common denominator, he will destroy us. If we surrender to him the traits that make us unique, we will fade into a shadow and a caricature of what we might have otherwise been.

26. "No stopping – avalanche area." If we do not choose to follow the Savior, we have implicitly chosen to follow another path, upon which we stand a good chance of being blind-sided.

We have all witnessed "that after a people have been once enlightened by the Spirit of God, and have had great knowledge of things pertaining to righteousness, and then have fallen away into sin and transgression, they become more hardened, and thus their state becomes worse than though they had never known these things." (Alma 24:30).

Joseph Fielding Smith, Jr. taught: "Before you joined the church you stood on neutral ground. When the gospel was preached, good and evil were set before you. You could choose either or neither. There were two opposite masters inviting you to serve them. You left the neutral ground and you can never get back on to it. Should you forsake the Master you enlisted to serve, it will be by the instigation of the evil one, and you will follow his dictation and be his servant." ("C.E.S. Manual," p. 258).

27. "Cross winds." We are continually buffeted by both the winds of adversity and the roaring category 5 hurricane of the adversary.

If we allow the maelstrom to disorient us from our sense of direction, or from our purpose, or "when we undertake to cover our sins, or to gratify our pride, our vain ambition, or to exercise control or dominion or compulsion upon the souls of the children of men, in any degree of unrighteousness, behold, the heavens withdraw themselves; the Spirit of the Lord is grieved; and when it is withdrawn, Amen to the priesthood or the authority of that man." (D&C 121:37).

When that happens, we will be as Alma the Younger, who was "racked with eternal torment, for (his) soul was harrowed up to the greatest degree and racked with all (his) sins." He "remember(ed) all (his) sins and iniquities, for which (he) was tormented with the pains of hell…. The very thought of coming into the presence of…God did rack (his) soul with inexpressible horror" to the point that he was "racked, even with the pains of a damned soul." (Alma 36:12-16).

When Satan has breached the firewalls of our spiritual security systems, has neutralized our body's defense mechanisms, and his infectious virus has spread uncontrollably, the effect of the resulting contamination is compromise, confusion, conflict, and chaos.

28. "One way." Jesus said: "I am the way, and the truth, and the life; no one comes to the Father but through me." (John 14:6). "This is the way; and there is none other way nor name given under heaven whereby man can be saved in the kingdom of God. (2 Nephi 31:21).

We will exclaim, as did those in Zarahemla so long ago: "The Spirit of the Lord Omnipotent…has wrought a mighty change in us, or in our hearts, that we have no more disposition to do evil, but to do good continually. And we, ourselves, also, through the infinite goodness of God, and the manifestations of his Spirit, have great views of that which is to come; and were it expedient, we could prophesy of all things. And it is (our) faith…that has brought us to this great knowledge, whereby we do rejoice with such exceedingly great joy." (Mosiah 5:2-4).

Those who have certain knowledge of their spiritual identity understand their relationship with the Lord. As Benjamin instructed the saints in Zarahemla: "Now, because of the covenant which ye have made ye shall be called the children of Christ, his sons, and his daughters; for behold, this day he hath spiritually begotten you; for ye say that your hearts are changed through faith on his name; therefore, ye are born of him and have become his sons and his daughters. And under this head ye are made free." (Mosiah 5:7-8). As a grateful father said of his prodigal son: "This thy brother was dead, and is alive again; and was lost, and is found." (Luke 15:32).

We do not need to suffer the consequences of spiritual identity theft. In 2008, 8.4 million people in the United States had their identities stolen at a total cost of $49.3 billion. How many more have had their spiritual identities stolen, and at what a cost? It is better to act preventively rather than redemptively. The poor example of a lack of planning set by the world emphasizes the need for conscious efforts to resist Satan. The Saints plan for the worst even as they hope for the best.

29. "Quiet – hospital zone." The church is a hospital for sinners, and obedience to the doctrines of the Kingdom provides an opportunity for triage for those who are in desperate need of immediate spiritual attention.

The following are adapted from the Twelve Steps of Addiction Recovery. (See L.D.S. Social Services). We must acknowledge to ourselves that we are at risk of the constant and unrelenting assaults of Satan upon our spiritual identities. We must come to believe that only the power of God can restore us to complete spiritual health. We must turn our lives over to the care and keeping of God. We must constantly re-evaluate the stability and integrity of our moral defensive shields. We must acknowledge the power of the priesthood as a key ally in our fight against, and resistance to, Satan's onslaughts. We must be ready to allow the power of God, and not our own, to defeat Satan. We must ask Jesus Christ to come to our defense, and in particular to help us to heal the damage done in consequence of the weaknesses in our armor. We must be true to our friends, family, and acquaintances; to be true to our word, and to honor our commitments, in order to draw upon the power of God through ordinances and covenants. We must be absolutely honest in our dealings with our fellow warriors, and insofar as it is possible, right whatever wrongs for which we are responsible. We must constantly monitor our defensive network of systems designed to resist Satan, recognize when they weaken or fail, accept responsibility for consequences that have been under our control, and take steps to restore the integrity of the network. We must do everything we can to maintain open lines of communication with the powers of heaven. We must not only believe in Christ, but also believe Him when He says that He can heal us through the power of His Atonement. We must then use the Atonement as our secret weapon against Satan in the defense of our spiritual identity.

30. "Lane ends – merge right." Whenever we feel that we are out of options, and the way before us is hedged up, it always pays to turn to the right. I am reminded of my experiences in the woods when antler-shed hunting. As I have followed game trails and they have split to the right and left, with an equal chance of success by following either one, I have habitually turned to the right. No offense intended to those who are right-brained, but I just feel uncomfortable going to the left.

When we turn to the right, forewarned and forearmed with the teachings of the gospel, we profitably expend our energy as we ascend the hill of the Lord, trimming away the fat of indolence, mediocrity, laziness, and inattention. Our positive lifestyle choices make it easier for us to obey the principles of good spiritual and emotional nutrition. As we observe a steady diet of discipleship, ultimately "all things (are) restored to their proper order, every thing to its natural frame – mortality raised to immortality, corruption to incorruption." (Alma 41-4).

We recognize that only organically grown spiritual food is wholesome, delicious, and high in moral fiber content, and we are able to easily distinguish it from the empty calories of carnality, sensuality, and devilishness, and from the malnourishment that is caused by the mold of misinformation. We learn to identify the noxious weeds of worldliness that lie in the path that leads to the left, and we listen for the poisonous pandering that is so characteristic of the uncommitted and unconverted. We resolve to avoid the excesses of those who are slothful, and who fail to regularly exercise their faith and diligence. (See Alma 37:41).

31. "Traction tires advised." We need the comfort of the additional grip provided by correct principles, and the sure-footed stability of doctrine, as we negotiate the slippery slopes that lie above personality precipices.

We learn the art of defensive driving, as we speed down life's highways and byways, for we know that the fiery darts of the adversary will streak across the threatening skies that lie ahead. We become immersed in the construction of an all-terrain vehicle that will provide a fortress of security to guard against the day when the adversary's assaults will surely come. With our memory of the ideological War in Heaven still fresh in our minds, we renew our resolve to keep both hands on the wheel with our minds clear and focused as we valiantly and pointedly promote the cause of Zion with serious defensive driving.

32. "Seat belts mandatory." We need all the protection we can get from the spiritual equivalents of directives and bulletins from the National Highway Traffic Safety Administration.

In our pre-earth life, we didn't need government agencies to formulate safety protocols. Instead, on our own initiative, we surely rolled out of bed very early every morning to do mind-bending stretching exercises leading to intellectual flexibility, interpersonal pliability, and spiritual capability. Even before breakfast, we may have climbed the stadium steps of discipline before running several laps around the scriptures and engaging in refreshingly repetitive rehearsals that would prepare us for life's educational experiences. Each wind-sprint through The Book of Mormon would have brought familiarity and clarity, paving the way for later religious recognition, purposeful preparation, and affirmative action.

After thus awakening and arousing our faculties, perhaps we then sat down to a satisfying serving of restraint, fortified with the nutritional supplement of principle. This would have prepared us to renew our strength, mount up as on the wings of eagles, and run and not be weary, and walk, and not faint. (See Isaiah 40:31). Our thirst would have been quenched, not by supposed energy drinks laced with sweeteners and stimulants, but by water springing forth from a living fountain. Our hunger would have been met by the performance potential found in the bread of life.

Such a bountiful boot camp experience would have provided balanced stimulation designed to ward off the rigidity, inflexibility, and fanaticism of spiritual sclerosis. It would have promoted the concept of aerobic fitness to a group already determined to "press forward with a steadfastness in Christ, having a perfect brightness of hope, and a love of God and of all men." (2 Nephi 31:20). It would have renewed our resolve to persevere when we were introduced to a world where, due to neglect, many would suffer from the atrophy of their spiritual muscles leading to emaciation.

33. "**Watch for wildlife.**" All around us, the world is self-absorbed in partying, as if there were no tomorrow. Its philosophy is: "Eat, drink, and be merry, for tomorrow we die." (2 Nephi 28:7).

The world simply does not recognize the value of nourishment from the good word of God. Instead, it embraces the fleeting rush of artificial sweeteners, the empty calories of convenience, and the hypoglycemia of hypocrisy. The world jostles to and fro on a precarious platform of platitudes before it boards the Excess Express in a vain search for a shortcut to success. But the day will come when the worldly-wise will look in the mirror and see themselves for who they really are; that their spiritual bodies have become "one sorry sight! No more than skeletons, covered with skin. They will get up to heaven, but never get in. 'Another soul's mine!' they will hear Satan scream. 'Give man something nice, and he'll take the extreme!' OK, I'll admit it; I'll outright confess. For the fast way to hell, take the Excess Express." (Anonymous).

In our own pre-mortal life, we must have recognized that strenuous spiritual exercise would give us vigorous vitality and leave us stronger, and so we surely learned to use our recovery time wisely. We must have developed the capacity to carefully monitor our bodies' vital signs; to feel the spiritual equivalents of oxygen-debt and lactic acid buildup; to monitor the efforts of our minds to keep pace with our spiritual development. We surely experienced brief bursts of energy resulting in spectacular achievement, but more importantly, we discovered that sustained effort would carry us further along the road leading to eternal life. In that setting, we must have learned the value of developing endurance, so that when the time would come to go the second mile or turn the other cheek, instead of embracing the lascivious lifestyle of the rich and famous, it would be easier simply because of the force of habit.

34. "**Blowing dust.**" Satan's smokescreens are nothing more than billowing clouds of the dust of dissention, discord, deviancy, disproportion, and disagreement, kicked up by the winds of rebellion as they blow across his familiar desert wastes.

Lucifer was very influential in the pre-mortal world of spirits. In Hebrew, his name means "bright morning star." The name has also been translated as "Light Bearer," and so he was. In the Council, he offered to redeem all mankind. But even then, he lacked the faith necessary to allow agency to rule. He was so obsessed by his quest for power that he concocted a plan that was, in fact, an inoperative counterfeit. It would not work because it would not permit its participants to exercise free will. This is why Satan is called "the father of lies," and "a liar from the beginning." He promoted a bogus plan that, if embraced by a majority of God's spirit children, was calculated to elevate its author to a position of power.

35. Wildlife crossing." "God doth not walk in crooked paths, neither doth he turn to the right hand nor to the left, neither doth he vary from that which he hath said, therefore his paths are straight, and his course is one eternal round." (D&C 3:2). We can be sure that many who are walking in darkness at noonday will cross our paths. But they have no idea where they are going. We should try to be at least as obedient as J. Golden Kimball, who is reported to have said: "I may not always walk the straight and narrow, but I sure as hell try to cross it as often as I can."

In the pre-earth existence, when we were as spiritual toddlers, and were just learning how to walk the strait and narrow path, we must have taken our Father at His word when He assured us that "resistance" training would one day pay big dividends. When He urged us to do 10 push-ups through The Book of Mormon, we probably voluntarily tacked on another 13, all the way through the Articles of Faith. Instead of bench-pressing only the Aaronic Priesthood, we added on the additional weight of The Oath and Covenant of The Melchizedek Priesthood, because we knew we'd need additional muscle fiber and strength down the road. When He asked us to get our heart rate up to a steady 75 verses a day to facilitate our comprehension of gospel principles, we instead pushed our limits to whole chapters and even books of scripture. The elliptical trainer of consecration, the stationary bike of service, and the treadmill of sacrifice put us through the whole range of motion to develop and strengthen our core, and our reward was the increased capacity of our hearts to pump the life-giving element of the spirit through our bodies. We knew that one day our hearts would enlarge to encompass empathy for our fellow men, and that our bowels would be filled with compassion as we witnessed their struggles.

36. "Road narrows." If we want to be born again, we must negotiate the narrow constrictions of the birth canal of obedience and repentance. It is only after we have emerged on the other side of this hourglass of opportunity that we will find expanded horizons and limitless vistas stretching out before us, inviting us to travel to a far country, there to receive a kingdom for ourselves. (See Luke 19:12).

Portland, Oregon lies on the Columbia River, over 75 miles from the Pacific Ocean. Yet, ocean-going ships regularly cross the treacherous Columbia Bar at the mouth of the river, to steam upstream to deliver and take on cargo at Portland's bustling wharves. There are easier ports of call, but a trip to Portland every now and then is worthwhile for at least one special reason.

The barnacles that attach to the hulls can proliferate and create significant drag as the ship makes its way through the water. This creates inefficiency that translates into increased fuel costs that can become prohibitively expensive. Additionally, if the barnacles work their way onto the rudder mechanism, they can seriously compromise the ability of the captain to move the ship forward toward its intended destination.

But those barnacles thrive only in salt water. Fresh water kills them, and when they die, they lose their grip on the ship's hull and fall off in the water. Thus, the accumulation from months or years of contamination can be eliminated in just a few days as the ship moves through fresh river water, leaving it "as good as new."

In a similar fashion, we can rid ourselves of "the barnacles of life" that would otherwise compromise our mission or purpose. This can be done by completely immersing ourselves in cleansing water that leave us afresh and anew, and with a feeling afterward that can be almost indescribable.

37. "Keep right." Closely associated with "merging to the right," is "keep right." It helps if we never allow ourselves to wander into compromising territory. When in doubt as to the direction we should go, we will never go wrong if we rely upon the exhortation to "keep right."

We knew that while clothed in mortality, with good fortune and the favor of God, we would be wrought upon and cleansed by the power of the Holy Ghost, to be numbered among the people of the Church of Christ; and our names would be taken, that we might be kept in the right way, and be continually watchful unto prayer, relying alone upon the merits of Christ, who even while we were in Spiritual Boot Camp was already the author and finisher of our faith. (See Moroni 6:4).

As I probe the deep recesses of memory, and I think about what it must have been like for us before we embarked upon this incredible journey to a far country, I can still hear the Voice gently urging me: "O.K. Buttercup. One more lap around the scriptures!" Today, when my obedience seems inconvenient, I try to remember that long ago I learned that perspiration always precedes inspiration and that the dictionary is the only place where success comes before work. When my fragile faith is faltering, I try to remember that, although it is darkest just before the dawn, the new day always holds the promise of rebirth, recommitment, renewal, and redemption.

38. "High winds." In the Last Days, as the Spirit is withdrawn in the face of increasing wickedness, hurricane force winds of destruction will rake the earth, and the righteous will find sanctuary only by standing in holy places.

The faithful will enjoy "the power of God unto salvation" and become the architects of their own fate, in a very real sense. (Romans 1:16). They will be given the skills and the materials to build either a shanty or a temple in which to live their lives. Which one it will be, will depend on them. The outcome will be determined largely by their perspective. If they can face the challenges in their lives "with understanding, faith, and courage, they will be strengthened and comforted, and spared the torment which accompanies the mistaken idea that all suffering comes as chastisement for transgression." (Marion G. Romney, C.R., 10/64).

Sometimes bad things happen to good people, and life can be unpredictable. There are uncertainties with which each of us must deal, but if our foundation is solid and our footing secure, we will be able to successfully adapt to every circumstance and maintain our focus. We will remember the counsel of Paul, who was familiar with adversity: "Work out your own salvation with fear and trembling." (Philippians 2:12).

39. "Take the high road." Unto those to whom much is given, much is expected. The gospel standard demands an uncommonly high level of commitment that is forged in the crucible of experience, and quenched in the rarified atmosphere of ordinances and covenants.

Many in the church find it easy to "Follow the Prophet" on well traveled avenues dotted with conveniently located sidewalk cafes, and on brightly lighted world stages filled with appreciative applause and laudatory complements. But when no-one is looking, and there are no positive peer pressures to sustain correct choices, only undeviating commitment to the principles of the gospel will give us the strength to carry on.

40. "Oncoming traffic." Sometimes, the light at the end of the tunnel is the headlamp of an approaching train. But at other times, it can be the gathering light of a new day. Which it is, largely depends upon us.

Sometimes, the "no" comes as an answer to the "specifications set forth in our petitions." (Neal A. Maxwell). We express thanks for our Father's greater vision and are prepared for negative responses. We learn from them as much as we do from affirmations, for we know that whom the Lord loves, He also chastens. (See D&C 95:1). When we receive a bouquet of roses, we accept the thorns as well as the buds. Some people grumble that roses have thorns. We try to maintain our perspective, to be thankful that thorns have roses.

"Why is it," asked the poet, "whenever I reach for the sky to climb aboard cloud nine, it evaporates and rains upon my dreams? Is it a matter of science, or simply a matter of fact, that not even a cloud with a silver lining can hold the weight of our dreams without some precipitation? I think I've found the answer to this dilemma. Keep on reaching for the sky, but don't forget your umbrella." (Susan Stephenson).

41. Steep incline / grade." Sometimes, the path that stretches out before us seems too steep, or too tortuous, or just too hazardous to even attempt. Sometimes we just need to trust in the Lord, Who sees the end from the beginning, and Who has been there before us, as a trailblazer. (See D&C 122:8).

Wrote the poet: "My life is but a weaving between my Lord and me; I cannot choose the colors. He worketh steadily. Oft times He weaveth sorrow, and I, in foolish pride, forget He sees the upper, and I the under side. Not 'til the loom is silent, and the shuttles cease to fly, shall God unroll the canvas, and explain the reason why. The dark threads are as needful in the Weaver's skillful hand, as the threads of gold and silver in the pattern He has planned." (B.M. Franklin).

42. "Merging traffic." Many concerns will push and pull, bump and grind, and tug at our coat tails, as they jostle for our attention. As long as we keep our eye on the prize, when our eye is single, our whole bodies will be full of light. (See Luke 11:34). Even in heavy traffic, we will be able to "advance the cause, which (we) have espoused, to the salvation of man, and to the glory of (our) Father who is in heaven." (D&C 78:4).

Life is enough of a pressure cooker, as it is, without introducing unneeded additional stress. Many events "remain to (be) overcome through patience (in order to) receive a more exceeding and eternal weight of glory." (D&C 63:66). The Lord told Joseph Smith: "Be patient in afflictions, for thou shalt have many, but endure them, for, lo, I am with thee, even until the end of thy days." (D&C 24:8). Therefore: "In everything (we) give thanks, waiting patiently on the Lord." (D&C 98:1-2). We seek His face "always, that in patience (we) may possess (our) souls, and… have eternal life." (D&C 101:38).

43. "Pull over when drowsy." Sometimes we need to take time to sharpen the saw. Having said that, after a refreshing pause, we need to be able to recognize when "it is high time to awake out of sleep: for now is our salvation nearer than when we believed." (Romans 13:11).

Awakened and reinvigorated to clearly order our priorities, we seek "the kingdom of God, and his righteousness; (then) all these things shall be added" unto us until ultimately we enjoy eternal life. (Matthew 6:33). When our senses are dulled and our priorities are out of order, however, we lose power. If we choose mediocrity, rationalization, selfish pleasure, things of the world, the honors of men, or disobedience, we lose power. As long as we remain in this state, we will never partake of the fruit of the tree of life, enjoy its delicious fruit, or feel real gratitude. After taking a deep cleansing breath, we should first seek to obtain the word of truth, for then our tongue will be loosed, and we will have the Spirit and "the power of God unto the convincing of men." (D&C 11:21).

44. "No waiting." Gospel principles make provision for an immediate confrontation with unresolved sin.

Without repentance, the past would forever hold the future hostage and the Plan of Salvation would be thwarted. "Rejoice, O my heart," sung Nephi, "and give place no more for the enemy of my soul. Do not anger again because of mine enemies. Do not slacken my strength because of mine afflictions. Rejoice, O my heart." (2 Nephi 4:28-30).

45. "Reduce speed at night." Sometimes it is helpful to ratchet down the hectic pace of our lives, in order to stop and smell the roses that have been carefully planted and lovingly cultivated along the path of progress.

When we contemplate the word of God, we pause to pray. We slow down our minds, and free ourselves from the cares and concerns of the world. As we read the scriptures, and the solemnities of eternity illuminate our minds, or as we have questions, we continue to pray for understanding. We keep writing materials handy, knowing that reading will be a stimulating activity, and often, ideas or original thoughts that we will want to develop later will germinate within our minds. We read slowly. For a change, this study is not a race. No longer do we have to finish a prescribed number of chapters or verses each day. We spend several days pondering a single chapter or verse. We read topically if we want to. We stop to find out what other prophets have said about the same subjects. As we memorize scripture passages, they bloom with hidden meanings we hadn't been aware of, and from time to time the memory of relevant life experiences pops into our minds, just when we need it the most.

We ask questions as we read. We desire the companionship of the Holy Ghost as we read, and we recognize His illuminating influence as our minds are flooded with answers. We take a break from our busy activities to think about the relevance of the passages we are currently studying. We pause to let our minds work on their application to our life's experiences.

46. "Check brakes – steep grade ahead." There are going to be daunting obstacles that seem to frustrate our progress along the highways and byways of life. So we had better make sure all of the resources we will need are fully operational before embarking upon the journey.

Demosthenes overcame a lisp to become one of the greatest orators of all time.

Beethoven composed some of his finest music after he had become deaf. Long before he won his first and only election, Abraham Lincoln said: "I will prepare myself, and some day my chance will come." Helen Keller triumphed over the silence and darkness in her life to write that "faith, the spiritual strong searchlight, illuminates the way, and although sinister doubts lurk in the shadow, I walk unafraid towards the Enchanted Wood where the foliage is always green, where joy abides, where nightingales nest and sing, and where life and death are one in the presence of the Lord." As a young man, Heber J. Grant couldn't carry a note. Later, he became well known for his singing abilities. He said of his own experience: "That which we persist in doing becomes easier for us to do; not that the nature of the thing is changed, but that our power to do is increased."

47. "Flooded." When our lives seem to be in turmoil, and the water is rising until it seems ready to breach the sandbags of our spiritual and temporal defenses, we need to pause, take a deep cleansing breath, and trust in the Lord.

Even in our most difficult times, we can find much for which to be grateful. We need to turn the expression: "Thanks for nothing!" into a positive statement that affirms our faith in God's ultimate wisdom. We also need to realize that God "maketh his sun to rise on the evil (as well as) on the good, and sendeth rain on (both) the just and the unjust." (Matthew 5:45).

48. "Road may be icy." The most dangerous road conditions, like black ice, are those that we cannot see, that take us by surprise, catch us off-guard, and blind-side us with devastating consequences.

Perhaps our moments of greatest challenge will come when we are placed in compromising social situations where it seems easier to homogenize our standards. Maybe they will come when we are climbing the ladder of success and are tempted to scramble over those who are supposedly in our way and might be impeding our progress. The decisive moment could come when we are alone with our computer and surfing the web, and are more prone to visit sites of questionable value. It may come at the end of the month when we are reconciling our checkbook and balancing our budget, and are tempted by the glitter of telestial treasures and trinkets, but have not yet paid our tithing. It may be when we have not yet completed our home teaching, visiting teaching, or have not attended the temple in a while, and worldly desires compete for our time and attention.

49. "Scenic byway." When the Lord created the earth, He pronounced it "Good." (Genesis 1:10). And when He looked over all of His creations at the end of the sixth day, He pronounced His work "Very Good." (Genesis 1:31).

Let' face it; the world is a pretty special place, and the sooner we cultivate feelings of gratitude, the better off we will be. With gratitude, wonderful things happen. Good outweighs evil. Love overpowers jealousy, hate, and prejudice. Light drives out darkness and bats. Knowledge banishes ignorance. Humility displaces pride. Courtesy overwhelms rudeness. Appreciation overcomes thanklessness. Abundance supersedes poverty. Well-being replaces weakness. Simplicity overshadows perplexity. Harmony supplants discord. Faith controls fear. Hope casts out despair. Charity subdues selfishness. Joy deposes unhappiness, sadness, dejection, and misery. Confidence is substituted for timidity. Certainty dethrones bewilderment. Assurance unseats discouragement and even despair. Gratitude is a variation on the Golden Rule: "Fear not to do good, my sons, for whatsoever ye sow, that shall ye also reap; therefore, if ye sow good ye shall also reap good for your reward." (D&C 6:33).

"Those who live in thanksgiving daily have a way of opening their eyes and seeing the wonders and beauties of this world as though seeing them for the first time. Those who live in thanksgiving daily are usually among the happiest people on earth." (Joseph Wirthlin, "Ensign," 9/2001).

50. "Cross traffic." There will always be those who try to cross us, and particularly to "wrest the scriptures." (Alma 41:1). The proud often have only a weak foundation of doctrinal understanding of the gospel, and risk falling into transgression in consequence of their shallow comprehension of principles. As they pick apart the scriptures or the words of those who preach the gospel, the doctrines can be distorted into meaningless fragments without any coherent connection. As Alma declared to the inhabitants of Ammonihah: "Behold, the scriptures are before you; if ye will wrest them it shall be to your own destruction." (Alma 13:20).

Members of the church who have made covenants with God in the temple are not tormented by such confusion or wracked by doubt. They understand the meaning behind the question Paul asked of the Galatian saints: "Do I now persuade men, or God?" (Galatians 1:10). They are eager to make promises with God, for they have personally witnessed the effects of such actions. They understand that "until one is committed there is hesitancy, the chance to draw back, always ineffectiveness. Concerning all acts of initiative, there is one elementary truth, the ignorance of which kills countless ideas and splendid plans: that the moment one definitely commits oneself, then Providence moves too. All sorts of things occur to help one that would never have otherwise occurred. A whole stream of events issues from the decision, raining in one's favor all manner of unforeseen incidents and material assistance, which no man could have dreamed would have come his way." (Thomas F. Hornbein, "Everest: The West Ridge," p. 100).

51. "Pedestrian crossing." Mortality was designed with good reason to be a journey that was intended to be taken by foot. For most of recorded history, walking has been the primary means of transportation all over the world. If we spend too much time traveling at 75 mph in the fast lane of the highways and byways of life, we will miss the essence of what could have been a profoundly enjoyable experience. The Savior walked all over Galilee, but there is only one reference in the scriptures that he ever traveled by any means other than foot. (See John 12:14 & Matthew 21:7). The Apostle John declared: "He that saith he abideth in (the Savior) ought himself also so to walk, even as he walked." (1 John 2:6).

Walking is good for our bodies. In addition to journeying by foot, work, cleanliness, rest, and exercise are important and positive components of the Word of Wisdom. Therefore, the Lord commanded: "Cease to be idle; cease to be unclean; cease to find fault one with another; cease to sleep longer than is needful; retire to thy bed early, that ye may not be weary; arise early, that your bodies and your minds may be invigorated." (D&C 88:124). In the end, "they that wait upon the Lord shall renew their strength; they shall mount up with wings as eagles; they shall run, and not be weary; and they shall walk, and not faint." (Isaiah 40:31).

52. "Farm equipment." It is probably no coincidence that Adam and Eve were commanded to till the ground, and that it was ordained that it would be by the sweat of their brow that they were to eke out their existence. (See Genesis 3:19). Agriculture and animal husbandry have been the norm for most of recorded history, and it has, for the most part, been exhausting for farmers.

Nevertheless, farming is literally the ordained way to make a living. "I want to bear you my testimony," said Ernest L. Wilkinson, "that if you develop the habit of work, it will be the most invigorating, satisfying, even relaxing and greatest blessing of your life. The opportunity to work is God's greatest blessing to mankind, and this means six days of each week." Neal A. Maxwell called work a spiritual necessity, and said that we avoid it at peril to our souls. A favorite saying of Harold B. Lee was: "Work without vision is drudgery. Vision without work is dreamery. But work with vision is destiny."

Make no small plans," declared Daniel Burnham, "for they have no magic to stir men's souls." "Cease to be idle; cease to be unclean; cease to find fault one with another; cease to sleep longer than is needful; retire to thy bed early, that ye may not be weary; arise early, that your bodies and your minds may be invigorated." (D&C 88:124). We should think big as we put our minds and our bodies to work.

53. "Gas, food, lodging." Obedience to gospel principles satisfies every spiritual need, and puts our temporal concerns in perspective, often relegating them to second-tier status.

We have learned by experience that there is a direct correlation between physical and spiritual energy and vitality. From our quickening in the womb, our first stirrings of life signaled a tangible message of hope, spanning the eternities, as it traveled from our heavenly home into the mortal world.

Now, our commission is to awaken and arouse our faculties, to nurture the word in our hearts, so that it might swell by faith. We try to wrap out minds around the concept that our spirits will one day be inseparably joined to our physical bodies, and that our soul will "be restored to the body, and the body to the soul; yea, and every limb and joint…to its body." (Alma 40:23).

54. "Follow pilot car." We know to Whom it is that we look for guidance. It is in Him that "we live and move and have our being." (Acts 17:28).

This truth is indisputable, for "the Spirit itself beareth witness with our spirit, that we are the children of God." (Romans 8:16). We know this intuitively. How sweet it is to hear Primary age children as young as three sing the song that reinforces what the Spirit whispers to each soul: "I am a child of God, and he has sent me here, has given me an earthly home with parents kind and dear. I am a child of God, and so my needs are great. Help me to understand his words before it grows too late. I am a child of God. Rich blessings are in store. If I but learn to do his will, I'll live with him once more. Lead me, guide me, walk beside me; help me find the way. Teach me all that I must do to live with him someday." (Naomi Randall, "I am a Child of God").

55. "Children at play." How refreshing that Heavenly Father organized the world in such a way that in it, life begins with babies, who with untinctured innocence teach the world about unconditional love.

Love underlies our quest for perfection, and when we learn to pray and to repent, it is natural to feel the love of God and fellowmen swell our hearts. A heart that is "past feeling" is insensitive. It is mortally wounded and is immune to any nurturing influence. The qualities of a noble character are admirable, but they need the softening influence of love before they can become celestial qualities. Love is an aether that permits us to catch a glimpse of heaven. It allows us to bridge the gulf between the world of everyday, and the land unpromised and unearned that is felt only with the Spirit.

56. "No cell phone use." We can thank God that He did not provide inspiration to develop cell phone technology until the Last Days. How different the world might have been if the use of Personal Digital Assistants had become commonplace even a generation ago. Who knows what the consequences of laziness, entitlement, selfishness, and narcissism might now be, had digital communication gotten a 20 year head-start?

Let's end our reliance upon social media to relate to others, and live in a daily, personal thanksgiving to God. Christianity only began to thrive when it left the cloistered confines of monastic life, and its teachings became the personal possession of the people. Now, technology threatens to become the new god of this world.

When the masses are given the opportunity to follow the Plan of Salvation, not in cyberspace, but in the trenches where they are rubbing shoulders with each other, they learn how to use their means wisely, manage their time carefully, keep their priorities in order, maintain their perspective even when their days seem purposeless, change their hearts through faith on His name, accept responsibility for their actions and use their agency wisely, use their failures as learning experiences, bear adversity well, recognize the seeming detours and distractions in their lives as opportunities for personal growth, continue to express their gratitude in times of adversity, maintain a cheerful attitude, sacrifice (seemingly), be anxiously engaged, perform acts of quiet Christianity, open their arms to those around them, love their neighbors, do missionary work, acknowledge the qualities of goodness in others, express appreciation to others, recognize how precious their divine attributes are, read the scriptures, promote the cause of Zion, magnify their callings, shout Hosannas to the Lord, be valiant in their testimony of Jesus, worship God in the temple and honor their temple covenants, observe the Word of Wisdom, be temperate and not easily provoked to anger, have integrity, view education as a life-long process, learn how to work, nurture family relationships, and take their responsibilities as teachers seriously.

As we learn to express in thought, word, and deed our gratitude to God, it will come to "include thanksgiving for his tutoring of us to aid our acquisition of needed attributes and experiences while we are in mortality. (Our thanksgiving will come because) we trust his design of life itself!" (Neal A. Maxwell, "Ensign," 7/1982). That design relies upon face to face, and skin to skin contact with each other.

As Tiny Tim put it: "God bless us, everyone!" And so, we remember the Lord's blessing as we brim with emotion in gratitude for His personal involvement in our lives: "The Lord bless thee and keep thee. The Lord make his face shine upon thee, and be gracious unto thee. The Lord lift up his countenance upon thee, and give thee peace." (Numbers 6:24-26).

57. "Deaf child." "Behold, the days come, saith the Lord God, that I will send a famine in the land, not a famine of bread, nor a thirst for water, but of hearing the words of the Lord." (Amos 8:11). "Hear now this, O foolish people, and without understanding; which have eyes, and see not; which have ears, and hear not." (Jeremiah 5:21).

The Lord realizes that our minds are generally locked on telestial targets, and that when we even attempt so-called higher-level thinking we risk becoming "as sounding brass, or a tinkling cymbal." (1 Corinthians 13:1). "For my thoughts are not your thoughts," He chided. "Neither are your ways my ways.... For as the heavens are higher than the earth, so are my ways higher than your ways, and my thoughts than your thoughts." (Isaiah 55:8-9). The best of life seems always to be "further on. Its real lure is hidden from our eyes somewhere behind the hills of time." (Sir William Murdock). In the end, good things come to those who are willing to wait.

58. "Pull over for emergency vehicles." There are times and circumstances when we will see red, white, and blue strobe lights in our rear view mirrors as we plod along the highways and byways of life. If we pull over at such times, the police car or ambulance might just whiz by, and we can avoid interfering with the management of the emergencies that are a part of life. If the situation somehow involves us, however, interacting calmly and cooperatively with the authorities who demand our attention will improve our chances of a successful resolution to the problem.

The Savior involves Himself in our lives under two distinct circumstances: when things are going well, and when thing are not going well. Longfellow memorably wrote about the footprints that we leave behind on the sands of time. Sometimes, however, there are two sets of footprints, one His and one ours, as we walk together, but during times of particular difficulty, there may be only one set. Of course, it is during those trying times that the Savior lifts us onto his shoulders. We are comforted that He will lead us out of the bondage of ignorance "by power, and with a stretched-out arm." (D&C 103:17). The very fact that He is "mighty to save" suggests that we must allow Him to become involved in our lives, so He may rescue us. (2 Nephi 31:19).

59. "No compression brakes." We really don't want the very engine that drives us forward to somehow slow us down. When we ease off the accelerator pedal, as sometimes we must, we want to avoid losing our forward momentum, because soon enough we will be back on the gas.

The process of sanctification by which we are cleansed from the effects of sin requires that we keep on the gas. If our engines are truly high performance, the gospel will drive the law into our inward parts. (See Jeremiah 31:33). We will become "firmer and firmer in the faith of Christ." (Helaman 3:35). If we sanctify ourselves, our minds will "become single to God, and the days will come that (we) shall see him; for he will unveil his face" unto us. (D&C 88:68). Our spiritual preparation will move us forward to enter His presence.

By avoiding the use of compression brakes; by not subverting our own power in a process that actually slows us down, we will be able to bind ourselves by our own integrity to act with nobility. Our covenants will bring a sense of responsibility that in turn becomes a powerful reinforcement for positive action. Making these solemn promises with God will help us to break bad habits as we establish a means of accountability by making our commitment known to others. We can unify the forces within ourselves, and channel them into constructive forces without backpressure, to secure the blessings of heaven

60. "No Littering." We must not discard trash along the way as we negotiate the scenic highways and byways of life. We need to visualize the Savior's name on the "Adopt a Highway" signs by the side of the road. As soon as we realize that He is willing to pick up all of our discarded garbage, we will be on the pathway to celestial law, and His burden will be lighter.

The Atonement's invitation to forgive and be forgiven is a counterpoint to the inevitable sense of empty despair, despondency, misery, and hopelessness related to the failings that have been, and will continue to be, an integral part of our schooling in mortality. The Atonement stands independent and alone in the face of an avalanche of wickedness that has been poured out all over the highways and byways of life with increasing fury in the Last Days.

The Atonement is the only reasonable alternative to an otherwise overwhelmingly negative power competing for influence in the affairs of our affairs. The only stipulation of the Atonement is that we recognize our disobedience and go through the process of repentance wherein we recognize our transgression, experience remorse, renounce the self-defeating behavior, resolve to do better, make restitution where possible, and then do our part to establish a reconciliation with the Spirit, and ultimately receive a remission of sin. If we go through this process, we will be as those in The Book of Mormon who "cried with one voice, saying: Yea, we believe all the words which thou hast spoken unto us; and also, we know of their surety and truth, because of the Spirit of the Lord Omnipotent, which has wrought a mighty change in us, or in our hearts, that we have no more disposition to do evil, but to do good continually." (Mosiah 5:2). We will have only completed the process of repentance when forgiveness, painted with a broad brush, is at its foundation. For as the Lord said: "I...will forgive whom I will forgive, but of you it is required to forgive all men." (D&C 64:10).

61. "H.O.V. Lane." The Plan of Salvation was created with families in mind. No-one is going to reach the gates of the Celestial Kingdom by himself or herself. We are all in this together.

Remember that the magic of Camelot was that Arthur had a round table constructed for his royal court. In his kingdom, all were as one, and there was a fleeting wisp of glory in the air. After all, "the crown had made it clear. The climate must be perfect all the year. A law was made a distant moon ago here. July and August cannot be too hot. And there's a legal limit to the snow here in Camelot. The winter is forbidden 'til December, and exits March the second on the dot. By order, summer lingers through September, in Camelot. I know it sounds a bit bizarre, but in Camelot that's how conditions are. The rain may never fall 'til after sundown. By eight, the morning fog must disappear. The snow many never slush upon a hillside. By nine p.m. the moonlight must appear. In short, there's simply not a more congenial spot for happily-ever-aftering than here, in Camelot." (Alan J. Lerner).

We can be sure that the Lord designed Camelot; but also that, for Him, it was only a trial run. For "since the beginning of the world have not men heard nor perceived by the ear, neither hath any eye seen, O God, besides thee, how great things thou hast prepared for him that waiteth for thee." (D&C 133:45).

"After a coherent and
vigorous presentation, B.H. Roberts
said that he loved books, and that in some
degree books had made him. But then, in a most
vehement way, he said: "But I am not dependent
on books. I am dependent for what I really know
and trust on the direct experience of God."
("Defender of The Faith," p. 374).

The Holy Ghost:
Getting to Know Him

Happiness smells like bread baking in the oven, looks like a bright smile, makes us feel warm and cozy inside, sounds like children laughing in the park, and tastes like an ice cream sundae. Apples smell like cider, look like big red balls, feel smooth and hard, sound crunchy when biting into them, and taste sweet and juicy.

Smell, sight, touch, sound, and taste are the passport stamps that attest to our involvement in the world around us. They are critical to our interaction with the environment. Our brains have been created in such a way that they become blenders that take these sensations and whip them up into frothy virgin piña colatas of perception that become our own inimitable windows on the world. Life's experiences create zesty signature specialty drinks complete with little umbrellas that catch our attention, maraschino cherries that hold our interest, and whipped cream that keeps us coming back to the server asking for more, please.

But, as common as our five physical senses are, none of us see things in exactly the same way. Closely associated with intimate experiment, experience testifies to the recognition of our individuality by the Author of the Plan of Salvation. It is within the divinely conceived and ordained process of the marriage of sense and perception that our personalities enjoy their greatest elasticity. The resulting originality allows us to savor the gentle tug of non-conformity. Just as wind and water shape the landscape, the Master Potter takes our pliant mortal clay and fashions His magnum opus, with each piece of the puzzle expressing its own unique character. We are works in progress, stanzas in His unfinished symphony, and are continually evolving in an eternal progression.

It is only when we stop living that we start dying. We move and have have our being through sense and perception that blend into a refreshing elixir preventing us from becoming too set in our ways. These form an unlikely union, that by intelligent design has been created to upset the status-quo, expand every experience, weather every storm, and meet every challenge. At the end of the day, it is "by the experiment of this ministration" utilizing our senses, that we are able to "glorify God for (our) professed subjection unto the gospel of Christ." (2 Corinthians 9:13). It was ordained in the heavens that as we internalize the doctrine, we feel the exertion of an equalizing influence, for "all are alike unto God." (2 Nephi 26:33). But at the same time, sense and perception flavor a painstakingly crafted formula that enhances the distinctive qualities that make each of us unique.

We have other senses, as well, such as temperature (thermoception), body position (proprioception) pain (nociception), balance (equilibrioception), and time (chronoception). Together, like hormones, they subtly catalyze our environmental awareness. There are other senses that we do not have, or have only in diminished capacity, such as the ability to detect electrical and magnetic fields, polarized and infrared light, water pressure, pheromones, and the ability to utilize sonar. But we do not have a lock on the senses that we do enjoy; they are not uniquely ours. Bears have a better sense of smell, eagles a better sense of sight, catfish (believe it or not) a better sense of touch and taste, and dogs a better sense of sound. But what we do have seems to be in a perfect balance and harmony that is individually tailored to our specific needs.

Roughly 30 percent of the neurons in our cerebral cortex are devoted to vision, 8 percent to touch, 3 percent to hearing, and 0.1% to smell. It is unknown how many of the brain's neurons in the gustatory cortex are related to taste. There are roughly 100 billion neurons in our grey matter with 100 trillion connections (synapses) and a processing capacity of ten trillion instructions per second. The electrical output that would be required to simulate this brain function in a laboratory setting is equivalent to ten megawatts. A phenomenal amount of activity is going on in our brains to accommodate virtually limitless perceptions that take the philosophical supposition "cogito ergo sum" to incomprehensible levels.

Our senses are real, and when our bodies are in homeostasis, or in a state of equilibrium, we experience all of them, often unconsciously. They blend together in harmony to give us all the information we need in order to interact with our environment. But they do more than just that, by magically transforming raw data into perception, and in so doing they enrich our lives. Perception confirms that the sum is greater than its parts. It sweeps aside the simple math of stimulus and response, nullifying the argument that we simply react to our surroundings, and it introduces the intriguing element of uncertainty that give vitality and vibrancy to life, and new meanings to self-awareness. Perception opens up unknown possibilities of existence that we may have never before considered.

Our senses allow us to communicate, but our perceptions make our lives complete. Take even one sense from us, however, and we may be labeled as handicapped, be thought to have diminished capacity, or made to feel that we are somehow impaired. Our senses are so powerful that it we lose one, by substitution the others will move in with increased acuity to fill the void.

Sometimes, our senses can run wild. Hypersensitivity to auditory, visual, and tactile stimuli comes to mind. We all attempt, with varying levels of success, to compartmentalize endless data streams that unceasingly threaten to overwhelm us. A relentless flood of neural information may so overpower us that we suffer a breakdown of our nervous system. We may have a panic attack, or worse. Einstein described sensory overload as a storm that had broken loose in his mind. As a disciplined physicist, he was able to quantify, process, and control the barrage of mathematically complex information to which his brain was subjected. The therapy of his own design was an attempt to wrap his mind around a grand unifying principle that he hoped would harmonize the four fundamental forces of nature. Even with his prodigious mental calisthenics, he was unable to quantify and define that elusive equation, but if the Plan of Salvation is perfect, an equivalent principle must surely exist. It seems certain that God's Plan must hold the key that allows us to create order out of the chaos that is the milieu of mortality.

Some have defined His remedy as a spiritual "sixth sense," like the elusive dark matter that has been postulated to fill the void of space. Some believe that it is intuition, or the ability to take raw data and make sense of it and understand it immediately, without the need for conscious reasoning, interpretive analysis, or cerebral scrutiny. To accommodate the phenomenon of having the strong sensation that a current event has been experienced in the past, we have coined the phrase déjà vu, from French, literally meaning "already seen." The answer could be extrasensory perception, or the reception of information gained with the mind, rather than through the recognized physical senses. Perhaps it is clairvoyance, or the faculty of perceiving things or events in the future or beyond normal contact. Maybe it is premonition, or a strong feeling that something is about to happen. It may be all of the above, and more.

God's whole is surely greater than the sum of His parts, just as our perceptions are more than the sum of the sensory stimulations codified by our cerebral cortices. His spiritual sixth sense must be described by a common denominator that is the elusive theory of everything. Surely, there is a grand unifying principle underlying His Plan, but it probably defies explanation on a chalkboard, cannot be quantified by attaching electrodes to neurons, and will never be explained by dissecting a brain. No matter how far the neural net is cast, it will not be wide enough to catch God's vision for the education and exaltation of His children. His thoughts are not our thoughts, and His ways are not our ways.

The Higgs Boson may be "the God particle" that confirms "the Standard Model," a theory that attempts to harmonize the forces that govern the natural world. But if there is another power that supersedes the discipline of physics, that generates more energy than the Large Hadron Collider, a revision of the basic principles relating to "Philosophiæ Naturalis Principia Mathematica" will be required. (Sir Isaac Newton, 7/5/1687). That revision has always existed, quietly humming along in the background, flying beneath the radar, as it were. We know it as the Plan of Salvation.

Those of us with a strong Judeo-Christian background describe the commanding force the drives the execution of the Plan as the Holy Ghost. We believe that He is real, and that we all experience His influence. We submit that when our bodies are perfectly attuned to celestial rhythms, we often don't even consciously think about Him. We testify that the Holy Ghost has the ability to enrich our lives without dominating or overpowering our interaction with the world, thereby elegantly preserving the principle of free will. Our experience suggests that, with His input, we are given just the right amount of information we need in order to relate more comprehensively with our environment, while at the same time retaining ownership for our actions. And yet, we affirm that He is our fountain of facts and figures, our storehouse of knowledge, our lifetime of learning, our repository of reassurance, our spring of sagacity, our talisman of talents, and our warehouse of wisdom.

He is the author of acumen, the avatar of agency, the architect of aptitude, the benefactor of blessings, the champion of committed Christians, the craftsman of comfort, the designer of our discipleship, the engineer of erudition, the guarantor of gifts, the initiator of insight, the inventor of intelligence, the patron of perception, the provider of praise, the sponsor of scholarship, and the ultimate source of understanding. He testifies of truth, and provides the aether within which we communicate with our Heavenly Father. He makes our lives complete. However, we have also seen that by accident or by intention, we can lose the blessings of His influence. We can find ourselves in a state that is "past feeling," and lose the precious perception that He provides. (Ephesians 4:19).

We do Him little justice if we regard the Holy Ghost as only a spiritual sixth sense. His influence exceeds our ability to understand something immediately, without the need for conscious reasoning; is greater than the gathering of information not gained through the recognized physical senses but grasped with the mind; surpasses a strong feeling that something is about to happen, is superior to the strong sensation that an event has been experienced in the past; and transcends the faculty of perceiving things or events in the future or beyond normal contact.

It is a worthwhile endeavor getting to know the Holy Ghost, "getting to know all about Him, getting to like Him, and getting to hope He like us. Putting it another way, but nicely, He is precisely our cup of tea, getting to feel free and easy when we are with Him. Haven't you noticed, suddenly we're bright and breezy, because of all the beautiful and new things we're learning about Him day by day." (Adapted from "The King and I," "Getting to Know You," lyrics by Lorenz Hart and Richard Rodgers).

The Holy Ghost is real. "We believe in God, the Eternal Father, and in His Son, Jesus Christ, and in the (third member of the Trinity, the) Holy Ghost." (1st Article of Faith). The Savior promised: "When he, the Spirit of truth, is come, he will guide you into all truth: for he shall not speak of himself; but whatsoever he shall hear, that shall he speak: and he will shew you things to come." (John 16:13). He is in the form of a man and has a Spirit body. "The Father," said the Prophet Joseph Smith, "has a body of flesh and bones as tangible as man's; the Son also; but the Holy Ghost has not a body of flesh and bones, but is a personage of Spirit." (D&C 130:22). His mission, after bestowing all of the other blessings of which He is capable of providing, is ultimately to bear witness of the Father and the Son. "Wherefore I give you to understand," wrote Paul, "that no man speaking by the Spirit of God…can say that Jesus is the Lord, but by the Holy Ghost." (1 Corinthians 12:3).

The Holy Ghost manifests truth to the honest in heart. He is a revelator through Whom prophecy comes. By His power we "may know the truth of all things." (Moroni 10:5). "No prophecy of the scripture is of any private interpretation," said Peter. "For the prophecy came not in old time by the will of man: but holy men of God spake as they were moved by the Holy Ghost." (2 Peter 1:20-21). When we, at last, come back into the presence of God our Father, it will be through the tender guidance, concerned supervision, nurturing influence, dizzying inspiration, and powerful witness of the Holy Ghost. His spirit will authoritatively justify us before the throne of God. (Moses 6:60). We will be weighed and measured according to His equitable and unimpeachable testimony.

He is the Holy Spirit of Promise. "Concerning them who shall come forth in the resurrection of the just - They are they who received the testimony of Jesus, and believed on his name and were baptized after the manner of his burial… That by keeping the commandments they might be washed and cleansed from all their sins, and receive the Holy Spirit by the laying on of the hands of him who is ordained and sealed unto this power; And who overcome by faith, and are sealed by the Holy Spirit of promise, which the Father sheds forth upon all those who are just and true." (D&C 76:50-53).

After giving us our physical senses, God paused for a moment, and then also gave us a Divine Companion that we may think of as "the breath of life." (Genesis 2:7). Joseph Fielding Smith (who surely was in a position to know) said the Spirit of God "has power to impart truth with greater effect and understanding than the truth can be imparted by personal contact even with heavenly beings. Through the Holy

Ghost, the truth is woven into the very fibre and sinews of the body so that it cannot be forgotten." ("Doctrines of Salvation," 1:47-48). The Holy Ghost weaves golden threads into the tapestry of our lives so that we may take steady steps with the confidence born of its vibrant inner light.

"My life is but a weaving between the Lord and me," wrote the poet. "I cannot choose the colors; He worketh steadily. Oft-times, He weaveth sorrow, and I, in foolish pride, forget that He seeith the upper, and I, the underside. Not 'til the loom is silent and the shuttles cease to fly, shall God unroll the canvas and explain the reasons why. The dark threads are as needful in the Weaver's skillful hand, as the threads of gold and silver, in the pattern He has planned." (B.M. Franklin). If we allow Him to, the Holy Ghost will tailor our lives so that when we present ourselves before the throne of God, our garments will be free of the soil of sin, and we will be neatly dressed in our Sunday best that is a coat of many colors.

In the meantime, one of the principal responsibilities of the Holy Ghost is to anticipate and eliminate the culture shock that we might otherwise feel when we make the inevitable transition from a telestial tenement to a celestial station. We think of Paul's description of a "building fitly framed together (that) groweth unto an holy temple in the Lord." (Ephesians 2:21). C.S. Lewis suggested: "Imagine yourself as a living house. God comes in to rebuild that house. At first, perhaps, you can understand what He is doing. He is getting the drains right and stopping the leaks in the roof and so on. You knew that those jobs needed doing and so you are not surprised. But presently, He starts knocking the house about in a way that hurts abominably and does not seem to make any sense. What on earth is He up to? The explanation is that He is building quite a different house from the one you thought of - throwing out a new wing here, putting on an extra floor there, running up towers, making courtyards. You thought you were being made into a decent little cottage, but He is building a palace." ("Mere Christianity").

We make initial preparations to take up eventual residence in the mansions that have been prepared for us, by submitting ourselves to baptism by water. But that demonstration of faith and obedience only unlatches and nudges open the gate that exposes the pathway leading to the Celestial Kingdom. "For the gate by which ye should enter is repentance and baptism by water; and then cometh a remission of your sins by fire and by the Holy Ghost." (2 Nephi 31:17). Without baptism, we cannot take advantage of the Atonement, but without the gift of the Holy Ghost, we cannot even make the vital distinctions between truth and error. That requires perception on a plane that is more profound than that which is provided by our organs working in concert with our central nervous systems. It comes only to those who perceive themselves as acorns of a mighty oak. When we chart the course we would hope our lives might take, we cannot navigate past dangerous shoals and jagged reefs without the assistance of a trustworthy Pilot with unfathomable experience.

The Plan of Salvation cannot operate to our benefit without discernment. Were it not for the gift of the Holy Ghost, the Plan would work to our damnation. Its elements would be thrown into turmoil without the moral element of responsibility that He provides. Joseph Smith was able to enjoy the promptings of the Spirit and exercise his powers of discernment long before he became a member of The Church of Jesus Christ. As Peter said: "God is no respecter of persons; but in every nation he that feareth him, and worketh righteousness, is accepted" by him. (Acts 10:34-35).

Today, those who are led by the Light of Christ to seek out the truth may also enjoy the promptings of the Holy Ghost. In the closing chapter of The Book of Mormon, Moroni promised: "And when ye shall receive these things, I would exhort you that ye would ask God, the Eternal Father, in the name of Christ, if these things are not true; and if ye shall ask with a sincere heart, with real intent, having faith in Christ, he will manifest the truth of it unto you, by the power of the Holy Ghost." (Moroni 10:4).

Joseph Fielding Smith said: "We can receive a manifestation of the Holy Ghost, even when we are out of the church, if we are earnestly seeking for the light and for the truth. The Holy Ghost will come and give us the testimony we are seeking, and then withdraw." He continued: "There is no need for anyone to remain in darkness; the light of the everlasting gospel is here; and every sincere investigator on earth can gain a personal witness from the Holy Spirit, of the truth and divine nature of the Lord's work." ("Ensign," 6/1971). Heaven, then, waits upon our initiative.

Then, when we become members of the church, we need the special gift of the Holy Ghost to help us to be true to our blossoming faith. Joseph Fielding Smith said: "We may, after baptism and confirmation, become companions of the Holy Ghost, who will teach us the ways of the Lord, quicken our minds and help us to understand the truth." ("Doctrines of Salvation," 1:42). He can be our ever-faithful companion throughout the course of our mission in mortality, no matter in what areas we might serve, or how surprising to us our transfers might seem.

We need the gift of the Holy Ghost to eliminate ambiguity in our lives, clarify the elements of the Plan of Happiness, and bring accountability into sharp focus, so we may amend our behavior with the help of the Atonement. Joseph Fielding Smith said: "We are promised that when we are baptized, if we are true and faithful, we will have the guidance of the Holy Ghost. What is the purpose of it? To teach us, to direct us, to bear witness to us of the saving principles of the gospel of Jesus Christ." (C.R., 10/1959).

With the gift of the Holy Ghost, the plain and simple truths of the gospel of Jesus Christ, "even the key of the knowledge of God," will be unfolded to our view. (D&C 84:19). Joseph Fielding Smith said: "What a glorious privilege this is to be guided constantly by the Holy Ghost and to have the mysteries of the kingdom of God made manifest." ("Answers to gospel Questions," 4:90).

The Holy Ghost orients us toward the Celestial Kingdom. Joseph Fielding Smith said: "After we are baptized, we are confirmed to make us companions with the Holy Ghost; to give us the privilege of the guidance of the third member of the Godhead, that our minds might be enlightened, and that we might be quickened to seek for knowledge and understanding concerning all that pertains to our exaltation." ("Ensign," 6/1972).

The Holy Ghost endows us with spiritual and priesthood power. Marion G. Romney said: "The gift of the Holy Ghost is an endowment which gives us the right to enjoy the enlightenment, companionship, and guidance of the Spirit, as long as we comply with the commandments of God." He went on to say: "Receiving the Holy Ghost is the therapy which effects forgiveness and heals the sin-sick soul." (C.R., 4/1974).

When we view the gift of the Holy Ghost as an endowment, we can see that only those who are on a path leading to exaltation (through participation in the saving principles of the gospel) need healing at the level and intensity that is provided by intimate association with the third member of the Godhead. After our baptism and confirmation to receive the gift of the Holy Ghost, we receive the priesthood-administered ordinances of the temple. Brigham Young said our endowment of power received there gives us instruction sufficient to lay hold of eternal life, and consists of receiving all those ordinances "which are necessary for you, after you have departed this life, to enable you to walk back to the presence of the Father, passing the angels who stand as sentinels, being enabled to give them the key words, the signs and tokens, pertaining to the Holy Priesthood, and gain your eternal exaltation in spite of earth and hell." (J.D., 2:31).

In a way that presages the endowment in the temple, the gift of the Holy Ghost provides the power to perform whatever work is necessary for us to achieve our exaltation. Joseph Fielding Smith said: "The Holy Ghost is the Messenger, or Comforter, which the Savior promised to send to his disciples after He was crucified. This Comforter is, by His influence, to be a constant companion to every baptized person, and to administer unto the members of the church by revelation and guidance, knowledge of the truth that they may walk in its light. It is the Holy Ghost Who enlightens the mind of the truly baptized member. It is through Him that individual revelation comes, and the light of truth is established in our hearts." ("Answers to gospel Questions," 2:149-150). He ministers to our needs "with healing in his wings." (Malachi 4:2).

Because the gift of the Holy Ghost is an endowment from on high, it is reserved for the faithful who have entered in at the strait gate of baptism. It is bestowed by those who hold the authority of the priesthood. Joseph Fielding Smith said: "You cannot get the gift of the Holy Ghost by praying for it, by paying your tithing, by keeping the Word of Wisdom, not even by being baptized in water for the remission of sins. You must complete that baptism with the baptism of the Spirit. The Prophet said on one occasion that you might as well baptize a bag of sand as not confirm a man and give him the gift of the Holy Ghost, by the laying on of hands. You cannot get it any other way." ("Doctrines of Salvation," 1:41).

The gift of The Holy Ghost is bestowed under special terms and conditions. Marion G. Romney said: "The promise that God shall give unto (us) knowledge 'by the unspeakable gift of the Holy Ghost' (D&C 121:26), poses the question as to the manner in which we may receive this gift. It is by the laying on of hands following faith in the Lord Jesus Christ, repentance from sin, and baptism by immersion for the remission of sins." (C.R., 4/1974). We receive the gift of the Holy Ghost by obedience to the first principles of the gospel. (See the 4th Article of Faith).

And yet, there are baptized and confirmed members of the church who do not enjoy "the companionship of the Holy Ghost (because it) is available only to those who prepare themselves to receive it," said Joseph Fielding Smith. "It is my judgment," he continued, "that there are many members of this church who have been baptized for the remission of their sins, and who have had hands laid upon their heads for the gift of the Holy Ghost, but who have never received it. They listen (to heretical teachings) and the first thing you know, they find their way out of the church, because they do not have understanding." ("Seek Ye Earnestly The Best Gifts," p. 3). Without the guidance of the Holy Ghost, "their ears are dull of hearing, and their eyes have they closed." (Acts 28:27). "Noses they have they, but they smell not." (Psalms 115:6).

Our God-given senses cannot replace the influence of the Spirit. "The wind bloweth where it listeth, and thou hearest the sound thereof, but canst not tell whence it cometh, and whither it goeth: so is every one that is born of the Spirit." (John 3:8). Even if we use our physical senses to excess, relying on our intellect and instinct, while ignoring spiritual promptings that are provided in a rarified atmosphere like a refreshing breeze on a hot summer day, we will fall short of our perception potential provided by the pattern of the Plan.

If we do not know, or choose to ignore the Holy Ghost, we become susceptible to three dangers. The first is indifference, or a lack of commitment. If we do not know the Master, how can we be expected to serve Him with all our heart, might, mind, and strength? The second is waywardness, or straying from the gospel standard. If we are unprincipled and believe in nothing, how can we be expected to stand for something? The third is rebellion, or active opposition to the principles of truth. If we extinguish the light, in the gathering gloom how can we avoid stumbling over the obstacles to our progression? King Benjamin cautioned his people: "This much I can tell you, that if ye do not watch yourselves, and your thoughts, and your words, and your deeds, and observe the commandments of God, and continue in the faith of what ye have heard concerning the coming of our Lord, even unto the end of your lives, ye must perish." (Mosiah 4:30).

We may excel in sports, have the I.Q. of a genius, have perfect pitch, receive the accolades of men, spend our days in the heady atmosphere of the ivory towers of academia, jet-set with celebrities, hobnob with princes and potentates, or be the richest person in Babylon, but in the end, if we have not enjoyed the companionship of the Holy Ghost, none of it will be worth the ashes of a rye straw. Perhaps, when the last chapters of our lives are written, teachability and malleability will prevail, rather than sense or sensibility. The Holy Ghost cannot summarily rewrite the chapters of our lives, but it can help us to begin a new ending to the story.

Joseph Fielding Smith counseled: "If we find ourselves in a condition of unbelief or unwillingness to seek for the light and the knowledge which the Lord has placed within our reach, then we are in danger of being deceived by evil spirits and the doctrines of devils. When these false influences are presented before us, we will not have the distinguishing understanding" by which we can recognize them for what they are. (C.R., 10/1952). Not only our physical senses, but also our spiritual acuity will have failed us in our times of greatest need. Lacking inspiration, we will face eternity short of the breath of the Almighty that might have otherwise sustained our lives. (See Job 33:4). Our final expiration of the celestial aether that filled our lungs at birth will be utterly complete.

Some have received the gift of the Holy Ghost, but then have let it slip between their fingers. Joseph Fielding Smith said: "The Spirit of the Lord will not dwell in unclean tabernacles, and when a person turns from the truth through wickedness, that Spirit does not follow him but departs, and in the stead thereof comes" the overwhelming influence of the physical senses, manifest as the "spirit of error, the spirit of disobedience, the spirit of wickedness, (and) the spirit of eternal destruction." (C.R., 4/1962).

He also taught: "It is the privilege of every member of the church to know the truth, to speak by the truth, to have the inspiration of the Holy Ghost. It is our privilege, individually, to receive the light and to walk in the light; and if we continue in God, that is, keep all of His commandments, we shall receive more light until eventually there shall come to us the perfect day of knowledge." ("Relief Society Magazine," 1/1941).

At that day, "by the power of the Spirit our eyes (will be) opened and our understanding (will be) enlightened, so as to see and understand the things of God." (D&C 76:12). Our physical senses will have finally harmonized with our spirit. We will feel the truth as it swells within our bosom, as it did for the two disciples on the road to Emmaus, who said of the resurrected Lord: "Did not our heart burn within us, while he talked with us by the way, and while he opened to us the scriptures?" (Luke 24:32). We will touch eternity as our cheeks "brush against the veil, as goodbyes and greetings are said almost within earshot of each other. In such moments, this resonance with realities on the other side of the veil is so real that it can be explained in only one way." (Neal A. Maxwell, "All These Things Shall Give Thee Experience," p. 6-27).

We will smell the sweet fragrance of celestial gardens, and hear the Spirit of truth speak "of things as they really are, and of things as they really will be," and these things will be "manifested unto us plainly, for the salvation of our souls." (Jacob 4:13). We will hear a voice saying "well done thou good and faithful servant...enter thou into the joy of the Lord." (Matthew 25:21). At last, we will come back into the presence of God our Father, through the nurturing guidance of the Holy Ghost.

If all truth can be
circumscribed into one great
whole, then the Plan of Salvation
is the Holy Grail of religious doctrine.
It is the spiritual equivalent of the theory of
everything (physics' Unified Field Theory).
It explains our place in the cosmos, and
defines and gives substance and
meaning to our existence.

The Holy Grail of Religious Doctrine

The Book of Abraham describes "their plan" meaning the plan of the Gods. (Abraham 4:21). Jacob refers to it as: "The plan of our God." (2 Nephi 9:13). Its keystone is the Atonement of Jesus Christ, and so Alma called it "the plan of mercy." (Alma 42:15). Later in the same address, Alma acknowledged its grand nature by calling it "the great plan of mercy." (Alma 42:31).

Its elements predate the organization of worlds without number. It is "the merciful plan of the great Creator" (2 Nephi 9:6), conceived to redeem us from death. Thus, it is "the plan of redemption" (Alma 12:25), even "the great plan of redemption" (Alma 34:31), or "the great and eternal plan of redemption." (Alma 34:16). From our perspective, it is "the plan of redemption, which was prepared from the foundation of the world." (Alma 18:39). It is all-inclusive, inasmuch as it is "the great and eternal plan of deliverance from death." (2 Nephi 11:5).

It is commonly called "the plan of salvation." (Alma 24:14). Moses acknowledged the benevolent nature of God when he described it as "the plan of salvation unto all men." (Moses 6:62). It applies to all mankind without exception, so it comes as no surprise that Alma called it "the great plan of salvation." (Alma 42:5). He also called it "the plan of restoration," (Alma 41:2), since its design is to bring us, pure, spotless, and innocent, back into the presence of our Heavenly Father. He knew that with this restoration we would experience indescribable joy, and so he also called it "the great plan of happiness." (Alma 42:8). It is "the plan of happiness, which (is) as eternal also as the life of the soul." (Alma 42:16).

Ultimately, it is "the great plan of the eternal God" (Alma 34:9), that caused us to sing together and shout for joy when its elements were first explained to us. (See Job 38:7).

"In a Wonderland they lie, dreaming as the days go by, dreaming as the summers die: Ever drifting down the stream. Lingering in the golden gleam. Life, what is it but a dream?" (Lewis Carroll, "Through the Looking Glass").

The Hourglass of Life

If mortality could be visualized in spatial dimensions, it would take the shape of an hourglass, with the strait gate its narrow midsection. After passing through that constriction, unparalleled vistas would open up to reveal untapped potential and unequalled opportunity. But initially, many of us would be caught in conceptually confusing cul-de-sacs that would prevent us from comprehending the purpose of the Plan. We would wander to and fro, dazed and disoriented, like flotsam and jetsam on the sea of life.

Some of us would be stalled in telestial traffic jams that would overheat our engines, foul our lubricants, seize our moving parts, and restrict our access to freely flowing spiritual energy. Others would lack restraint, as if their brake pads were worn, interfering with their ability to slow down, in order to avoid the sand traps of transgression, as they negotiated the minefields of mortality. Their ability to move forward with purpose might be compromised. They might lose their traction as they tried to move upward, and they might feel as if their gears were grinding and their clutch plates were slipping.

A few of us might squander scarce resources, as if our thermostats were inoperable, causing our cooling systems to boil over from the excitement of excessive exertion in the steam plant of sin. All these mechanical issues might combine to overwhelm us in a perfect storm of trial and temptation, forcing, as it were, lifestyle compromises that would make self-control and self-actualization all the more difficult, while making rationalization and self-justification more tempting options.

But for the few of us who were lucky enough to finally reach the constriction in the hourglass, there would come a realization that the time to stand and deliver had arrived. As Brutus observed, we would face that "tide in the affairs of men which, taken at the flood, leads on to fortune. Omitted," we would realize that the voyage of our lives would be condemned to be "bound in shallows and in miseries. On such a full sea," however, we would find ourselves "afloat, and we" would "take the current when it serves, or lose our ventures." (Shakespeare, "Julius Caesar," Act 4, Scene 3).

Those who made it through the strait and narrow way, would be fortunate, indeed, to find that by following the blueprints of the Plan, they would be able to successfully flex their spiritual muscles and exercise their moral agency in a forum of free will that engaged opposition in a vigorous tug-of-war. They would realize that the Plan works best when its participants are able to make excellent choices in the midst of less attractive competing options. They would hope to be sensitive to spiritual promptings, to be stimulated by the light of Christ, to receive the Gift of the Holy Ghost, to be thereby guided, and to be replenished with the high octane fuel of faith that would ignite the fire of their fortitude and propel them forward.

Those who would seize the moment, thread the eye of the needle, and negotiate the strait and narrow path would realize that what at the outset had felt like a confinement, and a constraint, was in fact a birth canal, or a portal through which all must pass in order to progress eternally. They would feel as if they had literally been born again. Expanding circles of opportunity that had beforehand been hidden from their view would snap into sharp focus. They would see beyond the limited horizon of their sight, and comprehend a vision in which the perfect law of liberty stretched out before them in a vista of incomprehensible proportion. They would see that God's Plan rests on solid footings that are reinforced with the rebar of our resolve, and that it is upon the foundation of the covenants that we make with Him that celestial sureties are constructed, leading to eternal life in His mansions above.

"We are divine sparks
struck off the white
hot anvil of God."
(B.H. Roberts).

The Light of The World

Light is used throughout the scriptures as a symbol for Jesus Christ. The Savior himself said: "I am the true light that lighteth every man that cometh into the world." (D&C 93:2).

The New Testament records that He taught in the temple during the Feast of Tabernacles that was a commemoration of the Lord's blessings to the children of Israel during their journey in the wilderness. It also celebrated the end of the harvest season. The Jews considered this the greatest and most joyful of all their feasts.

"Now about the midst of the feast Jesus went up into the temple, and taught. And the Jews marvelled, saying, How knoweth this man letters, having never learned? Jesus answered them, and said, My doctrine is not mine, but his that sent me. If any man will do his will, he shall know of the doctrine, whether it be of God, or whether I speak of myself." (John 7:14-18). He was referring to the spiritual enlightenment we receive as we strive to live in obedience to gospel principles.

During the Feast of Tabernacles, the temple in Jerusalem was illuminated by four enormous golden candelabra that were strategically placed on the temple mount above the city of Jerusalem. According to the Mishnah, the oral rabbinic tradition, each was around 75 feet tall with four branches, at the top of which were large bowls, each filled with 10 gallons of oil. When these were ignited, the flames were a spectacular sight for the entire city to see. To complete the sound and light show, musicians played harps, lyres, cymbals, and trumpets to make joyful music in a glorious celebration.

Tradition identifies both Mount Moriah, where Abraham took Isaac to be sacrificed, and Mount Zion, where the original Jebusite fortress stood that had been conquered by David, as encompassed by present day Mount Zion. It is the holiest site in Judaism, where God's divine presence is manifested. Both Solomon's Temple and the Temple of Zerubabel, later expanded by Herod, are believed to have stood on Mount Zion. According to Jewish tradition, a third temple will also be built there. Today, many Jews will not walk on Mount Zion, for fear of treading upon the Holy of Holies, where the high priest anciently communicated directly with God.

This was the setting for the celebration of the Feast of Tabernacles, and possibly, while standing before the dancing light coming from the blazing bowls of oil, Jesus declared: "I am the light of the world: he that followeth me shall not walk in darkness, but shall have the light of life." (John 8:12).

To the Nephites, the Savior explained: "Behold, I am the law, and the light. Look unto me, and endure to the end, and ye shall live; for unto him that endureth to the end will I give eternal life." (3 Nephi 15:9). Joseph Smith received revelation relating to "the light of truth; Which truth shineth. This is the light of Christ. As also he is in the sun, and the light of the sun, and the power thereof by which it was made. As also he is in the moon, and is the light of the moon, and the power thereof by which it was made; As also the light of the stars, and the power thereof by which they were made; And the earth also, and the power thereof, even the earth upon which you stand. And the light which shineth, which giveth you light, is through him who enlighteneth your eyes, which is the same light that quickeneth your understandings; Which light proceedeth forth from the presence of God to fill the immensity of space— The light which is in all things, which giveth life to all things, which is the law by which all things are governed, even the power of God who sitteth upon his throne, who is in the bosom of eternity, who is in the midst of all things." (D&C 88:6-13).

As we strive to be like Jesus, we reflect His light. We can be as the candelabra during the Feast of Tabernacles. "Ye are the light of the world," the Savior taught. "A city that is set on an hill cannot be hid." (Matthew 5:14). We can help others come to know Him by letting our light "so shine before men, that they may see (our) good works, and glorify (our) Father which is in heaven." (Matthew 5:16). We can also become more committed to obedience if we "continue in (His) word, then are (we His) disciples indeed; And (we) shall know the truth, and the truth shall make (us) free" from the burdens of sin. (John 8:31-32). We will bask in the glow of the light of the world, and be guided to spiritual safety.

"They that wait upon the
Lord shall renew their strength;
they shall mount up with wings as
eagles; they shall run, and not
be weary; and they shall
walk, and not faint."
(Isaiah 40:31).

The Lord's Patient Protection and Affordable Healthcare Act

Heavenly Father is the penultimate holistic health care provider. By following the principles of His patient protection and affordable healthcare act, a cooperative relationship with His children is fostered, leading to optimal physical, mental, emotional, social, and spiritual health, without the use of chemo-therapeutics or invasive therapies, not to mention onerous premium payments.

In everything He does, in every program that has been initiated by His able assistants, the advantages of evaluating the whole person is emphasized, including an analysis of their physical, nutritional, environmental, emotional, social, spiritual and lifestyle values. The scope of His Plan encompasses all conventional modalities of diagnosis and treatment, as well as alternative remedies, all with an emphasis on the healing powers of obedience to true principles, as well as on the regenerative power of ordinances and covenants. The doctrine upon which His program is based is grounded on continuing education as well as on personal responsibility for behavior and outcomes, with the objective of the achievement of balance and well-being.

The scriptures are replete with instances of physical disease caused by disobedience to His laws of emotional and spiritual health. "Zeezrom, for example, lay sick "with a burning fever, that was caused by the great tribulations of his mind on account of his wickedness. ...His many other sins, did harrow up his mind until it did become exceedingly sore, having no deliverance; therefore he began to be scorched with a burning heat." (Alma 15:3). Alma wrote: "I was racked with eternal torment, for my soul was harrowed up to the greatest degree." (Alma 36:12). Jeremiah reported that his recalcitrant brethren had "eaten a sour grape, and the children's teeth (were) set on edge." (Jeremiah 31:29). Peter said of those who had forsaken righteous lifestyle choices: "The dog is turned to his own vomit again; and the sow that was washed, to her wallowing in the mire." (2 Peter 2:22). Belshazzar became aware of his spiritual bradycardia, that his "countenance was changed, and his thoughts troubled him, so that the joints of his loins were loosed, and his knees smote one against another." (Daniel 5:6).

In a worst-case scenario, spiritual sicknesses mimics the symptoms of those with advanced diabetes whose peripheral circulation has been so compromised that they can no longer feel. As we experience the hard lessons of life that the Plan purposely throws our way with frustrating regularity, we may become numb to the better angels of our nature and lose our capacity to touch and be touched by those around us. We will then find ourselves more and more isolated from the sensitivity to our surroundings that is critical to our full participation in the Lord's healthcare system. We will find ourselves in a spiritual vacuum, gasping for life-sustaining celestial air.

In His holistic approach to our spiritual well-being, if we wish to run and not be weary, and walk and not faint, all we need to do is let our sins trouble us, with that trouble that shall bring us down unto repentance. (See Alma 42:29).

Touchstone

"Prosperity is the measure or touchstone of virtue,
for it is less difficult to bear misfortune than
to remain uncorrupted by pleasure."
(Tacitus).

The Lord's Touchstone

Anciently, the purity of gold was tested with a smooth rock called a touchstone. When the metal was rubbed across the touchstone, it left a mark on its surface that was matched to a color on a chart. The higher the percentage of gold, the more yellow would be the mark.

The concept of determining the amount of gold in an alloy gives a whole new meaning to the scriptures that speak of a "refiner's fire." For "who may abide the day of his coming? And who shall stand when he appeareth? For he is like a refiner's fire." (Malachi 3:2). For he is like fuller's soap; and he shall sit as a refiner and purifier of silver, and he shall purify the sons of Levi, and purge them as gold and silver, that they may offer unto the Lord an offering in righteousness." (D&C 128:24). God's influence is like a refiner's fire in the sense that it burns the dross, detritus, and impurities out of our nature, leaving only "24 karat gold."

It goes without saying that each of us would like to be pure gold, and not the 10 to 18 karat variety that is alloyed with other metals. Costume jewelry is not fit for the disciples of Christ. In fact, the beautiful streets of the Celestial Kingdom have "the appearance of being paved with gold" that has not been mixed with nickel, copper, tin, manganese, cadmium, or zinc. (D&C 137:4). As it turns out, gold never tarnishes, but retains its brightness, and it is malleable. (See Alma 37:5). In spiritual terms, we would say that those who are 24 karat gold are untarnished by sin, and are teachable.

Having said that, we are constantly assaulted by worldly influences that can corrupt, compromise, and canker our character so that it is only 18 karat, or even 14 karat. For that matter, sometimes our character may be further cheapened by fool's gold, if we are not being true to ourselves; for example, when we are being hypocritical.

Anyone who has done centrifugal casting knows that the gold in the crucible needs to be heated up until it is white-hot and "spinning" before the wound-up casting arm is released, throwing the gold into a refractory material within which a wax pattern has been invested. That wax pattern is a detailed and accurate representation of a final product that can be created only if the gold is thrown by centrifugal force during the casting process into every nook and cranny. In this vein, I am reminded of something B.H. Roberts said of the saints, that they are "as white-hot sparks struck off the divine anvil of God."

In the casting process, gold needs to be heated to at least 1,064 degrees Celsius, which is its melting point, in order for it to flow into the wax pattern. So too, do we need to raise our core testimony temperature until we are "white-hot," so that we can be molded into the pattern God has planned for us.

The touchstone of compassion, that measures our love of God and of each other, will determine our discipleship; if we are 24 karat gold. I am reminded of a story about John K. Edmunds, who enjoyed a distinguished legal career in Chicago, and who also, after his retirement, served as the President of the Salt Lake Temple. On one occasion, a widow came to him for legal advice, and when they were finished, she apprehensively asked: "How much do I owe you?" Gently, he responded, "Why don't you pay me what you think it's worth." Greatly relieved, she got out her coin purse, fished around for a quarter, and pressed it into his hand. He looked at the quarter, looked at her, and then got out his own coin purse, and gave her ten cents change. Brother Edmunds knew what it meant to follow in his every day life the Savior's example of charity.

You see, more than law, he was practicing benevolent blindness. He was able to look beyond the monetary demands of his profession, and relate to a poor widow in the same way the Savior, out of the abundance of His heart, spoke to the downtrodden, little children, farmers and fishermen, and those who tended goats and sheep.

The Savior related to strangers and foreigners, to the rich as well as to the poor, to the politically powerful, as well as to unfriendly scribes and Pharisees. He ministered to the hungry, the deprived, and the sick. He blessed the lame, the blind, the deaf, and other people with physical disabilities. He drove out demons and evil spirits that had caused mental or emotional illness. He purified those who were burdened with sin. He taught lessons of love and repeatedly demonstrated unselfish service to others. All were recipients of His love.

The benevolently blind who follow in the footsteps of the Savior look the other way, above and beyond the faults of others. They give the benefit of the doubt, turn the other cheek, go the second mile, obey the Golden Rule, turn a blind eye when others fall short of expectations, and are tolerant when they fail to measure up. Benevolent blindness is another of the Lord's touchstones that is an easy measure of our discipleship. He said: "Thou shalt love the Lord thy God with all thy heart, and with all thy soul, and with all thy strength, and with all thy mind; and thy neighbour as thyself." (Luke 10:25-28).

The Savior taught us to love those who are difficult to love. When He powerfully related the parable of the Good Samaritan, He pointedly chose an individual from a class whom the Jews despised. But having done so, He pointedly asked the lawyer, "Which now of these three, thinkest thou, was neighbour unto him that fell among the thieves?" (Luke 10:36). The question articulated the touchstone that defined His ministry. Our answer to the same question measures our mark, and determines if we are 24 karat gold, simply gold that has been alloyed to metals of lesser quality, or worst of all, fool's gold.

Howard W. Hunter said: "The Samaritan gave us an example of pure Christian love. He had compassion; he went to the man who had been injured by the thieves and bound up his wounds. He took him to an inn, cared for him, paid his expenses, and offered more if needed for his care. This is a story of the love of a neighbor for his neighbor." ("Ensign," 11/1986). He performed a labor that C.S. Lewis called: "Quiet Christianity." Such acts touch our spiritual sensitivities. It was with no little inspiration that State Farm Insurance Company has adopted the slogan: "Like a good neighbor, State Farm is there!" As it speaks to our spirit with the affirmation of truth, who wouldn't want to be protected by the encircling arms of a company like State Farm?

If we find it difficult to think of similar modern day examples of The Good Samaritan in our own lives, perhaps we could ratchet down our expectations and just concentrate on being good neighbors. We could take our cue from Mr. Rogers, who said: "I've always wanted to have a neighbor just like you. I've always wanted to live in a neighborhood with you. So, let's make the most of this beautiful day. Since we're together we might as well say: Would you be mine? Could you be mine? Won't you be my neighbor?"

How might the world change if each of us consciously tried to be a Good Samaritan, or even a Good Neighbor, just once a week, or even once a month? We would be successful if we remembered that, although it is we who make our friends, it is God Who has made our neighbors. Our "love should have no boundary, and we should have no narrow loyalties," taught Howard W. Hunter. ("Ensign," 11/1986). For as Christ said: "If ye love them which love you, what reward have ye? Do not even the publicans the same?" (Matthew 5:46).

If we are to be good neighbors, we simply need to love them and serve them. As Joseph Smith taught: "It is a duty which every Saint ought to render to his brethren freely - to always love them, and ever succor them. To be justified before God we must love one another; we must overcome evil; we must visit the fatherless and the widow in their affliction, and we must keep ourselves unspotted from the world, for such virtues flow from the great fountain of pure religion. Strengthening our faith by adding every good quality that adorns the children of the blessed Jesus, we can pray in the season of prayer; we can love our neighbor as ourselves, and be faithful in tribulation, knowing that the reward of such is greater in the kingdom of heaven. What a consolation! What a joy!" (H.C., 2:229).

If you were asked to do so, would you lay down your life for your family, your friends, your neighbors, or those who treat you unkindly? We remember the Amish, who seem to have perfected the quality of loving their neighbors as themselves. "Next to the Bible, the most important book in any Amish household is 'The Martyr's Mirror,' which documents the persecution suffered by the Anabaptists in Europe in the 16th and 17th centuries. This book is read aloud to Amish families nearly every day. Among the stories, is the tale of one Amishman who was being pursued by a bounty hunter across a frozen lake. The ice cracked, and the bounty hunter fell in. The Amishman stopped and pulled the bounty hunter from what would have surely been an icy death, only to then be taken into custody and later executed for his faith." ("Christian Science Monitor").

If it is hard to relate to that story, we might ask ourselves: On our own touchstone, will we leave a mark of pure gold or, like the priest and the Levite, pass by on the other side? Can we find the power and the purpose to walk along the path of charity? Joseph Smith said: We must love others, even our enemies as well as friends. Christians should cease wrangling and contending with each other, and cultivate the principles of union and friendship in their midst." (H.C., 5:498–499).

"That is magnificent counsel today, even as it was then," declared Howard W. Hunter. "The world in which we live, whether close to home or far away, needs the gospel of Jesus Christ. It provides the only way the world will ever know peace. We need to be kinder with one another, more gentle and forgiving. We need to be slower to anger and more prompt to help. We need to extend the hand of friendship and resist the hand of retribution. In short, we need to love one another with the pure love of Christ, with genuine charity and compassion and, if necessary, shared suffering, for that is the way God loves us.

We need to walk more resolutely and more charitably the path that Jesus has shown. We need to pause to help and lift another and surely we will find strength beyond our own. If we would do more to learn the healer's art, there would be untold chances to use it, to touch the wounded and the weary and show to all a gentler heart." ("Ensign," 5/1992).

Charity encompasses all other godly virtues, and defines both the beginning and the end of the Plan of Salvation. When all else fails, charity will not. It is the greatest of the attributes of God. At the end of the day, all you really need is love. If you have love, "there's nothing that can't be done; nothing that can't be sung; nothing you can say; but you can learn how to play the game. It's easy. Nothing that can't be made; no one that can't be saved. You can learn how to be you in time. It's easy. All you need is love. Love is all you need. There's nothing you can know that isn't known; nothing you can see that isn't shown. There's nowhere you can be that isn't where you're meant to be. It's easy. All you need is love. Love is all you need." (John Lennon, 1967).

Loving others is "a more excellent way." (1 Corinthians 12:31). As Moroni declared: "Wherefore, whoso believeth in God might with surety hope for a better world." (Ether 12:4). Today, perhaps with more urgency than ever before, we need a better world.

The prophet Elijah wore a mantle, apparently a cloak made of cloth. The passing of the mantle from Elijah to Elisha symbolized the passing of prophetic authority to Elisha.

The Mantle
of The Prophet

In modern times we sometimes speak of the "mantle" of authority that the prophet receives when he is ordained and set apart. Although the prophet today does not wear a cloak or piece of cloth that is uniquely his, God bestows upon him the keys of the priesthood, or the power to act in His name as the leader of the church on the earth. When a prophet dies, this mantle of authority passes to the new prophet.

Elisha succeeded Elijah as the prophet. These two priesthood leaders shared a special relationship. Before Elijah was taken up unto heaven, "fifty men of the sons of the prophets went, and stood to view afar off: and they two stood by Jordan. And Elijah took his mantle, and wrapped it together, and smote the waters, and they were divided hither and thither, so that they two went over on dry ground. And it came to pass, when they were gone over, that Elijah said unto Elisha, Ask what I shall do for thee, before I be taken away from thee. And Elisha said, I pray thee, let a double portion of thy spirit be upon me." (2 Kings 2:7-9). Clearly, Elisha was quite impressed with his mentor's display of priesthood power, and looked forward to exercising it, as well.

"And it came to pass, as they still went on, and talked, that, behold, there appeared a chariot of fire, and horses of fire, and parted them both asunder; and Elijah went up by a whirlwind into heaven. And Elisha...took up...the mantle of Elijah that fell from him, and went back, and stood by the bank of Jordan. And he took the mantle of Elijah that fell from him, and smote the waters, and said, Where is the Lord God of Elijah? and when he also had smitten the waters, they parted hither and thither: and Elisha went over. And when the sons of the prophets which were to view at Jericho saw him, they said, The spirit of Elijah doth rest on Elisha." (2 Kings 2:11-15).

Today, when the prophet dies, the mantle of authority is transferred in an orderly manner to his successor, one might even say with equally spectacular results. Joseph Fielding Smith explained: "There is no mystery about the choosing of the successor to the President of the Church. The Lord settled this a long time ago, and the senior apostle automatically becomes the presiding officer of the church, and he is so sustained by the Council of the Twelve, that becomes the presiding body of the church when there is no First Presidency. The President is not elected, but he has to be sustained both by his brethren of the Council and by the members of the church." ("Doctrines of Salvation," 3:156).

Gordon B. Hinckley explained to the saints how this procedure was followed when he was ordained and set apart as the prophet and President of the church following the death of Howard W. Hunter. "With President Hunter's passing, the First Presidency was dissolved. Brother Monson and I, who had served as his counselors, took our places in the Quorum of the Twelve that became the presiding authority of the church. (A few days later) all of the living ordained Apostles gathered in a spirit of fasting and prayer in the upper room of the temple. Here we sang a sacred hymn and prayed together. We partook of the Sacrament of the Lord's Supper, renewing in that sacred, symbolic testament our covenants and our relationship with Him who is our divine Redeemer. The Presidency was then reorganized, following a precedent well established through generations of the past. (This precedent has been explained in the statement above by Joseph Fielding Smith). There was no campaigning, no contest, and no ambition for office. It was quiet, peaceful, simple, and sacred. It was done after the pattern which the Lord Himself had put in place." (C.R., 4/1995).

As He did anciently, the Savior has given the keys of the kingdom to each of the latter-day Apostles. However, only the President of the church, who is the senior living Apostle, and the President of the Quorum of The First Presidency, may use these keys (or authorize others to use them) on behalf of the entire church. The Lord explained: "I have appointed unto my servant Joseph to hold this power in the last days, and there is never but one on the earth at a time on whom this power and the keys of this priesthood are conferred." (D&C 132:7).

When the mantle of authority fell upon Elisha, and he duplicated Elijah's miracle of parting the waters of Jordan, the people immediately accepted and sustained him, as today we do the newly ordained President of the church. "This ye shall know assuredly—that there is none other appointed unto you to receive commandments and revelations until he be taken, if he abide in me. ...For verily I say unto you, that he that is ordained of me shall come in at the gate and be ordained as I have told you before, to teach those revelations which you have received and shall receive through him whom I have appointed." (D&C 43:2-3 & 7).

Soon after Elijah had been taken into heaven, the people wanted to send 50 strong men to look for him. But Elisha said: "Ye shall not send. And when they urged him till he was ashamed, he said, Send. They sent, therefore, fifty men; and they sought three days, but found him not." (2 Kings 2:16-17). It may have been no coincidence that it was not long thereafter that Elisha healed Naaman of leprosy, for his story teaches us to follow the counsel of the prophet even when we may not understand it, or when it may concern small and simple matters.

"Naaman, captain of the host of the king of Syria…was a leper." (2 Kings 5:1). He "came with his horses and with his chariot, and stood at the door of the house of Elisha. And Elisha sent a messenger unto him, saying, Go and wash in Jordan seven times, and thy flesh shall come again to thee, and thou shalt be clean. But Naaman was wroth, and went away, and said, Behold, I thought, He will surely come out to me, and stand, and call on the name of the Lord his God, and strike his hand over the place, and recover the leper. Are not (the) rivers of Damascus better than all the waters of Israel? May I not wash in them, and be clean? So he turned and went away in a rage." (2 Kings 5:10-12).

We all know how the story ended. "And his servant came near, and spake unto him, and said, My father, if the prophet had bid thee do some great thing, wouldest thou not have done it? How much rather then, when he saith to thee, Wash, and be clean? Then went he down, and dipped himself seven times in Jordan, according to the saying of the man of God: and his flesh came again like unto the flesh of a little child, and he was clean." (2 Kings 5:13-14).

Frequently, we are asked to do small things by the prophet or other ecclesiastical authorities. "The way of the gospel is a simple way. Some of the requirements may appear to you as elementary and unnecessary. Do not spurn them. Humble yourselves and walk in obedience. I promise that the results that follow will be marvelous to behold and satisfying to experience." (Gordon B. Hinckley, C.R., 10/1976).

Even when Israel was at war with Syria, Elisha guided the people. The Syrian leaders so feared the power of the prophet, that their king was told: "Elisha, the prophet that is in Israel, telleth the king of Israel the words that thou speakest in thy bedchamber. And he said, Go and spy where he is, that I may send and fetch him. And it was told him, saying, Behold, he is in Dothan. Therefore, sent he thither horses, and chariots, and a great host: and they came by night, and compassed the city about." (2 Kings 6:12-14).

"And when the servant of the man of God was risen early, and gone forth, behold, an host compassed the city both with horses and chariots. And his servant said unto him, Alas, my master! how shall we do? And he answered, Fear not: for they that be with us are more than they that be with them. And Elisha prayed, and said, Lord, I pray thee, open his eyes, that he may see. And the Lord opened the eyes of the young man; and he saw: and, behold, the mountain was full of horses and chariots of fire round about Elisha." (2 Kings 6:15-17).

Today, some fear that latter-day Israel is helpless to stand against the evils of the world. But as Dallin H. Oaks taught: "When I read this wonderful story as a boy, I always identified with the young servant of Elisha. I thought, If I am ever surrounded by the forces of evil while I am in the Lord's service, I hope the Lord will open my eyes and give me faith to understand that when we are in the work of the Lord, those who are with us are always more powerful than those who oppose us." (C.R., 10/1992). The Lord promised Joseph Smith: "I will go before your face. I will be on your right hand and on your left, and my Spirit shall be in your hearts, and mine angels round about you, to bear you up." (D&C 84:87). The President of the church is a prophet of God. We sustain him and follow his counsel, for his power, the power of God, is greater than any other.

"The tyrant dies and his rule is over;
the martyr dies and his rule begins."
(Soren Kierkegaard).

The Martyr's Mirror

Next to the Bible, the most important book in any Amish household is "der Martyrspeigel" ("The Martyr's Mirror") that documents the persecution suffered by the Anabaptists in Europe in the 16th and 17th centuries. This book is read aloud to the family nearly every day. Among the stories is the tale of one Amishman being pursued by a bounty hunter across a frozen lake. The ice cracked, and the bounty hunter fell in. The Amishman pulled the bounty hunter from what would have surely been an icy death, and then was himself taken into custody and later executed for his faith. With such stories told time after time, it is not surprising that there is within the Amish psyche a deep reservoir of forgiveness and grace.

As I have thought about the example of the Amish, and the lessons they teach us in the conduct of their lives, I have begun to see the stories of our own pioneer forefathers in a new light. I used to think that the Willie and Martin Handcart Companies pretty much got what they deserved, that Joseph Smith's martyrdom, although a tragedy, was the logical conclusion to an unfortunate stream of events, and that Zion's Camp was a somewhat overblown example of the privation that was common in those times.

I thought that the Mormon Battalion's trek to California was no more than the equivalent of many other westward migrations, and that the scourge of locusts, accompanied by flocks of gulls from the Great Salt Lake, could have been an article straight out of any random "Audubon Society" magazine. Even the Pioneer Trek seemed unremarkable, if only because it was an example from among hundreds, or perhaps thousands, that were undertaken in the 1840s.

Having said all that, it may just be that as Mormons endlessly recount these stories in firesides, Sacrament meetings, and even in General Conference, the purpose is to solidify our roots, particularly if we are not of pioneer stock and cannot claim membership in the Sons of Utah Pioneers, or count early leaders of the church or polygamous families among our direct-line ancestors.

Perhaps we tell these stories simply because, in an age of social media, personal information devices, computer generated images, and real-time video, they are completely alien to our experience. Maybe we all need an occasional dose of reality to jar us out of our complacency and recalibrate our senses.

Perhaps we need these stories to bolster our faith in a God Who is more focused on our visceral needs, than He is on which car we should buy, which college our children should attend, or which vacation we should take.

Maybe we need more icy rivers to cross, more adversaries with whom we could contend, more hot desert winds to parch our throats and crack our lips, more dry water holes to test our faith, and more starving livestock to drive us to our knees.

Maybe we have forgotten how to make ourselves comfortable while sleeping on the hard ground, how to pray fervently over our crops when clouds of locusts threaten, and how to feel genuine appreciation for the sacrifices of our forbearers.

On one occasion, after Joseph Smith had petitioned the Lord for redress and relief, he was told: "All these things shall give thee experience, and shall be for thy good." (D&C 122:7). His subsequent letters to the Saints reveal how he responded to this counsel, and his conduct thereafter gives us a pretty good indication that he went right back to work.

Two years earlier, Joseph had been told: "Gird up thy loins for the work…for thou art chosen, and thy path lieth among the mountains." (D&C 112:7). In fact, the saints were enjoined no fewer than eleven times in the Doctrine & Covenants to cast aside their apprehensions and get to work. They were told to look past the towering mountains that lay before them, and to seek the valleys the Lord had provided for their safe passage.

We need not worry about the future, but neither should we allow ourselves to be held hostage by the past. Worry is interest on a debt that never comes due, and if we are paralyzed by a fear that history will repeat itself, it is because we have not listened carefully enough to the counsel of our priesthood leaders. Joseph encouraged the saints, when they were building the Nauvoo Temple: "Brethren, shall we not go on in so great a cause? Go forward and not backward. Courage, brethren; and on, on to the victory! Let your hearts rejoice, and be exceedingly glad." (D&C 128:22).

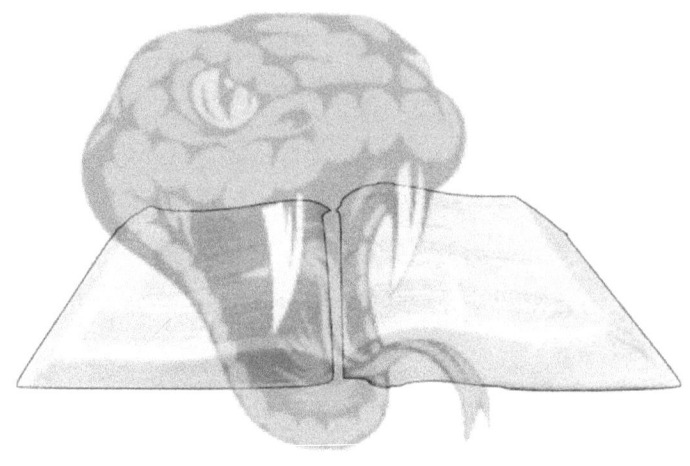

Martin Luther said that
the danger of uninspired versions of
scripture is that its meaning is wrested and the
commandments are neglected. Those who worship in
the synagogues of Satan, he declared, prescribe sin and
prohibit righteousness. These are the abomination of
antichrist and the furious harlots of the devil.
(See: "What Luther Says," 1/1,019).

The New American Bible: Uninspired Version

There are at least 75 different versions of the Bible, among them the American Standard Version, the American King James Version, the Amplified Bible, An American Translation, the Berkeley Version, the Bible in English, the Bible in Living English, the Bishop's Bible, the Catholic Public Domain Version, the Christian Community Bible, the Clear Word Bible, the Common English Bible, the Complete Jewish Bible, the Contemporary English Version, the Concordant Literal Version, the Coverdale Bible , the Dabhar Translation, the Darby Bible, the Divine Nature King James Bible, the Douay-Rheims Bible, the Easy English Bible, the Easy to Read Version, the Emphasized Bible, the English Jubilee 2000 Bible, the English Standard Version, the Ferrar Fenton Bible, the Geneva Bible, God's Word, the Good News Bible, the Great Bible, the Hebraic Roots Version, the Inclusive Bible, the International Standard Version, the Jerusalem Bible, the Julia E. Smith Parker Translation, the King James 2000 Version , the King James Easy Reading Version, the King James Version, the Lamsa Bible, the Literal Translation of the Bible, the Living Bible, Matthew's Bible, the Modern English Version, the Modern King James Version, the Modern Language Bible, the New American Bible, the New Century Version, the New English Bible, the New English Translation, the New International Reader's Version, the New International Version, the New Jerusalem Bible, the New Life Version, the New Living Translation, the New Messianic Version, the New Revised Standard Version, the New Word Translation of the Holy Scriptures, the Orthodox Study Bible, the Quaker Bible, the Recovery Version of the Bible, the Revised Version, the Revised Standard Version, the Revised English Bible, the Simplified English Bible, Tavener's Bible, Thompson's Translation, Today's New Bible, the International Version, the Millennium Bible, the Tree of Life Bible, Tyndale's Bible, the Updated King James Version, the Voice Bible, Webster's Revision, the Westminster Bible, Wycliffe's Bible, and the Young's Liberal Translation.

It is little wonder that members of The Church of Jesus Christ of Latter-day Saints "believe the Bible to be the word of God, (only) as far as it is translated correctly." (8th Article of Faith). Long ago, in a psalm of lamentation, David cried: "Be merciful unto me, O God: for man would swallow me up... In God, I will praise his word, in God, I have put my trust; I will not fear what flesh can do unto me. Every day they wrest my words." (Psalms 56:1-5). Those who wrest the words of the prophets pick them apart, and distort the doctrine into meaningless fragments without any coherent connection. They fall into transgression in consequence of their shallow comprehension of principles.

The wresting of the word of God is real, and finds expression in the New American Bible Uninspired Version. In The Book of Mormon, Alma warned: "Some have wrested the scriptures, and have gone far astray. (Alma 41:1). Elsewhere, he warned his own brethren: "Behold, the scriptures are before you; if ye will wrest them it shall be to your own destruction. (Alma 13:20).

The author of such confusion is clear. The Lord told Joseph Smith: It is Satan who "doth stir up the hearts of the people to contention concerning the points of my doctrine; and in these things they do err, for they do wrest the scriptures and do not understand them." (D&C 10:63).

The twisting of the meaning of doctrine is not a new phenomenon. Isaiah was speaking dualistically, when he prophesied: "The earth also is defiled under the inhabitants thereof; because they have transgressed the laws, changed the ordinance, (and) broken the everlasting covenant." (Isaiah 24:5). Later, Nephi wrote: "There are many plain and precious things taken away from the book, which is the book of the Lamb of God." (1 Nephi 13:28). Speaking prophetically of the Last Days, he wrote: "The Gentiles do stumble exceedingly, because of the most plain and precious parts of the gospel of the Lamb which have been kept back by that abominable church, which is the mother of harlots." (1 Nephi 13:34). "And also many covenants of the Lord have they taken away." (1 Nephi 13:26). These prophecies teach by indirect reference of an apostasy, and beg for a restoration of truth, for "at the time the book proceeded out of the mouth of the Jew, the things which were written were plain and pure, and most precious and easy to the understanding of all men." (1 Nephi 14:23).

In His introduction to the Doctrine & Covenants, the Lord said of the inhabitants of the earth: "They have strayed from mine ordinances, and have broken mine everlasting covenant. They seek not the Lord to establish his righteousness, but every man walketh in his own way, and after the image of his own god, whose image is in the likeness of the world, and whose substance is that of an idol, which waxeth old and shall perish in Babylon, even Babylon the great, which shall fall. Wherefore, I the Lord, knowing the calamity which should come upon the inhabitants of the earth, called upon my servant Joseph Smith, Jun., and spake unto him from heaven, and gave him commandments" that directly related to the prophesied Restoration. (D&C 1:15-17). Paul had foreseen our day, when a restoration of truth would shed light on the doctrines of the kingdom, whose principles had become distorted through error and apostasy. (See 2 Thessalonians 2:3).

For thus shall my church be called in the last days," declared the Lord, "even The Church of Jesus Christ of Latter-day Saints. Verily I say unto you all: Arise and shine forth, that thy light may be a standard for the nations." (D&C 115:4-4). The light would sweep away the gossamer threads of factious secular religion, obviating the need for 75 different translations of the Bible. There would be one standard, and that bar would be set by the Lord. As Paul had foreseen, He would give "some, apostles, and some, prophets, and some, evangelists, and some, pastors and teachers; for the perfecting of the saints, for the work of the ministry, for the edifying of the body of Christ. Till we all come in the unity of the faith, and of the knowledge of the Son of God, unto a perfect man, unto the measure of the stature of the fulness of Christ; that we henceforth be no more children, tossed to and fro, and carried about with every wind of doctrine, by the sleight of men, and cunning craftiness, whereby they lie in wait to deceive; but speaking the truth in love, may grow up into him in all things, which is the head, even Christ." (Ephesians 4:11-15).

In the nineteenth century, the Prophet Joseph Smith was a true witness and a wonderful guide to those seeking pure and undefiled religion, and even today he leads those who lack wisdom to the fountain of all truth. (See James 1:27). His presence dominates our history. He has brought millions to the point where they need "not teach every man his neighbour, and every man his brother, saying, Know the Lord: for all shall know me, from the least to the greatest." (Hebrews 8:11).

From his birth to his martyr's death at the age of thirty-eight, we feel the power and influence of Joseph Smith. "He emerges the prophet, seer, organizer, lawgiver, promoter, architect, and teacher. His religious concept includes fashioning the kingdom of God upon the earth, changing the lives of men and women, and preparing everyone who will listen for Christ's advent." (Ivan Barrett, "Joseph Smith & The Restoration").

Footnote: To learn more about how latter-day revelation has come about, see Robert J. Matthews, "Joseph Smith's Inspired Translation of the Bible," "Ensign," 12/1972.

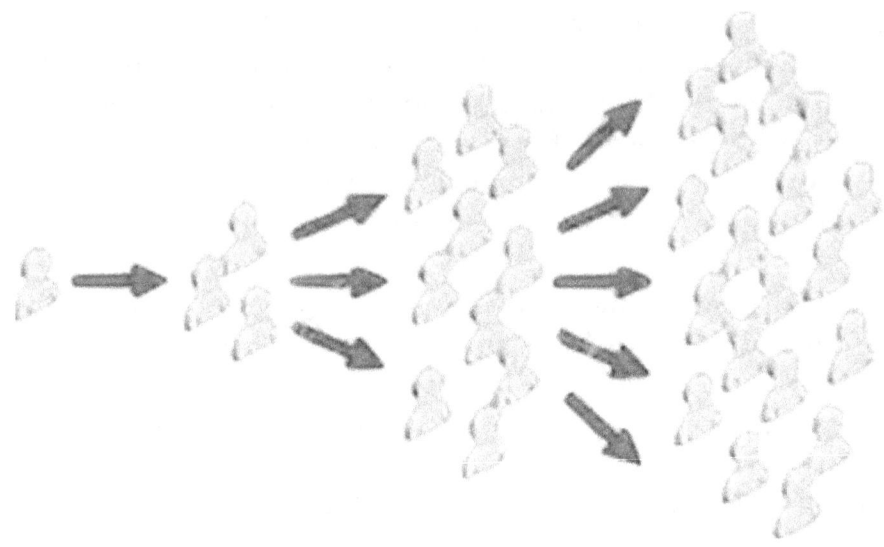

The Apostle Paul compared the
members of the church to the parts of the body.
Just as the head, the ears, the eyes, the nose, the mouth,
the neck, the shoulders, the back, the breast, the vitals and
bowels, the arms and hands, the loins, and the legs and
feet are important in their different functions, so
are all members of the church important
with their different skills and talents.

The Number of The Disciples Was Multiplied

"For the body is not one member, but many. If the foot shall say, Because I am not the hand, I am not of the body; is it therefore not of the body? And if the ear shall say, Because I am not the eye, I am not of the body; is it therefore not of the body? If the whole body were an eye, where were the hearing? If the whole were hearing, where were the smelling? But now hath God set the members every one of them in the body, as it hath pleased him. And if they were all one member, where were the body? But now are they many members, yet but one body. And the eye cannot say unto the hand, I have no need of thee: nor again the head to the feet, I have no need of you." (1 Corinthians 12:14-21). All are equally important; the head, ears, eyes, nose, lips, neck, shoulders, back, breast, vitals and bowels, arms and hands, loins, and legs and feet.

During the Apostolic ministry, the church grew rapidly. This was cause for great rejoicing, but it also created some challenges. As the church grew, the Apostles needed other members to help direct and build up the kingdom of God. "And in those days, when the number of the disciples was multiplied, there arose a murmuring of the Grecians against the Hebrews, because their widows were neglected in the daily ministration. Then the twelve called the multitude of the disciples unto them, and said, It is not reason that we should leave the word of God, and serve tables. Wherefore, brethren, look ye out among you seven men of honest report, full of the Holy Ghost and wisdom, whom we may appoint over this business. But we will give ourselves continually to prayer, and to the ministry of the word. And the saying pleased the whole multitude: and they chose Stephen, a man full of faith and of the Holy Ghost, and Philip, and Prochorus, and Nicanor, and Timon, and Parmenas, and Nicolas a proselyte of Antioch: Whom they set before the apostles: and when they had prayed, they lay their hands on them. And the word of God increased; and the number of the disciples multiplied in Jerusalem greatly; and a great company of the priests were obedient to the faith." (Acts 6:1-7).

Today, the unique needs of diverse members of the church can be equally challenging, but they also enrich and strengthen the body of Christ. Zion comes in many different colors. It speaks Aymara, Dutch, Fijian, French, Mandarin, Russian, Slovene, and dozens of other languages. It lives in over 3,000 stakes in practically every country in the world, (1,579 in the United States, and 1,661 outside the United States as of 2016) from Argentina to Zimbabwe. It has over 15 million members (2016) who are red, yellow, brown, black, and white. Zion wears a sarong, a grass skirt, a blue collar, a lava lava, a kilt, and a business suit. It lives in igloos, bamboo huts, double-wides, townhomes, cardboard shacks, and high-rises. Most important of all, it shares a common testimony that Jesus is the Christ, and that His love, indeed, makes the world go round. Today it is more important than ever to remember that there is no United States of America in heaven. The great equalizer in the sight of God is obedience by His children to His will. Thus, we may be at-one with Christ.

It is remarkable that although members of the church differ from each other and live in strikingly different cultures, they are still unified. Coast redwoods are among the largest living things. The tallest known tree reaches a height of 368 feet, weighs hundreds of tons, and has been living for well over 2,000 years. But, curiously, while most other trees of massive size have deep roots to support their great weight, the root system of the redwood is very shallow. The key to its survival is the intertwining of the roots of one tree with those of several of its neighbors. Redwoods live in groves; they cannot stand alone. Interdependence is critical to the stability and longevity of each individual tree.

In our day, the Lord has initiated organizational changes as the church has grown, that are similar to the interdependence of the redwoods. These changes have helped meet the needs of church members throughout the world. The Quorums of the Seventy and Area Presidencies, for example, have created an interdependency that fosters strength and unity.

Snowflakes are at the other extreme from coast redwoods, and are one of nature's most fragile creations. Although delicate in structure, look at what these unique individuals can do when they stick together. As in the case of redwoods or snowflakes, so it is with the church, which "hath need of every member," that the whole may be kept in perfect working order, and so that each individual within the organization may perform to the level of his or her potential. (D&C 84:110).

Church members echo Paul, who declared from imprisonment in Rome: "We, being many, are one body in Christ." (Romans 12:5). Today, there are many striking evidences of the spiritual and intellectual unity of the church. For example, in spite of subtle textual variations within the many translations of the scriptures used by members worldwide, there is remarkably little disagreement as to their meaning. In church organization and church government, ecclesiastical leaders enjoy virtual harmony in spite of individual cultural, social, political, and economic differences. The ordinances of the gospel, from baptism to the endowment in the temple, are universally understood and faithfully administered by Latter-day Saints whose sense of community overshadows any perceived differences.

Stephen, one of the original Seventy who were called to help the Twelve Apostles, testified before the Sanhedrin, was arrested on false charges of blasphemy, and was brought to the Jewish council. (Acts 6:11-15). "When they heard these things, they were cut to the heart, and they gnashed on him with their teeth. But he, being full of the Holy Ghost, looked up steadfastly into heaven, and saw the glory of God, and Jesus standing on the right hand of God." (Acts 7:54-55).

His last words reveal the depth of his discipleship. As he was stoned, he called upon God, "saying, Lord Jesus, receive my spirit. And he kneeled down, and cried with a loud voice, Lord, lay not this sin to their charge. And when he had said this, he fell asleep." (Acts 7:59-60).

Philip, another of the original Seventy, preached and performed miracles in Samaria, but somehow had not been given the authority to bestow the gift of the Holy Ghost. "Now when the apostles which were at Jerusalem heard that Samaria had received the word of God, they sent unto them Peter and John: Who, when they were come down, prayed for them, that they might receive the Holy Ghost: (For as yet he was fallen upon none of them: only they were baptized in the name of the Lord Jesus). Then laid they their hands on them, and they received the Holy Ghost." (Acts 8:14-17).

"And when Simon (the sorcerer) saw that through laying on of the apostles' hands the Holy Ghost was given, he offered them money Saying, Give me also this power, that on whomsoever I lay hands, he may receive the Holy Ghost." (Acts 8:18-19). "But Peter said unto him, Thy money perish with thee, because thou hast thought that the gift of God may be purchased with money. Thou hast neither part nor lot in this matter: for thy heart is not right in the sight of God. Repent therefore of this thy wickedness, and pray God, if perhaps the thought of thine heart may be forgiven thee. For I perceive that thou art in the gall of bitterness, and in the bond of iniquity." (Acts 8:20-23).

James E. Faust said: "This greatest of all powers, the priesthood power, is not accessed the way power is used in the world. It cannot be bought or sold. Worldly power often is employed ruthlessly. However, priesthood power is invoked only through those principles of righteousness by which the priesthood is governed." (C.R., 4/1997). We can all hear the voice of the Lord. "What I the Lord have spoken, I have spoken, and I excuse not myself; and though the heavens and the earth pass away, my word shall not pass away, but shall all be fulfilled, whether by mine own voice or by the voice of my servants, it is the same." (D&C 1:38).

Many of us can relate to the experience of Oliver Cowdery, who was told: "Did I not speak peace to your mind concerning the matter? What greater witness can you have than from God?" (D&C 6:23). Later, Oliver was told: "I will tell you in your mind and in your heart, by the Holy Ghost, which shall come upon you and which shall dwell in your heart." (D&C 8:2).

The counsel of the Lord has come to all of us, through Joseph Smith: "These words are not of men nor of man, but of me; wherefore, you shall testify they are of me and not of man; For it is my voice which speaketh them unto you; for they are given by my Spirit unto you, and by my power you can read them one to another; and save it were by my power you could not have them; Wherefore, you can testify that you have heard my voice, and know my words." (D&C 18:34-36).

Robert D. Hales said: "For the most part, conversion happens over a period of time as study, prayer, experience, and faith help us to grow in our testimony." (C.R., 4/1997). We, like the early saints, are living in a time when the church is growing rapidly. The Lord wants each of us to serve in his kingdom as it grows. Each of us needs to recognize and appreciate the qualities, talents, and experiences that different members bring to the Lord's service, but at the same time, we need to be sensitive to the voice of the Spirit that speaks personally and privately to each of us at sundry times and in diverse places. (See D&C 128:21).

"The woods are lovely, dark and deep,
But I have promises to keep, and
miles to go before I sleep,"
(Robert Frost).

The Parable of
The Hiawatha Trail

Not long ago, I had the opportunity to ride my bicycle along the Hiawatha Trail with my nine year old granddaughter, Haidyn. The route of the Hiawatha mountain biking and hiking trail winds its way for 15 miles through the Bitterroot Mountains of North Idaho and Western Montana, while traversing 10 train tunnels and negotiating 7 sky-high trestles. Still called the Milwaukee Road, when it was completed over a century ago it was one of the most scenic stretches of railroad in the country. The "Route of the Hiawatha" is most famous for the Taft Tunnel, that burrows for 8,771 feet (1.66 miles) under the Bitterroots at the state line.

As we started our bike ride, the thought struck me that Haidyn had reached the age of accountability and now found herself in the valley of decision. As we entered the first tunnel, I thought about the physical, emotional, and even the doctrinal switch points that she would face along the ride.

Of all things, I thought about NASAs moon missions, each of which was dependent upon a precise trajectory that would bring the command module back to earth. To accomplish that, during the 240,000-mile passage from the moon, a number of course corrections had to be made, utilizing rocket "burns" of precise duration. Upon reaching the earth's atmosphere, the entry window was less than 2 degrees. If the earth were a basketball, and the space capsule a grain of sand, it would have to enter the atmosphere at a trajectory with a margin of error no wider than a piece of paper. Otherwise it would either come in at too steep an angle and burn up, or it would come in too shallow, skip off the atmosphere and bounce back into space and away from the earth. There would be no second chance to make a good first impression on Mission Control in Houston.

Although the terrain at the crest of the Bitterroot Mountains appeared challenging, to be sure, the consequences of poor decision-making on Haidyn's part were not as significant as that of lunar astronauts. Still, with every pedal stroke, her commitment level to successfully complete the 15 miles of the Milwaukee Road increased. For a terrestrial explorer suited up in a nine year old's body, it would still be a daunting task, even though the constant downgrade of 1.25% would ameliorate the physical stress of the ride.

Haidyn had barely started on the trail, when she encountered her first obstacle, the

Taft Tunnel beneath the crest of the Bitterroots. Negotiating the tunnel would take Haidyn from her Montana starting point westward into Idaho. Two hundred yards into the tunnel, the light creeping in from the entrance was smothered by a blackness that was the equivalent of pitch dripping over and slowly smothering the eyes. Even the water that we could hear seeping from the rock walls and ceiling was black. It had a certain texture, but no form and no real substance. It was a vaguely wet aether. All Haidyn could do was keep her eyes fixed on the light from the headlamps of cyclists ahead of her, and keep pedaling steadily forward. The beam from her own headlamp only faintly illuminated the walls of the tunnel, and as I observed her she seemed to be standing still, while the silent rock passed by like a ghost ship in the night.

The darkness seemed to suck at our lungs, and we were unable to focus our eyes on the encroaching walls of granite that seemed ready to reach out and grab us. As Haidyn resolutely moved along, I thought of a message Boyd K. Packer once shared with the saints. He said: "Shortly after I was called as a General Authority, I went to Elder Harold B. Lee for counsel. He listened very carefully to my problem and suggested that I see President David O. McKay. President McKay counseled me as to the direction I should go. I was very willing to be obedient but saw no way possible for me to do as he counseled.

I returned to Elder Lee and told him that I saw no way to move in the direction I was counseled to go. He said, 'The trouble with you is you want to see the end from the beginning.' I replied that I would like to see at least a step or two ahead. Then came the lesson of a lifetime: 'You must learn to walk to the edge of the light, and then a few steps into the darkness. Then the light will appear and show the way before you.' Then he quoted from The Book of Mormon: 'Dispute not because ye see not, for ye receive no witness until after the trial of your faith.' (Ether 12:6)." ("B.Y.U. Magazine," 3/1991).

Haidyn had a long 15 minute ride inside the Taft Tunnel to put into practice that wise counsel. At one point, she called out to her dad, who was riding nearby, and actually asked if she could turn off her light. I am not sure why she did that, but it may be because she wanted to savor the raw, untinctured experience of walking (or pedaling) by faith. Perhaps she wanted to focus on the uncommon opportunity to literally wrap all of her physical senses around adversity, and call upon her spiritual reserves to carry the day. She may have intuitively realized that she was being given a unique chance to increase her confidence, to control and master her emotions, and to confront and overcome her fears. She may have known that the experience would provide unprecedented preparation for her encounter with the next tunnel on her journey through life, providing her with invaluable experience so that it would not take her by surprise.

When Haidyn was a few hundred yards from the end of the tunnel, she could begin to vaguely see what at first appeared to be only a tiny pinpoint of light. But as she pedaled on, that pinpoint grew larger and larger until it assumed the shape of an exit. In the gathering light, she began to be able to make out features within the tunnel itself, and to see the pedals, handlebars, and handgrips of her bicycle. She could see her hands and her feet, as well as the forms of those who had been steadily cycling nearby, but who, until this point, had been beyond the veil of darkness, and invisible to her eyes.

Haidyn knew that they had been there all along, because from time to time they had called out words of encouragement to her, and had it not been so dark, the frost on their breath would have betrayed the temperature inside the tunnel, that was 40 degrees colder than the ambient air temperature on the trail. Haidyn had taken fresh courage each time she had heard those familiar voices, but now, as she moved into the light, she was infused with an overwhelming sense of courage that replaced her hesitancy and dissipated her fears that evaporated with her return to the heat of the day.

As her eyes re-adjusted to the brilliant sunlight, Haidyn was quick to notice that she could little afford even a moment's distraction from the task that now lay before her. For as far as she could see on the trail that stretched off into the distance, there were rocks on the path, and she soberly realized that they would, without relief, present challenges to her cycling skills. It was little consolation to her that many of the big rocks had been previously cleared, because they were the ones that would have been easiest to see in the first place. She would have had little difficulty avoiding them. It was the little rocks and the gravel surface of the roadbed that would prove to be most hazardous, should her concentration falter.

It became clear to Haidyn that she would need to move forward purposefully and steadily. She could not allow herself to weave back and forth across the straight and narrow path that lay before her. To do so would be to invite disaster. In fact, as she continually adjusted to the conditions of the trail, she could feel her front wheel washing out on the gravel. At these moments, the impending peril jerked her attention back to the road.

She quickly learned to roll with these obstacles, and to her delight, found that, with practice, they would take care of themselves without her conscious attention. She realized, however, that if she braked too hard, her rear wheel would lock up and she would lose control. So, instead of quickening her pace and risking blowing a corner, she maintained steady forward momentum to maximize her progress and minimize risk. She learned that if she pedaled too fast, turned too sharply, or made adjustments too quickly, she would find herself in trouble without any viable options to re-establish control.

That is not to say that Haidyn was able to eliminate opposition along the trail. The trip may have only taken 2 or 3 hours, but to her it felt like a lifetime. She put to use the skills she had learned while snow skiing, and remembered that when she had been gliding smoothly and effortlessly along a run, she had been going downhill. The Hiawatha Trail was an unforgiving teacher, but Haidyn was a quick study, who discovered that her best strategy would be to control her cadence and her breathing, and to push evenly against the pedals no matter the incline, or how far away was the next rest stop.

She had only one crash, but it hurt a lot. It happened so fast that she barely had time to react as her hand, forearm, and hip skidded along the ground. As I picked her up and held her closely, I thought about the fallen giants in the forest whose rings we have all traced with our fingers. We notice that the spacing between the rings is irregular, because the years of greatest growth are represented by the widest rings, reflecting years of abundant moisture, but from rain, rather than from tears, as was the case with Haidyn.

Yes, tears were shed, but bravely she got back on the bike. I knew that Haidyn would be wiser for the experience, and would be better prepared down the trail to avoid another close encounter of the dirt kind. I hope she was able to take away something positive from the crash. Maybe dumping her bike gave her a chance to reflect on the fact that we can be zooming along, standing on our pedals without a care in the world, with the wind in our faces and enjoying the freedom of the trail. Then, almost without warning, we might hit an obstacle that jerks our handlebars sideways, causes us to lose our sure grip, throws our inertia out of balance, and we suddenly find ourselves one with mother earth.

How Haidyn handled her crash was similar to how she dealt with the tunnels that we encountered throughout our ride. Some, like the Taft Tunnel, were so long you couldn't see the end from the beginning. Others had enough of a curve to them that, even though they were not very long, the light at the end was hidden from view as we started out. In any event, the darkness in many of them seemed to compress our chests and make breathing more labored. They were "un-nerving," in that they caused a sensory deprivation that actually made us more acutely aware of our internal defense mechanisms designed to combat and triumph over unavoidable stress. I hope that Haidyn was able to realize that in some of the tunnels that we encounter in life, the Sprit may seem to abandon us. We may have to suck it up, when we feel that we have been forsaken. In the case of the Taft Tunnel, the longest and hardest one to be negotiated, it had to be tackled from both directions, at the beginning and then again at the very end of the trip, inasmuch as the shuttle bus return dropped us off at the outbound exit of the tunnel. The greatest tests, it seems, are sometimes saved for last.

A word about those seven trestles. They soared above the valley floor. As intimidating as they may have initially seemed, it was clear that the trestles were our "friends" that had been provided by the engineers who constructed the road, in order to avoid hundreds or even thousands of feet of vertical loss and gain. The thought came to my mind as we approached the first trestle that it was within our power to be as eagles, and we had chosen to fly rather than to walk as turkeys.

I thought of the inspiring poem, penned by John Magee, entitled "High Flight." "Oh, I have slipped the surly bonds of earth and danced the skies on laughter-silvered wings. Sunward I've climbed, and joined the tumbling mirth of sun-split clouds, and done a hundred things you have not dreamed of; wheeled and soared and swung high in the sunlit silence. Hovering there, I've chased the shouting wind along, and flung my eager craft through footless halls of air. Up, up the long, delirious, burning blue I've topped the windswept heights with easy grace, where never lark, or even eagle flew. And, while with silent lifting mind I've trod the high untrespassed sanctity of space, I put out my hand, and touched the face of God." On those trestles, it seemed like we didn't need an airplane to experience High Flight. I hoped that the joy of the moment would not be lost on Haidyn.

I pointed out to her that as we make our way along the strait and narrow path, across the canyons that we encounter in life, we are protected on both sides by an iron rod of security. In the case of the Hiawatha Trail, these were taut steel cables strategically stretched at a height of 6, 12, and 18 inches, on up to 4 feet, to keep us out of harm's way. The only way we could put ourselves in jeopardy of serious injury or death would have been if we were to have made a conscious and deliberate effort to disregard the safety mechanisms that had been provided by those who had carefully planned out the route of the Hiawatha.

There did come a point when Haidyn asked: "How much further do we have to go?" To her credit, there was no hint of complaint in her innocent inquiry. I think she only wanted some perspective. She was beginning to feel that she was approaching the limits of her endurance, never having before pedaled so far. She may have never been so tired, so hungry, or so thirsty. She wanted to finish what she had set out to do, but she realized that she had finite physical resources. It was at this point that she and I began to have a serious conversation about the emotional and spiritual reserves upon which she could draw in this time of real need. We talked about the relationships between ability, inability, and availability, about how inspiration precedes perspiration, and about how the dictionary is the only place where success comes before work. We discussed what it means to go the second mile.

We talked about the qualities of high-achievers, those who dream big, who have developed spirituality and are persons of known character, who have clearly defined and realistic goals, who do not procrastinate but accept responsibility, who establish priorities and stick with them, who consciously choose which habits will unconsciously govern much of their lives, who have single-minded concentration, who never consider the possibility of failure, who recognize and act upon the switch-points in their lives, who seize the moment, and who persist until they succeed.

When high achievers like Haidyn see a turtle on a fence post, they know one thing for certain; he had help getting up there. They draw upon their experiences to influence outcomes. They know that if you put roller skates on an octopus, you won't necessarily know where it will go, only that it is sure to be a wild ride. As Haidyn pedaled long, I thought of the poem that reads: "The stars fade away, the sun himself grow dim with age, and nature sink in years. They shall flourish in immortal youth, unhurt amidst the war of elements, the wreck of matter, and the crash of worlds." (Joseph Addison, "Cato," Act 5, Scene 1).

Howard W. Hunter told the following story: "It was on a summer day early in the morning. I was standing near the window. The curtains obstructed me from two little creatures out on the lawn. One was a large bird and the other a little bird, obviously just out of the nest. I saw the larger bird hop out on the lawn, then thump his feet and cock his head. He drew a big fat worm out of the lawn and came hopping back. The little bird opened its bill wide, but the big bird swallowed the worm. There was squawking in protest. The big bird flew away, and I didn't see it again, but I watched the little bird. After a while, the little bird hopped out on the lawn, thumped its feet, cocked its head, and pulled a big worm out of the lawn." At one point, as Haidyn and I stopped for a nutrition break, I offered a silent prayer of gratitude that she liked worms.

I briefly shared with her an experience I had as a young man. It had been my habit to run 5 or 10 miles every morning, for an hour or two before sunrise. I ran through the Santa Monica Mountains, above Pacific Palisades, in Southern California. One day, as I neared the end of my run, I regained the surface streets and began to trace my way back to my home. I stopped at an intersection, waiting for the traffic signal to change, and put my hands on my knees. With the sweat dripping off the end of my nose, I thought about throwing in the towel, stopping right then and there, and giving my complaining muscles a much deserved rest. However, through sweat-soaked eyes, I looked up, and saw as it were, a vision before me. Insistently flashing red with neon brightness, directly in front of me, were these words that urged me on: "Don't walk!"

That message, as if from God Himself, prompted me to wonder: "What happens to us when we go the second mile?" As we learn to confront our trials and tribulations, by pushing just a little harder, we grow in the spirit. It is no coincidence that these two scriptures are linked together: "And whosoever shall compel thee to go a mile, go with him twain," and then: "Be ye, therefore, perfect, even as your Father which is in heaven is perfect." (Matthew 5:38 & 48).

I hoped that as Haidyn approached the limits of her physical endurance, she would be pushing her spiritual boundaries, as well. I thought that as she discovered reserves of physical energy that she had not known she possessed, she would simultaneously be making deposits to her spiritual bank account, to be held in reserve for the moment when a desperate withdrawal might be required. I believed, and I think Haidyn might have also felt, that pushing our physical boundaries expands our spiritual boundaries, and vice versa. Stretching our capacity enlarges the circle of our experience and creates new opportunity for growth.

As Teddy Roosevelt famously observed: "It is not the critic who counts; not the one who points out how the strong stumble, or where the doer of deeds could have done them better. The credit belongs to the one who is actually in the arena, whose face is marred by dust and sweat and blood; who strives valiantly; who errs, who comes short again and again, because there is no effort without error and shortcoming; but who actually strives to do the deeds; who knows great enthusiasms, the great devotions; who recognizes a worthy cause; who at the best knows in the end the triumph of high achievement, and who at the worst, at least fails while daring greatly, so that a place shall never be with those cold and timid souls who neither know victory nor defeat." ("Citizenship In A Republic," 4/23/1910).

As we neared the end of the trail, I was confident that no matter how tired Haidyn had felt, she would not experience defeat. She would triumph over every obstacle. In the future, she would be able to measure the difficulty of her challenges against her experience on the Hiawatha Trail. We talked about different scenarios. For example, in the future, as Haidyn would face the minefields of mortality, she would be able to say: "If I can do that (the Hiawatha), I can do this!" Or: "I know that I can do this, because I did that (the Hiawatha)." In the future, because she had built new spiritual muscle, Haidyn would be able to exercise and stretch her mortal frame to new limits.

I warned her that she might be sore the day following such strenuous exercise. But I also reminded her that perspiring every day is good therapy, and that breaking a soul-sweat is even better. If she could view her experiences on the Hiawatha Trail from a spiritual perspective, she would be doubly blessed. Spiritually aerobic exercise would be the best way to keep her body attuned to the Infinite. The process might take her breath away, but at the same time it would give her an increased capacity to fill her lungs with celestial air, and to experience the refreshing breeze that washes over the eternal world. It would allow her to feel the power of the Force.

I told Haidyn that, as far as I was concerned, she had become a Jedi Knight, for it is they who serve and utilize that mystical power described as the Force to assist them as the guardians of peace and justice in the galaxy. The philosophy of self-denial that is embraced by the Jedi stands in sharp contrast to that of their arch-enemies, the Sith, who use the dark side of the Force to usurp power.

"May the Force be with you!" declared General Dodonna, before the Death Star battle in Episode 4 of the Star Wars saga. Obi-Wan Kenobe described the Force as "what gives a Jedi power. It's an energy field created by all living things. It surrounds us and penetrates us. It binds the galaxy together."

I reminded Haidyn how the Master Teacher Yoda had explained to young Luke Skywalker: "A Jedi's strength flows from the Force. But beware of the dark side; anger, fear, aggression. The dark side are they. Easily they flow; quick to join you in a fight. If once you start down the dark path, forever will it dominate your destiny; consume you, it will." Haidyn's Jedi training on the Hiawatha Trail would enhance her power to resist the temptation to yield to the dark side.

She was not alone on her journey. She was constantly shepherded by her parents and grandparents to keep her out of harms way, and they were pleased that she listened carefully to their counsel. They knew that she valued their experience, but she still had to travel her own path, as she passed one milepost after another on her quest. No one else could do it for her. That was as it should have been, because that level of personal commitment helped Haidyn to see beyond limited horizons and remove the veil of insensitivity to her divine destiny.

We were close to the end of the ride when Haidyn, to my great surprise, asked: "When we get there, do we have to go back up again?" I thought: "Bless her heart!" She didn't ask in complaint, or whine about the possibility. She just wanted to know. I reassured her that there would be a bus waiting for us, that would take us back to our car up at the trail head, but at the same time, I thought to myself that she had asked a pertinent question, because the journey is never really over.

As Q told Captain Picard: "You just don't get it do you, Jean Luc? The trial never ends. We wanted to see if you had the ability to expand your mind and your horizons. And for one brief moment you did. For that one fraction of a second, you were open to options you had never considered. That is the exploration that awaits you. Not mapping stars and studying nebula, but charting the unknown possibilities of existence." ("Star Trek, The Next Generation," Episode 185).

I hope that one of the things that Haidyn has learned from her experience on the Hiawatha Trail is this: We left our heavenly home so that we might chart for ourselves the unknown possibilities of existence. We have come "like gentle rain through darkened skies, with glory trailing from our feet as we go, and endless promise in our eyes. We are strangers from a realm of light, who have forgotten all - the memory of our former life and the purpose of our call. And so, we must learn" for ourselves "why we're here, and who we really are." (Adapted from "Saturday's Warrior," lyrics by Doug Stewart).

Earlier, I mentioned the bus at the end of the Trail that was waiting to take us back to our car. Those who devised the Hiawatha for cyclists provided a plan for all of its participants to follow, that included the convenience of a bus that was designed to take them back home. In all fairness, it was not a very pretty bus, and Haidyn may have been initially disappointed in its lack of amenities. As a matter of fact, the driver told us that there were a dozen or so buses, 4 or 5 of which were operable at any one time, the rest being held in reserve to be used for spare parts to keep at least a few running at any given time.

As Haidyn and I stood waiting to board our bus, I thought about the thousands of workers who, over a hundred years ago, toiled to make the Route of the Hiawatha a reality. It was with my nine year old granddaughter in mind that they designed, built, and maintained the roadbed. It was envisioned and constructed so that Haidyn might have a life-altering experience. When the rock was quarried, the trees felled, and the timbers sawn and hauled to the site, the grade surveyed, the rock blasted from the mountainsides, the ties and the track laid, and the spikes pounded in place, it was with Haidyn in mind. Their planning, construction, and preservation guaranteed that her experience in June 2015 would be a positive one.

Even the grade had been surveyed to Haidyn's benefit. Its gentle slope allowed her to set and maintain a pace that would not tempt her to run faster than she had strength and means. The constant grade spoke to her in a physical and tangible way, reminding her that the race is not to the swift, nor the battle to the strong.

All that was necessary was for her to position herself in the zone, with her face oriented to the light, where she could face obstacles in order to develop physical toughness, and then to square off against mental and emotional challenges, so that she could experience fortitude, and finally to enjoy a spiritual harmony that would allow her to conquer adversity.

As I watched her, I realized that what was responsible for her commendable performance was something that was more than physical, it was more than endorphins kicking in, and it was something greater than adrenaline that had given her a second wind. It was something metaphysical, as unconscious mechanisms guided her, and spiritual energy charged her resolve. I know that if I had been able to put electrodes on her chest, I would have seen on the screen of the EKG that her heart was performing at an unusually high level of efficiency. She was not only burning fat, but also lethargy, indifference, mediocrity, and laziness. She was being infused with an inner peace that surpasses understanding. After the Hiawatha, I am certain that she will never be the same. Nothing will rattle her cage.

We boarded the bus hot and sweaty, tired and dusty, and thirsty and hungry. But at the end of a long ride, that old bus seemed to Haidyn as a chauffeured limousine. I thought of something Boyd K. Packer said in a General Conference address, to the membership of the church, many of whom must have felt as Haidyn did, hot and sweaty, and tired and thirsty from the exigencies of their mortal experience.

Elder Packer told the story of a World War II naval aviator, who left the security of his aircraft carrier to embark upon a dangerous mission. True to the predictions of his superior officers during the pre-flight briefing, he endured enemy anti-aircraft fire and engaged in potentially lethal dogfights. His plane was hit numerous times by flack that tore away parts of his wings. His plexi-glass canopy was shattered and he could hardly see through blood-splattered goggles to navigate in bad weather back to his ship. As he came in for a landing on the pitching deck of the carrier, his controls were nearly useless, his descent too steep, and his angle all wrong. He was frantically waved off by the crewman on deck who was guiding him in, but he figured he had only one chance, and this was it, and he would take it. With a sickening thump, as he pancaked his aircraft on the deck, the belly tank burst into flame, and the tail hook failed to engage the cables that would have jerked him to a halt. As he careened into the safety net at the far end of the flight deck, what was left of his plane crumpled into twisted metal. A rescue crew in asbestos suits rushed to his aid, smothered the burning wreckage in fire-retardant foam, clamored up to the cockpit, cut through his safety harness, grabbed him by the shoulders, and dragged him to safety. Doctors and nurses attended to his wounds even as he was carried to sick-bay. Due to their skill and attention, as well as to his unconquerable spirit, he made a remarkable and full recovery, and was awarded the Distinguished Flying Cross for uncommon valor. This, Elder

Packer suggested, is how most of us will return from our mortal mission to the presence of our Father. God help us all!

The hidden blessing that await those who have successfully navigated the Hiawatha Trail is that they will find shelter from the vicissitudes and vagaries of life. Over thirty years ago, Vaughn Featherstone told the saints that they should get on their bikes and start pedaling! In essence, he said that the season of the world before us will be like no other in the history of mankind. It is clear that Satan has unleashed every evil, every scheme, every blatant, vile perversion ever known to man in any generation. Just as this is the dispensation of the fullness of times, so it is also the dispensation of the fullness of evil. We must find safety, and it is not to be found in the world. Wealth cannot provide it, law enforcement agencies cannot assure it, and membership in the church alone cannot bring it.

As the evil night darkens upon this generation, we must create sanctuaries for light and safety, places that will be quiet; sacred havens where the storm cannot penetrate to harm us. There will be hosts of unseen sentinels watching over and guarding us, he assured us. Angels will attend us, and it will be as it was in the days of Elisha. Those that be with us will be more than they that be against us.

Before the Savior comes, the world will darken, he warned. There will come a period of time where even the elect of God will lose hope. The world will be so filled with evil that the righteous will only feel secure within the sacred walls of their homes and their temples that provide safe havens of peace.

Elder Featherstone declared: "I believe we may well have living on the earth now or very soon the boy or babe who will be the prophet of the church when the Savior comes. Those who will sit in the Quorum of Twelve Apostles are here. There are men in our homes and communities who will have apostolic callings. We must keep them clean, sweet, and pure in a wicked world."

Our garments will clothe us in a manner as protective as temple walls. Our covenants and the ordinances of the priesthood will fill us with faith as a living fire. In a day of desolating sickness, scorched earth, barren wastes, sickening plagues, disease, destruction, and death, we as a people will rest in the shade of trees, we will drink from the cooling fountains. We will abide in places of refuge from the storm, we will mount up as on eagles wings, we will be lifted out of an insane and evil world. We will be as fair as the sun and clear as the moon.

The Savior will come and will honor His people. Those who are spared and prepared will know Him. They will cry out 'blessed be the name of He that cometh in the name of the Lord; thou art my God and I will bless thee; thou art my God and I will exalt thee." Our children will bow down at His feet and worship Him as the Lord of Lords, the King of Kings. They will bathe His feet with their tears and He will weep and bless them for having suffered through the greatest trials ever known to man. His bowels will be filled with compassion and His heart will swell wide as eternity and He will love them. He will bring peace that will last a thousand years and they will receive their reward to dwell with Him. Let us prepare them with the faith to surmount every trial and every condition. (Adapted from an address delivered to the Utah South Stake, 4/1987).

Haidyn is well on her way to enjoying that level of temporal and spiritual security and symmetry. The Hiawatha Trail, it seems, has provided her with more than a recreational opportunity. Like the Plan of Salvation itself, it has become a temporal microcosm of that blueprint for her survival in the Last Days.

There
is no revelation
where there is no student.
(See Proverbs 29:18).

The Plan of Salvation:
15 Names

In the New Testament, there are tantalizingly few verses that speak of the Plan of Salvation. In Titus 1:2, Paul spoke of the promise of "eternal life, which God, that cannot lie, promised before the world began." (Titus 1:2). Peter wrote that Jesus Christ was "foreordained before the foundation of the world," to be the Redeemer. (1 Peter 1:20). In his letter to the Hebrews, he wrote that the Savior "became the author of eternal salvation" (Hebrews 5:9).

Abraham wrote of the creative process, and of the Gods' reasoning in creating the earth: "And we will prove them herewith, to see if they will do all things whatsoever the Lord their God shall command them; And they who keep their first estate shall be added upon; and they who keep not their first estate shall not have glory in the same kingdom with those who keep their first estate; and they who keep their second estate shall have glory added upon their heads for ever and ever." (Abraham 3:25-26). Moses spoke of "the Plan of Salvation unto all men. (Moses 6:62).

But it is in The Book of Mormon that we really get a feel for the Plan. In several verses, (1 Nephi 13:26, 29, 32, 35, 35, & 40, 1 Nephi 14:23, & 1 Nephi 19:3), Nephi explained that in the Last Days, the Gentiles would "stumble exceedingly, because of the most plain and precious parts of the gospel of the Lamb" that had been distorted within or deleted from the scriptures. (1 Nephi 13:34).

But there would be a light provided at the end of the tunnel, for those whose minds had been "blinded by the subtle craftiness of men." (D&C 123:12). Through His prophet, the Lord promised: "I will proceed to do a marvellous work among this people, even a marvellous work and a wonder: for the wisdom of their wise men shall perish, and the understanding of their prudent men shall be hid." (Isaiah 29:14).

The Merciful Plan of the Great Creator (2 Nephi 9:6).

"Mercy claimeth the penitent, and mercy cometh because of the Atonement; and the Atonement bringeth to pass the resurrection of the dead; and the resurrection of the dead bringeth back men into the presence of God. For behold, justice exerciseth all his demands, and also mercy claimeth all which is her own; and thus, none but the truly penitent are saved." (Alma 42:23-24). Our conscience is a celestial spark that

God has put into each of us. It is part of the Merciful Plan of the Great Creator Whose purpose is the saving of our souls.

The Plan of our God (2 Nephi 9:13).

The "great and eternal purposes" of the Plan of our God, "were prepared from the foundation of the world." (Alma 42:26). John Taylor taught: "To the Son is given the power of the resurrection, the power of the redemption, the power of salvation, the power to enact laws for the carrying out and accomplishment of the design. Hence, life and immortality are brought to light, the gospel is introduced, and He becomes the Author of eternal life and exaltation." ("Mediation and Atonement," p. 171-172).

The Great and Eternal Plan of Deliverance from Death (2 Nephi 11:5).

One of the foundation teachings of the gospel is that we came into this world to die. "And now behold, I say unto you that if it had been possible for Adam to have partaken of the fruit of the tree of life at that time, there would have been no death, and the word would have been void, making God a liar, for he said: If thou eat thou shalt surely die." (Alma 12:23). It was clearly understood before we came here that our experience would be part of the Great and Eternal Plan of Deliverance from Death. When Adam was sent into the Garden of Eden, it was with the understanding that he would violate or transgress a law in order to bring to pass mortality for the human family.

The Plan of Salvation (Alma 24:14).

The Plan of Salvation is the Plan of Redemption, the Plan of Mercy, and the Plan of Happiness, because it makes possible the resurrection of otherwise imperfect mortals to an eternal life of glory. "Now, if it had not been for the plan of redemption, which was laid from the foundation of the world, there could have been no resurrection of the dead; but there was a plan of redemption laid, which shall bring to pass the resurrection of the dead." (Alma 12:25).

The Plan of Redemption (Alma 29:2).

"According to justice, the plan of redemption could not be brought about" and "mercy could not take effect except it should destroy the work of justice." (Alma 42:13). The beauty of the Plan of Redemption, then, is that it meets the demands of justice through the infinite mercy of a loving Heavenly Father. The Plan allows God to be both just and merciful at the same time.

The Great Plan of the Eternal God (Alma 34:9).

None of us can hope to find meaning in our lives if we treat the integral elements of the Plan superficially or carelessly. A conscious appreciation of its value must be earned. If we take it for granted or if we abandon its core principles, its power to bless our lives may slip away and be lost forever. While the Great Plan of the Eternal God guarantees free will, it also gives us wide latitude to use our agency inappropriately to make poor choices. It provides us with currency sufficient for our needs, but also allows us to substitute for legal tender wads of counterfeit cash with which late payments may be made with interest tacked on for bad behavior. If we attempt to subvert the Plan in futile efforts to obtain and retain blessings we do not deserve, our destabilizing efforts will reward us with a pyrrhic victory at best.

The Great and Eternal Plan of Redemption (Alma 34:16).

Nephi clearly taught that "it is by grace that we are saved, after all we can do." (2 Nephi 25:23). Latter-day Saints, however, tend to emphasize works to the point that it may seem to others that the grace of God takes a back seat to their own efforts to earn salvation. In spite of their focus on accountability, agency, industry, and labor, as they are exhorted to greater dedication, diligence, and duty, the truth is that nothing we can do will ever qualify us to enjoy eternal life. It is only because of the Great and Eternal Plan of Redemption that we are saved. Paul and Luke echoed Nephi, writing that it is "by grace ye are saved, through faith, and that not of yourselves. It is the gift of God." (Ephesians 2:8). "We believe that through the grace of the Lord Jesus Christ we shall be saved." (Acts 15:11). It is "the grace of God that bringeth salvation." (Titus 2:11).

The Great Plan of Redemption (Alma 34:31).

The Great Plan of Redemption required that "an Atonement should be made; therefore God Himself atoneth for the sins of the world, to bring about the plan of mercy, to appease the demands of justice, that God might be a perfect, just God, and a merciful God also." (Alma 42:15). The Atonement allowed God to satisfy justice and still mercifully reclaim us from physical and spiritual death. The Savior thus became the Master of the situation. In His sacrifice, the debt would be paid, redemption made, the covenant fulfilled, justice satisfied, the will of God done, and all power, including the keys of resurrection, given to the Son.

The Plan of Restoration (Alma 41:2).

The Book of Mormon clearly teaches that the purpose of the Fall was to give us the opportunity to come to the earth in order to prepare for a resurrection. "And we see that death comes upon mankind, yea, the death which has been spoken of by Amulek, which is the temporal death; nevertheless there was a space granted unto man in which he might repent; therefore this life became a probationary state; a time to prepare to meet God; a time to prepare for that endless state which has been spoken of by us, which is after the resurrection of the dead." (Alma 12:24). The Atonement is the keystone of the Plan of Restoration, that allows us to be raised in the resurrection clothed in exactly the kinds of bodies for which we have prepared ourselves.

The Great Plan of Salvation (Alma 42:5).

Without its light, we are doomed to suffer in the shadows where we experience only illusions and caricatures of reality. The discrepancy between our marginalized behavior and the ideals of the Great Plan of Salvation will become so great that our short-lived pleasure in worldly ways will surely evaporate as the morning dew in the full light of day. Sooner or later, when this disparity has become so great that it reaches "critical mass," a requisite readjustment will tear down the façade of corruption and hypocrisy to allow the cultivation of a more nurturing lifestyle made possible by obedience to the principles of the Plan.

The Great Plan of Happiness (Alma 42:8).

Alma taught that in the absence of repentance for our sins, and without the benefit of saving principles of the Plan, we must ultimately be in a wretched state, living forever in our sins. "And now behold, if it were possible that our first parents could have gone forth and partaken of the tree of life they would have been forever miserable, having no preparatory state; and thus the plan of redemption would have been frustrated, and the word of God would have been void, taking none effect." (Alma 12:26). Without redemption from sin, if Adam and Eve were to have partaken of the fruit of the tree of life, without first having received a remission of their sins through the Atonement of Christ, it would not have been possible for them to sustain a celestial existence, inasmuch as in their fallen condition they would have been incapable of obedience to celestial principles. Thus, the Great Plan of Happiness would have been forever frustrated.

The Plan of Mercy (Alma 42:15).

One of the foundation teachings of the gospel is that we came into this world to die. "And now behold, I say unto you that if it had been possible for Adam to have partaken of the fruit of the tree of life at that time, there would have been no death, and the word would have been void, making God a liar, for he said: If thou eat thou shalt surely die." (Alma 12:23). It was clearly understood before we came here that our experience would end in the deaths of our mortal bodies as part of the Plan of Mercy.

The Plan of Happiness (Alma 42:16).

The cherubim guaranteed that the Plan of Happiness would not be frustrated. "For behold, if Adam had put forth his hand immediately, and partaken of the tree of life, he would have lived forever, according to the word of God, having no space for repentance." (Alma 42:5). This would have posed an immediate problem that begged a solution. Because of the transgression in the Garden, justice demanded that "man became lost forever, yea, they became fallen man. And now, ye see by this that our first parents were cut off both temporally and spiritually from the presence of the Lord." (Alma 42:6-7). So it was, that "they became subject to follow after their own will." The crowning principle of agency was to be honored, even if it meant that justice must be served. Therefore, "it was appointed unto man to die" (Alma 42:6), rather than to reclaim him "from this temporal death, for that would destroy the great plan of happiness." (Alma 42:8).

The Great Plan of Mercy (Alma 42:31).

The Great Plan of Mercy gives us the opportunity to live our lives, push the envelope, and dare to take risks. When we fail to measure up to its laws, Jesus Christ intervenes in our behalf. When we Recognize our mistakes, when we experience Remorse for having made them, when we attempt to make Restitution if our behavior has wronged others, when we learn from the mistake and Reform our ways, and Resolve to Refrain from Repeating it, we will be free to continue the path of progress, with a complete Resolution of what would have otherwise been an incapacitating shortcoming.

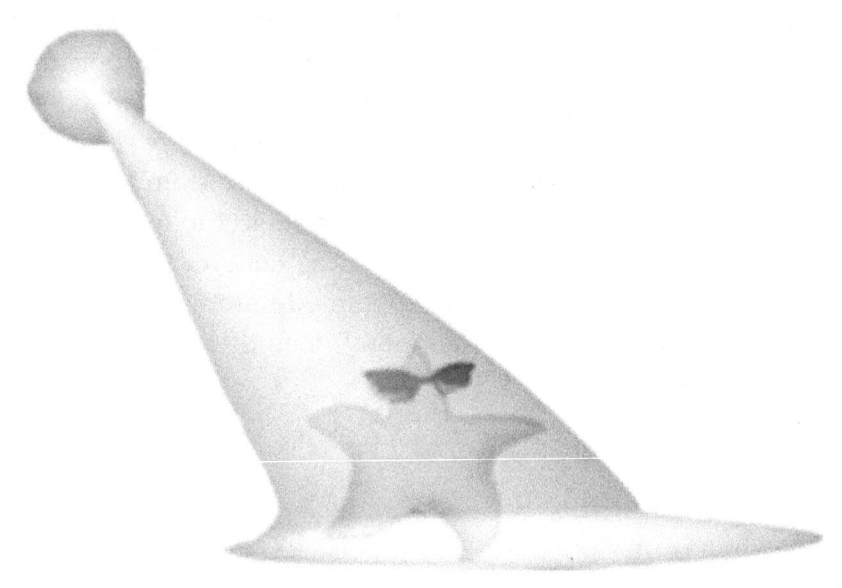

Let us hope that America has
become a place where we may all worship
"Almighty God according to the dictates of our
own conscience, and (where all have) the
same privilege (to) worship how,
where, or what (we) may."
(11th Article of Faith).

The Political Spotlight

"Whereas it is the duty of nations as well as men to own their dependence upon the over-ruling power of God, to confess their sins and transgressions in humble sorrow, yet with assured hope that genuine repentance will lead to mercy and pardon, and to recognize the sublime truth, announced in the Holy scriptures and proven by all history, that those nations only are blessed whose God is the Lord and inasmuch as we know that by his divine law, nations like individuals are subjected to punishments and chastisements in this world, may we not justly fear that the awful calamity of civil war, which now desolates the land may be but a punishment inflicted upon us for our presumptuous sins to the needful end of our national reformation as a whole people." (Abraham Lincoln: "Proclamation Appointing a National Fast Day," 3/30/1863).

In our day, would, or could, a sitting President of the United States dare to proclaim a National Fast Day? Would it be wise or prudent for those who run for the highest public office to vehemently profess deep religious belief? This became a pertinent question in the presidential campaign of 2012. Latter-day Saints, many of whom at least spiritually identified with the Republican presidential candidate, were tantalized by a statement made by Thomas Paine in "Common Sense," over 200 years earlier. He wrote: "We have it in our power to begin the world over again. A situation similar to the present has not happened since the days of Noah." (P. 103). Many members of the church wanted to believe that "there is a serene Providence that rules the fate of nations. It makes its own instruments, creates the man for the time...inspires his genius, and arms him for his task." (Ralph Waldo Emerson, "Oration on the Death of Lincoln," 4/19/1865). Many of them thought Mitt Romney was the man for the season.

An unprecedented opportunity seemed to be in the works. It appeared that, with a Latter-day Saints in the political spotlight, the church would have an unparalleled chance to explain its religious and historical traditions to the public. But its critics would have a bigger platform, too. Mormon leaders have stated time and again that the church does not "endorse, promote or oppose political parties, candidates or platforms." And yet, "The Latter-day Saints began running a multimillion-dollar series of ads, called "I'm a Mormon," in 2010, to dispel stereotypes by telling the stories of individual Mormons.

In surveys of non-Mormons, only a small minority said they were familiar with the Church. FAIR ("The Foundation for Apologetic Information & Research," a volunteer Mormon anti-defamation group) launched a website (MormonVoices.org), to combat misinformation about the church, in anticipation of attention that would surely be given to the faith. On an informal level, instructional sessions were organized for church members so that they might better deal with potential issues about Mormonism in the upcoming general election.

The problem Latter-day Saints faced was articulated in blogs and posts that went something like this: "Really, you don't want a Mormon in the White House. If it comes down to it, the devil you know is better than the devil you don't know. Being an informed voter and not voting for a Mormon is not bigoted. It's smart."

But, members of the church were encouraged by something that Teddy Roosevelt had long ago declared, that they now hoped would bear sway: "Discrimination against the holder of one faith means retaliatory discrimination against men of other faiths. The inevitable result of entering upon such a practice would be an abandonment of our real freedom of conscience and a reversion to the dreadful conditions of religious dissention that in so many lands have proven fatal to true liberty, to true religion, and to all advance in civilization." (John Meacham, "An American Gospel," p. 148).

Supreme Court Justice Sandra Day O'Conner wrote: "Reasonable minds can disagree about how to apply the Religion Clauses in a given case. But the goal of the Clauses is clear: To carry out the Founders' plan of preserving religious liberty to the fullest extent possible in a pluralistic society. By enforcing the Clauses, we have kept religion a matter for the individual conscience, not for the prosecutor or the bureaucrat. At a time when we see around the world the violent consequences of the assumption of religious authority by government, Americans may count themselves fortunate: Our regard for constitutional boundaries has protected us from similar travails, while allowing private religious exercise to flourish." ("An American Gospel," p. 238-239).

Although religious affiliation should not be an issue in a presidential campaign, Mitt Romney's religion came up time and again in 2011-2012, and members of the church were repeatedly asked by their friends and neighbors to defend not the candidate, but the church. Rather than ignoring them, it became necessary to somehow put a more positive spin on the unfair statements and biased questions with which they were bombarded. Romney's political aspirations are now over, but the following questions may still be applied to any practicing Latter-day Saint with the temerity to run for political office.

Unfair Question: Isn't a vote for a Latter-day Saint, a vote for Satan?

Fair Question: I don't know much about the Mormon Church, but is it true what my pastor says, that it is a cult?

Worldwide, there are over 15 million Mormons, (as of 2016), nearly the same as the number of Jews. In the United States the LDS Church is the 4th largest individual denomination with over 6.3 million members. Only 12% of all Mormons live in Utah. In all fairness, if it could ever have been accurately characterized as such, the church has moved far beyond cult status, and it could even be argued that it is moving forward into the mainstream of religious thought in the United States of America, and beyond.

In fact, "any objective definition of 'cult' that can be applied to The Church of Jesus Christ of Later-day Saints can also be applied to the Christian church of the New Testament, and to most of today's mainline denominations when they were in their infancy." (Steven Robinson, "Are Mormons Christians?" p. 25).

Cults: 1) Started by strong and dynamic leaders who are in complete control of their followers. 2) Possess scripture that is either added to or that replaces the Bible as God's Word. 3) Rigid standards for membership. 4) Often recruit members from other "cults." 5) Are actively evangelistic and proselytize new converts. 6) Have leaders that are not professional clergymen. 7) Have a system of doctrine and practice that is in a state of flux. 8) Believe there is continual, ongoing communication from God. Such communication can contradict, or even supersede God's revelation, as found in the Bible. 9) Have truth not available to any other group or individuals. 10) Have an initiate vocabulary by which they describe the truths of their revelations. They may even coin new words or phrases.

Andrew Jackson said: "I do not believe that any who shall be so fortunate as to be received to heaven through the Atonement of our blessed Savior will be asked whether they belonged to the Presbyterian, the Methodist, the Episcopalian, the Baptist, or the Roman Catholic faiths. All Christians are brethren, and all true Christians know they are such because they love one another. A true Christian loves all, immaterial to what sect or church he may belong." ("An American Gospel," p. 112).

Unfair Statement: I'm not familiar with The Church of Jesus Christ of Latter-day Saints, but I mistrust Mormons.
Fair Question: "I'm not familiar with your church. Can you tell me a little bit about it, to help me understand you better?

"Mormons are like artichokes. At first encounter, you either like them or you don't. But those who have unfavorable first impressions often find that once the outer layers are peeled away, both Mormons and artichokes are most likable. In fact, most people who get to know Mormons become their friends. And a little objective research on Mormon beliefs reveals that, except for a few doctrinal differences, these people who call themselves Latter-day Saints are just like the rest of us...very human beings." (The Boston Globe, 1967)

Unfair Question: Wouldn't the Mormon prophet tell an elected official who is a member of his church what to do?
Fair Question: Are the political decisions of Latter-day Saints founded on impressions that they receive in answer to prayer?

At a Democratic political rally in the Bronx, Catholic candidate for President John F. Kennedy "claimed to have spoken recently with Francis Cardinal Spellman, the powerful archbishop of New York. 'I sat next to Cardinal Spellman at dinner the other evening, and asked him what I should say when voters question me about the doctrine of the Pope's infallibility.' 'I don't know, Senator,' the Cardinal told me. 'All I know is, he keeps calling me Spillman.' ("An American Gospel," p. 183-184).

Responding to the Supreme Court Decision in 1962 forbidding the reading of an official prayer in public schools, J.F.K. said: "We have in this case a very easy remedy and that is to pray ourselves. I would think that it would be a welcome reminder to every American family that we can pray a good deal more at home, we can attend our churches with a good deal more fidelity, and we can make the true meaning of prayer much more important in the lives of all our children." ("An American Gospel," p. 188).

"May not and ought not the children rightly say: "Our fathers were Englishmen who came over this great ocean, and were ready to perish in this wilderness; but they cried unto the Lord, and he heard their voice." (William Bradford, "An American Gospel," p. 38).

At the end of the day, Mitt Romney said: "I will take care to separate the affairs of government from any religion, but I will not separate us from the God who gave us liberty."

Unfair Question: Don't Mormons participate in secret rituals in their temples?
Fair Question: Is it true that Mormons attend church regularly, and participate in sacred ordinances in the temple, to recharge their spiritual batteries?

Even Lyndon B. Johnson, in his Inaugural Address, declared: "We have made covenants with the land itself." Our forefathers "came here...to make a covenant with this land. Conceived in justice, written in liberty, bound in union, it was meant one day to inspire the hopes of all mankind, and it binds us still. If we keep its terms, we shall flourish."

James Madison said: "If angels were to govern men, neither external nor internal controls on government would be necessary." ("An American Gospel," p. 84).

Unfair Question: If a Mormon President were elected, wouldn't grape juice, instead of wine, be served at official functions?
Fair Question: Would Latter-day Saint elected officials obey the Word of Wisdom while serving in public office?

On some constitutional matters, "the best that can be done may be to apply to the Constitution the maxim of the law, "de minimis no curat," or 'the law does not concern itself with trifles." Some causes are not worth fighting, where the wall of separation between church and state is very low to the ground (e.g. the motto on our coins, the Pledge of Allegiance, or the Chaplain of the Congress). ("An American Gospel," p. 228).

Unfair Question: With strict Mormon upbringing, would Latter-day Saint public servants lack the political toughness to survive?
Fair Question: Would the discipline and structure that is characteristic of Latter-day Saint culture and tradition favor those who desire to bring order out of chaos?

In an example of his wit, John F. Kennedy said: "One of the inspiring notes in the last debate was struck by the Vice President in his very moving warning to the children of the nation and the candidates against the use of profanity by Presidents and ex-Presidents when they are on the stump. And I know after 14 years in the Congress with the Vice President that he was very sincere in his views about the use of profanity. But I am told that a prominent Republican said to him yesterday in Jacksonville, Florida: "Mr. Nixon, that was a damn fine speech." And the Vice President said, "I appreciate the compliment but not the language." And the Republican went on, "Yes, sir, I liked it so much that I contributed a thousand dollars to your campaign." And Mr. Nixon replied, "The hell you say." (Al Smith Memorial Dinner, Waldorf-Astoria Hotel, New York, NY, 11/19/1960).

Unfair Question: Would church-related responsibilities distract a Latter-day Saint from the important affairs of government?
Fair Question: Would they take all of their public responsibilities seriously, and still be able to pay attention to their core values?

"I have been driven many times to my knees by the overwhelming conviction that

I had nowhere else to go." (Abraham Lincoln, "An American Gospel," p. 224). "I know not how philosophers may ultimately define religion, but from Micah to James it has been defined as service to one's fellowmen rendered by following the great rules of justice and mercy, and of wisdom and righteousness." (Theodore Roosevelt).

Unfair Question: Could the heritage of persecution of the Latter-day Saints negatively influence the decision-making capability of an L.D.S. public servant?
Fair Question: Would the cultural heritage of the church help Latter-day Saints to have a more sympathetic perspective regarding the rights of minorities?

"The bosom of America is open to receive the oppressed and persecuted of all nations and religions; whom we shall welcome to a participation of all our rights and privileges. They may be Mohometans, Jews or Christians of any sect, or they may be atheists." (George Washington, "An American Gospel," p. 245-246).

"I have sworn upon the altar of God eternal hostility against every form of tyranny over the mind of man." (Thomas Jefferson. This quotation is inscribed inside the frieze of the Jefferson Memorial, in Washington, D.C.).

Unfair Question: Mormons seem to be committed to their faith, but don't we need those in public office who can focus on the job at hand?
Fair Question: Could the religious background of a Latter-day Saint public servant be an asset when dealing with the affairs of the government?

"Those of us in the political world need to be reminded that our fast-paced existence can sometimes be an obstacle to quiet reflection and deep commitment, that we can easily forget the ideas and principles that brought us into the public arena in the first place." (Ronald Reagan, "An American Gospel," p. 224).

Unfair Question: Could church responsibilities prove to be a distraction for a Latter-day Saint public servant?
Fair Question: Could their heritage of service in the church make them better public servants?

Latter-day Saints believe: "When ye are in the service of your fellow beings ye are only in the service of your God." (Mosiah 2:17).

Unfair Question: Do Latter-day Saints read their "Mormon Bibles" every day?
Fair Question: Will Latter-day Saint public servants regularly turn to the scriptures, and to other great books, for daily inspiration?

"Seek ye diligently and teach one another words of wisdom; yea, seek ye out of the best books words of wisdom; seek learning, even by study and also by faith." (D&C 88:118).

Unfair Question: While in office, would a Latter-day Saint continue to wear his or her special underwear?
Fair Question: Would a Latter-day Saint public official honor his or her sacred covenants when making difficult decisions?

Some clerics wear their vestments on the outside. Latter-day Saints wear the reminders of their sacred covenants on the inside. "I will remember the works of the Lord: surely I will remember the wonders of old." (Psalms 77:11). "Some trust in chariots, and some in horses: but we will remember the name of the Lord our God." (Psalms 20:7).

Unfair Question: I've heard that Mormons like to recite: "Every member is a missionary." Will Latter-day Saints public officials who have served full-time missions have a hidden agenda, and covertly try to impose their religion on others?
Fair Question: Will Latter-day Saint public servants do anything other than bring out the best in others?

"Let your light so shine before men, that they may see your good works." Matthew 5:16).

Unfair question: Will Latter-day Saint public officials want to take time off from the civic responsibilities to attend church services, including their semi-annual General Conferences?
Fair Question: Will they be able to successfully juggle their public and private responsibilities? For example, will they read and seek inspiration from the scriptures every day of the year, or only on Sundays?

"I shall need the favor of that Being in whose hands we are, who led our forefathers, as Israel of old, from their native land, and planted them in a country flowing with all the necessaries and comforts of life." (Thomas Jefferson's second Inaugural Address).

Unfair Question: Will they surround themselves with like-minded advisors, who are nothing more than "yes men"?
Fair Question: Does their tradition help them to understand the concept of having "counselors" to assist them in their decision-making?

"If there is anything virtuous or lovely or of good report, we seek after these things."

(13th Article of Faith). Lyndon B. Johnson's favorite scripture from the Old Testament was Isaiah's counsel: "Come now, and let us reason together." (Isaiah 1:18).

"Abraham Lincoln once told visiting ministers that he did not worry whether God was on his side or not. 'For I know that the Lord is always on the side of the right.' It was, Lincoln said, 'my constant anxiety and prayer that I and this nation should be on the Lord's side.'" ("An American Gospel," p. 24).

Unfair Question: Wouldn't the personal convictions of a Latter-day Saint who had been entrusted with the responsibility to care for the public welfare, stand in the way of the law of the land?
Fair Question: Would the teachings of their church help them to focus on their responsibility to support the Constitution?

"I believe that since Roe v. Wade has been the law for 20 years, that we should sustain and support it and the right of a woman to make that choice, and my personal beliefs, like the personal beliefs of other people, should not be brought into a political campaign. I have my own beliefs, and those beliefs are very dear to me. One of them is that I do not impose my beliefs on other people." (Mitt Romney).

"And that law of the land which is constitutional, supporting that principle of freedom in maintaining rights and privileges, belongs to all mankind, and is justifiable before me. Therefore, I, the Lord, justify you, and your brethren of my church, in befriending that law which is the constitutional law of the land." (D&C 98:5-6).

This passage of scripture goes on to explain: "As pertaining to law of man, whatsoever is more or less than this, cometh of evil." (D&C 98:7). Hence, George Washington's observation: "Whatever may be conceded to the influence of refined education on minds of peculiar structure, reason and experience both forbid us to expect that national morality can prevail in exclusion of religious principle." ("An American Gospel," p. 28).

"At this moment, I have in my heart a prayer. As I have assumed my duties, I humbly pray Almighty God, in the words of King Solomon: 'Give, therefore, Thy servant an understanding heart to judge Thy people, that I may discern between good and bad: for who is able to judge this so great a people?' I ask only to be a good and faithful servant of my Lord and my people." (Harry S. Truman, in his first address to Congress following the death of President Franklin D. Roosevelt).

Unfair Question: Isn't it true that a Latter-day Saint public servant would attempt to undermine gay and lesbian marriage laws?

Fair Question: Would they use the influence of their position to promote the core values that have made America great?

"I believe that the family is the foundation of America - and that it needs to be protected and strengthened." (Mitt Romney).

Unfair Question: Aren't Mormons intolerant and bigoted toward other religions, and even other Christian religions?
Fair Question: Does the religion of the Latter-day Saints teach them to tolerate the religious viewpoints of others?

"I should like to assure you, my Islamic friends, that under the American Constitution, under American tradition, and in American hearts, this center, this place of worship, is just as welcome as could be a similar edifice of any other religion. Indeed, America would fight with her whole strength for your right to have here your own church and worship according to your own conscience. This concept is indeed part of America, and without that concept we would be something else than what we are." (Dwight D. Eisenhower, remarks at the opening of the Islamic Center in Washington, D.C., "An American Gospel," p. 181).

We might pose the question: "How can Mormon candidates, in any hotly contested election, deflect some of these hard questions? Again, we might take a cue from the wit of John F. Kennedy.

The year was 1958 and then-Senator Kennedy was already at the front of the pack for the Democratic presidential nomination that was still two years away. Inside a white-tie ballroom full of everyone who mattered in Washington D.C., the conventional wisdom was that young Jack Kennedy was both pawn and proxy for his powerful, unscrupulous father Joe. But that did not stop Kennedy from delivering a joke that night that was nothing less than audacious. Pulling a piece of paper from his pocket, he read a telegram he said had been sent by his father, regarding the upcoming 1960 presidential election: "Jack – Don't spend one dime more than is necessary. I'll be damned if I am going to pay for a landslide."

It was brilliantly funny, but upon further reflection, it was the Rosetta Stone of political humor. Just imagine what might have happened that night if someone else had gone to the podium and told that very same joke. It would have been repeated a million times over, each time at Kennedy's expense. Instead, he took the punch-line for himself and applied the loud laughs he earned as an inoculation against an insidiously poisonous idea. Indeed, if anyone who had yet to speak had planned to joke about the ripe topic of Kennedy's rich daddy, they had little choice but to erase it from their draft. (See Mark Katz, "The Daily Beast").

And so, we come to the story told of the Lutheran who died and went to heaven. When he was ushered past the pearly gates by St. Peter, he first saw a large mansion where a loud and boisterous party was in full swing. "Who are those people?" he asked his guide. St. Peter answered, and said, "Oh, they're the Presbyterians." Further down the road, there was another group making merry. "Those are the Methodists." And so it went. Finally, toward the end of the road, there were signs posted along the way that warned: "Quiet!" "Speak in whispers, only!" "Headlights off!" In the distance was a mansion with curtains drawn, shutters latched, and doors securely bolted shut. "Who lives there? asked the Lutheran. "Oh," said St. Peter. "Those are the Mormons. They think they are the only ones here."

A final thought. "The liberality and virtue of America in establishing perfect equality and freedom among all religious denominations and societies, will no doubt produce to us a great reward, for when news of it reaches the oppressed dissenters from the establishment churches of Europe, and they find it encourages both Protestants and Catholics, they will at once cry out, America is the Land of Promise." (Tench Coxe, delegate from Pennsylvania to The Continental Congress, "An American Gospel," p. 98).

Let us hope that America has become a place where we may all worship "Almighty God according to the dictates of our own conscience, and (where we all have) the same privilege (to) worship how, where, or what (we) may," no matter what our political affiliation or aspirations might be. (11th Article of Faith).

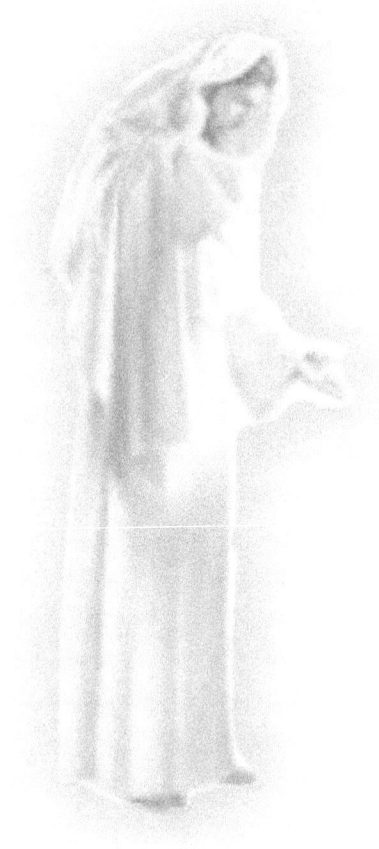

The wife of Albert Einstein was once asked whether she understood everything her husband had written. "I understand the words," she replied, "but not the sentences."

The Power of Proverbs

"And (Solomon) spake three thousand proverbs and his songs were a thousand and five." (1 Kings 4:32). The Proverbs emphasize the importance of wisdom, and illustrate the differences between being learned and being wise. They teach us about the distinguishing features of wisdom and earthly treasures, urge us to trust in the Lord, counsel us to speak carefully, illustrate the pitfalls of pride, illuminate principles relating to friendship, happiness, and good humor, and provide instruction regarding how to raise our children.

"The fear of the Lord is the beginning of knowledge, but fools despise wisdom and instruction." (Proverbs 1:7). Jacob put it this way: "O the vainness and the frailties, and the foolishness of men! When they are learned they think they are wise, and they hearken not unto the counsel of God, for they set it aside, supposing they know of themselves, wherefore, their wisdom is foolishness and it profiteth them not. And they shall perish. But to be learned is good if they hearken unto the counsels of God." (2 Nephi 9:28-29). These warnings against the pitfalls of intellectual apostasy remind us that access to the Spirit must accompany true learning, and that an appeal to vanity is the devil's way of turning our minds against the Plan of Salvation.

The Book of Proverbs emphasizes the worth of wisdom compared to the emptiness of earthly treasures. "Happy is the man that findeth wisdom, and the man that getteth understanding. For the merchandise of it is better than the merchandise of silver, and the gain thereof than fine gold. She is more precious than rubies: and all the things thou canst desire are not to be compared unto her." (Proverbs 3:13-15).

The Book of Proverbs teaches us about our dependence upon God. "Trust in the Lord with all thine heart; and lean not unto thine own understanding. In all thy ways acknowledge him, and he shall direct thy paths. Be not wise in thine own eyes: fear the Lord, and depart from evil." (Proverbs 3:5-7).

The Book of Proverbs teaches us to speak carefully: "These six things doth the Lord hate: yea, seven are an abomination unto him: A proud look, a lying tongue, and hands that shed innocent blood, An heart that deviseth wicked imaginations, feet that be swift in running to mischief, a false witness that speaketh lies, and he that soweth discord among brethren." (Proverbs 6:16-19).

The Book of Proverbs teaches us to speak gently. "A soft answer turneth away wrath: but grievous words stir up anger." (Proverbs 15:1). Gordon B. Hinckley said: "We seldom get into trouble when we speak softly. It is only when we raise our voices that the sparks fly and tiny molehills become great mountains of contention." ("New Era," 10/1999). "Even a fool, when he holdeth his peace, is counted wise, and he that shutteth his lips is esteemed a man of understanding." (Proverbs 17:28). Sometimes it is better to keep our mouths shut, and be thought fools, rather than open them and remove all doubt.

The Book of Proverbs condemns pride. "The fear of the Lord is to hate evil: pride, and arrogancy, and the evil way, and the froward mouth, do I hate." (Proverbs 8:13). "Pride goeth before destruction, and an haughty spirit before a fall." (Proverbs 16:18).

Ezra Taft Benson said: "The central feature of pride is enmity toward God and toward our fellowmen. Enmity means 'hatred toward, hostility to, or a state of opposition.' It is the power by which Satan wishes to reign over us. Pride is essentially competitive in nature. We pit our will against God's. When we direct our pride toward God, it is in the spirit of 'my will and not thine be done.' As Paul said, they 'seek their own, not the things which are Jesus Christ's.' (Philippians 2:21). When our will is in competition with God's will, our desires, appetites, and passions go unbridled. (See Alma 38:12 & 3 Nephi 12:30). The proud cannot accept the authority of God giving direction to their lives. (See Helaman 12:6). They pit their perceptions of truth against His great knowledge, their abilities against His priesthood power, and their accomplishments against His mighty works. Our enmity toward God takes on many labels, such as rebellion, hard-heartedness, and stiff-neckedness, (and those who are proud are) unrepentant, puffed up, easily offended, and sign seekers. The proud wish God would agree with them. They aren't interested in changing their opinions to agree with His. Pride is a damning sin in the true sense of that word (because) it limits or stops progression." (C.R., 4/1989).

The Book of Proverbs counsels us: "Only by pride cometh contention." (Proverbs 13:10). President Benson said: "Arguments, fights, unrighteous dominion…all fall into this category of pride. Contention drives the Spirit of the Lord away. Pride adversely affects all our relationships." (C.R., 4/1989).

The Book of Proverbs addresses friendship. "He that walketh with wise men shall be wise: but a companion of fools shall be destroyed." (Proverbs 13:20). "Make no friendship with an angry man…lest thou learn his ways, and get a snare to thy soul." (Proverbs 22:24-25). "A friend loveth at all times." (Proverbs 17:17). "Ointment and perfume rejoice the heart: so doth the sweetness of a man's friend by hearty counsel." (Proverbs 27:9). "Two are better than one; because they have a good reward for their labour. For if they fall, the one will lift up his fellow: but woe to him that is alone when he falleth; for he hath not another to help him up." (Ecclesiastes 4:9-10).

Marvin J. Ashton said: "A friend is a person who is willing to take me the way I am.' Accepting this as one definition of the word, may I quickly suggest that we are something less than a real friend if we leave a person the same way we found him. No greater reward can come to any of us as we serve, than a sincere 'Thank you for being my friend.' When those who need assistance find their way back through and with us, it is friendship in action. When the weak are made strong and the strong stronger through our lives, friendship is real. If a man can be judged by his friends, he can also be measured by their heights. Yes, a friend is not only a person who is willing to take me the way I am, but who is also willing and able to leave me better than he found me." (C.R., 10/1972).

The Book of Proverbs teaches us how to raise our children. "Train up a child in the way he should go: and when he is old, he will not depart from it." (Proverbs 22:6). Richard G. Scott said: "You must be willing to forgo personal pleasure and self-interest for family-centered activity, and not turn over to church, school, or society, the principal role of fostering a child's well-rounded development. It takes time, great effort, and significant personal sacrifice, to 'train up a child in the way he should go.' Where can you find greater rewards for a job well done?" (C.R., 4/1993).

"Chasten thy son while there is hope, and let not thy soul spare for his crying." (Proverbs 19:18). "Correct thy son, and he shall give thee rest; yea, he shall give delight unto thy soul." (Proverbs 29:17). "My son, keep thy father's commandment, and forsake not the law of thy mother: Bind them continually upon thine heart, and tie them about thy neck. When thou goest, it shall lead thee; when thou sleepest, it shall keep thee; and when thou awakest, it shall talk with thee. For the commandment is a lamp; and the law is light; and reproofs of instruction are the way of life." (Proverbs 6:20-23).

The Book of Proverbs teaches us about happiness and good humor. A merry heart maketh a cheerful countenance: but by sorrow of the heart the spirit is broken." (Proverbs 15:13). "A merry heart doeth good like a medicine: but a broken spirit drieth the bones." (Proverbs 17:22). Hugh B. Brown said: "I would like to have you smile because, after all, we must keep a sense of humor whatever comes. I think that of all the people in the world, we should be the happiest. We have the greatest and most joyous message in the world. I think that when we get on the other side, someone will meet us with a smile (unless we go to the wrong place and then someone will grin), so let us be happy. But let our happiness be genuine - let it come from within" ("The Abundant Life," p. 83).

The Book of Proverbs teaches us about criticism: "Yea, my reins shall rejoice, when thy lips speak right things." (Proverbs 23:16). "He, that being often reproved hardeneth his neck, shall suddenly be destroyed, and that without remedy." (Proverbs 29:1). "The tongue of the wise useth knowledge aright: but the mouth of fools poureth out foolishness." (Proverbs 15:2). Almost half a century ago, Gordon B. Hinckley said: "Surely this is the age and place of the gifted pickle sucker. The tragedy is that this spirit is epidemic. Criticism, fault-finding, evil speaking - these are of the spirit of the day. They are in our national life. To hear tell these days, there is nowhere a man of integrity among those holding political office. In many instances this spirit has become the very atmosphere of university campuses. The snide remark, the sarcastic gibe, the cutting down of associates - these, too often, are of the essence of our conversation. In our homes wives weep and children finally give up under the barrage of criticism leveled by husbands and fathers. Criticism is the forerunner of divorce, the cultivator of rebellion, and sometimes the catalyst leading to failure. Even in the church, it sows the seed of inactivity and finally apostasy. I come this morning with a plea that we stop seeking out the storms and enjoy more fully the sunlight. I am suggesting that we accentuate the positive. I am asking that we look a little deeper for the good, that we still our voices of insult and sarcasm, that we more generously compliment virtue and effort. I am not asking that all criticism be silenced. Growth comes of correction. Strength comes of repentance. Wise is the man who can acknowledge mistakes pointed out by others and change his course. I am not suggesting that our conversation be all honey and blossoms. Clever expression that is sincere and honest is a skill to be sought and cultivated. What I am suggesting and asking is that we turn from the negativism that so permeates our society and look for the remarkable good in the land and times in which we live, that we speak of one another's virtues more than we speak of one another's faults, that optimism replace pessimism, that our faith exceed our fears." ("B.Y.U. Devotional," 10/29/1974).

Joseph Smith declared that happiness "is the object and design of our existence and will be the end thereof, if we pursue the path that leads to it; and this path is virtue, uprightness, faithfulness, holiness, and keeping all the commandments of God." ("Teachings," p. 255). Our serious contemplation of The Book of Proverbs can help us to follow that path.

"We believe that we
have in this church the answers to all
questions, for the Lord is the head of the church,
and He has given us the program. Our message
is what it has always been, and our hope is that
our people will live the commandments of the
Lord. They have been revealed in the holy
scriptures and by living prophets."
(Spencer W. Kimball).

The Priests of Baal
in Our Lives

"Born in poverty but nurtured in faith, José García prepared for a mission call. I was present the day his recommendation was received. There appeared the statement: 'Brother García will serve at great sacrifice to his family, for he is the means of much of the family support. He has but one possession, a treasured stamp collection, that he is willing to sell, if necessary, to help finance his mission.' President Spencer W. Kimball listened attentively as this statement was read to him, and then he responded: 'Have him sell his stamp collection. Such sacrifice will be to him a blessing.'

Then, with a twinkle in his eye and a smile on his face, this loving prophet said: 'Each month at church headquarters we receive thousands of letters from all parts of the world. See that we save these stamps and provide them to José at the conclusion of his mission. He will have, without cost, the finest stamp collection of any young man in Mexico.'" (Thomas S. Monson, C.R., 10/1978).

When we put the things of God first in our lives, the rewards we receive are far greater than anything we may have had to sacrifice along the way. But we sometimes don't receive these blessings right away. More often than not, we need to be patient.

Jeroboam, who led the Kingdom of Israel into idolatry, was followed by a succession of idolatrous kings. Of those rulers, Ahab was the worst. He "did more to provoke the Lord God of Israel to anger than all the kings of Israel that were before him." (1 Kings 16:33). He married Jezebel, adopted the worship of Baal, and encouraged his people to join him in the worship of false gods.

In consequence of their idolatry, the prophet Elijah was sent to deliver words of warning to Ahab and his kingdom. Because of the wickedness of Ahab and his people, Elijah declared, "There shall not be dew nor rain these years, but according to my word." (1 Kings 17:1).

In The Book of Mormon, Nephi, the son of Helaman, was given the same power: "Blessed art thou, Nephi, for those things which thou hast done; for I have beheld how thou hast with unwearyingness declared the word, which I have given unto thee, unto this people. And thou hast not feared them, and hast not sought thine own life, but hast sought my will, and to keep my commandments. And now, because thou hast done this with such unwearyingness, behold, I will bless thee forever; and I will make thee mighty in word and in deed, in faith and in works; yea, even that all things shall be done unto thee according to thy word, for thou shalt not ask that which is contrary to my will." (Helaman 10:4-5).

After Elijah declared that no rain would fall in the kingdom, the Lord commanded him to flee from the presence of Ahab. "And the word of the Lord came unto him, saying, Get thee hence, and turn thee eastward, and hide thyself by the brook Cherith, that is before Jordan. And it shall be, that thou shalt drink of the brook; and I have commanded the ravens to feed thee there. So he went and did according unto the word of the Lord." (1 Kings 17:2-5).

Gordon B. Hinckley, a latter-day counterpart to the Prophet Elijah, said: "I draw strength from a simple statement made concerning the Prophet Elijah: 'So he went and did according unto the word of the Lord.' (1 Kings 17:5). There was no arguing. There was no excusing. There was no equivocating. Elijah simply 'went and did according unto the word of the Lord.' And he was saved from the terrible calamities that befell those who instead scoffed and argued and questioned." (C.R., 10/1971).

After the brook in the wilderness dried up, the Lord sent Elijah to the Widow of Zarephath. "And it came to pass after a while, that the brook dried up, because there had been no rain in the land. And the word of the Lord came unto him, saying, Arise, get thee to Zarephath...and dwell there: behold, I have commanded a widow woman there to sustain thee. So he arose and went to Zarephath. And when he came to the gate of the city, behold, the widow woman was there gathering of sticks: and he called to her, and said, Fetch me, I pray thee, a little water in a vessel, that I may drink. And as she was going to fetch it, he called to her, and said, Bring me, I pray thee, a morsel of bread in thine hand.

And she said, As the Lord thy God liveth, I have not a cake, but an handful of meal in a barrel, and a little oil in a cruse: and, behold, I am gathering two sticks, that I may go in and dress it for me and my son, that we may eat it, and die. And Elijah said unto her, Fear not; go and do as thou hast said: but make me thereof a little cake first, and bring it unto me, and after make for thee and for thy son. For thus saith the Lord God of Israel, the barrel of meal shall not waste, neither shall the cruse of oil fail, until the day that the Lord sendeth rain upon the earth. And she went and did according to the saying of Elijah: and she, and he, and her house, did eat many days. And the barrel of meal wasted not, neither did the cruse of oil fail, according to the word of the Lord, which he spake by Elijah." (1 Kings 17:7-16).

The Lord often helps those in need through the service of other people. Jeffrey

Holland said: "I know we can each do something, however small that act may seem to be. We can pay an honest tithe and give our fast and freewill offerings…and we can watch for other ways to help. To worthy causes and needy people, we can give time if we don't have money, and we can give love when our time runs out. We can share the loaves we have and trust God that the cruse of oil will not fail."

Elder Holland said that the widow's response when Elijah asked her for food was an "expression of faith, as great, under these circumstances, as any I know in the scriptures. Perhaps uncertain what the cost of her faith would be, she first took her small loaf to Elijah, obviously trusting that if there were not enough bread left over, at least she and her son would have died in an act of pure charity."(C.R., 4/1996).

Ezra Taft Benson counseled: "When we put God first, all other things fall into their proper place or drop out of our lives. Our love of the Lord will govern the claims for our affection, the demands on our time, the interests we pursue, and the order of our priorities. May God bless us to put Him first and, as a result, reap peace in this life and eternal life with a fulness of joy in the life to come." (C.R., 4/1988).

When the widow's son later became sick and died, Elijah "carried him up into a loft, where he abode, and laid him upon his own bed. And he cried unto the Lord, and said, O Lord my God, I pray thee, let this child's soul come into him again. And the Lord heard the voice of Elijah; and the soul of the child came into him again, and he revived." (1 Kings 17:17-22).

The priesthood power of Elijah did not go unnoticed in the land. Before long, he found it necessary to contend with all of the priests of Baal, who were the lackeys of Ahab and Jezebel: "Now therefore send, and gather to me all Israel unto mount Carmel, and the prophets of Baal four hundred and fifty, and the prophets of the groves four hundred, which eat at Jezebel's table. So Ahab sent unto all the children of Israel, and gathered the prophets together unto mount Carmel." (1 Kings 18:19-20).

When the people gathered to hear Elijah speak, he asked them, "How long halt ye between two opinions?" (1 Kings 18:21). To halt between two opinions is to serve two masters. But no-one can do this, "for either he will hate the one, and love the other; or else he will hold to the one, and despise the other. Ye cannot serve God and mammon." (Matthew 6:24). A house divided against itself cannot stand.

We sometimes halt between two opinions in our struggle to be obedient. There is a constant battle between maintaining church dress standards and adopting the standards of the world, keeping the Sabbath or enjoying the weekend, honoring the Word of Wisdom or pushing the envelope in the cafés of convenience that are scattered all along the broad boulevards of Idumea, memorizing the Thirteenth Article of Faith or practicing it, following the counsel of the brethren or analyzing it to find some weakness within it, or some way around it, so that we can justify our behavior and feel better about our disobedience.

Sometimes, we must contend with "the Priests of Baal" lurking in our own lives. "The stirring words of the prophets urge us to choose, to decide, and not to halt. Elijah's message has tremendous relevancy today, for all must finally choose between the gods of this world and the God of eternity." (Neal A. Maxwell, "That My Family Should Partake," p. 22).

Following Elijah's spiritually exhausting confrontation with the priests of Baal, (1 Kings 18) he was comforted by the Holy Ghost and was instructed to continue in God's work. (1 Kings 19). He became discouraged, just as we sometimes do in our daily struggles. "There are 1,200 kids in my high school, and I'm the only member." "None of my teammates support my standards." "I've tried giving out copies of The Book of Mormon, but all I seem to get is rejection." "Everyone else got to date at 14, but I have to wait 'til I'm 16." "While everyone else is out enjoying the weekend, I'm on a service project on Saturday, and in church on Sunday."

Elijah said: "The children of Israel have forsaken thy covenant, thrown down thine altars, and slain thy prophets with the sword; and I, even I only, am left; and they seek my life, to take it away." (1 Kings 19:10). Despite God's spectacular display of power on Mount Carmel (see 1 Kings 18:30-40), Elijah still felt that he was the only Israelite left who worshiped the true God.

The Lord responded to Elijah by declaring: "Yet I have left me seven thousand in Israel, all the knees which have not bowed unto Baal, and every mouth which hath not kissed him." (1 Kings 19:18). In the midst of the community of unbelievers (and apostate members of the church) there were thousands who were still faithful to their covenants (or who, as the elect of God, would respond enthusiastically to overtures from members of the church). Today, there are many who just don't know where to find the truth. If we are sensitive to the whisperings of the Spirit, the Lord will direct us to them.

The Lord communicated with Elijah in the same way He often counsels us. (See 1 Kings 19). Gordon B. Hinckley said: "I think the best way I could describe the (communication) process is to liken it to the experience of Elijah as set forth in the book of First Kings. Elijah spoke to the Lord, and there was a wind, a great wind, and the Lord was not in the wind. And there was an earthquake, and the Lord was not in the earthquake. And there was a fire, and the Lord was not in the fire. And after the fire, a still, small voice, which I describe as the whisperings of the Spirit." (C.R., 10/1996).

Ezra Taft Benson asked that we take time to listen to these promptings of the Spirit. "Answers to prayer," he said, "come most often by a still voice and are discerned by our deepest, innermost feelings. I tell you that you can know the will of God concerning yourselves if you will take the time to pray and to listen." (C.R., 10/1977). The lesson of Elijah contending with the priests of Baal teaches us that we will be comforted and guided as we put God first and heed the whisperings of the Holy Ghost.

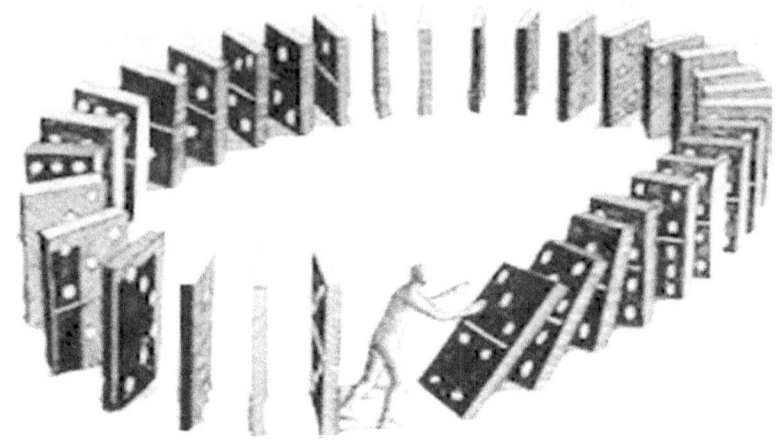

"The catalogue
of a man's discipline he must
compile for himself. He cannot be guided
by any rule that others may lay down, but is
under necessity of tracing it himself through
every avenue of his life. He is obliged
to catechize and train himself."
(Brigham Young).

The Principle
of Agency

The term "agency" is used only six times in the scriptures, in D&C 29:36, 64:18, 93:31, 107:78, Moses 4:3, & 7:32. It is interesting that such an important principle is so infrequently mentioned, and yet we incessantly talk about it in gospel discussions. Then again, the term "free agency" is never found in the scriptures, although in years past, the term was in common usage in the church. "More recently, we have taken note of our being "free to choose" and "free to act"(2 Nephi 2:27 & 10:3. See also Helaman 14:30), and of our opportunity to do many things of our own "free will." (D&C 58:27 & Mosiah 18:28). When we use the expression "moral agency," found just once in the scriptures, in D&C 101:78, we appropriately emphasize accountability. We have the capacity for free will, but are moral beings who are responsible for not only our decisions, but also for the consequences that follow.

We have purchased our agency at great cost and sacrifice. Knowing what we do about the War in Heaven, it is no wonder that our youth are so zealous regarding the exercise of their agency. They were among the most valiant in the pre-earth existence, and during the ideological War in Heaven, that was fought by Lucifer for mind control, they must have been zealous in their defense of agency.

During that conflict, agency did prevail, and when the victorious spirits came to the earth clothed in bodies of flesh and bone, they did so with a passion for the freedom to choose their own destiny. Therefore, when those embodied spirits are controlled by compulsion, "in any degree of unrighteousness", it is ingrained within their nature to resist. It is helpful to understand why they feel as passionately as they do, and to be very cautious when questions arise that involve their exercise of agency.

The most powerful weapons used in warfare today, and the most coldly efficient ways to take life, utilize the exercise of chemical, nuclear, and biological agents. But the most coldly efficient way to kill another's spirit is through the manipulation of ideology.

Agency is the lynchpin of the Plan of Salvation. Its righteous application, that is fundamental to the operation of the Plan, is difficult to master. All one has to do is read the "News" to see how the battle is going, and to see who seems to be winning. But here's the really amazing thing about agency: The more it is exercised with responsibility, the more of it there is to use. The less wisely it is used, the less of it there is to use.

Making correct choices very subtly increases our power to make more correct choices. "You may know me," said the personality trait. "I'm your constant companion. I'm your greatest helper; I'm your heaviest burden. I will push you onward or drag you down to failure. I am at your command. Half the tasks you do might as well be turned over to me. I'm able to do them quickly, and I'm able to do them the same every time if that's what you want. I'm easily managed; all you have to do is be firm with me. Show me exactly how you want it done; after a few lessons I'll do it automatically. I'm the servant of all great men and women, and the servant of failures, too. But I work with all the precision of a marvelous computer. You may run me for profit, or you may run me to ruin; it really makes no difference to me. Work with me. Be easy with me and I will destroy you. Be firm with me and I'll put the world at your feet. For I am Habit!" (Anonymous).

It only takes about three to four weeks of consciously and consistently using agency to create a "good" habit. That's also about how long it takes to break "bad" habits. Consistently attending church services is a good example of the creation of a good habit.

Following Satan limits our choices and subsequently hobbles our freedom to make good choices. Anyone who has suffered the consequences of bad choices knows firsthand what it means to be snared in Satan's strong cords and feel the downward drag of the weight of the chains of hell.

This begs the obvious question: Why, then, do we seem to find it so easy to follow Satan? There are always two voices operating, "two voices are calling, one coming out from the swamps of selfishness and force, where success means death, and the other from the hilltops of justice and progress, where even failure brings glory. Two lights are seen on your horizon, one, the last fading marsh light of power, and the other the slowly rising sun of human brotherhood. Two ways lie open for you, one leading to an ever lower and lower plane, where are heard the cries of despair and the curses of the poor, where manhood shrivels and possessions rot down the possessor, and the other leading to the highlands of the morning, where are heard the glad shouts of humanity, and where honest effort is rewarded with immortality." (Commencement Address to Queen Margaret College, Glasgow, Scotland, June 15, 1932, in "Helen Keller: Sightless but Seen; Deaf but Heard," p. 113).

The kicker is that we can we use agency, the very principle Satan uses to get us to follow him, to withstand His temptations. The correct application of moral agency can be used to set us free from enslavement to self-defeating behaviors. At the end of the day, agency is both the beginning and the end of the Plan. Finally, the Judgment will hinge upon how we exercised our agency.

Contemporary prose illustrates the principle: "My father focuses heart-gripping flashes across the wall screen. Family slides. I am small, my brother is smaller, and my sister is smallest. Days now dead re-open like old storybooks from memory's heaped box. Pulling out pictures of cooking in grandfather's dutch oven; playing cheetah on our backyard monkey-jungle; being beautifully Easter-bested with my coat buttoned wrong; hugging a mommy minus grey hair. Soberly, I think of another Father, Who someday shall open my mind, and flash reeling remembering of every day's minute across my soul, across the heavens, and kindly ask me to narrate." (Lora Lyn Stucker, "New Era," 8/1973).

Perhaps we can start now to make a conscious effort to be aware of the number of times we exercise our agency, and make mental notes relating to its righteous application. We can then thank God each time, not only for the gift, but also for our power to make correct choices, and for the ripple effect it has in our lives.

"I feel like shouting hallelujah,
when I think that I ever knew
Joseph Smith the Prophet."
(Brigham Young).

The Prophet Joseph Smith:
The Third of The Three Pillars of Testimony

When we depart this life, wouldn't it be wonderful if one of the first things we did after we passed through the veil was to warmly embrace the Prophet Joseph Smith. On one occasion, anticipating his own family reunion, he said: "I will tell you what I want. If tomorrow I shall be called to lie in yonder tomb, in the morning of the resurrection let me strike hands with my father." (H.C., 5:361).

The Three Pillars of Testimony are the Lord Jesus Christ, The Book of Mormon, and the Prophet Joseph Smith. So, if beyond the veil, we should meet Brother Joseph, what will our reaction be, just after we have struck hands with him? B.H. Roberts, born 13 years after the martyrdom, was once asked a question on the life and teachings of the Prophet. "As he answered, the elders saw their beginning curiosity expanded to vast proportions. They nodded in grateful admiration. All of a sudden, he looked up, raised his hands, and exclaimed: "Brother Joseph, I have fought for you, I have defended you, I have loved you!" ("Defender of The Faith," p. 388). I hope, when we have that veil experience, we will have a strong testimony of the prophet, because it is he who "holds the keys of this last dispensation, and no man or woman in this dispensation will ever enter into the Celestial Kingdom of God without the consent of Joseph Smith." (Brigham Young, J.D., 7:289-290).

There are certain things we know in this life with undeviating, absolute, unshakeable certainty. We must obey the laws of physics. The sun will rise tomorrow morning. If we step off a curb, our feet will eventually strike pavement, or perhaps a mud puddle. We e must balance eating, sleeping, and working to be consistently successful.

We also know things of a metaphysical nature. We know who we are. We know Joseph Smith. We know things about him that cannot be rationally explained. Boyd K. Packer described a conversation he had with an atheist friend, who pressed him about his testimony. He asked Elder Packer: "Tell me how you know." Elder Packer said he remembered something Joseph Smith had said: "A person may profit by noticing the first intimation of the spirit of revelation; for instance, when you feel pure intelligence flowing into you, it may give you sudden strokes of ideas…and thus by learning the Spirit of God and understanding it, you may grow into the principle of revelation." ("Teachings," p. 151). And then he simply asked his friend, "Tell me what salt tastes like." Some explanations are so unusual that they defy description; others are so unremarkable that they fail to generate even a blip on the radar of our consciousness.

That is not to say, however, that we should not try to bring order and transparency to what has heretofore been characterized as inexplicable. "In recent years, the church has undertaken the monumental task of publishing every extant document written by Joseph Smith or by his scribes in his behalf, as well as other records that were created under his direction or that reflect his personal instruction or involvement. It is contemplated that the print edition of The Joseph Smith Papers will consist of about two dozen volumes, divided into six series: Documents, Journals, Revelations and Translations, Histories, Administrative Records, and Legal and Business Records. In addition, transcripts of all known and available Joseph Smith documents will be published on the Joseph Smith Papers website, along with the annotation from the printed volumes and images of almost all of the documents." (See: JosephSmithPapers.org).

While it is the intention of those who are involved in the project to present their findings in an academic manner, it cannot be disputed that there is another legitimate avenue of scholarship. For, it is when we feel the Spirit that we "hear truth spoken with clarity and freshness; uncolored and untranslated, it speaks from within ourselves in a language original but inarticulate, heard only with the soul." (Hugh B. Brown). For example, Daniel D. McArthur, who led one of the first handcart companies to Salt Lake City, declared: "It always seemed to me that if I ever did know anything on this earth, I surely knew that he was a Prophet."

If we rely upon the media to learn about Joseph Smith, we may be confronted by doubt, skepticism, cynicism, ridicule, contempt, hostility, derision, suspicion, disparagement, and even scorn. But there is another side to the prophet. On one occasion, he said: "I can taste the principles of eternal life, and so can you. They are given to me by the revelations of Jesus Christ; and I know that when I tell you these words of eternal life as they are given to me, you taste them, and I know that you believe them. You say honey is sweet, and so do I. I can also taste the spirit of eternal life. I know that it is good; and when I tell you of these things which were given me by inspiration of the Holy Spirit, you are bound to receive them as sweet, and rejoice." (H.C., 6:304).

But even Moroni cautioned him: "Wherever the sound (of the marvelous work) shall go, it shall cause the ears of men to tingle, and wherever it shall be proclaimed, the pure in heart shall rejoice, while those who draw near to God with their mouths, and honor him with their lips, while their hearts are far from him, will seek its overthrow, and the destruction of those by whose hands it is carried. Therefore, marvel not if your name is made a derision and had as a by-word among such, if you are the instrument in bringing it, by the gift of God, to the knowledge of the people." ("The Messenger and Advocate," 2/1835).

Joseph has been described as a prism of the Lord Jesus Christ. In other words, "he reduced his teachings to the capacity of every man, woman and child, making them as plain as a well defined pathway." (Brigham Young). Mercy Fielding Thompson, whose husband served as a clerk to Joseph Smith, said: "I have listened to his clear and masterly explanations of deep and difficult questions. To him all things seemed simple and easy to be understood, and thus he could make them plain to others as no other man could that I ever heard."

After experiencing General Conference via satellite, it's hard to imagine how significant must have been the communication challenges faced by the early saints, as they made extraordinary efforts to listen to the counsel of their leaders. A contemporary named Amos Potter described a sermon Joseph Smith gave in Nauvoo: When the Prophet began his address, he said: "I have three requests to make of the congregation: The first is, that all who have faith will exercise it and pray the Lord to calm the wind; for as it blows now, I cannot speak long without seriously injuring my health; the next is that I may have your prayers that the Lord will strengthen my lungs, so that I may be able to make you all hear; and the third is, that you will pray for the Holy Ghost to rest upon me, so as to enable me to declare those things that are true." When he "had spoken about thirty minutes there came up a heavy wind and storm. The dust was so dense that we could not see each other any distance, and some of the people were leaving when Joseph called out to them to stop and let their prayers ascend to Almighty God that the winds would cease blowing and the rain stop falling, and it should be so. In a very few minutes the winds and rain ceased and the elements became calm as a summer's morning. The storm divided and went on the north and south of the city, and we could see in the distance the trees and shrubs waving in the wind, while where we were it was quiet for one hour, and during that time one of the greatest sermons that ever fell from the Prophet's lips was preached."

What might we have felt, if we had been privileged to hear the Prophet thus speak? Harold B. Lee once counseled the saints at the conclusion of a General Conference: "If you want to know what the Lord has for this people at the present time, I would admonish you to get and read the discourses that have been delivered at this conference, for what these brethren have spoken by the power of the Holy Ghost is the mind of the Lord, the will of the Lord, the word of the Lord, and the power of God unto salvation." (C.R., 4/1973).

Those who knew the Prophet spoke of his honesty. Eliza R. Snow declared: "His integrity was as firm as the pillars of heaven." John M. Bernhisel, who boarded in Joseph and Emma's home in Nauvoo, recalled: "He is naturally a man of strong mental powers, and is possessed of much energy and decision of character, great penetration, and a profound knowledge of human nature. He is a man of calm judgment, enlarged views, and is eminently distinguished by his love of justice. He is kind and obliging, generous and benevolent, sociable and cheerful, and is possessed of a mind of a contemplative and reflective character. He is honest, frank, fearless and independent, and as free from (false appearances) as any man to be found."

His contemporaries spoke of his happiness, although he was well acquainted with grief. Parley P. Pratt described him as "mild, affable, beaming with intelligence; mingled with a look of interest and an unconscious smile, or cheerfulness…his benevolence unbounded as the ocean." Joseph recognized that "happiness is the object and design of our existence, and will be the end thereof, if we pursue the path that leads to it, and this path is virtue, uprightness, faithfulness, holiness, and keeping all the commandments of God." ("Teachings," p. 255).

Those with whom he labored in the ministry recognized the clarity and power of his mission. Lorenzo Snow said: "The people loved to hear him, because he was full of revelation." Mary Ann Stearns Winters, a stepdaughter of Parley P. Pratt, remembered: "The Holy Spirit lighted up his countenance till it glowed like a halo around him, and his words penetrated the hearts of all who heard him." Orson Spencer declared: "At his touch, the ancient prophets spring into life, and the beauty and power of their revelations are made to commend themselves with thrilling interest to all that hear." Edward Stevenson recalled: "The Prophet testified with great power concerning the visit of the Father and the Son, and the conversation he had with them. Never before did I feel such power."

There are specific things we can do to treasure up the words of Joseph Smith, and to live by the principles he taught. Brigham Young said: "From the first time I saw the Prophet Joseph…I did hearken to (his words), and treasured them up in my heart, laid them away, asking my Father in the name of His Son Jesus to bring them to my mind when needed. I treasured up the things of God, and this is the key that I hold today. I was anxious to learn from Joseph and the Spirit of God." (Logan Conference, 5/25/1877).

Harold B. Lee quoted the following passages from the Doctrine & Covenants, that relate to the mission of Joseph Smith: "Thou shalt give heed unto all his words and commandments which he shall give unto you as he receiveth them, walking in all holiness before me; For his word ye shall receive, as if from mine own mouth, in all patience and faith. For by doing these things the gates of hell shall not prevail against you; yea, and the Lord God will disperse the powers of darkness from before you, and cause the heavens to shake for your good, and his name's glory." (D&C 21:4-6, a revelation received on the occasion of the organization of the church, 4/6/ 1830).

President Lee then taught: "The only safety we have as members of this church is to do exactly what the Lord said to the church in that day when the church was organized. There will be some things that take patience and faith. You may not like what comes from the authority of the church. It may contradict your political views. It may contradict your social views. It may interfere with some of your social life. But if you listen to these things, as if from the mouth of the Lord himself, with patience and faith, the promise is that the gates of hell shall not prevail against you. (C.R., 10/1970).

Even now, we sense his presence. Mary Alice Cannon Lambert, who lived in Nauvoo, said: "Saints and sinners alike felt and recognized a power and influence which he carried with him." Howard Coray remembered: "I sat and listened to his preaching... when I have been completely carried away with his indescribable eloquence and power of expression, speaking as I have never heard any other man speak." Wilford Woodruff testified: "In his public and private career he carried with him the Spirit of the Almighty, and he manifested a greatness of soul which I had never seen in any other man."

When we study his life, and our testimony of his mission becomes more powerfully entrenched in our hearts, we are drawn inevitably to the conclusion that, when he receives his exaltation in the Celestial Kingdom of God, he "will be seated on the right hand of Christ." (Bruce R. McConkie, C.R., 10/1949). One of his greatest contributions "was his knowledge of what is to come after death. He did much to clarify men's understanding of heaven and to make it seem worth working for." ("My Religion & Me" course manual). Every time we think of him and his mission, we are moved to rededicate ourselves to honoring the principles of heaven for which he gave his life.

If all of our sins smelled like tobacco,
none of us would come to church.

The Sacrament

If you have ever witnessed an automobile accident, you may have seen everything related to it unfold in slow motion. At the same time, it's like your brain sped up, allowing you to process information more comprehensively, so that you could see every element in fine detail. I have had such an experience, and it reminded me of the account of Moses, who "cast his eyes and beheld the earth, yea, even all of it; and there was not a particle of it which he did not behold, discerning it by the Spirit of God." (Moses 1:27). Although neuroscientists cannot tell us why, in extreme situations we sometimes have this ability. In the case of Moses, he was able to see in fine detail because he was full of the Spirit of God.

When we consider the Sacrament, it is helpful to step back and view it in slow motion, if you will. We are able to do so, particularly because of the influence of the Spirit that is woven into the tapestry of the ordinance. As we listen to the prayer, we are struck by how deliberately the powers of heaven are invoked in our behalf. "O God, the Eternal Father." Immediately after beseeching God, there is often a "pregnant pause" suggesting that birth is imminent. Something wonderful is about to happen, and we're waiting with bated breath to find out what it is.

The Sacramental Prayer is part of a priesthood ordinance, and is not an ordinary prayer of thanksgiving in the traditional sense. After addressing God, the prayer gets right down to the business at hand: "We ask thee in the name of thy Son Jesus Christ….." Now this really grabs our attention, positioning us squarely in the center of the petition, catapulting us into a highly emotional state, and getting the tightly wound chords of our spiritual sensitivities vibrating with intensive anticipation. We've just invoked the name of the Son of God!

There follow several entreaties, each charged with a rising tide of energy, and the prayer is closed with one final plea: "That they may always have His spirit to be with them." The power and promise of this final appeal calls to mind practical benefits that we've all experienced. Fundamentally, the Spirit influences us to ratchet down the hectic pace of our lives. The Lord knows how busy we are. He also knows what it feels like to be neglected, to be ignored, and to be in competition with telestial trivialities. In fact, He may have been thinking of the Sacrament when He urged David: "Be still, and know that I am God." (Psalms 46:10).

The Spirit clears our minds, and impels us to see things unambiguously. Once, in preparation for the holidays, I was hanging strings of lights on the outside of my house. Unraveling them as I took them out of the boxes in which they had been stuffed the previous winter, I realized I was faced with a hopelessly tangled mess. We can compare that Gordian Knot of tangled wires and bulbs with the cacophony of the "Christmas Lights of Confusion" that are so prevalent in the world today.

So what can we do "to have His Spirit to be with us," to be able to see, and hear, and feel, with unmitigated transparency? First of all, let's consider the Pandora's Box of social media, that once opened, can be used for good or for evil. For better or for worse, it has become part of our experience, if it is not already firmly entrenched as part of our lives. If you haven't already done so, read or watch David Bednar's address at the 2014 B.Y.U. Education Week Devotional, that explores this subject. (Available at LDS.Org, in its Media Library).

Elder Bednar warned of the dangers related to the improper use of technology. "Too much time can be wasted, too many relationships can be harmed or destroyed, and precious patterns of righteousness can be disrupted," he said. "We should not allow even good applications of social media to overrule the better and best uses of our time, energy, and resources." If we want to have His Spirit to be with us, instead of texting, surfing the net, twittering, or feeding our dependency on Facetime, Pinterest, or Instagram, we might consider spending our time in other, arguably more worthwhile, activities.

If we want to have His Spirit to be with us, we might want to turn off our cell phones and put away our tablets, especially during Sacrament meeting. Instead of answering e-mail, we might quietly use our time seeking answers to prayer. Instead of focusing our attention on the cares of the world, and sampling the flavor of the day, we could instead savor the moment and relish our relationship with our Father in Heaven. Instead of burning the candle at both ends, or trying to run faster than we have strength, we could step back, take a deep breath, and realize that when we have given our best, it is good enough. If we want the Spirit to be with us, we will re-group, re-assess, re-prioritize our time, re-focus on matters of substance, and get to work, while ignoring petty pursuits. We will cultivate the feeling I had when I witnessed that automobile accident. We will learn to speed up our brains, even as we quietly perceive things in slow motion. In a world that is filled with smoke and mirrors and artful deception that can only lead to conceptual cul-de-sacs, doctrinal dead-ends, and religious round-abouts, we will more clearly see what is real because we have moved to a more spiritually advantageous point of view

The Sacrament has the power to do this because it immobilizes time, which reminds me of a line from the motion picture "Frozen." "For the first time in forever, nothing's in my way!" So too, nothing gets in the way of the Sacrament. There is no pomp or circumstance, no splendid celebration with ceremony or fuss, and no histrionics to detract from the simplicity of the ordinance. No outside interferences compete for our attention, and there are no distractions to obstruct the direct conduit to God's listening ear. For the first time in forever, nothing's in our way!

Administered at the beginning of a week that is sure to have its ups and downs, the Sacrament is an independent constant with a powerful and influential capacity. It is a bastion of stability in the midst of turmoil, and it never gets old. There is no update 10.4.1 to worry about. There is enough Random Access Memory within the Sacrament to bind us to unchanging principles, and the code of its working vocabulary calls us to action in a clear and unmistakable voice. The language of the Sacrament is simply the gospel Standard, whether it is expressed in English or any of the other 188 languages spoken in the Lord's Church. (Source: "LDS Newsroom," 11/21/2014).

Its irreducible elements define a lowest common denominator that breaks down the Plan of Salvation into easily digestible bite-sized principles. At the same time, the Sacrament positions the solemnities of eternity right in the cross hairs. We can take our understanding as far as our capacity allows us to go, because the Sacrament is individually tailored to suit our circumstances, and yet it is collectively understood and is universally applicable. Insofar as the Sacrament is concerned, God "doeth nothing save it be plain unto (us); and he inviteth (us) all to come unto him and partake of his goodness; and he denieth none that come unto him… and all are alike unto God." (2 Nephi 26:33).

Many years ago, Melvin J. Ballard counseled: "The road to the Sacrament table is the path of safety for the Latter-day Saints." ("Improvement Era," 10/1919). We live in a different world today, almost a century after Elder Ballard made that remark. One thing that hasn't changed, however, is that we still place a high priority on our personal security. It has been said that there are only two or three places where one can find maximum security: in a prison cell, in a hospital's intensive care unit, or possibly in a doomsday prepper's panic room.

We don't want or need that kind of security because we have Elder Ballard's "path of safety" that leads us to the emblems of Christ. It makes us wonder: Why would anyone willfully neglect to follow that clearly marked "path of safety?" Who would say to themselves: "I think I'll just blow off Sacrament Meeting this week." It just doesn't make sense to do so.

Our testimonies grease the wheels and allow us to move us along on the Path of

Safety. It's no coincidence that our hearts swell during its administration, and that immediately thereafter, on Fast Sunday, it's customary to pour out their contents in testimony of the truths of the gospel. In sharp contrast to the world's orientation toward confrontation and its insatiable appetite for conflict, the spirit of the ordinance bears a witness of peace. Its inarticulate stirrings are evidence of personal revelation, as we remember the powerful promise "that His spirit might be with (us)."

Joseph Smith said we "may profit by noticing the first intimation of the spirit of revelation; for instance, when you feel pure intelligence flowing into you, it may give you sudden strokes of ideas… By learning the Spirit of God and understanding it, you may grow into the principle of revelation." The Sacrament, then, is the perfect schoolmaster to bring us to Christ. (See Galatians 3:24).

When we stop to think about it, everything about the church is revelatory. We've all had these experiences. Hugh B. Brown spoke for all of us, when he said: "Sometimes during solitude, I hear truth spoken with clarity and freshness; uncolored and untranslated it speaks from within myself in a language original but inarticulate, heard only with the soul, and I realize I brought it with me, was never taught it nor can I efficiently teach it to another." But as Spencer W. Kimball observed: "Expecting the spectacular, (we) may not be fully alerted to the constant flow of revealed communication." (C.R., 4/1977). The Sacrament, that lowest common denominator that puts us all on an equal footing, gives each of us an opportunity to recognize these universal feelings and to act on them.

I've now taken the Sacrament close to 2,500 times. I'm not expecting the spectacular, and yet I recognize the repetitive nature of the ordinance as theatrical encore on a cosmic level. Like a beautiful sunset, or a rainbow after a summer shower, or a baby's birth, or the sound of a loved one's voice, or passing through the veil of the temple, it doesn't get old, it stirs my most intimate sensitivities, and it continues to amaze me.

The Sacrament raises our testimony temperature and gets our juices flowing. It gives us a healthy "whack" right in our status quo, where we need it the most. It makes us feel complete, whole, at peace, and it binds up our wounds. We feel forgiveness through the Atonement, and have a burning desire to re- commit ourselves to be disciples of Christ.

We understand what Joseph Smith meant, when he exclaimed: "I can taste the principles of eternal life, and so can you. They are given to me by the revelations of Jesus Christ."(H.C., 6:304-305, 312, & 317). We understand what it means when we hear the promise in the Sacrament prayer, that we may have His Spirit to be with us. In the church, we often hear a member of the Bishopric say: "We will now prepare for the Sacrament…by singing a hymn." We are encouraged to sing with devotion, worshipfully, reverently, fervently, with conviction, solemnly, thoughtfully, and with dignity. But at the end of the day, our preparation really begins in the hours immediately following our last Sacrament meeting. In this sense, also, the Sacrament is "frozen in time."

Of course, our preparation is tied to the Atonement of Jesus Christ, a process that began during our pre-earth existence. It's one of the reasons we "sang together and… shouted for joy." (Job 38:7). That spontaneous outburst of emotion was in response to the explanation that during mortality we would be able to partake of the Sacrament, to renew not only our covenant of baptism, but also, perhaps, the covenants we undoubtedly had made with our Father during that great council.

Groundwork for the ordinance of the Sacrament was laid during the mortal ministry of the Savior, with clarity first established in the upper room at Jerusalem. Luke recorded how the Savior taught His disciples to administer the Sacrament of the Last Supper. (See Luke 22). Later events in the Garden of Gethsemane give further context to the Sacrament, with unmistakable definition provided on the cross, and incontrovertible finality shaped by an empty tomb. For emphasis, Latter-day Saints have the additional witness of Book of Mormon scriptures that deal with the Savior's instruction to priesthood brethren during His post-mortal ministry among the Nephites. (See 3 Nephi 18:7).

These Book of Mormon scriptures also testify that the Sacrament is frozen in time. As pre-occupied as the prophet Moroni must have been after Cumorah, he was still able to write a few more things on The Plates of Mormon. Included in those precious engravings was specific instruction dealing with the ordinance of the Sacrament. (See Moroni 4). Moroni knew that the Sacrament would be "the path of safety" for his descendants, and even for his brethren the Lamanites. (See Moroni 1:4).

As Joseph Smith organized the latter-day church, he received a revelation known as The Lord's Preface to The Doctrine & Covenants. In it, he recorded a warning that was reminiscent of Isaiah, and meant for the world: "Prepare ye for that which is to come (for) they have strayed from mine ordinances, and have broken mine everlasting covenant." (D&C 1:12-13, see Isaiah 24:5). Through Joseph, the Lord would see to it that the ordinance of the Sacrament would be properly restored.

He prioritized the ordinance of the Sacrament when He revealed to His prophet specific instructions regarding its administration. (See D&C Section 20, recorded in its entirety soon after the church was organized on April 6, 1830). This revelation provides instruction not only on how the sacramental prayers should be offered, but also gives us insight into the necessity of our own preparation prior to participation in the ordinance. "The duty of the members after they are received by baptism - The elders or priests are to have a sufficient time to expound all things concerning the church of Christ to their understanding, previous to their partaking of the sacrament." (D&C 20:68).

To take advantage of the real power of the Sacrament, it is necessary to develop a solid foundation of doctrinal understanding through new member discussions, and then to participate in repetitive instruction in gospel Essentials and gospel Doctrine classes, and in Primary, Sunday School, Priesthood and Relief Society meetings. Continuing religious education is the constant companion of the priesthood-administered ordinances of the gospel.

D&C 20 continues: "And the members shall manifest before the church, and also before the elders, by a godly walk and conversation, that they are worthy of it, that there may be works and faith agreeable to the holy scriptures - walking in holiness before the Lord." (D&C 20:69). This is where works meet faith, where the rubber hits the road – walking in holiness before the Lord. As Martin Luther observed: "Good works do not make a good man, but a good man does good works. And what makes a man good? Faith in God, and Christ."

Then, in this same revelation, we have the Sacramental Prayer itself. Without the recurring, repetitive infusion of power through the Sacrament, living a Christ-centered life is possible and can be wonderful, but it is not ideal. Trying to negotiate the minefields of mortality on our own, without the protective priesthood ordinance of the Sacrament, we will fall short and cannot measure up. The Lord condemned the world specifically because it had "changed the ordinance, and (had consequently) broken the everlasting covenant." (D&C 1:13). Without the Sacrament, neither Latter-day Saints nor the world can hope to enjoy the protection of a covenant relationship with the Good Shepherd.

On September 30, 2014, I celebrated a milestone in my life: 25,000 days on earth. I hope if I have done anything with the indescribable gift of a long life, I have been able to teach my children and grandchildren about the importance of the Sacrament. My daughter Tara shared with me the following: "When I have a moment to breathe, be calm, and then watch my boys pass the Sacrament to the congregation, my spirit has a moment to be still. To some, that might not seem like a very long time, but in my busy life it seems like a lifetime!" The Sacrament, once again, is frozen in time.

My son-in-law Nate told me: "A couple of Sundays ago, as I sat down with my family on our favorite row and prepared my bag as a road block, in an attempt to keep the kids from escaping, I said a quick prayer that maybe today I could be a little more in tune during the Sacrament; that maybe I could direct my thoughts more toward the Savior and His Atonement. Almost immediately after that silent prayer, a young man tapped me on the shoulder and asked me if I would participate in the administration of the ordinance and help pass the Sacrament. It was a very humbling experience that I will record as an answer to a prayer for an increased desire to focus on the Sacrament and the Savior."

My daughter Elizabeth said: "The bishop challenged our ward to avoid distractions for our children during the Sacrament. So I made a book with pictures of Jesus and His life, and I have my 5 & 9 year-old boys look through it before the Sacrament. They have learned to listen and to feel the Spirit, and although it has taken them some time, they are now more accustomed to focusing on the words of the prayers."

One of my heroes is William Tyndale, who has been called "the mostly unrecognized translator of the most influential book in the world." He was an English priest, who died a martyr, on October 5, 1536, 481 years ago. He is one, like Joseph Smith, whose influence defies measurement. He has helped countless millions make the transition to a higher spiritual plane. He was the first to translate the Bible and publish it in English, the language of the people. He did this in 1526, only 72 years after Gutenberg turned the world upside down with his publication of a Latin Bible utilizing his invention of the printing press, in 1454.

In order to accomplish the task, Tyndale studied the New Testament in its original Hebrew and Greek. He was a true polyglot, fluent in Greek, Latin, French, German, Italian, and Spanish in addition to his native English. The result of his scholarship was so spectacular that, in the following century, the theologians revising the Bible relied heavily on his interpretations when creating the King James Version. 83% of the New Testament in the K.J.V. can be attributed to Tyndale. With feeling, passion, and excitement, he bequeathed to us its poetical language. These same emotions wash over us as we listen to the recitation of the sacrament prayer.

Tyndale crafted familiar phrases that flow like honey from our lips: "Let there be light." "In the beginning, God created the heaven and the earth." "In the beginning was the Word and the Word was with God and the Word was God." "Our Father, which art in heaven, hallowed be thy name." "The spirit is willing but the flesh is weak." "Blessed are they that mourn, for they shall be comforted." And even "It came to pass," that familiar phrase found 1,407 times in The Book of Mormon, and 672 times in the K.J.V.

Tyndale wrote about "the tongues of men and of angels, "sounding brass and tinkling cymbals," "the salt of the earth," "the signs of the times," and "Atonement. He is responsible for these expressions, as well: "Blessed are the peacemakers," "Seek and ye shall find," "Ask and it shall be given you, "The Lord bless thee and keep thee. The Lord make his face to shine upon thee and be merciful unto thee. The Lord lift up his countenance upon thee, and give thee peace. "

It would be nice if Tyndale were responsible for the word "Sacrament," but alas, he is not – it derives from the ecclesiastical Latin sacrāmentum, from sacrō ("hallow, or consecrate"), and from sacer ("sacred, or holy").

One day, a priest visiting his parish openly attacked Tyndale's beliefs. He replied: "If God spare my life, before very long I shall cause a plough boy to know the scriptures better than you do!" In fulfillment of that prophetic statement, as of November 2014, the Bible has been translated into 531 languages, and 2,883 languages have at least a portion. (Source: Wikipedia).

The next time we partake of the Sacrament, we might ask ourselves: "Who are the modern day plough boys, of whom Tyndale referred?" Surely, they are our 16 year-old Priests, our 14 year-old Teachers, and our 12 year-old Deacons, who know the scriptures better than many theologians. Tyndale's prophetic vision has come true.

Thanks to the restoration of the gospel, each of us, proverbial "plough-boys" and commoners in the church, can understand the scriptures as well as any. The Restoration has calibrated our heartstrings to vibrate in harmony with celestial melodies, as when we listen to the sacramental prayers. In the musicality of these prayers, we can "taste" the principles of eternal life.

To quote two more of William Tyndale's contributions to our liturgy, and these may be my favorites: By the "still small voice" we can know the truth of all things. And second: "In him we live, and move, and have our being."

Thank God for all those who have sacrificed so much that we might enjoy the Sacrament, and for all that it means to us. Within its administration lies the key to our perfection. According to Brigham Young, "The sin that will cleave to all the posterity of Adam and Eve is, that they have not done as well as they knew how." (J.D., 2:130). The road to the Sacrament table is our path of safety. May we resolve, from this hour, to better understand and to keep the covenant of the Sacrament, by doing as well as we know how.

"The second mile is a gift of spiritual independence that removes the veil of insensitivity to our destiny."
(Richard L. Gunn).

The Second Mile

"And, behold, one came and said unto him, Good Master, what good thing shall I do, that I may have eternal life? And he said unto him…if thou wilt enter into life, keep the commandments. He saith unto him, Which?" (Matthew 19:16-17). Jesus then enumerated a number of commandments.

"The young man saith unto him, All these things have I kept from my youth. What lack I yet?" (Matthew 19:20). This young man had been a good and faithful member of the church. He had attended Primary and Sunday School, never missed a Seminary class, and had been ordained a Deacon at age twelve. He had been a faithful home teacher with his father, and had accepted opportunities to speak in church. He had done temple baptisms for the dead. He had attained the rank of Eagle Scout. He had received his endowment in the temple, had accepted the Law of the gospel by covenant, and had faithfully served a two year full time mission for the church. In his obedience to the letter of the law, he had been perfect.

But the Savior knew his heart, and perceived that there was something missing from his life that was preventing him from achieving the gift of spiritual independence that would remove the veil of insensitivity to his destiny. What he lacked was not necessarily the same thing that was absent from the personal lives of his contemporaries. His challenges had been carefully tailored by a wise Father to meet his circumstances, that he might grow through opposition that had been specifically and pointedly fashioned to address his needs. The Savior knew this young man's heart, and perceived that obedience to the Law of Consecration would be his greatest challenge.

And so, He "said unto him, If thou wilt be perfect, go and sell that thou hast, and give to the poor, and thou shalt have treasure in heaven: and come and follow me." The Savior knew this would have been an easy thing to do if the young man had been poor and destitute. "But when the young man heard that saying, he went away sorrowful: for he had great possessions." (Matthew 19:16-22).

This impressionable young man, like so many in the church, had not developed the seasoned maturity that comes with age. From the opposite end of the temporal spectrum near the end of his life, William Tyndale said that he would rather "be blessed with Christ, in a little tribulation, than to be cursed perpetually with the world for a little pleasure. Prosperity is a right curse," he wrote, "and a thing that God giveth to his enemies."

For each of us, mortality is a probationary state; a time in which we will be individually tried to see if we will put to the proof those things that we have been taught we must do if we are to inherit eternal life. In short, we are tested and tempted so that God can see if we are willing to "go the second mile." When I was younger, I ran 5 or 10 miles every morning, for an hour or two before sunrise. I ran through the Santa Monica Mountains, above Pacific Palisades, in Southern California. One day, as I neared the end of my run and began to retrace my route over the surface streets back to my home, I stopped at an intersection, waiting for the traffic signal to change. I put my hands on my knees and allowed the perspiration to drip off the end of my nose. I thought about aborting my run, stopping right then and there, and letting my complaining muscles cool down. However, through sweat-soaked eyes, I looked up, and saw as it were, a vision before me. Insistently flashing red with neon brightness, directly in front of me, were these words that urged me on: "Don't walk!"

That message, as if it had come from God Himself, urged me to go the second mile, and the experience has since prompted me to reflect upon this question: "What happens to us when we go the second mile?" I have come to the conclusion that as we learn to confront our trials and tribulations, by pushing just a little harder, we grow in the spirit. It is no coincidence that these two scriptures are linked together: "And whosoever shall compel thee to go a mile, go with him twain," and then: "Be ye therefore perfect, even as your Father which is in heaven is perfect." (Matthew 5:38-48).

I have been a member of the church for long enough to have experienced the exhilaration of temporal, spiritual, emotional, and intellectual symmetry. But the world still tugs at me. I am in a probationary state. My life is a time of testing, to see if I "will do all things whatsoever the Lord (my) God shall command (me)." (Abraham 3:25). We all have crosses to bear, and the ominous warning applies to every one of us: "Whosoever doth not bear his cross, and come after me, cannot be my disciple. …Whosoever he be of you that forsaketh not all that he hath, he cannot be my disciple." (Luke 14:27 & 33).

The question remains: What and who do I think the Savior was talking about when he said: "Whosoever shall compel thee to go a mile, go with him twain. "(Matthew 5:41). When I joined the church, I was asked to go the first mile. I started to attend church on a weekly basis. I began to regularly repent. I established the habit pattern of consistently partaking of the Sacrament. I learned what it means to keep the Sabbath day holy, and I adjusted my habit patterns to do so to the best of my ability. I accepted a home teaching assignment together with its related responsibilities. I learned to express myself by employing modest speech that reflected the higher standard to which I aspired. I began to consistently pay my tithes and offerings. I worked to sustain my temple worthiness. I accepted and tried to magnify ward callings. I began to appreciate the temporal and spiritual benefits of obedience to the Word of Wisdom. I made regular deposits to my spiritual bank account by praying daily to my Heavenly Father, and learned how to make withdrawals in times of need. I made a conscious effort to internalize the Ten Commandments, and tried to be ever mindful of my baptismal covenants.

However, after a period of time I began to recognize that Heavenly Father had something more in mind for me, and I felt the urge to go the second mile. I had been attending church, but the second mile compelled me to take advantage of opportunities such as B.Y.U. Education Week, and other conferences and symposia, and to really internalize the scripture that encouraged me to seek "out of the best books words of wisdom," and to "seek learning even by study and also by faith." (D&C 109:7).

I had been repenting regularly, but His admonition to go the second mile put the Atonement in a new perspective. Against the backdrop of His marvelous light, my sins brought me real sorrow. I felt terrible about them. I felt profoundly filthy. I wanted to unload and abandon them. I became almost obsessive-compulsive about cleansing my soul. I was broken in heart, and had the spirit of contrition, and became zealous in my preparation to receive the Spirit, that I might be teachable. At a heightened level of preparation, I began to consistently ask, as did those on the Day of Pentecost: "What shall I do?" I listened for answers, and began to feel with greater intensity the promptings of the Spirit.

I had been receiving the Sacrament each Sunday, but the second mile urged me to be consistently receptive to new ways to have His spirit to be with me. I determined to prepare for the ordinance of the Sacrament hours and even days ahead of time, and to treat the service itself with newfound respect.

I felt that I had been keeping the Sabbath day holy, but the second mile encouraged me to visit the sick, and the elderly, and to look for opportunities to provide compassionate service and to perform other acts of Quiet Christianity.

I had been doing my home teaching, but I began to realize that if I wanted to go the second mile, that responsibility would never be over, no matter the day of the month. I began to take an active interest in the on-going affairs of my families, and to be sensitive to their spiritual, emotional, intellectual, and temporal needs. With a second mile perspective, I began to see hidden truth in the scripture that related to my responsibilities: "Verily I say unto you, Inasmuch as ye have done it unto one of the least of these my brethren, ye have done it unto me." (Matthew 25:40).

I had established habit patterns that supported my desire to express myself with soft and considerate words, but I took to heart the second mile admonition of Paul, who wrote: "Let no corrupt communication proceed out of your mouth, but that which is good to the use of edifying, that it may minister grace unto the hearers." (Ephesians 4:29).

I had been paying my tithing, but I began to regularly ponder the significance of the second mile covenant to obey the Law of Consecration.

I had maintained temple worthiness, and had received my own endowment, but I began to appreciate the second mile requirement to do my own family history work, and to expand my temple service by participating in baptismal, initiatory and sealing ordinances, in addition to proxy endowments for the dead.

I had consistently accepted a succession of ward callings, but realized that my second mile commitment would require me to go beyond an hour or two of service each week, and would compel me to consecrate my time and talents to the needs of those for whom I had a stewardship responsibility. I began to appreciate the observation of Job, who wrote: "For God speaketh once, yea twice, yet man perceiveth it not. In a dream, in a vision of the night, when deep sleep falleth upon men, in slumberings upon the bed; Then he openeth the ears of men, and sealeth their instruction." (Job 33:14-16).

I had learned to be undeviating in my obedience to the Word of Wisdom, but when I applied the second mile principle to this law of health, I began to see it in its greater context, as a conduit to enlightenment, and so I began to pay more strict attention to the spirit of the law, and to the delicate relationships between physical and spiritual stability, and between physical health and personal revelation.

I was praying daily to my Heavenly Father, but the second mile urged me to ask for His influence at the break of day, and to return and report at its end. The second mile reminded me of the Lord's commandment: "Go to the house of prayer and offer up thy sacraments upon my holy day; For verily this is a day appointed unto you to rest from your labors, and to pay thy devotions unto the Most High; Nevertheless thy vows shall be offered up in righteousness on all days and at all times." (D&C 59:9-11).

I had been obeying the Ten Commandments to the best of my ability, but the second mile asked me to live according to principles defined by a higher spiritual law, to develop real compassion for others, and to shun the siren song coming from great and spacious buildings.

I had been mindful of my baptismal covenants, but the second mile focused my thoughts on the command to be "willing to mourn with those that mourn; yea, and comfort those that stand in need of comfort, and to stand as witnesses of God at all times and in all things, and in all places that ye may be in, even until death." (Mosiah 18:9). I learned that the second mile would expose me to experience God's love, and to understand what Paul meant when he said: "By the grace of God I am what I am: and his grace which was bestowed upon me was not in vain; but I laboured more abundantly than they all: yet not I, but the grace of God which was with me." (1 Corinthians 15:10).

The General Authorities of the church urge us to go the second mile, when they speak in General Conference. They talk about the first principles and ordinances of the gospel, because they are mindful that they may be instructing non-members and less-active members, but they realize that they are also speaking to members of the church who have already committed themselves to obedience. Their messages have multiple layers of meaning and application. They speak to the basic principles in such a way that non-members are encouraged to take the first steps toward commitment, while at the same time, seasoned members are encouraged to commit to go the second mile.

As Paul traveled along the road to Damascus, he learned what it meant to go the second mile. He later ministered among the Corinthian Saints, whom he was pleased to discover had a working relationship with the laws of a gospel whose expression he characterized as being written upon "tables of stone." But he also took pains to explain their second mile commitment: "Ye are manifestly declared to be (living examples of) the epistle of Christ ministered by us, written not with ink, but with the Spirit of the living God; not in tables of stone, but in fleshy tables of the heart."(2 Corinthians 3:3).

Those who commit to the second mile are as the Nephites of old, who were encouraged by the sermon of King Benjamin. The scriptures record: And now, it came to pass that when king Benjamin had thus spoken to his people, he sent among them, desiring to know of his people if they believed the words which he had spoken unto them. And they all cried with one voice, saying: Yea, we believe all the words which thou hast spoken unto us; and also, we know of their surety and truth, because of the Spirit of the Lord Omnipotent, which has wrought a mighty change in us, or in our hearts, that we have no more disposition to do evil, but to do good continually. And we, ourselves, also, through the infinite goodness of God, and the manifestations of his Spirit, have great views of that which is to come; and were it expedient, we could prophesy of all things. And it is the faith which we have had on the things which our king has spoken unto us that has brought us to this great knowledge, whereby we do rejoice with such exceedingly great joy." (Mosiah 5:1-4).

Sooner or later, every member of the church is a second miler, who is manifestly encouraged to endure to the end in righteousness. During His mortal ministry, the Savior said "he that shall endure unto the end, the same shall be saved." (Matthew 24:13). Going a little further, He explained to Joseph Smith: "If you keep my commandments (the first mile) and endure to the end (the second mile) you shall have eternal life, which gift is the greatest of all the gifts of God." (D&C 14:7).

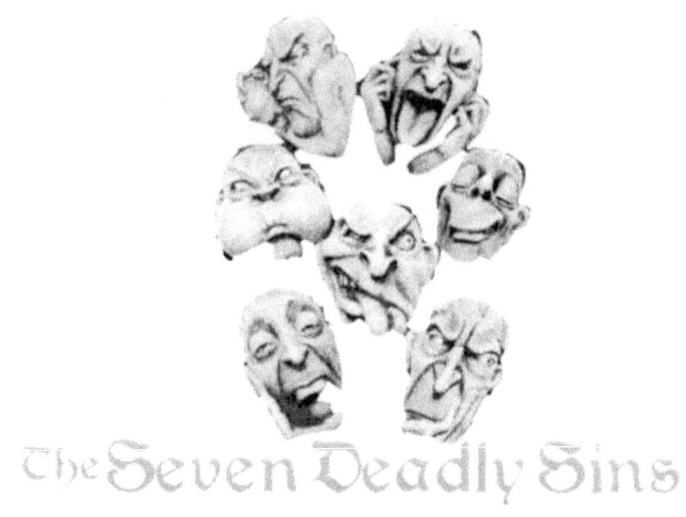

The Seven Deadly Sins

"These six things
doth the Lord hate: yea
seven are an abomination unto
him: A proud look, a lying tongue, and
hands that shed innocent blood, an heart that
deviseth wicked imaginations, feet that be swift
in running to mischief, a false witness that speaketh
lies, and he that soweth discord among brethren."
(Proverbs 6:16-19).

The Seven Deadly Sins

It is easy to look around and see all that is bad in the world, but it is harder to put a positive spin on what seems like an avalanche of bad press on the 5 o'clock news. Nevertheless, that is exactly what we should attempt to do when we are assaulted on a daily basis by the Seven Deadly Sins, for "a merry heart maketh a cheerful countenance: but by sorrow of the heart the spirit is broken. (Proverbs 15:13).

1). Solomon tells us that the Lord hates "a proud look." Every character trait that has been tainted by pride has a counterpart in humility. For example, pride looks over to man and argues who is right, while humility looks up to God and cares about what is right. Pride asks only: "What do I want out of life?" while humility quietly inquires: 'What would God have me do?' Pride is motivated by selfish desire, while humility is inspired by God's will. Pride is driven by the fear of man, while humility is nurtured by the love of God. The applause of the world rings in the ears of the proud, while the accolades of heaven warm the hearts of the humble.

The self-centered, conceited, boastful, arrogant, and haughty nature of the proud is easily trumped by the modest, self-effacing, and deferential behavior of the humble. Hatred, hostility, blind opposition, and enmity are the raw manifestations of pride, but these are overwhelmed by the sociability, approachability, accommodation, faith, hope, and charity of the humble.

The proud feel more comfortable with their own perception of truth than they do with God's omniscience. They pit their own abilities against His priesthood power, their own paltry accomplishments against His mighty works, and their stubborn will against His gentle counsel. Those who refuse to accept His authority have hard-hearts, stiff-necks, and are overtly and covertly rebellious. They lack the pliability and malleability of the humble. The proud are unrepentant because they are smitten with themselves, while the humble experience remorse with the realization that they are less than the dust of the earth. The proud are easily offended and are sign seekers, and because they are past feeling, they require greater and greater intensities of stimulation to receive the same level of temporal or theological gratification. The humble are long suffering and faithful, and when things seem that they could not be worse, they are at their best, because then they are particularly sensitive to the whisperings of the Spirit.

The proud are uninterested in changing their opinions or in aligning themselves with God's direction. They consume themselves in a senseless scramble of self-serving interest. The humble, on the other hand, foster an atmosphere of cooperation, collaboration, and conciliation, and they pool their resources with those with whom they work in order to achieve mutually agreeable solutions to their problems.

The proud argue, fight, exercise unrighteous dominion, and abuse their position, while the humble speak softly, seek peaceful solutions, invite the Spirit to guide them in their interpersonal relationships, and recognize the priesthood of God as the engine that drives their righteous behavior. The proud set the stage for secret combinations that are built up with one purpose in mind: To get gain and the glory of the world. The humble, on the other hand, work openly, knowing that "nothing is secret, that shall not be made manifest; neither any thing hid, that shall not be known and come abroad." (Luke 8:17).

In their assessments and judgments, the humble are prone to praise loudly and blame softly. They understand that when straightening a bent nail, a pat on the back is better than a bump on the head. Before being critical of others, the humble remember that they might not have had the same advantages. They have learned to seek out supportive and sustaining spiritual experiences in the peaceful countryside of cognitive clarity, and they encourage others to remove themselves from the madding crowd, to clear their heads, to listen more attentively and see more plainly, to breathe more deeply as they inhale the fresh air of truth, and to be caressed by its gentle breeze, if they have not beforehand been refreshed by such influences and invigorated by such whisperings.

We can choose to humble ourselves by receiving counsel and chastisement, by forgiving those who have offended us, by rendering selfless service, and by our good example that teaches others. We can unconsciously choose to be humble by adopting a lifestyle that complements and honors God, and that acknowledges His "glory, honor, power, majesty, might, dominion, truth, justice, judgment, mercy, and an infinity of fulness, from everlasting to everlasting." (D&C 109:77).

The antidote to pride is frustratingly simple. The quiet example of the Savior is illustration enough. Humility will conquer our pride and cleanse our inner vessel as we yield to the enticings of the Holy Spirit, put off the natural man, and become Saints through the Atonement of Christ.

2). Solomon tells us that the Lord hates "a lying tongue."

The process by which honesty is woven into and entrenched within our character is that of testing the mettle of our convictions. We have no proof until we act on the basis of trust. Then comes the confirmation of the reality, as feelings of self-confidence grow and purposeful actions replace tentative overtures. Truly did Paul declare: "God hath not give us the spirit of fear, but of power, and of love, and of a sound mind." (2 Timothy 1:7). Honesty is clothed with the power stemming from a grateful heart and the love that only a sound mind is capable of expressing. Honesty motivates us to do what is right, rather than what is expedient. Peter's admonition strikes a resonant chord within those whose actions are consistent with honesty: "We ought to obey God rather than men." (Acts 5:29).

As Josiah Gilbert Holland wrote: "God, give us Men! A time like this demands strong minds, great hearts, true faith, and ready hands. Men whom the lust of office does not kill. Men whom the spoils of office cannot buy. Men who possess opinions and a will. Men who have honor; men who will not lie. Men who can stand before a demagogue and damn his treacherous flatteries without winking. Tall men, sun-crowned, who live above the fog in public duty and in private thinking. For while the rabble, with their thumb worn creeds, their large professions and their little deeds, mingle in selfish strife, Lo! Freedom weeps, Wrong rules the land, and Justice sleeps." ("God, Give us Men").

All of us are repeatedly faced with occasions when withdrawals must be made from our spiritual bank accounts. Honest individuals, however, do not write checks that they cannot cash. They realize that only after regular deposits have been faithfully made over a period of time, can they rely on the cornucopia of comfort created by the cushion of confidence that becomes a currency that is supported by consistently honest conduct.

Honest individuals never thirst, because they have sent taproots down through deep gospel topsoil directly into a flowing fountain of living water. Well did the poet write about a message that relates to the challenges faced by each of us in every day experiences that are tailored by a wise Heavenly Father, that we may be encouraged to seek out that which is honest, true, chaste, benevolent, and virtuous. "The tree at the church next door to me turned up its roots and died. They had tried to brace its leaning, but it lowered and lowered, and then there it lay leaves in grass and matted roots in air, like a loafer on a summer day. 'Look there,' said the gardener. 'Short roots - all the growth went up. Big branches - short roots.' 'How come?' I asked. 'Too much water. This tree never had to hunt for drink.' Especially in thirsty times, my memory steps outside and looks at the tree at the church next door to me that turned up its roots and died." (Carol Lynn Pearson).

As those with honest hearts quietly carry out their work, the righteousness of their cause will be revealed to them in marvelous simplicity and plainness. Walls of opposition to their progress will crumble and fall away. The Lord will comfort and succor them with the bread of life. As they travel through the harsh environment of mortality, oases will spring up in the desert and living waters will slake their thirst. Their roots will be deeply embedded in gospel soil that is buttressed by the bedrock of eternally valid principles.

Those who are honest are the architects of their own fate, even as they draw upon powers greater than themselves. Perhaps Victor Hugo heard that majestic clockwork when he wrote: "Be like a bird that pausing in her flight a while on boughs to light, feels them give way beneath her and yet sings, knowing that she hath wings." Those who are honest are busily engaged fashioning defensive weapons on the forge of faith in the armory of thought. These are the tools with which they will build for themselves heavenly mansions of joy and strength and peace. Those who are honest with themselves, with others, and with God "are the masters of thought, and the shapers of condition, environment, and destiny." (Spencer W. Kimball, "The Miracle of Forgiveness," p. 103).

Angels will attend the honest in heart: "For I will go before your face," promised the Lord. "I will be on your right hand, and on your left, and my Spirit shall be in your hearts, and mine angels round about you, to bear you up." (D&C 84:88). Once we have received the holy anointing of honesty, we "can never rest until the last enemy is conquered, death destroyed, and truth reigns triumphant." (Parley P. Pratt, "Deseret News," 4/30/1853).

3). Solomon tells us that the Lord hates "hands that shed innocent blood."

In addition to His obvious condemnation of murder, (see Exodus 20:13), the Lord hates those who prevent the innocent from embracing the truth, or who destroy the faith and confidence of those who have accepted the truth. The scriptures record Alma's confession that, during the rebellious years of his youth, he "had murdered many of (Heavenly Father's spirit) children," but add the clarification that he had "rather, led them away unto destruction." (Alma 36:14). That he had contributed to their spiritual demise later caused him to be "racked, even with the pains of a damned soul." (Alma 24:15). "So great had been (his) iniquities, that the very thought of coming into the presence of (his) God did rack (his) soul with inexpressible horror." (Alma 36:14).

When Captain Moroni addressed the gross negligence on the part of the government officials of his day, he asked: "Can you think to sit upon your thrones in a state of thoughtless stupor, while your enemies are spreading the work of death around you?" (Alma 60:6-7). One cannot but help to think of those in our day who are in positions to intervene, but instead choose to sit on their hands, look the other way, or even encourage the institutionalized mass murder of the unborn innocent.

Isaiah declared: "Behold, a king shall reign in righteousness, and princes shall rule in judgment." (Isaiah 32:1). But when bureaucrats lose their sense of divine purpose, the temporal and spiritual equilibrium of the citizens of their society hangs in the balance. Heaven sometimes holds its breath while waiting upon the initiative of those who are charged with the sacred responsibility to lead by precept as well as by example.

In The Book of Mormon, we learn about Nephi, the son of Helaman, who found it necessary to withdraw from among the people, because "they did reject all his words, insomuch that he could not stay among them." Wicked leaders had "usurped the power and authority of the land, laying aside the commandments of God, and... doing no justice unto the children of men; condemning the righteous because of their righteousness; letting the guilty and the wicked go unpunished because of their money; and moreover to be held in office at the head of government, to rule and do according to their wills, that they might get gain and glory of the world, and, moreover, that they might the more easily commit adultery, and steal, and kill." (Helaman 7:2-5).

4). Solomon tells us that the Lord hates "a heart that deviseth wicked imaginations."

This is why He particularly loves the innocence of little children. While they drew, a kindergarten teacher walked up and down the rows in her classroom, observing the work of her students. She stopped at the desk of one little girl and asked what her drawing was. The girl replied, "I'm drawing a picture of God." The teacher paused, and then tentatively said, "But no one knows what God looks like." Without missing a beat or looking up from her paper, the five year old replied, "They will in a minute." Though tender in years, this child had what we might call pure and untinctured imagination.

When adults are equally pure in heart, they enjoy an intrinsic and self-reinforcing countermeasure to wicked imaginations. Their behavior is driven by altruism, self-denial, self-discipline, self-restraint, and self-sacrifice. The pure in heart are not easily offended, nor do they hold grudges. They never rationalize their weaknesses, frailties and failures; rather, they seek the peace that comes with repentance and forgiveness of God. Their self-esteem hinges upon approval by God, and not of the world.

What should we do when we are faced with wicked imaginations? Sometimes, the very "deceitfulness of riches choke(s) the word," and we are blinded to our characteristic good judgment, insomuch that we act irrationally. (Matthew 13:22). That is to say, the temptation of wicked imaginations clouds our vision and compromises our ability to make correct and prudent choices.

Every day, we are blitzed by any number of offers to spend obscene amounts of money so we can save, and it is only natural to assume that some of the purveyors of promises "too good to be true" lie in wait to "falsify the balances by deceit." (Amos 8:5). They infiltrate the media, and like sharks circling near the shore, wait for the unwary to move into dangerously deep water. They disguise their telestial temptations with tinsel, and invite the innocent to gamble away their fortunes and forfeit their birthright for a mess of pottage. Like the tangled Christmas lights of confusion, they play upon our innate trust and the better angels of our nature, twisting the truth into caricatures of reality. Wicked imaginations get our heads spinning so wildly with distracting disorientation that just about any outlandish offer has the power to draw our unfocused eyes to shimmering pots of gold at the end of rainbows.

Wicked imaginations deform our comprehension of credibility, causing us to stand unsteadily on our spiritual tip-toes, roll the dice, and capitulate the determination of our destiny to the hands of lady luck. When wicked imaginations have so distorted our better judgment, it may be that the source of our improbable hope is the great deceiver himself, for Alma clearly taught: "Whatsoever is good cometh from God, and whatsoever is evil cometh from the devil." (Alma 5:40). To narrow our search parameters, however, and to steer us back on course, Paul reminded us: "If there is anything virtuous, lovely, or of good report or praiseworthy, we seek after these things." (Philippians 4:8).

Paraphrasing the Apostle Paul, we should abhor wicked imaginations, and instead cleave to that which a reasonable person would presume to be true. (See Romans 12:9). Paul was all too familiar with those who sowed false hope, writing: "For they that are such…serve their own belly; and by good words and fair speeches deceive the hearts of the simple." (Romans 16:18). Such swindlers have sharpened their pencils and honed their skills as consummate con men.

When confronting such swindlers, we cannot descend to the lowest common denominator of their comfort level. Instead, we should yearn, as Paul did, for the light that will disperse their darkness, "that we henceforth be no more children, tossed to and fro," as flotsam and jetsam on the sea of life, "and carried about with every wind of doctrine, by the sleight of men, and cunning craftiness." (Ephesians 4:14). His simple counsel was: "Let no man deceive you with vain words." The trouble with vanity is that it relies on false hope, and upon the strength of false premises.

A wicked imagination is a pyramid scheme that cannot deliver on its promises. It writes checks it cannot cash because its spiritual reserves are running on empty and it is forever teetering on the brink of bankruptcy. In its worst form, wicked imagination is an abomination because it thwarts God's Plan of Happiness. No wonder Paul counseled: "Beware lest any man spoil you through philosophy and vain deceit, after the tradition of men, after the rudiments of the world." (Colossians 2:8). Not only can our travel plans be spoiled, but also the direction of our life's journey can be detoured when we succumb to wicked imaginations and to offers that seem too good to be true.

5). Solomon tells us that the Lord hates "feet that be swift in running to mischief."

We are slow to mischief when we possess the ability to look past telestial temptations and temporal trivia, and adjust our perspective so that righteous goals that are worthy of our energy expenditure become our quest. With enlightenment by the Spirit, we experience pure focus. Sensory input from the five natural senses is transformed by a spiritual sixth sense that orders our hierarchy of value and determines our priorities. When we have been conditioned through discipline, diligence, faith, and patience to be slow to run to mischief, we give the highest value to the people, interests, and activities that deserve our immediate attention. We draw upon all our physical and spiritual resources to address those concerns of greatest importance, while those whose feet are swift to run to mischief squander the enlightenment so freely given and yet so casually and carelessly received. The Lord warned: "Wo unto him ... that wasteth the days of his probation, for awful is his state!" (2 Nephi 9:27). Particularly when individuals groan "under darkness and under the bondage of sin," they grope about in a frantic and yet fruitless quest as they run to and fro, desperately searching for meaning, stability, and focus in their lives. (D&C 84:49).

If we ignore our innate urge to abhor mischief, and instead allow ourselves to be habitually distracted by trifling concerns, we sin by omission and risk settling for life in a marshland of mediocrity. There is, after all, "a tide in the affairs of men, which, taken at the flood, leads on to fortune. Omitted, all the voyage of their life is bound in shallows and in miseries." (Shakespeare, "Julius Caesar," Act 4, Scene 2). "How carefully most men creep into nameless graves, while now and again one or two forget themselves into immortality." (Wendell Phillips, "Speech on The Murder of Lovejoy").

There is always a price to be paid when individuals are quick to run to mischief. For example, when societal spiritual equilibrium is lost, its values are often adjusted in a vain attempt to re-establish a state of balance. When gods of wood and stone are nearly universally worshipped, it is justified as multiculturalism. If perversion is widely embraced, it is legitimized as an alternative lifestyle. When the poor are exploited, it is often disguised in the name of government-sponsored programs and policies. When unborn children are institutionally murdered, the collective conscience is soothed by coining terms like "pro-choice," and "women's rights" that deflect the issue away from the stark reality and brutality of the cold expression "late term abortion." When public figures are caught in a web of lies, the sin is mollified and excused as "hyper-exaggeration" or "factual extension." When power is abused, it is disguised as progressivism. When the media is polluted with obscenities, it is described as freedom of expression. We have gotten so many participation trophies growing up that we think that we are entitled to recognition and reward regardless of our lack of achievement. The target has been moved so many times that we think we are scoring repetitive bulls-eyes, when in reality the arrows have strayed far from the mark.

When individuals are drawn to mischief, they gradually lose their focus, just as eyesight may diminish over time. First they squint, and then they hold the page a little closer or a little further away. They compensate for their inability to see clearly, and whether it is the printed page or their character that they cannot read, it is being unconsciously compromised. The faithful don't consciously intend to lose their testimony of the Savior. Conviction just fades away like a slow leak from an automobile tire, and not as a sudden blowout, and it can all be traced back to a capitulation to the tendency toward mischief that began at a specific point in time. As Benjamin warned: "This much I can tell you, that if ye do not watch yourselves, and your thoughts, and your words, and your deeds, and observe the commandments of God, and continue in the faith," and avoid running to mischief, "even unto the end of your lives, ye must perish." (Mosiah 4:30).

6). Solomon tells us that the Lord hates "a false witness that speaketh lies."

Those who bear false witness and speak lies often have only a weak foundation of doctrinal understanding of the gospel. They fall into transgression in consequence of their shallow comprehension of principles. They pick apart the scriptures and the words of those who preach the gospel, distorting the doctrines into meaningless fragments without any coherent connection. As Alma declared to the inhabitants of Ammonihah: "Behold, the scriptures are before you; if ye will wrest them it shall be to your own destruction." (Alma 13:20).

The composite principles of the gospel are the consummate compilation of affirmative actions; together, they are as much the sum of "Thou shalt" commandments, as they are "Thou shalt not" commandments. Honesty, for example, is the mortar that holds together the building blocks of character, which is why the Lord hates a false witness that speaketh lies.

Those who are honest with themselves, their fellowmen, and the Lord have an unshakable moral and ethical standard upon which they can rely, and upon which their belief system is securely anchored. Others, who make value judgments based on endocrine secretions, rather than on the unchanging and eternally validated laws of the gospel, have no such foundation, but instead build their houses on the shifting sands of expediency, circumstance, and desire. Those who seek to be lights unto themselves, fail to improve the quality of their disposition because their intellect can never bridge the gap between rational behavior and faith, nor can it provide the mortar necessary to build character.

The Lord hates those who speak lies. A prospective employer asked a young man who had applied for a job, "If I hire you, can I count on you to be honest?" The young man replied, "You can count on me to be honest, whether you hire me or not." He delighted in being honest, and not because he was obligated to be so. Coercion counters agency, and those who are repetitively acted upon may ultimately forsake principles of conduct that are consistent with trustworthiness. Thus, the Lord instructed the Saints: "He that is compelled in all things, the same is a slothful and not a wise servant." Therefore, "men should be anxiously engaged in a good cause, and do many things of their own free will, and bring to pass much righteousness. For the power is in them, wherein they are agents unto themselves." (D&C 58:26-28).

Free will implies the power and opportunity to choose, but not as the man, we are told, who walked the straight and narrow path, who never lied, and who kept the commandments until he died; who never went to the theatres, and never learned to dance; who never once on shapely legs bestowed a wicked glance; who never smoked or kissed another's wife, and never took a bit of liquor in his life; who never let his temper rise, who never called his neighbor a fool, and kept strictly to the Golden Rule. Now you can be assured that he really lived on earth. But he was deaf, and dumb, and blind, and paralyzed from birth. (Anonymous).

Every day, we make choices that are illuminated by our values. We may have an examination in math, or history, or economics. But another will be in honesty. If we must fail one test, we need to make sure it is in math, history, or economics. There are many fine people in the world who are honest and successful and yet know nothing about these other subjects.

Long ago, Alexis de Tocqueville wrote: "I sought for the greatness and genius of America in her commodious harbors and her ample rivers, and it was not there; in her fertile fields and boundless prairies, and it was not there; in her rich mines and her vast world commerce, and it was not there. Not until I went to the churches of America and heard her pulpits aflame with righteousness did I understand the secret of her genius and her power. America is great because she is good, and if she ever ceases to be good, she will cease to be great." ("Reflections of Alexis de Tocqueville," p. 71). In the words of the Apostle Paul: "Thanks be made for all men…that we may lead a quiet and peaceful life in all godliness and honesty." (1 Timothy 2:1-2).

7). Solomon tells us that the Lord hates those who "soweth discord among brethren."

Murmuring is the subdued and continually repeated expression of indistinct or inarticulate complaints or grumbling. Like an earthquake, the murmuring of the disgruntled and malcontented can build into harmonic waves with the power to undermine the foundations of both relationships and institutions. Because they expect results without responsibility, their murmuring is a cowardly act. It is often conducted anonymously or behind the cloak of secrecy, but its effects are felt publicly. The pride of those who murmur compels them to expect a return without having made a legitimate investment. Especially in the case of those who murmur against priesthood authority, no tangible expenditure of faith has been made; and yet, they somehow expect results without responsibility.

Gossip is the bedfellow of murmuring, but it is more focused on mindless chatter and speaking without real purpose. It is just as damaging, however, because it feeds voraciously on rumor, hearsay, second-hand information, innuendo, and vanity. Left unchecked, it may build into a self-perpetuating chain reaction leading to a cascade of unfortunate consequences. In its many forms, gossip has one common characteristic. The words so loosely spoken cannot be gathered up later on. Like feathers left on the doorstep of those with whom one engages in idle conversation, gossip drifts to the four winds, and cannot be recalled. Words so carelessly scattered about in gossip suggest that the mouth has been brought on-line before the brain.

Those who murmur and gossip are fault-finders, who throw dirt but lose ground in the process. They are like flies that pass over healthy parts of the body to feed only at open sores. At the dedication of the Kirtland Temple, Joseph Smith referred to those predatory individuals who had sought to tear down the Latter-day work through fault finding. "We ask thee," he prayed, "to confound, and astonish, and to bring to shame and confusion, all those who have spread lying reports abroad, over the world, against thy servants, if they will not repent." (D&C 109:29).

Too often, those who murmur and gossip forget that when they point their finger at someone, there are three other fingers pointing right back at them. On the other hand, when the righteous seek to discover the best in others, they somehow bring out the finest in themselves. How refreshing, when their appraisals reflect a nobler estimate of others and their potential. Even if but little good is known, the faithful still speak in glowing terms of that which they do know to be true. If they are the first to discover a fault in others, they are the last to make it known to the world. They practice restraint, and are always ready to give courage and hope, and to speak kind words that come from the heart to awaken the soul to cheerfulness, "'til heart meets with heart and rejoices in friendship that ever is true." (Joseph L. Townsend, "Let Us Oft Speak Kind Words").

When we are assaulted by the Seven Deadly Sins, and confronted by compromise, we should remember the counsel of Alma, who taught: "For behold, it is as easy to give heed to the word of Christ, which will point to you a straight course to eternal bliss, as it was for our fathers to give heed to this compass, which would point unto them a straight course to the promised land." (Alma 37:44). As it was for Alma and his people, so it is for us. With our Liahona, we will find the strength to resist the seven deadly sins. We will discover that no wind can blow except it fills our sails and carries us ever closer to our intended destination, without delay or interruption, and without extra cost, loss, or sacrifice.

True disciples do the right things for the right
reasons, follow the Lord's example in prayer,
treat others kindly, exercise forgiveness,
judge righteously, obey the law, serve
God and do His will, observe the
Golden Rule, and actively seek
His kingdom.

The Strait and Narrow Path to Discipleship

Do the right things for the right reasons. "Take heed that ye do not your alms before men," cautioned the Savior, "to be seen of them: otherwise ye have no reward of your Father which is in heaven." (Matthew 6:1). Jesus referred to these people as hypocrites, those who pretend to have certain qualities but do not; who try to appear to be righteous but are not, or who do good things only to be seen by others. Hypocrites are wrapped up in themselves and tend to make very small packages. "They have their reward," cautioned the Savior. (Matthew 6:2). He also reminded us: "Where your treasure is, there will your heart be also." (Matthew 6:21).

William R. Bradford of the Seventy once spoke with the bishop of a ward whose youth had worked hard to earn money for an activity. The bishop asked Elder Bradford if he would help the youth receive recognition for what they had done. To the bishop's surprise, Elder Bradford said he would not. He said that he was glad that the young people had been so diligent, but that it was not important that they receive public acknowledgement for that work. When the youth decided to donate their money to the church's general missionary fund instead of using it for the activity, they asked if they could have their picture taken with Elder Bradford as they made the donation, and they wanted to have the photo and an article put into the newspaper. Again Elder Bradford surprised them by saying "no." He told the bishop: "You might consider helping your young people learn a higher law. Recognition from on high is silent. It is carefully and quietly recorded there. Let them feel the joy and gain the treasure in their hearts and souls that come from silent, selfless service." (C.R., 10/1987).

We can easily determine what we treasure by evaluating the resources we devote to obtaining it. Basically, we will be judged by the things for which we stand in line. Having said that, when we do something for the right reasons, we unconsciously "lay up for (ourselves) treasures in heaven, where neither moth nor rust doth corrupt, and where thieves do not break through nor steal." (Matthew 6:20). Our spiritual bank accounts will overflow with deposits that may later be withdrawn as an annuity of joy in the kingdom of heaven. (See D&C 18:14-16).

Express gratitude and follow the Savior's example of prayer. We would do well if our petitions would loosely follow this pattern: "Dear God, So far today I've done all right. I haven't gossiped. I haven't lost my temper. I haven't lied or cheated. I haven't been greedy, grumpy, nasty, selfish or overindulgent. I'm very thankful for that. But in a few minutes, I'm going to get out of bed, and from then on I'm probably going to need a lot more help. Amen." (Anonymous).

In fact, the Savior taught: "After this manner therefore pray ye: Our Father which art in heaven, Hallowed be thy name. Thy kingdom come. Thy will be done in earth, as it is in heaven. Give us this day our daily bread. And forgive us our debts, as we forgive our debtors. And lead us not into temptation, but deliver us from evil: For thine is the kingdom, and the power, and the glory, for ever. Amen." (Matthew 6:9-13).

Dallin Oaks said: "We should address prayers to our Heavenly Father in words (we) associate with love, respect, reverence, and closeness. Men and women who wish to show respect will take the time to learn the special language of prayer." (C.R., 4/1993). A favorite poem of David O. McKay reminds us: "The builder who first bridged Niagara's gorge, before he swung his cable, shore to shore, sent out across the gulf his venturing kite, bearing a slender cord for unseen hands to grasp upon the further cliff and draw a greater cord, and then a greater yet, 'til at last across the chasm swung the cable – then the mighty bridge in air. So may we send our little timid thoughts across the void, out to God's reaching hands. Send our love and faith to thread the deep, thought after thought until the little cord has greatened to a chain no chance can break, and we are anchored to the infinite!" (Edwin Markham).

Treat others kindly and fairly, remembering that "there is so much bad in the best of us, and so much good in the worst of us, that it hardly behooves any of us to talk about the rest of us." (Anonymous). The example of Joseph Smith speaks volumes: "I am calm as a summer's morning;" he declared on his way to Carthage. "I have a conscience void of offense towards God, and towards all men." (D&C 135:4).

Exercise forgiveness. "Those who do not forgive others when no fault was intended are fools, and those who do not forgive others when fault was intended are usually fools." (Attributed to Brigham Young). Forgiveness is a divine attribute that may exert a nurturing and healing influence, as does no other quality.

Obey the law. Disciples emulate he of whom it was said: "He kept all Ten Commandments until he died. He walked the straight and narrow path and never lied. He never went to the theatres. He never learned to dance. He never once on shapely legs bestowed a wicked glance. He never strayed or kissed another's wife. He never took a bit of liquor in his life. He never let his temper rise. He never called his neighbor a fool, but kept strictly to the Golden Rule. Now you can be assured that he really lived on earth. But he was deaf, and dumb, and blind, and paralyzed from birth." (Anonymous).

Judge righteously. How can we ensure that we "judge righteous judgment." (J.S.T. Matthew 7:2). Mormon was referring to the Light of Christ when he said: "Behold, my brethren, it is given unto you to judge that ye may know good from evil; and the way to judge is as plain, that ye may know with a perfect knowledge, as the daylight is from the dark night. For behold, the Spirit of Christ is given to every man, that he may know good from evil; wherefore, I show unto you the way to judge; for every thing which inviteth to do good, and to persuade to believe in Christ, is sent forth by the power and gift of Christ; wherefore ye may know with a perfect knowledge it is of God." (Moroni 7:15-16, see John 1:19). The Light of Christ bathes the universe in order. (See D&C 88:6-13).

Moroni continued: "But whatsoever thing persuadeth men to do evil, and believe not in Christ, and deny him, and serve not God, then ye may know with a perfect knowledge it is of the devil; for after this manner doth the devil work, for he persuadeth no man to do good, no, not one; neither do his angels; neither do they who subject themselves unto him. And now, my brethren, seeing that ye know the light by which ye may judge, which light is the light of Christ, see that ye do not judge wrongfully; for with that same judgment which ye judge ye shall also be judged." (Moroni 7:17-18).

"The Holy Ghost is not that which lighteth every man that comes into the world, which is the Spirit of God which proceeds through Christ to the world, that enlightens every man that comes into the world, and that strives with the children of men until it brings them to a knowledge of the truth and the possession of the greater light and testimony of the Holy Ghost." (Joseph F. Smith, "Millennial Star," 65:115). When we respond to the Light of Christ, we will be led to the Holy Ghost and will receive it by ordinance. The Holy Ghost is only given following demonstrable obedience to gospel principles, and the ordinance of baptism. Shades of grey should not exist for members of the Lord's church, because they have the greater light and knowledge given by the Holy Ghost.

Serve God and do His will. "No man can serve two masters: for either he will hate the one, and love the other; or else he will hold to the one, and despise the other. (We) cannot serve God and mammon." (Matthew 6:24). We should "seek not for riches but for wisdom; and, behold, the mysteries of God shall be unfolded unto (us), and then shall (we) be made rich. Behold, he that hath eternal life is rich. (D&C 11:7).

To understand spiritual things, we must have discernment or guidance from the Holy Ghost. Those who are sincerely investigating the merits of the gospel, are taught by the Spirit, and when they are confirmed as members of the church they receive the special gift of the Holy Ghost by ordinance. One of His purposes is to guide us from the covenant waters of baptism, along the strait and narrow path leading to the other ordinances and covenants of the priesthood that are necessary if we are to obtain eternal life. This is one reason why members of the church are given the Holy Ghost beside the waters of baptism.

Those who decline the offer of the riches of eternity that might have been unfolded to their view by the power of the Holy Ghost are doomed to live their lives in scarcity of their basic spiritual needs. They scratch out a life beneath the poverty level, but are not even be aware of it. They lack curiosity about the world around them, and are uninterested in exploring it or the people in it. Their potential is untested because of their self-imposed limitations. Their minds are numb, and their spirits are shriveled. Their clothes closets may be full, but they still complain that they haven't got a thing to wear. They may eat well, but are always thinking about going on a diet. They may be loaded down with toys at birthdays and Christmas, but they are still bored silly because there's nothing to do. They may have advanced degrees, but still feel unfulfilled in their jobs. They never stop to smell the roses.

Observe the Golden Rule. The "Law of Compensation" defines the behavior of the disciples of Jesus Christ. "Therefore all things whatsoever ye would that men should do to you, do ye even so to them: for this is the law and the prophets." (Matthew 7:12).

When we consider the question: "How can I tell if I am converted to the gospel of Jesus Christ?" we inevitably come to this conclusion: The best indicator that we are progressing spiritually and coming unto Christ lies in the way we treat other people. We tell on ourselves by the way we treat others; "by the friends we seek, by the very manner in which we speak, by the way we enjoy our leisure time, and by the use we make of dollar and dime. We tell who we are by the things we wear, and in the way we wear our hair, by the kinds of things that make us laugh, and by the records we play on the phonograph. We tell who we are by the way we walk, by the things in which we delight to talk, and by the books we choose from a well-filled shelf. In these ways and more, we tell on ourselves." (Anonymous).

Actively seek His kingdom. "Seek ye first the kingdom of God, and his righteousness; and all these things shall be added unto you." (Matthew 6:33). Disciples understand that worldliness can twist our thinking, distort our perspective, and turn our loyalty from God, while greed can weaken our resolve to put our own needs aside and serve Him first. Disciples do not take expensive vacations in Idumea, nor do they incur the hidden costs of self-indulgence. They do not procrastinate their enrollment in the

Lord's university system, or defer the curriculum of the gospel in favor of worldly pursuits that ask for pitifully little in terms of commitment or effort.

As Jesus neared the end of the Sermon on the Mount, He described the process of admission to the kingdom of heaven. "Enter ye in at the strait gate," He said, "for wide is the gate, and broad is the way, that leadeth to destruction, and many there be which go in thereat; Because strait is the gate, and narrow is the way, which leadeth unto life, and few there be that find it." (Matthew 7:13-14).

If mortality could be visualized in spatial dimensions, it would take the shape of an hourglass, with the strait gate its narrow midsection. After passing through that constriction, unparalleled vistas would open up to reveal untapped potential and unparalleled opportunity. But initially, many of us would be caught in conceptually confusing cul-de-sacs that would prevent us from comprehending the purpose of the Plan. We would wander to and fro, dazed and disoriented, like flotsam and jetsam on the sea of life.

Some of us would be stalled in telestial traffic jams that would overheat our engines, foul our lubricants, seize our moving parts, and restrict our access to freely flowing spiritual energy. Others would lack restraint, as if their brake pads were worn, interfering with their ability to slow down as they negotiated the minefields of mortality in order to avoid the terrain traps of transgression. Their ability to move forward with purpose might be compromised. They might lose their traction as they tried to move upward, and they might feel as if their gears were grinding and their clutch plates were slipping.

A few of us might squander scarce resources, as if our thermostats were inoperable, leaving our cooling systems to boil over from the excitement of excessive exertion in the steam plant of sin. All these mechanical issues might combine to overwhelm us in a perfect storm of trial, temptation, and transgression, forcing, as it were, lifestyle compromises that would make self-control and self-actualization all the more difficult, while making rationalization and self-justification more tempting options.

But for the few of us who were lucky enough to finally reach the constriction in the hourglass, there would come a realization that the time to stand and deliver had arrived. As Brutus observed, we would face that "tide in the affairs of men which, taken at the flood, leads on to fortune. Omitted," we would realize that the voyage of our lives would be condemned to be "bound in shallows and in miseries. On such a full sea," however, we would find ourselves "afloat, and we" would "take the current when it serves, or lose our ventures." (Shakespeare, "Julius Caesar," Act 4, Scene 3).

Those who successfully negotiated the strait and narrow way would be fortunate, indeed, to find that by following the blueprints of the Plan, they were to be given enough wiggle-room to be able to successfully flex their spiritual muscles and exercise their moral agency in a forum of free will that engaged opposition in a vigorous tug-of-war. They would realize that the Plan works best when its participants are able to make excellent choices that would propel them beyond less attractive competing options. They would hope to be sensitive to spiritual promptings, to be stimulated by the light of Christ, to receive the Gift of the Holy Ghost, to be thereby guided, and to be replenished with the high octane fuel of faith that would ignite the fire of their fortitude.

Those who would seize the moment, thread the eye of the needle, and negotiate the strait and narrow path would realize that what at the outset had felt like a confinement, and a constraint, was in fact a birth canal, or a portal through which all must pass in order to progress eternally. They would feel as if they had been literally born again. Expanding circles of opportunity that had beforehand been hidden from their view would snap into sharp focus. They would see beyond the limited horizon of their sight, and comprehend a vision in which the perfect law of liberty stretched out before them in a vista of incomprehensible proportion. They would see that God's Plan rests on solid footings that are reinforced with the rebar of our resolve, and that it is upon the foundation of the covenants that we make with Him that celestial sureties are constructed, leading to eternal life in His mansions above.

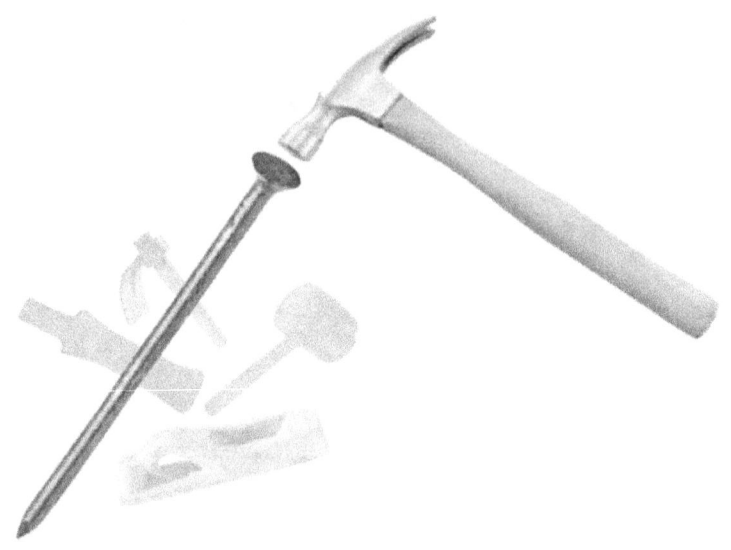

When
your only tool is
a hammer, you tend to
see every problem as a nail.

The Tools
of The Trade

Joseph, whose trade was carpentry, mentored Jesus from His youth. The boy must have developed considerable skill using the tools of Joseph's trade to craft many of the household items that would have made life in Israel more tolerable. Among other things, He surely learned three simple lessons from Joseph.

First, He learned to "measure twice and cut once." With the scarcity of wood in ancient Israel, Joseph couldn't afford to make mistakes. His example showed Jesus that He must know exactly what He was doing, why He was doing it, proceed carefully, delegate responsibility, accept accountability, earn trust, delight in appreciation, and feel satisfaction. Measuring twice and cutting once would reinforce the principle that proper prior priesthood planning prevents poor performance.

Secondly, He learned to "use the right tool for the job." In His youth, Jesus would have learned when and how to use chisels, drills, hammers, nails, pegs, and clamps. He would have learned how much pressure to apply with His adze, in order to shape either hard or soft wood, and how to deal with knots and other imperfections in the materials with which He was working. He would also have trusted His instincts, and relied upon relationship tools such as appreciation, benevolence, concern, empathy, encouragement, forgiveness, friendship, gentleness, humility, kindness, patience, persuasiveness, sincerity, tolerance, and understanding.

Thirdly, He would have learned that "by taking care of the tools of His trade, they would take care of Him." He would have learned how to use these tools without abusing or damaging them, how to coax the most out of them, and how to maintain them so that they would reliably provide for the temporal needs of His family. He would also have learned to use the spiritual tools of conviction, devotion, fasting, holiness, meditation, prayer, purity, reverence, scripture study, self-control, wisdom, and worship. In short, He would have learned to use both His head and his hands under the watchful eye of Joseph, but He would also have learned to use His heart, as His capacity for compassion and unconditional love expanded.

As His carpentry skills developed, He would have discovered a confidence born of the Spirit that would spill over into every other aspect of His life, for "he spake not as other men, neither could he be taught; for he needed not that any man should teach him." (J.S.T. Matthew 3:25). He would have mastered the innovative and original utilization of tools relating to priesthood keys, in a confirmation of that which had been spoken through His prophet Isaiah: "My thoughts are not your thoughts, neither are your ways my ways." (Isaiah 55:8). In the process, He would have nurtured in the armory of His own thoughts the devices to build bastions of joy and strategies of strength, as the Provider of peace. These tools would help Him to become the shaper of condition, environment, and destiny, and the author of salvation. (See Hebrews 5:9).

The Carpenter of Nazareth also utilized simple tools that relate to healthy and provident living. He knew that "when health is absent, then wisdom cannot reveal itself, culture cannot become manifest, strength cannot fight, and intelligence cannot be applied." (Heraclitus - Philosopher of the Golden Age of Greece). Truly, had Isaiah declared: "They that wait upon the Lord shall renew their strength, they shall mount up with wings as eagles, they shall run, and not be weary, and they shall walk, and not faint." (Isaiah 40:31). Isaiah recognized the tools that nurture the dependent relationship between obedience to the commandments and our physical and spiritual well-being.

Even trivial trappings can resonate with symbolism, and so the Carpenter of Nazareth used the simple telestial tools with which we are familiar to promote His celestial agenda. He used the color white as the symbol of purity. White bandages bind up our wounds. Flags of submission are white. Wedding dresses are white. Our venerable elders have white hair. When a wound has been cleaned with hydrogen peroxide, the flesh turns white. The linens used in the burial of the dead are white. The light at the end of the tunnel is a dazzling white. It may be no coincidence that our eyes are calibrated to see the stars in the heavens as a blaze of white light across the night sky that we call the Milky Way. Puffy white clouds stand out against blue skies and herald spring days filled with fields of beautiful white daisies. Healthy teeth are white, and a bright smile is the universal language and may be our best form of communication. The Lone Ranger and all the good cowboys have worn white hats. Satan tries to pervert white as the symbol of purity, and rationalizes falsehoods as nothing more than "white lies."

The Carpenter of Nazareth used "that for which all virtue now is sold, and almost every vice – almighty gold" as a symbolic tool, as well. (Ben Jonson, "Epistle to Elizabeth, Countess of Rutland"). While the desire for gold can obviously corrupt, the bright, shiny metal that cannot be corroded is also a symbol of purity that turns our thoughts to the inestimable worth of the Celestial Kingdom. Gold that has been heated in the crucible of the refiner's fire turns a dazzling white, and when the earth attains its celestial glory, the streets of its cities will be "pure gold, as it were transparent glass." (Revelation 21:21).

The Carpenter of Nazareth had at His disposal enough tools and to spare to build the incomparable Emerald City of Oz. We pat ourselves on the back and think that we have created palatial surroundings fit for kings with our telestial tools, but these temporal trappings provide nothing more than second-class accommodations in lodgings illuminated by a single bare bulb suspended from the ceiling by a frayed cord. Contrast that bleak existence with the experience of entering the prototype of heaven itself, the celestial room in the temple.

As breathtaking as that chamber in the House of the Lord might be, as much as it might orient our thoughts to eternity, it was still built by craftsmen utilizing corrupt tools with which we are largely familiar: hammers, nails, saws, levels, and tape measures. The celestial room is only a type or a shadow of the heavenly home that beckons to us, and that will be built with tools of a more enduring substance: faith, and charity, repentance and forgiveness, covenants and obedience, contrition and humility, ordinances and priesthood, and mercy and Atonement.

We realize that these spiritual tools provided by the Carpenter of Nazareth have such power to influence our destiny that our growth and development are meant to be of generation, and not just of maturation. We can be born again as new creatures in Christ by a mystical transformation utilizing otherworldly tools that we cannot explain. (See 2 Corinthians 5:17). The dismantling of our earthly clay may be traumatic, accomplished with the figurative equivalents of sledgehammers and crowbars, and the occasional small explosive, but through the lingering dust kicked up into the air we can see that God is up to something. The run-down cottage we had been living in is slowly being transformed by a celestial craftsman who visualizes the construction of a tabernacle fit to be the eternal dwelling place of our souls. We realize that Heavenly Father is using tools that run on the power of the priesthood, that have an infinite supply of energy from rechargeable spiritual batteries, that have been designed to create an environment for us that will be so much more than just an overnight stay in a cheap hotel.

The course of our development may involve costly change-orders, but the objective of the Master Carpenter is a remodel that will create a spiritual figure in the embodiment of our "perfect frame." The accounting of cost overruns will be measured only in terms of contrition, and will be swallowed up in His sacrifice. During construction, He will put the tape measure around our hearts, and not our heads. He will use blueprints that call for the use of tools upon which a monetary value cannot be placed. His workplace safety standards will far exceed those established by OSHA. The premium for Workman's Compensation Insurance will be paid for with the tool of repentance, and the insurance policy of the Atonement will provide the benefit of forgiveness.

During the process, not a hair of our heads will be lost. Our struggle to achieve the spiritual equivalent of cardiovascular fitness will be measured in soul-sweat, and somehow we will be able to call upon our bodies to produce more red blood cells. Their greater oxygen carrying capacity will enable us to go the second mile, to receive the tool of spiritual independence that eliminates our insensitivity to our destiny. The Savior's program of spiritual aerobics will allow us to run and not be weary, and to walk and not faint. Our capabilities will expand, and an organic transformation will no longer bind us to red blood cells, but to the life-generating tools of oaths and covenants, and promises and ordinances.

To facilitate our progression, the Carpenter of Nazareth will use a tool known as The Word of Wisdom. Its principles have been given to the Saints because of the particularly persuasive and well-entrenched influence of wickedness in our society, and "in consequence of the evil and designs which do and will exist in the hearts of conspiring men in the Last Days." (D&C 89:4). The Carpenter of Nazareth has leveled the playing field by giving us this important tool to combat the adversary. It nurtures our enjoyment of moral agency, while allowing its exercise to rule without abatement. The truth be told, we are given some wiggle room relating to our obedience to the laws of health, even as we are given pointed and specific tools to identify the pathway to happiness. Thus, is preserved the lynchpin of the Plan "that every man may act in doctrine and principle pertaining to futurity, according to the moral agency which (God has) given unto him, that every man may be accountable for his own sins in the day of judgment." (D&C 101:78).

In general, we are quite pleased with ourselves and with the sophisticated tools we use in our approach to Twenty-first century health care. The 1950s saw medical advances like the heart-lung machine that enabled surgeons to perform open-heart procedures that had been heretofore unthinkable. And yet, even today coronary artery disease remains one of our most daunting health care challenges. We prescribe a cornucopia of therapeutics like blood thinners, high blood pressure medications, and statin drugs, but these stopgap measures are largely ineffective tools that only skirt the real issues that concern a change of heart. The world has a ready diagnosis, but the gospel of Jesus Christ is a virtual war chest of tools that provide effective therapy for cold, stony, and hard hearts. The Atonement is the tool of choice for reconciliation, of which the Carpenter of Nazareth said: "If they harden not their hearts, and stiffen not their necks against me, they shall be converted, and I will heal them." (D&C 112:13).

Over time, we may build up cholesterol deposits in our arteries that choke the very life-blood from our hearts. Arteriosclerosis can threaten our physical lives. However, when we use gospel carpentry tools as the antidotes to the spiritual sclerosis jeopardizing our eternal stability, the pathways through which spirit flows will become as pliable clay in the hands of the Master Potter. The virtue of the massive collection of tools collectively known as the Plan of Salvation is its incredible power to touch our hearts, to change our nature, to soften us and to humble us, and to mold us as little children, to the end that our eternal happiness is secured.

We work hard to avoid physical obesity, but the Carpenter of Nazareth is also a personal trainer with celestial certification, Who encourages us to avoid the sugary temptations that contribute to spiritual obesity and flabbiness. They might taste good, but they pile on the calories of corruption. Indulgence makes delayed gratification more difficult, interferes with our awareness of personal responsibility and accountability, distorts healthy self-esteem, and damages the development of interpersonal relationships. The tools of the Carpenter that combat the obsession of our society with self-absorption include faith, divine nature, individual worth, knowledge, choice and accountability, good works, integrity, and virtue. (See "Young Women Values").

"Aha!" said the cartoon philosopher Pogo, who might have been talking about the reckless, self-centered, and self-destructive behavioral tools of the adversary. "Here we have someone paying for the sin of excess. The hobnailed boots of indiscretion's marathon dancer tap a rowdy two-step across the terracotta of his consciousness. Excess was his master. Reason was cast into the rumble seat of his libidinous juggernaut. Now the piper must be paid!" (Walt Kelly).

Indulgence in the self-defeating behaviors that neglect the tools of the Sabbath day, tithing, fasting, and prayer, comes at a heavy cost. For every physical regulation relating to our bodies, the Carpenter of Nazareth has provided tools that are their spiritual counterparts. To Him, a tool is a tool; He sees no distinction between the spiritual and the physical sides of our nature. (See D&C 29:34).

As we learn to use the tools of His trade, we will find "wisdom and great treasures of knowledge, even hidden treasures." (D&C 89:19). These include increased faith, spiritual power, and testimony. We will catch a glimpse of how Daniel must have felt in the worldly court of Darius, when he received the tools of "knowledge and skill in all learning and wisdom," and "understanding in all visions and dreams." (Daniel 1:17).

We live in the midst of Spiritual Babylon, adjacent to the wilderness of worldliness and the stench of sin, and an on-going trade show that hawks the wares of telestial temptation, but we must not compromise our standards, yield to the rising tide of mediocrity, or be swayed by the siren song of Satan's sentinels. The tools of the Savior's gospel trade allow us, as His disciples, to hold fast to the undeviating standard of celestial bound souls. Our eyes are fixed on the prize, because "vice is a monster of so frightful mien, as to be hated needs but to be seen; Yet seen too oft, familiar with her face, we first endure, then pity, then embrace." (Alexander Pope).

In the physical world, we have learned that if we do not ingest enough iron, we will become anemic. But there are also trace elements that are required to avoid spiritual anemia. The Carpenter of Nazareth employs metaphysical mechanisms as tools of His trade, that enable the Spirit to be bound to the blood flowing through our veins.

If pregnant women are deficient in folic acid, their babies will be at risk of neural tube defects, or serious spinal cord anomalies. Just so, if we do not consistently include in our diet the folic acid of faith, we will suffer spiritual spina bifida. We will be unstable in all our ways. (See James 1:8). We will be double-minded, and subject to spiritual anencephalia. For all practical purposes, a major portion of our brain, that would have otherwise meticulously monitored all aspects of our spiritual development, will be missing.

Just so, if the octane rating of the fuel that fires our faith is too low, we may limp along with our engines misfiring badly. Our fear will diminish our discipleship. The Carpenter of Nazareth has perfected a fuel additive that is designed to add needed horsepower during our push to the finish line. For example, He was able to power the performance of Paul, who provided us with the familiar endorsement: "I have fought a good fight, I have finished my course, I have kept the faith." (2 Timothy 4:7).

In the 1970s, a medical procedure was perfected to remove impurities from the bodies of those suffering from kidney failure. Today, those who go to dialysis centers do so to have contaminants removed from their blood, because their kidneys cannot accomplish the task on their own. The natural man is the spiritual equivalent of one who is in acute kidney failure, who "is an enemy to God, and has been from the fall of Adam, and will be, forever and ever, unless he yields to the enticings of the Holy Spirit...and becometh as a child, submissive, meek, humble, patient, full of love, willing to submit to all things which the Lord seeth fit to inflict upon him, even as a child doth submit to his father." (Mosiah 3:19). He is the stubborn individual who will not use the tools that have been providentially provided for him, who strikes out on his own, and fashions works of his own hands, worshipping "gods of wood or of stone," desperately clinging to the indefensible position that they are somehow the keys to his salvation. (Abraham 1:11).

The Sacrament has been provided as a tool so that we can remove impurities from our hearts. "Though your sins be as scarlet," counseled Isaiah, "they shall be as white as snow; though they be red like crimson, they shall be as wool." (Isaiah 1:18). There are gospel tools that effectively treat hostility, gall, rancor, and even bad blood. The Plan provides the gurney of the Sacrament service, where we may go to seek relief, where we may be given transfusions of the spiritual element to keep us going, at least until in a week's time it becomes necessary to repeat the process. The Carpenter of Nazareth learned that to be a master of His trade, He would need to be the servant of all, and for as long as we frequent His gospel blood-bank, we will be both recipients and donors, beneficiaries and benefactors.

The liver removes toxins from our bodies, but the tool of repentance removes the stain and the stench of sin from our souls. Reconciliation through the Atonement detoxifies us from the cares and the conditioning influences of the world, and from the process of homogenization that occurs as we are ground down by the vicissitudes of life.

Epinephrine secreted by the adrenal glands helps us to deal with every day stress. The tool of prayer helps us to deal with the stress that is built-in to mortality. The pituitary has been called the master gland that secretes hormones that regulate many of the vital functions of our bodies. As we draw closer to the Carpenter of Nazareth, its spiritual equivalent, the Holy Ghost, will comfort us and help us to maintain our overall spiritual equilibrium.

We give little thought to our autonomic nervous system, that regulates the day-to-day physical activities of our bodies. The Light of Christ nurtures our spirits, but most of us give it equally little attention. But as we study matters out in our own minds preparatory to receiving answers to our prayers, we become actively, rather than passively, involved in the process of inquiry. We dust off the tool of agency, and actually use it as it was envisioned. We move beyond the rusted tools of control, coercion, compulsion, intimidation, and external influence to the bright and shiny precision instruments of friendly persuasion and independence of action. We expand our capabilities, as we exercise the gifts, resources, and reserves provided by the perfect Plan of Salvation. Spencer W. Kimball promised: "If there be eyes to see, there will be visions to inspire. If there be ears to hear, there will be revelations to experience. If there be hearts that can understand, know this: that the exalting truths of Christ's gospel will no longer be hidden and mysterious, and all earnest seekers may know God and his program." (C.R., 10/1966).

We have the 5 physical senses of sight, hearing, smell, taste, and touch. But there is a spiritual sixth sense that is a tool of inestimable worth. The Holy Ghost is like a "Leatherman," the original multi-purpose tool. Lorenzo Snow recalled the cascade of feelings that poured forth at his baptism: "It was a tangible immersion in the heavenly principle or element, the Holy Ghost; and even more real and physical in its effects upon every part of my system than the immersion by water; dispelling forever, so long as reason and memory last, all possibility of doubt or fear in relation to the fact handed down to us historically, that the Babe of Bethlehem is truly the Son of God." ("Biography and Family Record of Lorenzo Snow," p. 7-9).

Our spiritual sixth sense is as a tool that allows us to see beyond the limited horizon of our vision, and to be touched by the virtue of the word of God so that we can savor eternal life with taste buds that are sensitive to eternal worlds. Our spiritual sixth sense helps us to smell the sweet fragrance of celestial gardens and hear their harmonic melodies, not just with our ears, but also with our joints and sinews. When we walk in the light and embrace the principles of truth, we brim over with charity as we find luxurious accommodations in the household of faith. We let virtue garnish our thoughts unceasingly. We cultivate a comfortable, contented, and confident companionship with the Spirit, and the doctrine of the priesthood washes over our minds and our hearts as the dews from heaven. We celebrate the light, and the Plan becomes a talisman of truth that is interwoven into the fabric of our being until its expression bursts forth as a coat of many colors. Its principles become elements of a tapestry that is everlasting, and without compulsion or coercion we become independent agents with the power to embrace our destiny and claim our eternal reward. (See D&C 121:45-46).

If, along the way, our spiritual muscles stretch a bit, the Carpenter of Nazareth can use that discomfort as a useful tool. It can even be our friend. Our pain receptors have practical purposes and tangible benefits. Diabetics are at real risk of injury because they cannot feel pain. Perhaps the Savior wanted us to be able to feel and deal with physical and emotional distress because we need to develop empathy for His sacrifice. Perhaps growing pains are necessary to really comprehend the Atonement.

The Carpenter of Nazareth uses perspiration as well as soul sweat, as tools to teach us about fortitude. If we can't stand the heat, we are admonished to get out of the kitchen! "I would thou wert hot or cold," said the Savior. (Revelation 3:14). The application of heat is an essential element in the process of purification. It ramps up our metabolism, gets our juices flowing, and stimulates us to move along on the path of progression. "Then flew one of the seraphims unto me," wrote Isaiah, "having a live coal in his hand, which he had taken with the tongs from off the altar. And he laid it upon my mouth, and said, Lo, this hath touched thy lips; and thine iniquity is taken away, and thy sin purged." (Isaiah 6:6-7).

The Carpenter of Nazareth also judiciously uses the tool of friendly persuasion. The word "beseech" is used in the scriptures 118 times, and 65 times in the New

Testament alone. When working with homeowners who didn't have a clear vision of what they wanted, or needed, to make their house a home, Joseph had to be a psychologist as well as a carpenter. He had a lot more experience than his neighbors when it came to crafting fine furnishings, and his suggestions would have been based not only on their perceived needs, but also on what would actually be the best fit for them, given their circumstances. Joseph would have been a good mentor to his Son, the Carpenter of Nazareth, as he groomed Him to become a motivational speaker who could change the world with the tools at hand, one Galilean at a time.

The Carpenter of Nazareth uses the tool of fatigue. Joseph must have had deadlines to meet, and customers with unreasonable expectations, but his work ethic kept him in his shop no matter what, until all of their orders had been successfully completed. We never read a bad review in the scriptures, that complains about careless or shoddy workmanship on the part of Joseph or his son. Jesus must have learned from Joseph that perfectionists can push themselves to the point that they feel they have no more to give.

But even then, we read His admonition: "Whosoever shall compel thee to go a mile, go with him twain," and we realize that He took His responsibilities to another level. (Matthew 5:41). The tool of fatigue can teach us a lot about ourselves, and about who we really are, especially when everything is on the line and all eternity hangs in the balance. Then, like the proverbial footprints in the sand, when we have utterly exhausted our own resources, the Carpenter of Nazareth will step up and carry our burdens for us. He will descend below any sacrifice we could ever make, for He is in a league all His own. (See D&C 122:8). His compassion is not something anyone could have taught Him, but it probably was to His advantage that He wasn't born with a silver spoon in His mouth.

The Carpenter of Nazareth uses the tool of testimony. All of us have been faced with times when withdrawals have needed to be made from our spiritual bank accounts. If we are fortunate, we have beforehand faithfully and consistently made deposits, in order to be prepared in our moment of need with a cushion of confidence that flows from our own courage and commitment, as well as from the condescension and compassion of our Creator. Testimony can be the financial tool of faith, to make sure we are not writing checks that cannot be cashed.

There is no monetary stipend associated with the Plan of Salvation, but it does provide us with the tools of the trade, that we might by the sweat of our brow earn enough of the currency of faith to secure our own accommodations, pay our bills on time, and occasionally indulge ourselves with some of the finer things of life. Interestingly, just as Millennials so often do in their relationships with their earthly parents, the Plan anticipates that eventually we'll return Home to move back in with our Heavenly Parents, and live under one roof, as we did at first.

One day, we may show up at Their doorstep in the same condition as the naval combat pilot who barely made it back to his ship. As the story goes, this World War II aviator had left the security of his aircraft carrier to undertake a dangerous mission over hostile territory. True to the predictions of his superior officers, he endured bad weather, flack from enemy anti-aircraft fire, and engaged in lethal dogfights with adversaries whose sole purpose was to kill him. His craft was hit numerous times by machine gun fire that riddled his fuselage, and by shrapnel that tore away parts of his wings. His Plexiglas canopy was shattered, and he could hardly see through blood-splattered goggles to navigate back to his ship.

As he came in for a landing in the midst of a storm on the pitching deck of the carrier, his controls were nearly useless, his descent was too steep and his angle was wrong. He was frantically waved off by the crewman on deck who was guiding him in, but he figured he had only one chance, and he would take it. With a sickening thump, as he pancaked his aircraft on the deck, its fuel tank burst into flame, and the tail hook failed to engage the cables that would have jerked him to a halt. Careening into the safety net at the far end of the deck, what was left of his plane crumpled into twisted metal.

A rescue crew in asbestos suits rushed to his aid, smothered the wreckage in fire-retardant foam, clamored up to the cockpit, cut him free of his safety harness, grabbed him by the shoulders, yanked him out of the plane, and dragged him to safety. Doctors and nurses attended to his wounds even before he arrived at sickbay. Due to their skill and attention, as well as to his unconquerable spirit, he made a remarkable and full recovery. For his heroism and gallantry in action, he was awarded the Distinguished Flying Cross, and given thirty days' leave for rest and recuperation. This is how most of us will return from our mortal mission to the presence of our Father. God-speed to us all. (Paraphrased from an address given by Boyd K. Packer).

At that joyful reunion, we'll probably hear Him tell us that all our trials and tribulations gave us experience, and were for our good. (See D&C 122:7). We will all be together again, and soon we will be busily engaged in the family business, utilizing tools of the trade with which we have gained an intimate familiarity.

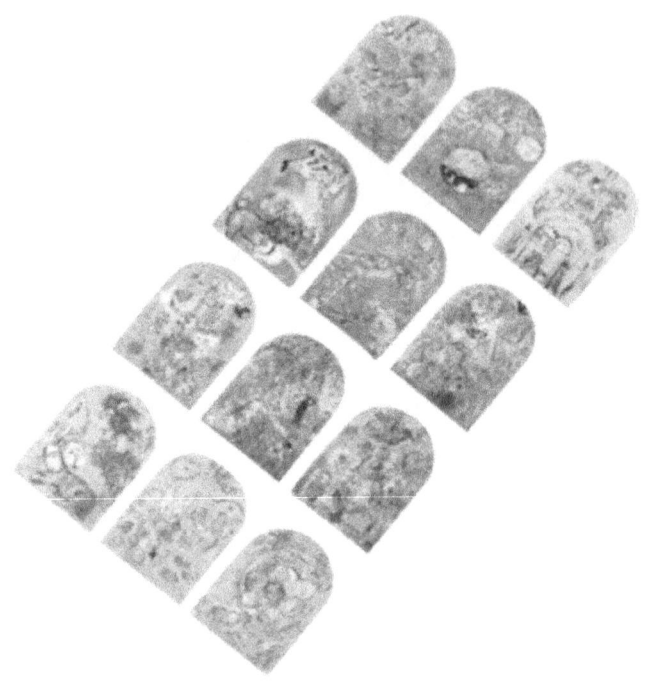

"The sons of Jacob were twelve: The sons of Leah;
Reuben, Jacob's firstborn, and Simeon, and Levi, and
Judah, and Issachar, and Zebulun: The sons of Rachel;
Joseph, and Benjamin: And the sons of Bilhah,
Rachel's handmaid; Dan and Naphtali:
And the sons of Zilpah, Leah's
handmaid; Gad and Asher."
(Genesis 35:22-26).

The Twelve Tribes of Israel

I can't take credit for all of the scholarship that went into this description of the Twelve Tribes of Israel, although I have significantly editorialized my sources that include the scriptures, Josephus, Wikipedia, and LDS.org., to name just a few. I have collated and organized diverse materials in an attempt to bring coherence to holy writ, doctrine, and historical, apocryphal, and pseudepigraphical accounts that have proven to be confusing to many students of the scriptures. My objective in studying the Twelve Tribes was simply to gain greater familiarity with my roots. I hope this collection of resources helps you to do that as well, whether you are a literal or adopted member of the House of Israel. At the end is a short discussion of the Ten Lost Tribes of Israel that is solely my own work.

The twelve sons of Jacob / Israel:

By Leah: Reuben, Simeon, Levi, Judah, Issachar, and Zebulun.
By Rachel: Joseph (Ephraim and Manasseh / a double portion), and Benjamin.
By Bilhah (Rachel's maid): Dan and Naphtali.
By Zilpah (Leah's maid): Gad and Asher

Reuben

Until the creation of the first Kingdom of Israel around 1050 B.C., Reuben was part of a loose confederation of Israelite tribes. No central government existed, and in times of crisis, the people were led by leaders known as Judges. With the threat of Philistine incursions, however, the twelve Israelite tribes formed a centralized monarchy (made up of the Kingdoms of Israel in the north, and Judah in the south) to meet the challenge. The new kingdom was called the United Monarchy, with Saul as its first king. After his death, all the tribes, with the exception of Judah in the south, remained loyal to the United Monarchy / Kingdom of Israel in the north. After the death of Saul's son and successor to the throne, Reuben joined the ten other northern Israelite tribes in making David, who was then the king of Judah in the south, the king of a re-united Kingdom of Israel.

According to the Book of Chronicles, Reuben aided David in conquering the Jebusite City of David, paving the way for the establishment of Jerusalem as the seat of

Israelite religion. However, when David's grandson Rehoboam took the throne around 930 B.C., the northern tribes split from the House of David / Kingdom of Israel / United Monarchy to re-form the Northern Kingdom. Reuben then remained part of the Northern Kingdom until it was conquered by Assyria around 723 B.C.. The tribes of the Northern Kingdom were deported, and from that time, Reuben was lost to history as one of the Ten Lost Tribes of Israel.

Simeon

Following the conquest of Canaan by the Israelites around 1200 B.C., Joshua allocated the land among the twelve tribes. At its height, the territory occupied by Simeon was in the southwest of Canaan, that was an insignificant rural backwater. Simeon was considered one of the less significant tribes in the Kingdom of Judah.

Simeon was the second son of Jacob and of Leah. Following the death of Joshua, the Israelites asked the Lord which tribe should be first to occupy its allotted territory, and Judah was chosen. Judah invited Simeon to fight with it in an alliance, in order to secure their allotted territories.

Simeon had been one of the strongest tribes during the wandering in the desert. But afterwards, the tribe seems to have dwindled in size, which was divine punishment for its reaction to the rape of Dinah.

As part of the kingdom of Judah in the south, what remained of Simeon was ultimately subjected to the Babylonian captivity, and when it ended, all remaining distinctions between Simeon and the other tribes in the Kingdom of Judah were lost, in favor of a common identity as "Jews." The Apocrypha reports that Simeon was deported by the Babylonians to Ethiopia. A few modern-day groups claim descent from the tribe of Simeon, with varying levels of academic and rabbinical support.

Levi

The Levites were the high priests of the Israelites, and descended from Levi, who was the third son of Jacob and Leah. Moses and his brother Aaron were both Levites. When Joshua led the Israelites into the land of Canaan, the Levites were the only tribe that received cities but not land, "because the Lord the God of Israel Himself (was) their inheritance." (Deuteronomy 18:2). The Levites had both religious and political responsibilities. In return, the landed tribes were expected to give tithes to the Levite priests who served in the temple. As Paul taught: "They that are of the sons of Levi, who receive the office of the priesthood, have a commandment to take tithes of the people according to the law." (Hebrews 7:5).

Samuel, Ezekiel, Ezra, and Malachi were all Levites. The descendants of Aaron, who was the first Levite high priest of Israel, continued in the priestly class. Even today, there are family dynasties within the tribe of Levi that have been integrated into Jewish and Samaritan societies.

When John the Baptist conferred the Aaronic Priesthood upon Joseph Smith and Oliver Cowdery, on April 15, 1829, he pronounced a blessing, saying: "Upon you my fellow servants, in the name of Messiah, I confer the Priesthood of Aaron, which holds the keys of the ministering of angels, and of the gospel of repentance, and of baptism by immersion for the remission of sins; and this shall never be taken again from the earth, until the sons of Levi do offer again an offering unto the Lord in righteousness." (D&C 13:1).

In an epistle to the Saints dated September 6, 1842, Joseph Smith wrote: "Behold, the great day of the Lord is at hand; and who can abide the day of his coming, and who can stand when he appeareth? For he is like a refiner's fire, and like fuller's soap; and he shall sit as a refiner and purifier of silver, and he shall purify the sons of Levi, and purge them as gold and silver, that they may offer unto the Lord an offering in righteousness." (D&C 128:24).

Judah

Judah was the fourth son of Jacob and of Leah. The tribe of Judah, its conquests, the centrality of its capital in Jerusalem, and the worship of Yahweh figure prominently in the books of Deuteronomy through 2 Kings. According to the Book of Joshua, following a partial conquest of Canaan by Israel shortly before 1200 B.C., land was allocated among the twelve tribes. Judah's divinely ordained inheritance encompassed most of the southern portion of the Land of Israel, including the Negev, the Wilderness of Zin, and Jerusalem.

In the Book of Judges, Judah is identified as the first tribe that was allowed to occupy the Promised Land. According to the Book of Judges, Judah invited Simeon to fight with it to secure their allotted territories.

The Book of Samuel describes God's repudiation of a budding monarchy initiated by the northern tribe of Benjamin. That honor was then bestowed upon the tribe of Judah for all time in the person of King David. In Samuel's account, after the death of Saul, all the tribes other than Judah remained loyal to the House of Saul, while Judah chose David as its king. However, after the death of Saul's son and successor to the throne of Israel, all the other Israelite tribes backed David, who was then the king of Judah, as the king of a re-united Kingdom of Israel. Ultimately, the Savior would come through David's line.

The Book of Kings follows the expansion and unparalleled glory of a united monarchy under David's son Solomon. However, with the accession of Solomon's son Rehoboam, around 930 B.C., the ten Northern Tribes, under the leadership of Jeroboam from the tribe of Ephraim, split from the House of David to create the Northern Kingdom. The Book of Kings is uncompromising in its low opinion of its larger and richer neighbor to the north, and portrays its conquest by Assyria in 722 B.C. as divine retribution for that Kingdom's return to idolatry.

Judah and Benjamin remained loyal to the House of David. These tribes formed the Kingdom of Judah, that existed until the Babylonian captivity around 586 B.C. when the population was deported.

Judah was the leading tribe of the Kingdom of Judah. David belonged to the tribe, and the royal line continued after the fall of the Kingdom of Judah. The traditional Jewish belief was that the Messiah would be of the Davidic line, based on the Lord's promise to David of an everlasting throne for his offspring.

Many Jewish leaders and prophets claimed membership in the tribe of Judah. For example, Isaiah, Amos, Habakkuk, Joel, Micah, Obadiah, Zerchariah, and Zephaniah all belonged to Judah. Later, after the Babylonian exile ended, Zerubbabel, who was the leader of the first Jews to return, was also said to be of the Davidic line, as was Nehemiah.

By lineage, Jesus was a member of the tribe of Judah. (See Matthew 1:1-6 & Luke 3:31-34). Because it was part of the Kingdom of Judah in the south, the tribe of Judah survived the destruction of Israel (the Northern Kingdom) by the Assyrians, only to be later subjected to the Babylonian captivity. When Judah and Benjamin returned from that Babylonian exile, tribal affiliations were abandoned, probably because of the impossibility of reestablishing previous land holdings. Only the special religious role of the Levites was maintained. Jerusalem became the sole place of worship and sacrifice among the returning exiles, northerners and southerners alike. The distinction between tribes was lost in favor of a common identity as Jews that has endured to this day. Since Simeon and Benjamin had been very much the junior partners in the Kingdom of Judah, it was Judah that gave its name, that of the Jews, to this identity.

After the fall of Jerusalem to the Babylonians, Babylonia became the focus of Jewish life for a thousand years. The first Jewish communities in Babylonia started with the exile of the tribe of Judah to Babylon in 597 B.C., as well as after the destruction of the temple in Jerusalem in 586 B.C..

Ethiopian tradition asserts descent from Israelites of the tribes of Dan and Judah, who returned with the Queen of Sheba after her visit to King Solomon in Jerusalem. Hence the phrase "The Lion of the Tribe of Judah has conquered," that is found in the Book of Revelation.

Haile Selassie was the emperor of Ethiopia from 1930 to 1974. His full title in office was "By the Conquering Lion of the Tribe of Judah, His Imperial Majesty Haile Selassie I, King of Kings of Ethiopia, Elect of God." This title reflects Ethiopian dynastic traditions, which hold that all monarchs must trace their lineage to the offspring of King Solomon and the Queen of Sheba.

Latter-day revelation describes how "the children of Judah may begin to return to the lands which (the Lord) didst give to Abraham, their father." (D&C 109:64). It also demands: "Let them who be of Judah flee unto Jerusalem, unto the mountains of the Lord's house." (D&C 133:13). Then, "they also of the tribe of Judah, after their pain, shall be sanctified in holiness before the Lord, to dwell in his presence day and night, forever and ever."(D&C 133:35). This corroborates Paul's teaching: "Behold, the days come, saith the Lord, when I will make a new covenant with the house of Israel and with the house of Judah." (Hebrews 8:8).

Dan

Dan and Naphtali were the sons of Jacob and Bilhah, Rachel's maidservant. The tribe of Dan was the second largest Israelite tribe, after Judah. Until the formation of the first united Kingdom of Israel around 1050 B.C., Dan was a part of a loose confederation of Israelite tribes. No central government existed, and in times of crisis the people were led by leaders known as Judges.

Following the conquest of Canaan by the Israelites around 1200 B.C., Dan was the last tribe to receive its inheritance, a small enclave in the central coastal area. Members of the tribe of Dan were seafarers, which was unusual for an Israelite tribe. Its territory, not very extensive initially, was further diminished by the incursions of its dangerous Philistine neighbors. The most celebrated Danite was Samson, who figured prominently in tales of conflict with the Philistines.

All twelve Israelite tribes formed a strong centralized monarchy (made up of the Kingdoms of Israel in the north, and Judah in the south) to meet the challenge from the Philistines. The new kingdom was called the United Monarchy, with Saul as its first king. After the death of Saul, all the tribes except Judah remained loyal to the House of Saul, but after the death of his son and successor to the throne of Israel, the tribe of Dan joined the other northern Israelite tribes in making David, who was already the king of Judah, the monarch of a re-united Kingdom of Israel.

However, on the accession of David's grandson Rehoboam, around 930 B.C., the Northern Tribes split from the House of David to re-invent a Kingdom of Israel known as the Northern Kingdom. The territory of Dan was conquered by the Assyrians, and exiled Dan was lost to history, as one of the Ten Lost Tribes of Israel.

Today, Ethiopian Jews claim descent from the tribe of Dan, claiming that its members migrated into the Kingdom of Kush, now Ethiopia and Sudan, along with members of the tribes of Gad, Asher, and Naphtali, after the destruction of the Temple of Zerubbabel.

Naphtali

Following the completion of the conquest of Canaan by the Israelite tribes around 1200 B.C., Joshua allocated the land among the twelve tribes. Naphtali's inheritance was along the Lower Galilee. In this region was the highly fertile plain of Gennesaret, that brought prosperity to the region.

Naphtali was the second son of Jacob and Bilhah, Dan being the first. Militarism figured prominently in Naphtali's history. In the Gideon narrative Naphtali is one of the tribes that joined in an attack against Midianite invaders.

Until the formation of the first Kingdom of Israel around 1050 B.C., Naphtali was a part of a loose confederation of Israelite tribes. No central government existed, and in times of crisis, the people were led by leaders known as Judges. With the threat of Philistine incursions, the Israelite tribes decided to form a strong centralized monarchy to meet the challenge, and Naphtali joined the new kingdom with Saul as the first king. After his death, all the tribes other than Judah remained loyal to the House of Saul, but after the death of Saul's son who was successor to the throne of Israel, the tribe of Naphtali joined the other northern Israelite tribes and made David, who was then the king of Judah, the king of a re-united Kingdom of Israel. However, on the accession of David's grandson Rehoboam, around 930 B.C., the northern tribes split from the House of David to re-create a Kingdom known as the Northern Kingdom.

Around 732 B.C., Napthali, one of the most northern tribes, was one of the first to be conquered and then deported by Assyria. With its exile, it was lost to history. The Kingdom of Israel continued to exist until around 723 B.C., when it was again invaded by Assyria and the balance of the population deported. From that time, the tribe of Naphtali has been counted as one of the Ten Lost Tribes of Israel. There has been speculation that the Bukharian Jews living in Central Asia today are descendants of Naphtali.

Gad

Gad was the seventh son of Jacob, one of the two descendants of Zilpah, his handmaid, the second being Asher.

After the Exodus from Egypt, and following the conquest of Canaan by the Israelites around 1200 B.C., Joshua allocated the land among the twelve tribes. Gad settled near the Jordan River, on land the tribe desired as soon as it saw it, before it had even crossed the Jordan. However, the location was never secure from invasion and attacks, since to the south it was exposed to the Moabites, and like the other tribes east of the Jordan, it was exposed on the north and east to the Assyrians.

Until the formation of the first Kingdom of Israel around 1050 B.C., Gad was a part of a loose confederation of Israelite tribes. No central government existed, and in times of crisis, the people were led by leaders known as Judges. With the threat of Philistine incursions, the Israelite tribes decided to form a strong centralized monarchy to meet the challenge, and Gad joined the new kingdom with Saul as the first king. After his death, all the tribes other than Judah remained loyal to the House of Saul, but after the death of Saul's son and successor to the throne of Israel, Gad joined the other northern tribes in making David, who was then the king of Judah, the king of a re-united Kingdom of Israel.

However, on the accession to the throne of Rehoboam, David's grandson, around 930 B.C., the northern tribes split from the House of David to re-create a Kingdom of Israel as the Northern Kingdom. Gad was a member of that kingdom until it was conquered by Assyria around 723 B.C.. The population was deported, and thereafter lost to history. It is now counted as one of the Ten Lost Tribes of Israel.

In the Talmud, it is Gad, along with the tribe of Reuben, that is portrayed as being the first tribe to be carried away by the Assyrians. Some members of Gad may have escaped and settled in southern Spain. The ancient name of the city of Cadiz was Gadir, that means city of Gad, and the people in Cadiz still call themselves Gaditanos, that means Gadites. The word Gad, which is Guad in Spanish, is found all over southern Spain. Written on the coat of arms of Cadiz is its Latin name, which is Gadium, or the city of Gad.

Asher

The tribe consisted of descendants of Asher, the eighth son of Jacob. Asher was one of the two descendants of Zilpah, a handmaid of Leah, the other being Gad.

Following the completion of the conquest of Canaan by the Israelites around 1200

B.C., Joshua allocated the land among the Twelve Tribes. To Asher, he assigned western and coastal Galilee, a region with cool temperatures and plentiful rainfall, making it some of the most fertile land in Canaan. It boasted rich pastures, wooded hills, and orchards. Consequently, Asher was particularly prosperous, and was known for its production of good quality olive oil.

Until the formation of the first Kingdom of Israel around 1050 B.C., Asher was a part of a loose confederation of Israelite tribes. No central government existed, and in times of crisis, the people were led by leaders known as Judges. With the threat of Philistine incursions, the Israelite tribes decided to form a strong centralized monarchy to meet the challenge, and Asher joined the new kingdom with Saul as the first king. After his death, all the tribes other than Judah remained loyal to the House of Saul, but soon thereafter, Asher joined the other northern Israelite tribes in making David, who was then the king of Judah, the king of a re-united Kingdom of Israel.

On the accession of Rehoboam, David's grandson, around 930 B.C., the northern tribes split from the House of David to re-form a Kingdom of Israel known as the Northern Kingdom. Asher was a member of that kingdom until it was conquered by Assyria around 723 B.C., when the population was deported. From that time, Asher was lost to history and became one of the Ten Lost Tribes of Israel. Interestingly, we learn in the New Testament that Anna the prophetess, and her father, Phanuel, belonged to the tribe of Asher.

Despite appearing to have had close contact with the markets of Phoenicia, Asher appears to have been fairly disconnected from the other tribes of Israel. Additionally, it seems to have taken little part in the antagonism between the Canaanites and the other tribes of Israel.

Issachar

Issachar was the ninth son of Jacob, and the fifth son of Leah, his wife. Traditionally, Issachar was dominated by religious scholars. Jewish religious scholars seem to have been either Levites, or from the tribe of Issachar.

Following the completion of the conquest of Canaan by the Israelites around 1200 B.C., Joshua allocated the land among the twelve tribes. Issachar's territory stretched from the Jordan River in the east, to the coast in the west. This region included the fertile Esdraelon plain.

Since the members of the tribe of Zebulun were traditionally seen as merchants, and

Issachar as religious teachers, Issachar and Zebulun were benefited by a mutually advantageous relationship, whereby Issachar would devote its time to the study and teaching of Torah, while Zebulun would provide financial support in exchange for a share of Issachar's spiritual reward.

As part of the Kingdom of Israel, the territory of Issachar was conquered by the Assyrians, and the tribe was lost to history, it becoming one of the Ten Lost Tribes of Israel.

Zebulun

Following the conquest of Canaan, Joshua allocated the land among the twelve tribes. Zebulun's territory was at the southern end of the Galilee. The tribe consisted of descendants of Zebulun, sixth son of Jacob and Leah. At the division of the land of Israel among the seven tribes not yet provided for, the lot of Zebulun was third. Jesus was raised within the territory of Zebulun.

In Jewish tradition, the tribe of Zebulun was considered to have a mutually advantageous relationship with the tribe of Isaachar. Issachar's devotion to the study and teaching of the Torah, was financially supported by Zebulun in exchange for a share of the spiritual reward gained from such learning. The terms Issachar and Zebulun came to be used by Jews for anyone engaged in such a symbiotic relationship.

Zebulun played an important part in the early history of Israel. At the census of the tribes while in the Desert of Sinai during the second year of the Exodus, Zebulun numbered 57,400 men fit for war. (1 Chronicles 12:33).

Joseph

The tribe of Joseph was descended from Joseph, the son of Jacob and Rachel. Joseph was the brother to Benjamin, the other son of Rachel and Jacob. The sons of Joseph were Ephraim and Manasseh, and together they traditionally constituted the tribe of Joseph. Consequently, Joseph is sometimes not listed as one of the tribes, in favor of Ephraim and Manasseh in its place. The tribe of Joseph is often termed the House of Joseph, or the "two half-tribes of Joseph." Scholars believe that Joseph was originally considered a single tribe, and only split into Ephraim and Manasseh later.

Joseph's inheritance in the land of Canaan was one of the most valuable parts of the country, and the House of Joseph became the most dominant group in the Northern Kingdom of Israel. Eventually, the territories of both Ephraim and Manasseh were conquered by the Assyrians, and the tribe was exiled and thereafter lost to history. Despite a familial connection to Ephraim, Benjamin associated with the southern tribes and became part of the Kingdom of Judah As a result, its people escaped Assyrian captivity, and were only subjected to the later Babylonian exile. When these exiles were allowed to return, the distinction between Benjamin and the other tribes in the kingdom of Judah was lost in favor of a common identity as "Jews."

Despite both Ephraim and Manasseh being led away as two of the Ten Lost Tribes of Israel, several modern-day groups claim descent from them, with varying levels of academic and rabbinical support. The Yusufzai tribe (literal translation: The Sons of Joseph) in Afghanistan and Pakistan, have a long tradition connecting them to the exiled Kingdom of Israel. The Samaritans claim descent from these tribes, as do many Persian Jews. In Northeast India, the Mizo Jews claim descent from Manasseh. Similar traditions are held by the Telugu Jews in Southern India, who claim descent from Ephraim.

Considered less plausible by academic and Jewish authorities are the claims of western Christian groups. Many members of The Church of Jesus Christ of Latter-day Saints identify themselves as descended from Ephraim and Manasseh, believing that the lost tribes will be restored in the latter days as prophesied by Isaiah. Some Mormons believe that this would be the fulfillment of part of the Blessing of Jacob, that states that Joseph is a fruitful bough, even a fruitful bough by a well; whose branches run over the wall, with the interpretation that the wall is the ocean. In fact, The Book of Mormon teaches: "Behold, our father Jacob also testified concerning a remnant of the seed of Joseph. And behold, are not we a remnant of the seed of Joseph?" (3 Nephi 10:17).

Benjamin

The tribe consisted of descendants of Benjamin, the youngest son of Jacob and Rachel. The temple in Jerusalem was traditionally said to be partly in the territory of the tribe of Benjamin, with the balance of it in that of Judah.

After the conquest of the Promised Land promised land until the formation of the first Kingdom of Israel around 1050 B.C., Benjamin was a part of a loose confederation of Israelite tribes. No central government existed, and in times of crisis the people were led by leaders known as Judges.

Following the conquest of Canaan by the Israelites around 1200 B.C., Joshua allocated the land among the twelve tribes. To Benjamin, he assigned the territory between that of Ephraim to the north and Judah to the south. The westward boundary of the tribe of Benjamin stretched as far as the Mediterranean Sea.

Responding to a growing threat from the Philistines, the Israelite tribes formed a strong, centralized monarchy. Its first king was Saul, from the tribe of Benjamin, that at the time was the smallest of the tribes. He reigned for 38 years. After his death, all the tribes other than Judah remained loyal to the House of Saul, but after the death of his son and successor to the throne of Israel, the tribe of Benjamin joined the northern Israelite tribes in making David, then king of the Southern Kingdom of Judah, king of the united Kingdom of Israel and Judah. On the accession of Rehoboam, David's grandson, around 930 B.C., the northern tribes split from the House of David to re-form a Kingdom of Israel. Benjamin remained a part of the Southern Kingdom of Judah, until it was conquered around 586 B.C., and the population deported to Babylonia.

The tribe of Benjamin is described in the Bible as being taught to fight left-handed, so as to be able to wrong-foot its enemies. (See Judges 3:15-21 & 20:16, & 1 Chronicles 12:2).

The Book of Judges recounts how the rape of a concubine who belonged to a member of the tribe of Levi, by members of the tribe of Benjamin resulted in a battle at Gibeah, in which the other tribes of Israel sought vengeance, and during which the members of Benjamin including women and children, were systematically slaughtered. With Benjamin nearly wiped out, it was decided that the tribe should be allowed to survive, and its last 600 men were married off to women who were descended from Manasseh, whose men had been killed when it was discovered that they had not participated in the war against Benjamin. (So much for a Band of Brothers!)

Initially, although Jerusalem was in the territory allocated to the tribe of Benjamin, it remained under the independent control of the Jebusites, until it was finally conquered by David in the 11th century B.C., and made the capital of the united Kingdom of Israel. After the breakup of that United Monarchy, Jerusalem continued as the capital of the Southern Kingdom of Judah.

After the dissolution of the United Kingdoms of Israel and Judah around 930 B.C., Benjamin joined Judah as a junior partner in the Kingdom of Judah, or the Southern Kingdom. The Davidic dynasty, that had roots there, continued to reign in Judah. As part of the Southern Kingdom of Judah, Benjamin survived the destruction of the Kingdom of Israel by the Assyrians, only to be later subjected to the Babylonian captivity. When that captivity ended, the distinctions between Benjamin and Judah was lost in favor of a common identity as Israel, though as late as the time of Jesus of Nazareth, Paul still identified himself by his Benjamite ancestry. "I also am an Israelite," he wrote, "of the seed of Abraham, of the tribe of Benjamin." (Romans 11:1).

Manasseh and Ephraim were of the House of Joseph (A Double Portion).

Manasseh (the older of the two brothers).

Along with Benjamin, Joseph was the son of Jacob and Rachel. Joseph's sons Ephraim and Manasseh received "a double portion," and together they are often described as being of the "House of Joseph."

Until the formation of the first Kingdom of Israel around 1050 B.C., the tribe of Manasseh was part of a loose confederation of Israelite tribes. No central government existed, and in times of crisis, the people were led by leaders known as Judges. With the threat of Philistine incursions, the Israelite tribes decided to form a strong centralized monarchy to meet the challenge, and Manasseh joined the new kingdom with Saul as its first king. After his death, all the tribes other than Judah remained loyal to the House of Saul, but after the death of Saul's son and successor to the throne of Israel, Manasseh joined the other northern Israelite tribes in making David, who was then the king of Judah in the south, king of a re-united Kingdom of Israel. However, on the accession of Rehoboam, David's grandson, around 930 B.C., the northern tribes split from the House of David to re-form a Kingdom of Israel as the Northern Kingdom. Manasseh was a member of that kingdom until, around 723 B.C., it was conquered by Assyria and the population deported. From that time, Manasseh has been numbered among the Ten Lost Tribes of Israel, although some modern groups claim descent from the tribe.

We do know from The Book of Mormon that, "Aminadi was a descendant of Nephi, who was the son of Lehi, who came out of the land of Jerusalem, who was a descendant of Manasseh, who was the son of Joseph who was sold into Egypt by the hands of his brethren." (Alma 10:3).

Ephraim (the younger of the two brothers).
The tribe of Ephraim was one of the tribes of Israel. The tribe of Manasseh, together with Ephraim, formed the House of Joseph. The descendants of Joseph became two of the tribes of Israel, whereas each of the other sons of Jacob was the founder of only one tribe. In the Blessing of Jacob, Ephraim and Manasseh are treated as a single tribe, making it likely that originally Ephraim and Manasseh were considered one tribe, that of Joseph.

Following the completion of the conquest of Canaan by the Israelites around 1200 B.C., Joshua allocated the land among the twelve tribes. The territory given to the tribe of Ephraim was at the center of Canaan. The region later named Samaria consisted mostly of Ephraim's territory. The area was mountainous, giving it protection, and also highly fertile, providing an opportunity for prosperity.

Ephraim was the second son of Joseph and Asenath. Contrary to tradition, Ephraim received the birthright blessing from his grandfather Jacob, that was the blessing of the firstborn, instead of Manasseh. Although Manasseh was the elder son, Jacob had foreseen that Ephraim's descendants would be greater than his brother's. In some accounts, Ephraim is portrayed as domineering, haughty, discontented, and jealous, but in classical rabbinical literature, the biblical founder of the tribe is described as being modest and unselfish. These rabbinical sources allege that it was on account of modesty and selflessness that Jacob gave Ephraim precedence over Manasseh, the elder of the two. In these sources, God upholds the blessing in honor of the righteousness of Jacob, and makes Ephraim the leading tribe.

Ephraim became the progenitor of the tribe of Ephraim. In the Last Days, their privilege and responsibility is to bear the priesthood, take the message of the restored gospel to the world, and raise an ensign to gather scattered Israel. The children of Ephraim will crown with glory those from the north countries who will return in the Last Days. (See D&C 133:26-34).

A written record of one group from the tribe of Ephraim that was led from Jerusalem to America about 600 B.C. is described in the scriptures as the stick of Ephraim or Joseph, commonly called The Book of Mormon. It and the stick of Judah, that is the Bible, form a unified testimony of the Lord Jesus Christ, His resurrection, and His divine work among these two tribes (Joseph and Judah) of the house of Israel.

According to Joseph Smith, a branch of Ephraim will be broken off and will write another testament of Christ. (See J.S.T. Genesis 50:24-26 & 30-31). The stick of Judah and the stick of Joseph will become one in the Lord's hand. (See Ezekiel 37:15-19). The writings of Judah and of Joseph shall grow together. (See 2 Nephi 3:12). In The Book of Mormon, the keys of power or control over the record of the stick of Ephraim were committed to the prophet Moroni. (See D&C 27:5).

Ephraim is often seen as the tribe that embodied the entire Northern Kingdom, and the royal house resided in its territory, just as Judah was the tribe that personified the Kingdom of Judah to the south, and provided its royal family.

From the end of the conquest of Canaan by Joshua, who himself was a descendant of Ephraim, the tribe of Ephraim was a part of a loose confederation of Israelite tribes. No central government existed, and in times of crisis the people were led by leaders known as Judges. With the threat of Philistine incursions, the Israelite tribes decided to form a strong centralized monarchy to meet the challenge, and the tribe of Ephraim joined the new kingdom, with Saul as the first king. After his death, all the tribes other than Judah remained loyal to the House of Saul, but after the death of Saul's son and successor to the throne of Israel, the tribe of Ephraim joined the other northern Israelite tribes and made David, who was then the king of Judah in the south, king of a re-united Kingdom of Israel.

However, on the accession of Rehoboam, David's grandson, around 930 B.C., the northern tribes split from the House of David to form the Northern Kingdom of Israel. Its first king was Jeroboam, who came from the tribe of Ephraim. (See 1 Kings 1:26).

The accents of the tribes were distinctive enough, even at the time of the confederacy, so that when the Israelites of Gilead, under the leadership of Jephthah, fought the tribe of Ephraim, their pronunciation of "shibboleth" as "sibboleth" was considered sufficient evidence to single out individuals from Ephraim, to be punished with immediate death at the hands of the Israelites of Gilead.

Ephraim remained a member of the Northern Kingdom until it was conquered by Assyria around 723 B.C. and the population deported. From that time, the tribe of Ephraim was lost to history and has been counted as one of the Ten Lost Tribes of Israel. In The Book of Mormon, the Savior revealed something about these lost tribes: "And verily, verily, I say unto you that I have other sheep, which are not of this land, neither of the land of Jerusalem, neither in any parts of that land round about whither I have been to minister. For they of whom I speak are they who have not as yet heard my voice; neither have I at any time manifested myself unto them. But I have received a commandment of the Father that I shall go unto them, and that they shall hear my voice, and shall be numbered among my sheep, that there may be one fold and one shepherd; therefore I go to show myself unto them." (3 Nephi 16:1-3).

Ephraim was the most dominant of the tribes in the Northern Kingdom, that led to "Ephraim" becoming a synonym for the entire kingdom. As part of that kingdom, the territory of Ephraim was conquered by the Assyrians, and the tribe exiled; the manner of their exile led to their further history being lost. However, several modern day groups claim descent, with varying levels of academic and rabbinical support. The Church of Jesus Christ of Latter-day Saints believes that a significant portion of its members are descended from, or have been adopted into, the tribe of Ephraim. They argue that they are charged with restoring the lost tribes in the latter days as prophesied by Isaiah, and that the tribes of both Ephraim and Judah will play important leadership roles for covenant Israel in the Last Days. Some believe that this would be the fulfillment of part of the Blessing of Jacob, that states that Joseph is a fruitful bough, even a fruitful bough by a well; whose branches run over the wall, interpreting the "wall" as the ocean. (See Genesis 49:22).

"And it shall come to pass in that day that the Lord shall set his hand again the second time to recover the remnant of his people which shall be left, from Assyria, and from Egypt, and from Pathros, and from Cush, and from Elam, and from Shinar, and from Hamath, and from the islands of the sea. And he shall set up an ensign for the nations, and shall assemble the outcasts of Israel, and gather together the dispersed of Judah from the four corners of the earth. The envy of Ephraim also shall depart, and the adversaries of Judah shall be cut off; Ephraim shall not envy Judah, and Judah shall not vex Ephraim." (2 Nephi 21:11-13).

In The Church of Jesus Christ of Latter-day Saints, patriarchal blessings include a declaration of lineage, typically stating that the person is of the house of Israel and a descendant of Abraham, belonging to a specific tribe of Jacob. Many Latter-day Saints are of the tribe of Ephraim, the tribe given the primary responsibility to lead the latter-day work of the Lord. Because each of us has many bloodlines running in us, two members of the same family may be declared as being of different tribes in Israel. It does not matter if a person's lineage in the house of Israel is through a bloodline or by adoption. Church members are counted as descendants of Abraham and heirs to all the promises and blessings contained in the Abrahamic covenant.

The Ten Lost Tribes of Israel

According to the Bible, the Kingdom of Israel (or Northern Kingdom) was one of the successor states to the older United Monarchy (also called the Kingdom of Israel), that came into existence around 930 B.C., after the northern Tribes of Israel rejected Solomon's son Rehoboam as their king. Nine landed tribes formed the Northern Kingdom: The tribes of Reuben, Issachar, Zebulun, Dan, Naphtali, Gad, Asher, and Ephraim and Manasseh through Joseph. In addition, some members of tribe of Levi, who had no land allocation, were found in the Northern Kingdom. The tribes of Judah and Benjamin remained loyal to Rehoboam, and formed the Kingdom of Judah in the south, sometimes called the Southern Kingdom.
Nephi said: "There are many who are already lost from the knowledge of those who are at Jerusalem. Yea, the more part of all the tribes have been led away; and they are scattered to and fro upon the isles of the sea; and whither they are none of us knoweth, save that we know that they have been led away." (1 Nephi 22:4-5).

Nevertheless, he prophesied: "The Lord God will proceed to make bare his arm in the eyes of all the nations, in bringing about his covenants and his gospel unto those who are of the house of Israel. Wherefore, he will bring them again out of captivity, and they shall be gathered together to the lands of their inheritance; and they shall be brought out of obscurity and out of darkness; and they shall know that the Lord is their Savior and their Redeemer, the Mighty One of Israel." (1 Nephi 22:11-12).

In order to accomplish this, "the Lord shall utterly destroy the tongue of the Egyptian sea; and with his mighty wind he shall shake his hand over the river, and shall smite it in the seven streams, and make men go over dry shod." (2 Nephi 21:15).

The Lord revealed to Joseph Smith: "And they who are in the north countries shall come in remembrance before the Lord; and their prophets shall hear his voice, and shall no longer stay themselves; and they shall smite the rocks, and the ice shall flow down at their presence. And an highway shall be cast up in the midst of the great deep." (D&C 133:26-27).

When speaking of Israel, most people think of the Jews, and when referring to the Gathering of Israel, they have in mind the return of the Jews to the land of Jerusalem. It should be remembered, however, that the Jews represent but one of the Twelve Tribes of the House of Israel. "For lo...I will sift the house of Israel among all nations." (Amos 9:9).

Isaiah spoke of the Last Days, when the Lord would set His Hand a second time to gather His people. The first time was either during the Exodus from Egypt, or during Israel's return from the Babylonian captivity, depending upon one's point of view. As Isaiah saw it, the House of Israel would return from the seven known countries of his day, "from Assyria, and from Egypt, and from Pathros (or upper Egypt), and from Cush (or Ethiopia), and from Elam (east of Babylonia), and from Hamath (Northern Syria), and from the isles of the sea (the rest of the world)." (2 Nephi 21:11).

The apocryphal writer Esdras recorded this version of the escape of the Ten Lost Tribes of Israel from Assyria: "Those are the ten tribes, which were carried away prisoners out of their own land in the time of Hosea the king whom Salmanasar the king of Assyria led away captive, and he carried them over the waters, and so came they into another land. But they took this counsel among themselves, that they would leave the multitude of the heathen, and go forth unto a further country, where never mankind dwelt, that they might there keep their statutes, which they never kept in their own land. And they entered into Euphrates by the narrow passage of the river. For the most High then shewed signs for them, and held still the flood, till they were passed over. For through that country there was a great way to go, namely, of a year and a half: and the same region is called Arsareth. Then dwelt they there until the latter times; and now when they shall begin to come, the Highest shall stay the stream again, that they may go through." (Apocrypha, 2 Esdras 13:40-47).

Interestingly, Esdras declared that the Ten Tribes determined to keep the statutes of the Lord, even though they had not kept them when they were living in the Northern Kingdom. Other scriptures attest to the facts that these tribes were led away by the Lord, have since been continually preserved by Him, have had their own prophets minister among them, had the Savior Himself visit them after His resurrection, have kept their own scriptures and records, keep the statutes of God, and will be led out of the North Country by His power to help build the New Jerusalem.

curiosity

"In the dark
recesses of memory, in
unbidden suggestions, in
trains of thought unwittingly
pursued in multiplied waves and
currents all at once flashing and rushing,
in dreams that cannot be laid to the force of
instinct, in the obscure, but certain intuitions
of the spiritual life, we have glimpses of a
great tide of life ebbing and flowing,
rippling and rolling and beating
about where we cannot see it."
(E.S. Dallas).

The Unknown Possibilities of Existence

Q: "You just don't get it, do you Jean Luc? The trial never ends. We wanted to see if you had the ability to expand your mind and your horizons. And for one brief moment you did. For that one fraction of a second, you were open to options you had never considered. That is the exploration that awaits you. Not mapping stars and studying nebula, but charting the unknown possibilities of existence." ("Star Trek, The Next Generation," Episode 185).

We left our heavenly home in order to do just as Q said; to chart the unknown possibilities of existence. We have come "like gentle rain through darkened skies, with glory trailing from our feet as we go, and endless promise in our eyes. We are strangers from a realm of light, who have forgotten all - the memory of our former life and the purpose of our call. And so, we must learn why we're here, and who we really are." (Adapted from "Saturday's Warrior," lyrics by Doug Stewart).

Life's greatest questions plumb the depths of the unknown possibilities of existence. Where did we come from? Why are we here? Where are we going? There are about 3,300 questions in the Bible, and many relate to these three basics, including "Adam, where art thou?" (Genesis 3:9). "Where is he that is born king of the Jews?" (Matthew 3:2). "Which is the greatest commandment in the law?" (Matthew 22:36). "Who is my neighbor?" (Luke 10:29). "Am I my brother's keeper?" (Genesis 4:9). "If a man die, shall he live again? (Job 14:14). "If God is with us, who can be against us?" (Romans 8:31). "What must I do to be saved?" (Acts 16:30).

Answers require that we embark upon personal journeys that are similar to the 5 year mission of the Starship Enterprise: "To explore strange new worlds, to seek out new life and new civilizations, to boldly go where no-one has gone before." We are reminded of Dag Hammarskjöld's observation: "The longest journey is the journey inward, for he who has chosen his destiny has started upon a quest for the source of his being."

When we chart the unknown possibilities of existence, we sweep aside the self-limiting belief that "the sky is the limit." We substitute the mind and soul expanding certainty that "heaven is the limit," in keeping with one of the greatest contributions of Joseph Smith, namely, the "knowledge of what is to come after death. For, he did much to clarify our understanding of heaven and to make it seem worth working for." ("My Religion & Me" course manual).

When we open our minds to options we have never before considered, we envision a special place called Kolob, signifying the first creation, nearest to the celestial, or the residence of God. Of our relationship to that realm, William W. Phelps wrote: "No man has found pure space, nor seen the outside curtains, where nothing has a place." In the matrix within which he imagined Kolob, there was no end to matter, space, spirit, or race; virtue, might, wisdom, or light; union, youth, priesthood, or truth; glory, love, or being; because these things are markers on the chart upon which are revealed the bounds and conditions of the unknown possibilities of existence. (See: "If You Could Hie to Kolob").

A point of reference like Kolob grounds us to certainties that are real, even if they remain elusive. As we chart the unknown possibilities of existence, we struggle to wrap our minds around an expansion of knowledge that doubles every 12 months, and with the realization that there is no way on earth to keep up. If we do not stay focused on Kolob, we risk succumbing to the pessimistic observation that not only has knowledge outpaced truth, but also that truth has a hard time even holding its own. Truth seems to be treading water, at best, and at worst, it appears to be mired in the quicksand that is the product of the evils and designs that exist in the hearts of conspiring men. (See D&C 89:4). Knowing that Kolob exists gives us a measure of hope that we will not only be able to distinguish between truth and error, but also between knowledge and wisdom, and to make correct choices based on the intelligent application of the former in order to experience the latter.

Accepting the challenge to expand our minds and our horizons forces us to ask ourselves difficult questions: Have we embraced the moral element of responsibility to goes hand in hand with knowledge? Do we have the spiritual and intellectual maturity to couple knowledge with accountability? When we dare to grapple with these interrogatives, we come to an epiphany, as we determine to do our best to be righteous stewards in all circumstances. It was with this in mind that Joshua asked Israel: "Choose you this day whom ye will serve." (Joshua 24:15).

We are blessed with the privilege to be bathed in an innervating vitality, and to be empowered with an otherworldly serenity. As Bagheera, the powerfully built black panther confided to Mowgli the man-cub: "I had never seen the jungle. They fed me behind bars from an iron pan until one night I felt that I was Bagheera the Panther, and no man's plaything, and I broke the lock with one blow of my paw, and I came away." (Rudyard Kipling, "The Jungle Book").

Voyagers on the sea of life who have embraced the task that lies ahead know that their undertaking is consistent with God's mission statement to bring to pass their immortality and eternal life. (See Moses 1:39). These enlightened explorers use the 3.3 pounds of grey matter with which they have been endowed (consisting of around 100 billion cells with 100 trillion - 100,000,000,000,000 - neural connections) to good advantage. Such a breathtaking network blesses them with enough resources and to spare, in order to expand their minds and their horizons. God has clearly provided sufficient wiggle room to allow them to do so. He has created the means for them to step off the edge of forever, and to cast off onto the uncharted ocean of eternity, to discover the unknown possibilities of existence.

In the process, they must abandon the idolatry that obstructs their vision, and they must conquer their self-deification. They must abandon the worship of their own creations, and liberate themselves from their lust for power, avarice, domination, and the cult of the state. They cannot chart the unknown possibilities of existence unless they first recognize their fundamental moral obligations as transcendent and divine.

Their physical well-being will not save them, because what is at stake is feeling and not raw knowledge. As they embark upon the long and arduous journey of discovery, they will change their hearts and their nature, the scales will fall from their eyes, and the course that lies before them will be illuminated, so that they may see with the eye of faith into eternity. God, Who is the Master Navigator, stands ready to bestow upon them that perspective, and only waits upon their initiative before He acts in their behalf.

In the aforementioned Star Trek episode, Captain Jean Luc Picard asked: "Q, what is it you're trying to tell me? To which, Q tantalizingly replied: "You'll find out."

The gospel anchors us to
the infinite, and confirms that
our destiny was prepared in the pre-
earth existence, is molded in mortality,
and will be established in eternity,
when the heavens will smile
upon us and we will
be clothed with
the glory of
God.

The Year Without Summer

According to William Humphreys, a Weather Bureau scientist writing almost a century later, the cold year of 1816 was caused largely by volcanic ash in the earth's atmosphere. Such ash partially shielded the earth from the sun's rays, but permitted heat to escape from the atmosphere, thus lowering the temperature. Three major volcanic eruptions took place between 1812 and 1817. Soufriere on St. Vincent erupted in 1812, Mayon in the Philippines in 1814, and Tambora on the island of Sumbawa, in Indonesia, in 1815. The worst was Tambora, a 13,000-foot volcano. It has been estimated that its titanic explosion blew up to 100 cubic miles of dust, ash, and cinder into the atmosphere, generating a globe-girdling veil of volcanic dust, in the largest eruption in recorded history. By comparison, the 1980 eruption of Mt. St. Helens, in Washington state, blew 0.3 cubic miles of ash into the atmosphere. (This would make Tambora's eruption 83 times as powerful as St. Helens').

The idea that volcanic ash suspended in the atmosphere might lower the earth's temperature can be traced to Benjamin Franklin. But it was not until 1913, that William Humphreys published a now classic paper documenting the correlation between volcanic eruptions and worldwide temperature depressions. He reported that volcanic ash is 30 times more effective in keeping the sun's radiation out than in keeping the earth's in. Once blown into the stratosphere, it can take years for the ash to settle to the ground. In the meantime, the average temperature of the world may drop precipitously.

The chief effect seems to be the dramatic depression of minimum temperatures during the summer. Humphreys showed that the most pronounced dips in the world temperature curve have been, without exception, associated with violent volcanic eruptions that have ejected large quantities of ash into the stratosphere.

An example is the famous cold year of 1785, that followed the eruptions of Mount Asama in Japan and Skaptar Jokull in Iceland. These produced a widely observed "dry fog," the phenomenon that led Benjamin Franklin to suspect a relationship between cold weather and volcanic eruptions.

Even relatively small variations in the earth's annual mean temperature can cause widespread changes in the arctic ice pack and world sea levels, in desert boundaries, and in the geographical limits of plant, animal, and even human life. According to Humphreys, volcanic ash blown into the stratosphere once every couple of years would continuously maintain temperatures low enough to cover the earth with a mantle of snow so extensive as to be self perpetuating, and thereby initiating an ice age.

The New England farmer of 1816, of course, knew nothing of such theories. He knew only that something had gone terribly wrong with the weather. When that dreadful summer was followed by a winter so severe that the mercury froze in thermometers, he must surely have thought the change was permanent.

In April 1815, Mt. Tambora's eruption could be heard 1,600 miles away, in Sumatra. Of the 12,000 inhabitants of the Indonesian island upon which Tambora was located, only 26 survived. Over 4,000 vertical feet of the volcano was blown away. Ash and sulphate aerosols took months to gradually settle back to the troposphere where weather systems could then wash them back to the ground.

The eruption was the biggest in perhaps the last 10,000 years, dwarfing Krakatoa (1883 - 4.5 cubic miles), The stratospheric cloud of ash circled the earth, spread throughout the northern hemisphere, and reflected enough sunlight to severely disrupt normal weather patterns. In southern latitudes, the impact was minor, but in much of Europe it caused near famine conditions. In New England, it helped changed religious history. (See below).

The year 1816 is legendary in the annals of weather. It has been called "the year without a summer." No subject in the weather history of New England arouses so much interest today as does the summer of 1816. From May through September, an unprecedented series of cold spells chilled the northeastern United States and adjoining Canadian provinces, causing a backward spring, a cold summer, and an early fall. There was heavy snow in June and frost in July and August. All across the Northeast, crops were repeatedly killed by the cold, raising the specter of widespread famine.

The amazing weather of 1816 is well documented in the diaries and memoirs of those who endured it. Benjamin Harrison, a farmer in Bennington, Vermont. termed it "the most gloomy and extraordinary weather ever seen." Since relatively few settlers had yet crossed the Mississippi, most of our weather observations for 1816 come from the eastern United States, particularly the Northeast, where there was already a long-established tradition of weather watching.

April and May 1816 were both cold months over the Northeast, with frost delaying spring planting. Flowers were late in blooming and many fruit trees did not blossom until the end of May, only to have their budding leaves killed by a hard frost that also destroyed corn and other crops. Warm weather finally came during the first few days of June, and farmers forgot the May frost and began replanting. But even as they labored, a cold front was approaching that would bring disaster. During its passage, temperatures tumbled dramatically under the onslaught of arctic-like air.

From June 6 to 9, severe frost occurred in a wide swath of destruction, from Canada to Virginia. Ice was reported in Philadelphia, and "every green herb was killed, and vegetables of every description very much injured," according to a contemporary report. In Vermont, the ice was an inch thick on standing water, and icicles were a foot long. Corn and other staple crops were killed to the ground, and the leaves of the deciduous trees withered and died, and fell to the ground, as in late fall.

People shivered, dug out their winter clothing, and built roaring fires to keep warm. Farmers watched helplessly as their fields and gardens blackened, and as newly shorn sheep, though sheltered, perished. Thousands of birds also froze to death.

The culmination of this remarkable wave of cold air came early on the 11th of June. An observer noted: "Heavy frost. Vegetables killed at 5 o'clock. Temperature 30.5 degrees." Overall, frost killed almost all the corn in New England, the main food staple, as well as most garden vegetables.

There were two snowfalls. The first on the 6th of June, brought relatively light snow to New York State, Vermont, New Hampshire, and Maine. The second occurred only a day later, following the passage of a second cold front. It brought moderate to heavy snow to northern New England.

This first summer cold spell was followed by 4 weeks of relatively good weather. Farmers again replanted, and crops were growing well when, at the end of the first week in July, a new, inexplicable, outbreak of cold mercilessly descended upon New England. It indiscriminately killed corn, beans, cucumbers, and squash, and soon had local farmers talking again about the threat of famine.

Then, the remainder of the month was more seasonable, although there was another onslaught of cold around the 18th of July. Hardier grains such as wheat and rye, however, endured well, and by August, farmers were joking about their earlier "famine fever."

On August 20th, however, yet another cold front arrived, and temperatures tumbled in New Hampshire by 30 degrees. During the next 2 days, frost was reported all across New England, and most of the remaining corn in low lying areas that had been afforded some protection, was destroyed. A more severe frost came at the end of August, that, with a note of finality, put an end to the hopes of many corn growers, and whole fields had to be cut up for fodder.

The first week of September was relatively warm, but around the 11th an outbreak of cold again visited the Northeast, with hard frost reported in northern and central New England. It was the widespread and killing frost of September 27th, however, that irrevocably closed out the dismal growing season, and destroyed all hope of even a small harvest in New England.

A Concord New Hampshire newspaper reported that throughout New England less than 10% of the normal crop was harvested. In Montreal, it was feared that many parishes in Quebec would be in a state of famine before winter set in. During the severe winter of 1816-1817 that soon followed, the spectre of starvation became a reality for many.

As would be expected, a general migration from New England to the Midwest occurred the following year. Vermont, New Hampshire, and Maine, the states that had borne the brunt of the cold weather, suffered the greatest exodus of bankrupt farmers. More than sixty Vermont towns experienced population losses. Most Vermonters who left headed westward, stirred by newspaper advertisements of available lands in New York, Pennsylvania, and Ohio, that promised "well-timbered, well-watered, easily accessible and undeniably fertile land, and all to be had on long-term payments for only two or three dollars an acre."

Although New England farmers considered their crop failures a local tragedy, they could not have known that the abnormal weather was widespread throughout the Northern Hemisphere. In England, it was almost as cold as in the United States, and 1816 was a famine year there, as it was in France and Germany.

The meager harvest of grain was nowhere near sufficient for the needs of the people, and every resource for sustenance was carefully husbanded. Even forest berries and roots were preserved. The spring of 1817 brought the worst want, and in many parts of the county, families were brought to the verge of starvation.

In Norwich, Vermont, the crops of Joseph Smith Sr. were frozen along with nearly everyone else's. Unaware of the cause of the killing frosts, and discouraged by successive crop failures, the Smiths dejectedly left Vermont, for good.

"In 1816, Joseph Smith Sr. went to Palmyra, Ontario County, New York, in the company of a Mr. Howard. Before departing he called on his creditors and debtors to settle existing accounts, but some of them neglected to bring their accounts to the settlement. Evidently their claims against him were satisfied either by payment of cash or by the transfer of claims Joseph had against his debtors. Believing that all accounts were settled, he proceeded to Palmyra and purchased land. He then sent a communication to Lucy instructing her to stow their belongings on a wagon and prepare to move. Joseph arranged with Caleb Howard, cousin of the Mr. Howard who had traveled with him to Palmyra, to drive the team and bring his family to New York. Before Lucy Smith left to join her husband, however, additional creditors appeared and presented their uncancelled accounts for payment. Lucy described this event: 'I concluded it would be more to our advantage to pay their unjust claims than to hazard a lawsuit. Therefore, by making considerable exertion, I raised the required sum, which was one hundred and fifty dollars, and liquidated the demand.' When well-meaning neighbors proposed to ease the burden by raising money through subscription, Lucy refused. 'The idea of receiving assistance in such a way as this was indeed very repulsive to my feelings.'

Accounts settled, Lucy and her eight children, ranging in age from the infant Don Carlos to seventeen-year-old Alvin, set out for New York with Caleb Howard. In South Royalton, Lucy's mother, Lydia, was injured by an overturning wagon. When Lydia was taken to her son's home in Tunbridge, mother and daughter tearfully exchanged goodbyes. The aged Lydia admonished her daughter: 'I beseech you to continue faithful in the service of God to the end of your days, that I may have the pleasure of embracing you in another and fairer world above.' Lydia died two years later in Royalton of the injuries she had received at that time.

As the Smith family continued their journey, it became apparent to Lucy that 'Mr. Howard, our teamster, was an unprincipled and unfeeling wretch.' He spent the money Joseph, Sr., had paid him to gather the Smith family to New York on drinking and gambling. Joseph Jr., at the time a boy of ten, later remembered that even though he had not yet fully recovered from his leg operation, Howard made him walk 'in my weak state through the snow forty miles per day for several days, during which time I suffered the most excruciating weariness and pain.'" ("Church History in The Fulness of Times" student manual, Chapter Two: Joseph Smith's New England Heritage).

You won't find the phrase "The Lord works in mysterious ways" in the Bible, although He certainly does. The line is a misquote of the words of a popular English hymn written by William Cowper in 1773 that reads: "The Lord moves in mysterious ways, His wonders to perform. He plants His footsteps in the sea, and rides upon the storm. Deep in unfathomable mines of never failing skill, He treasures up His bright designs, and works His sovereign will. Ye fearful saints, fresh courage take; the clouds ye so much dread are big with mercy and shall break in blessings on your head. Judge not the Lord by feeble sense, but trust Him for His grace. Behind a frowning providence He hides a smiling face. His purposes will ripen fast, unfolding every hour. The bud may have a bitter taste, but sweet will be the flower. Blind unbelief is sure to err, and scan His work in vain. God is His own interpreter, and He will make it plain."

It is thought that Cowper, as his inspiration for the poem, used these verses from Isaiah: "For my thoughts are not your thoughts, neither are your ways my ways, saith the Lord. For as the heavens are higher than the earth, so are my ways higher than your ways, and my thoughts than your thoughts." (Isaiah 55:8-9). Whatever spiritual insight may have prompted Cowper to pen the lines of what is now a popular hymn, they were surely prophetic, as they presage the events that drove the Smith family to Palmyra, New York, hard by the Hill Cumorah.

In the words of Joseph Smith: "I was born in the year of our Lord one thousand eight hundred and five, on the twenty-third day of December, in the town of Sharon, Windsor county, State of Vermont. My father, Joseph Smith, Sr., left the state of Vermont, and moved to Palmyra, Ontario (now Wayne) county, in the state of New York, when I was in my tenth year, or thereabouts. In about four years after my father's arrival in Palmyra, he moved with his family into Manchester in the same county of Ontario. Some time in the second year after our removal to Manchester, there was in the place where we lived an unusual excitement on the subject of religion. I was at this time in my fifteenth year. During this time of great excitement my mind was called up to serious reflection and great uneasiness; but though my feelings were deep and often poignant, still I kept myself aloof from all these parties, though I attended their several meetings as often as occasion would permit.

In the midst of this war of words and tumult of opinions, I often said to myself: What is to be done? While I was laboring under the extreme difficulties caused by the contests of these parties of religionists, I was one day reading the Epistle of James, first chapter and fifth verse, which reads: "If any of you lack wisdom, let him ask of God, that giveth to all men liberally, and upbraideth not; and it shall be given him."

At length I came to the conclusion that I must either remain in darkness and confusion, or else I must do as James directs, that is, ask of God. I at length came to the determination to 'ask of God,' concluding that if he gave wisdom to them that lacked wisdom, and would give liberally, and not upbraid, I might venture. So, in accordance with this, my determination to ask of God, I retired to the woods to make the attempt."

Joseph then recounted how, after kneeling in prayer, he saw two Personages, whose brightness and glory defied all description, standing above him in the air. One of them spake unto him, calling him by name and said, pointing to the other—This is My Beloved Son. Hear Him! (See Joseph Smith History).

And the rest, as they say, is history.

"No man has found pure space, nor seen the outside curtains, where nothing has a place."
(William W. Phelps).

Thoughts of Kolob

"The Lord's throne is in heaven," wrote the Psalmist. (Psalms 11:4). In the beginning when God created the heaven and the earth, He made them temporally and spatially separate. Their bounds and conditions were distinctly different. It was this stroke of genius on the part of our Father that allowed Him to manipulate the laws of physics to create a veil, as it were, so that we would forget all about our pre-mortal home, in order to take full advantage of our mortal condition that is central to His Merciful Plan.

Nevertheless, we do know something about heaven, because according to the Book of Abraham's Facsimile #2, a place exists that is named Kolob, signifying the first creation, nearest to the celestial, or the residence of God. Of our relationship to that realm, William W. Phelps wrote: "No man has found pure space, nor seen the outside curtains, where nothing has a place." In the matrix of the dimensional reality in which he envisioned Kolob, "there is no end to matter, space, spirit, or race, virtue, might, wisdom, or light, union, youth, priesthood, or truth, glory, love, or being," because these are defined by different bounds and conditions that are only comprehensible to God. ("If You Could Hie to Kolob").

Ultimately, said the Lord, "there shall be the reckoning of the time of one planet above another, until thou come nigh unto Kolob, which Kolob is after the reckoning of the Lord's time; which Kolob is set nigh unto the throne of God, to govern all those planets which belong to the same order as that upon which thou standest." (Abraham 3:9). Somehow, it is from Kolob that the order of the other creations of God is temporally and spatially governed, and from there the boundary of heaven is established in such a manner that it is beyond the reach of detection by even the most sophisticated and delicately calibrated instruments utilized by terrestrial scientists. The Hubble telescope can see 10 or 15 billion light years into our past, almost back to the moment of creation at the Big Bang, but it cannot gaze into heaven five minutes. If it could do that, we "would know more than (we) would by reading all that has ever been written on the subject." (Joseph Smith, H.C., 6:50). Especially in the case of higher temporal and spatial dimensions, it would seem that there are some things that need to be believed, to be seen.

Isaiah confirmed that heaven and earth are spatially and temporally separate. "The heaven is my throne," the Lord revealed, "and the earth is my footstool." (Isaiah 66:1).

It is the Spirit, however, that has the power to carry us beyond the perceptible and palpable confines of this world to a place where boundaries become blurred, and the barricade of borders disappears. As John the Revelator exclaimed when he received his apocalypse: "Immediately I was in the spirit, and, behold, a throne was set in heaven." (Revelation 4:2). Joseph F. Smith had a similar experience, when "the eyes of (his) understanding were opened, and the Spirit of the Lord rested upon (him)," and he too saw into the eternal world." (D&C 138:11). Normally, the veil functions as an event horizon that denies our senses any hint of what lies beyond. It is only by the Spirit that the power can be generated to penetrate the barrier that isolates us from the sum and substance of an eternal reality. It is the Spirit that will answer our questions: "O God, where art thou? And where is the pavilion that covereth thy hiding place?" (D&C 121:1).

In the beginning, it was "the Gods (who) organized and formed the heavens and the earth" by defining the boundaries of the temporal universe, not to mention the eternal world. (Abraham 4:1). They did this by the power of faith. They set the conditions "by which the worlds were framed, (and) all things in heaven, on the earth, or under the earth. (These) exist by reason of faith as it existed in (the mind of the Gods). Had it not been for this principle of faith, the worlds would never have been framed, neither would man have been formed of the dust. It is this principle by which Jehovah works, and through which he exercises power over all temporal as well as eternal things." (Joseph Smith, "Lectures on Faith," #1). Perhaps this is why it is only by exercising perfect faith that we can have a true understanding of God's creations, and begin to experience His reality. (See James 2:22). Ultimately, "truth is knowledge of things as they are, and as they were, and as they are to come." (D&C 93:24).

Physics tells us that there are no privileged frames of reference. The galaxies are imbedded in time and imprinted upon a space whose fabric is constantly expanding. If we ask where and when the creation took place, the answer is everywhere and forever. If the universe is warped through time and space into a fourth dimension, it just might expand like a balloon, creating in every instant more space. It seems reasonable that God would utilize our everyday laws of physics to accomplish these purposes within the framework of the eternal thrones, dominions and principalities that are His higher-dimensional reality. This may explain why the Lord said to Moses: "As one earth shall pass away, and the heavens thereof, even so shall another come, and there is no end to my works." (Moses 1:38). "For by him were all things created that are in heaven, and that are in earth, visible and invisible, whether they be thrones, or dominions, or principalities, or powers: all things were created by him." (Colossians 1:16).

For now, our poor lenses cannot discern what is really there. "No man hath seen God at any time in the flesh, except quickened by the Spirit of God." (J.S.T. John 1:18). If it is true that "the light of the body is the eye," then, when the eye is single to faith, our "whole body shall be full of light." (3 Nephi 13:22). On one occasion after having received revelation, Joseph Smith confirmed the veracity of that promise, and declared: "My whole body was full of light, and I could see even out at the ends of my fingers and toes." (N.B. Lundwall, "The Vision," p. 11). This may help to explain why the angel Moroni hovered in the air during his visits to Joseph Smith in his chamber, and why his hands and his feet were naked. (J.S.H. 1:31). He could "see" with every part of his body. Every child of God potentially possesses this gift, and the Lord has promised that it only waits to be revealed. "If your eye be single to my glory," He said, "your whole bodies shall be filled with light, and there shall be no darkness in you; and that body which is filled with light comprehendeth all things." (D&C 88:67). There will come a day when "the sun shall no more go down; neither shall (the) moon withdraw itself: for the Lord shall be (our) everlasting light." (Isaiah 60:20).

When each of us comes face to face with eternity, as surely we must, the spiritual element will transform our mortal clay. Beforehand, while we tarry in the flesh, we might ask under what circumstances does that element quicken us, and how is the pure knowledge that flows from it vitalized? "A man's wisdom maketh his face to shine, and the boldness of his face shall be changed." (Ecclesiastes 8:1). When we are at one with God, when we have spiritually been born of Him and have internalized His divine nature, we will receive His image in our countenances. (Alma 5:14). That image and His likeness will bridge the barriers of time and space to leave their mark as an irrefutable confirmation of our noble birthright. The genetic code that had heretofore defined our nature will be transformed to bless us with an endowment of unearthly powers.

When we move into eternity, time will lose all significance, and "See you later," will cease to be in our vocabulary. Time, that we too frequently viewed as a predator that stalked us all our lives, may then be fondly remembered as the companion that accompanied us on our journey through mortality, reminding us to cherish every moment. We will find that our mortal experience was a tiny fraction of a much larger reality, and that our perspective was faulty as long as we believed it to be unique. We may be shocked to learn that mortality was not our natural dimension, after all. We will come to understand why it was that we were never entirely comfortable in our mortal circumstances, and why we felt like "strangers and pilgrims on the earth." (Hebrews 11:13). This will, in turn, clarify our innate thrust always toward the future, always beyond the horizon, always upward.

While we remain trapped in time, we can only indirectly appreciate the eternities. As we seek learning, even by study and also by faith, "we can make our lives sublime, and departing, leave behind us footprints on the sands of time." (Henry Wadsworth Longfellow, "A Psalm of Life"). There is always the threat, however, that those footprints might be washed away by the incessant wave action of unappreciated temporal and spatial dimensions beating on our shores. "There is a tide (after all) in the affairs of men which, taken at the flood, leads on to fortune." (Shakespeare, "Julius Caesar," Act 4, Scene 2). The gospel anchors us to the infinite, and confirms that our destiny was envisioned in the pre-earth existence, is molded in mortality, and will be established in eternity, when the heavens will smile upon us and we will be clothed with the glory of God. The concept of an infinite hierarchy of temporal and spatial dimensions will finally allow us to make sense of God's mission statement, which is to bring about our immortality and eternal life. (See Moses 1:39).

The veil is almost transparent in our lives when we are spiritually sensitive and prepared to act. As our powers expand, we experience the glittering facets of the life of the Spirit. "To use the careful preparation and training we receive as a springboard, to be capable of disciplined, controlled procedure and to be receptive to flashes of insight, is what solid Latter-day Saints should have going for them in their inner lives. The gospel sets us free to be creative, and sets us creative to become more free. It is the perfect law of liberty." ("My Religion and Me," Lesson #9). Truly, the gospel amplifies the quiet spiritual stirrings that underlie our mortal experience. It is the catalyst that has been added to a celestial cocktail that has been designed to propel us into the presence of God.

"I wish I could remember the days before my birth, and if I knew the Father before I came to earth," mused the poet. "In quiet moments when I'm all alone, I close my eyes and try to see my heavenly home. Although I can't remember and cannot clearly see, I listen to the spirit and so I must believe. But still I wonder, and I hope to find the answer to the question that is on my mind. Where is heaven? Is it very far? I would like to know if it's beyond the brightest star." (Janice Kapp Perry, "Where is Heaven?").

No Jesus = No Peace
Know Jesus = Know Peace

Thou Hast Done Wonderful Things

The prophet Isaiah employed symbolic language that does not teach directly, so we must examine and ponder his words to discover the truths they convey. His most beautiful and profound symbolic language focused on the Savior, as, for example, this familiar expression: "For unto us a child is born, unto us a son is given, and the government shall be upon his shoulder, and his name shall be called Wonderful, Counsellor, the mighty God, the everlasting Father, the Prince of Peace." (Isaiah 9:6).

He described how the Savior has the power to admit or exclude any person from Heavenly Father's presence: "And the key of the house of David will I lay upon his shoulder; so he shall open, and none shall shut; and he shall shut, and none shall open." (Isaiah 22:22). Nephi, who was a great admirer of Isaiah, expanded upon this theme: "Behold, the way for man is narrow, but it lieth in a straight course before him, and the keeper of the gate (of heaven) is the Holy One of Israel; and he employeth no servant there; and there is none other way (we can enter into Heavenly Father's presence) save it be by the gate; for he cannot be deceived, for the Lord God is his name." (2 Nephi 9:41).

Isaiah described how those who did not receive the gospel while on the earth, or who were not valiant in their testimonies while they were here, will go to a spiritual prison, of sorts, where the Savior will show them how to obtain mercy. "And it shall come to pass in that day, that the Lord shall punish the host of the high ones that are on high, and the kings of the earth upon the earth. And they shall be gathered together, as prisoners are gathered in the pit, and shall be shut up in the prison, and after many days shall they be visited." (Isaiah 24:21-22).

Joseph F. Smith taught that the gospel was "preached to those who had died in their sins, without a knowledge of the truth, or in transgression, having rejected the prophets." (D&C 138:32). This makes clear Isaiah's prophetic message: "The Lord has called thee in righteousness, and will hold thine hand, and will keep thee, and give thee for a covenant of the people, for a light of the Gentiles; to open the blind eyes, to bring out the prisoners from the prison, them that sit in darkness out of the prison house." (Isaiah 42:6-7). "Say to the prisoners, Go forth; to them that are in darkness, Shew yourselves. They shall feed in the ways, and their pastures shall be in all high places. They shall not hunger nor thirst; neither shall the heat nor sun smite them: for he that hath mercy on them shall lead them, even by the springs of water shall he guide them." (Isaiah 49:9-10).

The Savior will be our sanctuary, our "strength to the poor and to the needy in his distress, a refuge from the storm, a shadow from the heat, when the blast of the terrible ones is as a storm against the wall. (Isaiah 25:4). He is "as an hiding place from the wind, and a covert from the tempest; as rivers of water in a dry place, as the shadow of a great rock in a weary land." (Isaiah 32:2).

"And in this mountain shall the Lord of hosts make unto all people a feast of fat things, a feast of wines on the lees, of fat things full of marrow, of wines on the lees well refined. And he will destroy in this mountain the face of the covering cast over all people, and the vail that is spread over all nations. He will swallow up death in victory; and the Lord God will wipe away tears from off all faces; and the rebuke of his people shall he take away from off all the earth: for the Lord hath spoken it. And it shall be said in that day, Lo, this is our God; we have waited for him, and he will save us: this is the Lord; we have waited for him, we will be glad and rejoice in his salvation." (Isaiah 25:6-9).

One interpretation of Isaiah 25:6-7, that is popular among Latter-day Saints, is that the mountain he described is a symbol of the temple. (See Isaiah 2:2 and D&C 58:8-9). The feast mentioned in Isaiah 25:6 could be a feast of the words and teachings of Christ. We know that the temple endowment can be like a feast. "And it shall come to pass in the last days, that the mountain of the Lord's house shall be established in the top of the mountains, and shall be exalted above the hills; and all nations shall flow unto it." (Isaiah 2:2).

A vail or veil is a thin covering. Symbolically, it often represented the unbelief that prevented people from embracing the Savior. "And he beheld Satan; and he had a great chain in his hand, and it veiled the whole face of the earth with darkness; and he looked up and laughed, and his angels rejoiced." (Moses 7:26). The "vail" of darkness that is over the earth can only be dismissed by the power of the priesthood.

The Savior will comfort His children, and "swallow up death in victory; and the Lord God will wipe away tears from off all faces." (Isaiah 28:5). There is a sense of intimacy in this tender gesture that is shared only by people who love and trust each other completely.

The Savior will exercise the keys of the Resurrection. "Thy dead men shall live, together with my body shall they arise. Awake and sing, ye that dwell in dust: for thy dew is as the dew of herbs, and the earth shall cast out the dead." (Isaiah 26:19).

The Savior is the bedrock of our faith. "Thus saith the Lord God, Behold, I lay in Zion for a foundation a stone, a tried stone, a precious corner stone, a sure foundation." (Isaiah 28:16). "And now, my sons," Helaman clearly explained to Lehi and Nephi, "remember, remember that it is upon the rock of our Redeemer, who is Christ, the Son of God, that ye must build your foundation; that when the devil shall send forth his mighty winds, yea, his shafts in the whirlwind, yea, when all his hail and his mighty storm shall beat upon you, it shall have no power over you to drag you down to the gulf of misery and endless wo, because of the rock upon which ye are built, which is a sure foundation, a foundation whereon if men build they cannot fall." (Helaman 5:12). He is "the good shepherd, and the stone of Israel. He that buildeth upon this rock shall never fail." (D&C 50:44).

The Savior will restore the gospel to the earth. "And thou shalt be brought down, and shalt speak out of the ground, and thy speech shall be low out of the dust, and thy voice shall be, as of one that hath a familiar spirit, out of the ground, and thy speech shall whisper out of the dust." (Isaiah 29:4). In the process, a most remarkable thing will happen: "I will proceed to do a marvelous work among this people, even a marvelous work and a wonder: for the wisdom of their wise men shall perish, and the understanding of their prudent men shall be hid." (Isaiah 29:14). "They also that erred in spirit shall come to understanding, and they that murmured shall learn doctrine." (Isaiah 29:24).

The Savior, Who knows our trials and directs our paths, used the prophetic powers of one of His favorite servants to reveal how He will influence our lives in the Last Days. Isaiah clothed the Savior and His ministry with beautiful, symbolic expressions, showing us how He has done wonderful things for us.

"I never count the cost of anything. I just find out what the Lord wants me to do, and I do it."
(Brigham Young).

Tithing

The temple is a beacon that orients mankind toward the path leading back home. Accordingly, attending the temple regularly is one of the most important things we can do while on the earth. When Moroni asked us to "come unto Christ" (Moroni 10:32), it was a plea to enter into the ordinances of His priesthood and make temple covenants that would bind us forever to our families. That is the essence of the gospel of Jesus Christ. Therefore, it makes no difference upon which principle of the gospel we may be focusing, the distance to the temple where we ultimately take our bearing on eternity is measured in faith, and not in miles. It may have been with this in mind that, in 1881, obedience to the law of tithing became a requirement for temple attendance for those with an income. (J.D., 22:207-208). Payment of a full tithe provides a good barometer of our spiritual maturity, and is an easy measurement of our core testimony temperature.

"Those who have been thus tithed shall pay one-tenth of all their interest annually; and this shall be a standing law unto them forever, for my holy priesthood, saith the Lord." (D&C 119:4). Of course, we know that tithing has been a part of the gospel since the time of the Patriarchs, but it has been firmly re-established as a foundation principle of the latter-day restoration. The "History of The Church" records that in 1834 Joseph Smith and Oliver Cowdery pledged one-tenth of all that the Lord should give them as an offering for the poor. (H.C., 2:174-175). "The term 'tithing' had been used in some revelations before 1838 (e.g. D&C 64:23; 85:3; & 97:11-12) but the term connoted all free-will offerings or contributions, whether they were more or less than 10 percent. Then, in 1838, the Prophet received the definitive law that would be binding upon the church. (D&C 119).

Prior to this revelation on tithing, an adaptation of the Law of Consecration of property was practiced by the saints to care for the poor, to purchase lands, and to build church facilities. (D&C 42:30-39). The declared spiritual objective of that law was to "advance the cause" of "the salvation of man" (D&C 78:4-7) by creating equality in both "earthly things" and "heavenly things." At the time, this proved to be too difficult to obey, especially under the disruptive conditions suffered by church members in Missouri, and the practice was temporarily suspended in 1840. (H.C., 4:93). The Law of Tithing was given in part to fulfill material needs and to prepare the membership of the church to live the temporal aspects of the Law of Consecration at some future time. Tithing has variously been described as the donation of (1) a tenth of what people owned when they converted; (2) a tenth of their "increase" or income each year; and (3) one workday in ten of their labor, teams, and tools to public projects. Today, tithe payers pay a tenth of their "increase," or income, consistent with the direction given in D&C 119.

A 1970 letter from the First Presidency stated that notwithstanding the fact that members should pay one-tenth of their income, "every member of the church is entitled to make his own decision as to what he thinks he owes the Lord and to make payment accordingly." (3/19/1970). Hence, the exact amount paid is not as important as that each member feels that he or she has paid an honest tenth." ("Encyclopedia of Mormonism").

In the church today, tithes are basically used to support the three-fold mission of the church, to preach the gospel, redeem the dead, and perfect the saints. "The collection of tithing is the responsibility of the bishop in each ward. Tithes are presented confidentially to him or to his counselors. He forwards the tithes collected locally to church headquarters, where a committee consisting of the First Presidency, the Presiding Bishopric, and the Quorum of the Twelve Apostles supervises the distribution and expenditure of tithing funds. (D&C 120). These are used for such purposes as the building and maintenance of meetinghouses, temples, and other facilities, as well as for the partial support of the missionary, educational, and welfare programs of the church." ("Encyclopedia of Mormonism").

Matthew Cowley gave a marvelous address that illustrates beautifully the relationship God can have with His children when they are obedient to His laws. He said: "God is a wonderful partner, isn't he. I would like to be in business with somebody like that, having my partner come up to me and say 'Here, I'll furnish all the capital to start the business. I will furnish all the blessings. Then, you look after the business. Don't forget me. When the increase comes, you keep ninety percent, and turn over to me ten percent. You use your ninety percent any way you want to, and I'll put my ten percent right back into the business.' Wouldn't that be wonderful? That's just the kind of partner we have in this church. We keep the ninety percent and use it any way we wish. We give Him the ten percent, and here stands a temple, (and there) stands a tabernacle. He puts it all right back into the business, into his business. God will finance the church, brothers and sisters, if you will obey the principles of the gospel." ("Matthew Cowley Speaks," p. 76-77).

Finally, Heber J. Grant bore testimony of the promise given by Malachi when that prophet spoke in the name of the Lord, declaring: "Prove me now herewith, saith the Lord of hosts, if I will not open you the windows of heaven, and pour you out a blessing, that there shall not be room enough to receive it." (Malachi 3:10). "I bear witness," Elder Grant said, "that men and women who have been absolutely honest with God, who have paid their one-tenth (have received) wisdom whereby they have been able to utilize the remaining nine-tenths, and it has been of greater value to them, and they have accomplished more with it, than they would if they had not been honest with the Lord." (C.R., 4/1912).

The Lord also declared, through Malachi, that he would "rebuke the devourer for your sakes, and he shall not destroy the fruits of your ground." (Malachi 3:11). This promise becomes increasingly important in the Last Days, as events are played out and the struggle with Spiritual Babylon intensifies. We must obey this law, said the Lord, "to prepare (ourselves) against the day of vengeance and burning," (D&C 85:3), when the wicked who do not obey the will of God will be visited with "sore affliction, with pestilence, with plague, with sword, with vengeance, (and) with devouring fire." (D&C 97:26). "Nevertheless, let it be read this once...that if (Zion) sin no more, none of these things shall come upon her. And I will bless her with...a multiplicity of blessings upon her, and upon her generations forever and ever, saith the Lord your God." (D&C 97:27-28).

It is not unusual to hear members of the church bear personal testimony of the blessings that come through their obedience to the Law of Tithing. It is a wonderful law, conceived in royal courts above, and designed to give God's children a means to taste the riches of eternity. It allows faithful members of the church to be junior partners of the Lord in His work that began even before our birth, which is to bring about our immortality and eternal life. (See Moses 1:39). It adds a whole new layer of meaning to the Savior's question: "Wist ye not that I must be about my Father's business?" (Luke 2:49). It adds depth to the question: "What think ye of Christ?" (Matthew 2242). It adds poignancy to the Savior's plea: "Will ye also go away?" (John 6:67).

It establishes a measure of equality to temporal circumstances that seem, at times, to be wildly out of balance. Obedience allows every faithful member to labor in the traces, yoked equally to the Master. It gives them a chance to wipe the sweat from their brows and to acknowledge talents and capacities that have come from God. The Law of Tithing transports its adherents through time to the altars of the ancient temple, there to offer sacrifice with the levitical priests, and to feel the stirrings of a spiritual reality from beyond the veil. It gives them the means to measure the fruits of their labor, and when their offerings are put to use, it allows them to experience confirmation of the immutable law that relates blessings to obedience. It is with tithing donation slips that faithful members bank the fires of their testimonies, and warm themselves beside their glowing embers. The Law of Tithing provides a bellows that fans the flames of their resolve, as they plunge themselves directly into the white-hot crucible of faith.

It asks the same of those who have been blessed with the Midas Touch, those who have been tenderly caressed by the hand of fate, and those who were born with silver spoons in their mouths, as well as of those who are enrolled in the school of hard knocks, whose mortal curriculum seems to be filled with elusive goals, cancelled classes, cranky professors, daunting tuition, exhausting prerequisites, repetitive lower-level classes, dismaying learning laboratories, demoralizing homework assignments, intimidating term papers, unfulfilled dreams, and one crisis of confidence after another.

The circumstances might have been exceptional, but when the Lord sent Elijah to the Widow of Zarephath, he saw her there gathering of sticks: and he called to her, and said, Fetch me, I pray thee, a little water in a vessel, that I may drink. And as she was going to fetch it, he called to her, and said, Bring me, I pray thee, a morsel of bread in thine hand. And she said, As the Lord thy God liveth, I have not a cake, but an handful of meal in a barrel, and a little oil in a cruse: and, behold, I am gathering two sticks, that I may go in and dress it for me and my son, that we may eat it, and die. And Elijah said unto her, Fear not; go and do as thou hast said: but make me thereof a little cake first, and bring it unto me, and after make for thee and for thy son. For thus saith the Lord God of Israel, The barrel of meal shall not waste, neither shall the cruse of oil fail, until the day that the Lord sendeth rain upon the earth. And she went and did according to the saying of Elijah: and she, and he, and her house, did eat many days. And the barrel of meal wasted not, neither did the cruse of oil fail, according to the word of the Lord, which he spake by Elijah. (1 Kings 17:7-16).

The Lord helps those in need through the tithes and offerings of the saints, and He has re-established the law in our day, that the door might swing both ways. We are both blessed, and our capacity to bless the lives of others increases, when we pay our tithing. "When we put God first, all other things fall into their proper place or drop out of our lives. Our love of the Lord will govern the claims for our affection, the demands on our time, the interests we pursue, and the order of our priorities. May God bless us to put Him first and, as a result, reap peace in this life and eternal life with a fulness of joy in the life to come." (Ezra Taft Benson, C.R., 4/1988).

The law was conceived, because "all are alike unto God." (2 Nephi 26:33). It allows Him to apply a fine line to the definition of stewardship, and to measure our devotions without ambiguity. It creates a celestial standard that permits Him to be fair and impartial in His dealings with His children, without risking accusations of favoritism given to one or to another. It provides a way for both the rich and the poor to participate equally in the expansion of the temporal and spiritual assets of the church and kingdom. It eliminates class distinction by evenly dividing the weight of responsibility among all the members of the church, regardless of their individual temporal circumstances. Its objective is to make both princes and paupers feel that they are "fellowcitizens with the saints, and of the household of God." (Ephesians 2:19).

Those who pay their tithes are blessed with an exalted view of the kingdom of God on the earth. They are empowered with the spirit of anticipation. When they live in strict conformity to the other laws of the gospel, they are blessed to participate in temple ordinances, and are prepared to kneel at holy altars to make sacred covenants of consecration with God. Tithe payers are blessed with both the temporal and spiritual means to do all that is required to bring to pass a new heaven and a new earth. As their lives play out joyfully, the price, once paid so dearly, is recalled in gladness. They receive full value. Brigham Young, in his inimitable way, said: "I never count the cost of anything. I just find out what the Lord wants me to do, and I do it." (2/17/1861). He knew from whence his blessings came. (See Mormon 5:10).

"Act now, before it is too late!" urged Spencer W. Kimball. "Now is the time to chart the course of action you will follow tomorrow, and next week, and next year. Now is the time to commit yourself to be as Abraham…to begin to keep those commandments you have been failing to live. Determine now to…pay your tithing faithfully. …Here, then, is the challenge the Lord gives (to) every single man and woman…in the church: "Go ye, therefore, and do the works of Abraham." (D&C 132:32). ("Ensign," 6/1975).

"I believe that our existence
must go beyond Euclidean or other
practical measuring systems, and
that it is part of a reality beyond
what we now understand."
(Jean Luc Picard).

Travel at
The Speed of Thought

In the television series "Star Trek: The Next Generation," the Traveler, whose real name was unpronounceable by humans, was a native of Tau Alpha C, who had the power to alter space, time and warp fields with his mind. He could phase in and out of time and dimension, based on his ability to focus the energy of thought.

We are not there yet, but give us time, no pun intended. The universe is 13.7 billion years old. On their journey to earth, photons from the most distant stars have been traveling across space, at a constant speed of almost 671 million miles per hour, that works out to 5.88 trillion miles per year. That's 5.88 thousand billion miles each and every year, for as many as 13.7 billion years. To put things in perspective, just 4,000 years ago, when the starlight just now reaching our eyes was a mere 23,520 trillion miles from earth, our ancestors were still fashioning tools out of stone, so we haven't been players on the universal stage for very long. Early civilizations somewhere out there could have had well over three million times as long as we have had to figure things out. What wondrous technologies might these alien civilizations have developed within a time span that is almost three and a half million times as long as 4,000 years!

Nevertheless, what we do have going for us is impressive, at least by our own standards. Since the 1970s, the Information Age, also known as the Digital Age, Computer Age, or New Media Age, has blessed our lives with a shift from industrialization to information computerization and a knowledge-based society embedded within a global economy. Amazon and Google are good examples of the practical benefits related to the explosion in information-based technology. The transition by society to the use of technology in daily life has been dramatic, with no end in sight, and is nowhere more profound than in the sphere of the acquisition and utilization of knowledge.

In 1900, at the dawn of the 20th century, it had taken 150 years to double all human knowledge. Today it takes only around 12 months, and soon it will be every 12 hours, according to reliable estimates. Where will we be in 10, 50, or 100 years? Maybe the sky is not the limit. (We've already been there, and beyond, after all). Our brains (the same ones that are "boggled" by the aforementioned numbers) contain several billion petabytes of information. (One petabyte is 1,000 terabytes, 1 terrabyte is 1,000 gigabytes and 1 gigabyte is 1,000 megabytes). Perhaps we just have to organize the information in our brains more efficiently, in order to utilize their resources to greater potential. We have the Internet for comparison, which is arguably not very well organized either, as presently constituted. Nevertheless, all of the information on the World Wide Web is currently estimated to be just 5 million terabytes (TB) of which Google has indexed roughly 200 TB or just .004% of its total storage capacity.

Consider transportation technology. Caesar rode a horse, but then again, so did George Washington, 2,000 years later. As a matter of fact, the gauge of railroad track in the nineteenth century was initially determined by the width of a horse's rear, specifically a Roman chariot horse's rear. (Verified by Snopes). In 1592, Richard III was prompted to exclaim: "A horse! A horse! My kingdom for a horse!" (Shakespeare, "Richard III," Act, 5, Scene 4). Until the invention of the steam engine that was the driving force behind the Industrial Revolution, the horse defined the absolute speed limit at which one could travel in a horizontal direction. Henry Ford is said to have remarked: "If I had asked people what they wanted, they would have said faster horses."

In the next 100 years, there were amazing advances in transportation technology, with train travel in 1900 achieving a top speed of about 40 mph. In the next 50 years, transportation technology took another giant leap forward. On July 23, 1949, the De Havilland Comet became the first commercial jet aircraft, with a cruising speed of 460 mph.

In the next 25 years, transportation technology took a quantum leap forward. The Saturn 5 rocket that propelled humans to the moon weighed 6.5 million pounds and had a payload capacity of 260,000 pounds. It developed almost 8 million pounds of thrust for eight and a half minutes, achieving a speed of 7 miles per second, or 24,593 miles per hour.

In the next 12.5 years, the Voyager 1 spacecraft launched by NASA on September 5, 1977, achieved the fastest heliocentric recession speed of any man-made object: 10.72 miles per second (38,592 miles per hour). It has sustained that speed for over 35 years, and has now left our solar system and entered interstellar space.

From the perspective of storing, retrieving, and transmitting information, the Internet has made communication lightning fast also, and the search bar on computer screens has become the Sippy Cup of our culture. Information technology is approaching light-speed.

On September 10, 2008, scientists created the Large Hadron Collider, the world's largest and most powerful particle accelerator. It was built in collaboration with over 10,000 scientists and engineers from over 100 countries, as well as hundreds of universities and laboratories, and remains the largest and most complex experimental facility ever built by humans. At a cost of over 7.5 billion Euros, it is arguably the most costly scientific instrument mankind has ever made. It consists of a 27-kilometer ring of superconducting magnets with a number of accelerating structures to boost the energy of the particles along its path. Inside the accelerator, two particle beams approach the speed of light, or 186,200 miles per second. The data collected from the operation of the Large Hadron Collider consists of tens of petabytes of information per year. It is being analyzed by the world's largest computing grid, comprising over 170 computing facilities in a worldwide network in 36 countries. As of this writing, (2017), fears of the "doomsday phenomenon" (particle collisions causing black holes) have proven to be unfounded. This is fortunate, inasmuch as their creation would result in the annihilation of the earth.

As we approach the cosmic speed limit, perhaps we should re-write the laws of physics to allow warp speed. Warp drive is a hypothetical faster-than-light propulsion system. A spacecraft equipped with a warp drive has been theorized to be able to travel at speeds greater than that of light by many orders of magnitude, (Warp 1 – Warp 10), while circumventing the relativity problem of time dilation. If warp drive technology were to create an artificial "bubble" of normal space-time surrounding the spacecraft, the vehicle would be able to maintain interaction with objects in normal space. A theoretical solution for faster-than-light travel that models the warp drive concept was formulated by physicist Miguel Alcubierre in 1994, and NASA scientists have begun preliminary research to learn more about the practical applications of the technology.

But what of the aforementioned Traveler, and his ability to alter space, time, and warp fields? In the "Star Trek: The Next Generation" episode entitled "Where Silence Has Lease," Captain Jean Luc Picard said: "Considering the marvelous complexity of the universe, its clockwork perfection, its balances of this against that, such as matter, energy, gravitation, time, and dimension, I believe that our existence must go beyond euclidean or other practical measuring systems, and that it is part of a reality beyond what we now understand."

After warp speed's wrinkles have been ironed out, will the next level be travel at the speed of thought, like the Traveler? Perhaps so, if mathematical equations can be formulated to embrace a time-space-thought continuum, as described by Prot, in the movie "KPax." He told the scientists examining his claims of extraterrestrial origin and travel at thought-speed: "Einstein never said that nothing can travel faster than the speed of light." What he did say is that something traveling slower than light is slower in all frames of reference, and cannot therefore accelerate to a speed above the cosmic speed limit.

Perhaps gravitational waves that propagate at the speed of thought, a concept first suggested by the physicist Arthur Stanley Eddington, in 1922, will allow us to jump past that theoretical limit. If we can somehow come to a meeting of the minds between the abstract reality that emerges from mathematics, and the warm body of nature that we can see and touch, we just might be able to ride the exponential expansion of knowledge to a destination that reveal the answers we are looking for, that relate to travel at the speed of thought.

Don't drive as if you owned
the road. Drive as if you
owned the car.

True Discipleship

The gospel is as much the sum of "Thou shalt" commandments, as it is "Thou shalt not" commandments. Its composite principles are the consummate compilation of affirmative actions. Thus: "We believe in being honest," because the principle of true discipleship is the mortar that holds together the building blocks of character. (13th Article of Faith).

"Fame is a vapor, and popularity is an accident. Those who cheer you today may curse you tomorrow. In the end, the only thing that endures is character." (Attributed to Horace Greeley). Honesty is a sense of integrity and of character that shines through the eyes like a beacon of hope. George Washington declared: "I hope I shall always possess firmness and virtue enough to maintain what I consider the most enviable of all titles, the character of an honest man."

General Washington wanted what we all desire: To be "distinguished for (our) zeal towards God, and also towards men, (to be) perfectly honest and upright in all things; and firm in the faith of Christ." (Alma 27:27). Nephi observed of those who built their society on the foundation of noble character, that there "could not be a happier people among all the people who had been created by the hand of God." (4 Nephi 1:16).

Disciples are honest to the faith of their fathers. "They tell on themselves by the friends they seek; by the very manner in which they speak; by the way they enjoy their leisure time; by the use they make of dollar and dime. They tell who they are by the things they wear, and in the way they arrange their hair. By the kinds of things that make them laugh; by the records they play on the phonograph. They tell who they are by the way they walk; by the things in which they delight to talk; by the books they choose from a well-filled shelf. In these ways and more, they tell on themselves." (Anonymous).

Perhaps as never before, our time demands "strong minds, great hearts, true faith and ready hands; men whom the lust of office does not kill; men whom the spoils of office cannot buy; men who possess opinions and a will; men who have honor; men who will not lie; men who can stand before a demagogue and damn his treacherous flatteries without winking! Tall men, sun-crowned, who live above the fog in public duty and in private thinking." (Josiah Gilbert Holland).

The honesty of true disciples is intrinsic to their nature. They simply cannot lie. They are valiant in the testimony of Jesus. A prospective employer asked a young man who had applied for a job, "If I hire you, can I count on you to be honest?" To which, the young man replied: "You can count on me to be honest, whether you hire me or not."

True disciples recognize the property rights of others. In church one day, a man gave a talk on the 7th Commandment. It was a very hard and biting address, and after he had finished, he said: "I hope we have all learned from my remarks, and that we will start now to deal honestly with the possessions of others." Then, he said: "One of you took my umbrella a few weeks ago, and I know it will be very hard for you to return it to me face to face, so I have decided that you can come to my home tonight after dark, and just leave it on my porch." The next morning there were 35 umbrellas lying on his door step.

True disciples obey the law, and pattern their behavior after him of whom it was said: "He kept all Ten Commandments until he died. He walked the straight and narrow path and never lied. He never went to the theatres. He never learned to dance. He never once on shapely legs bestowed a wicked glance. He never smoked or kissed another's wife. He never took a bit of liquor in his life. He never let his temper rise. He never called his neighbor a fool. He kept strictly to the Golden Rule. Now you can be assured that he really lived on earth. But he was deaf, and dumb, and blind, and paralyzed from birth." (Anonymous).

True disciples cannot cheat themselves or others. They may regularly take examinations in academia. But they also take a daily examination in honesty. If they have to fail one test, they make sure it is in math, or science, or history. They realize that there are many honest and successful people in the world, who know little about quadratic equations, or the Krebs Cycle, or ancient Rome.

True disciples will not murmur, or engage in the subdued and continually repeated expression of indistinct or inarticulate complaint or grumbling. They will not gossip. They recognize that there is so much good in the worst of us, and so much bad in the best of us, that it hardly behooves any of us to talk about the rest of us. They do not find fault, and will not pass the buck. They remember the story of the four people named Everybody, Somebody, Anybody, and Nobody, none of whom was honest with themselves or others. There was an important job to be done and Everybody was sure that Somebody would do it. Anybody could have done it, but Nobody did it. Somebody got angry about it because it was Everybody's job. Everybody thought that Anybody could do it, but failed to realize that Nobody would step up to the plate. It ended up that Everybody blamed Somebody when Nobody did what Anybody could have done.

True disciples will never need to make excuses about their character. "My father focuses heart-gripping flashes across the wall screen. Family slides. I am small, my brother is smaller, and my sister is smallest. Days now dead re-open like old storybooks from memory's heaped box. Pulling out pictures of cooking in grandfather's dutch oven; playing cheetah on our backyard monkey-jungle; being beautifully Easter-bested with my coat buttoned wrong; hugging a mommy minus grey hair. Soberly, I think of another Father, Who someday shall open my mind, and flash reeling remembering of every day's minute across my soul, across the heavens, and kindly ask me to narrate." (Lora Lyn Stucker, "New Era," 8/1973).

True disciples exercise the gift of repentance. Marion D. Hanks observed: "At the banquet of consequences, when we go with our loved ones, there will not be much that is satisfying at the table unless we are able to bow our heads in reverence, rather than hang them in shame, in the presence of God who will be there." ("B.Y.U. Speeches of The Year," 10/3/1967).

True disciples are warriors on the front lines of the battle raging in the hearts of men, women, and children in the Last Days, at a time in the history of the earth when it seems that basic principles of character have become forgotten values. Ezra Taft Benson declared: "I do not believe the greatest threat to our future is from bombs or missiles. I do not think our civilization will die that way. I think it will die when we no longer care, when the spiritual forces that make us wish to be right and noble die in the hearts of men, when we disregard the importance of law and order, and the basic principles upon which this nation has been built. Great nations are never conquered from outside, unless they are rotten inside. Our greatest national problem today is erosion of the national morality." (C.R., 4/1968).

Long ago, Alexis de Tocqueville wrote: "I sought for the greatness and genius of America in her commodious harbors and her ample rivers, and it was not there; in her fertile fields and boundless prairies, and it was not there; in her rich mines and her vast world commerce, and it was not there. Not until I went to the churches of America and heard her pulpits aflame with righteousness did I understand the secret of her genius and her power. America is great because she is good, and if she ever ceases to be good, she will cease to be great." (This has been cited to a quotation in "Picturesque America" by William Cullen Bryant, p. 502, first published in 1872, but such a statement has not been located in the 1874 or 1894 editions.)

"Teach me to
walk in the light of his love,
to pray to my Father above, (and) to
know of the things that are right. Together
we'll learn of his commandments, that
we may return home to his presence,
to live in his sight (and) always,
always, to walk in the light."
(Clara W. McMaster).

Walk in The Light

Walking in the light of the gospel endows us with a greater capacity to love the Savior, His work, and His children. As we embrace its principles, the Lord is good to us. Enlightenment dissipates the cobwebs of doubt, smooths out the rough edges of our testimonies, builds our self-confidence to tackle tough questions, and provides the self-aasurance we need to freely exercise our agency. Light bestows upon us the gifts of peace, comfort, and a clear conscience. It illuminates the gospel as the ultimate measure of truth. The light exerts a liberating influence, as it frees us from apprehension, despair, doubt, fear, ignorance, timidity, unsteadiness, and worry, It empowers us to keep that which we hold near and dear safe from those rodents who scurry about in the shadows, waiting for opportunities to ransack our treasury.

Light also energizes our ability to manage the gift of time. We learn to take time with discipline, bide our time with patience, make time with diligence, find time with care, spend time with thoughtfulness, invest time with wisdom, and share time with pleasure. Shedding light on the weightier matters of the law infuses us with a liberating sense of independence, as we learn something new every day. Our hearts and our minds are illuminated with a breathtaking expansion of understanding. As we learn to harmonize our learning style with the Spirit, we discover a pattern that soon becomes our norm.

The genius of the Plan is that in order to increase our understanding of the truth, further light and knowledge are available to create an atmosphere that is conducive to teaching by the Spirit. Truth bears its own independent witness, and it builds with steadiness on its own solid foundation. It requires no external warrant.

When we walk mildly and quietly in the light, we embrace truth. (See D.B.Y., p. 65). "The wisdom that is from above is first pure, then peaceable, gentle, and easy to be entreated, full of mercy and good fruits, without partiality, and without hypocrisy." (James 3:17). As the world grows increasingly noisy, we remember that inspiration comes more easily in peaceful settings. A quarter of a century ago, Boyd K. Packer lamented: "Clothing and grooming and conduct are looser and sloppier and more disheveled. Raucous music characterizes the drug culture, with obscene lyrics blasted through amplifiers, while lights flash psychedelic colors. This trend to more noise, more excitement, more contention, less restraint, less dignity, and less formality is not coincidental nor innocent nor harmless. The first order issued by a commander mounting a military invasion is the jamming of the channels of communication of those he intends to conquer. Irreverence suits the purposes of the adversary by obstructing the delicate channels of revelation in both mind and spirit." (C.R., 10/1991).

As we embrace the light we establish a prayerful attitude. Spencer W. Kimball promised: "The Lord is eager to see our first awakening desires and our beginning efforts to penetrate the darkness. Having granted freedom of decision, he must permit us to grope our way until we reach for the light. But when we begin to hunger, when our arms begin to reach, when our knees begin to bend and our voices becomes articulate, then and not till then does our Lord push back the horizons, draw back the veil, and make it possible for us to emerge from dim uncertain stumbling to sureness, in heavenly light." (Munich Germany Area Conference, 8/1973).

Light is like a deep-tissue massage that strengthens our core, stimulates our fast-twitch muscle fibers, and increases our flexibility and elasticity. Light warms up our juices, channels them, gets them flowing, and raises our core testimony temperature. The Prophet Joseph is our example, and his experiences underscore several basic principles relating to light and knowledge. What he did in preparation for his theophany in the Sacred Grove is our pattern, as well. His "mind was called up to serious reflection and great uneasiness." His "feelings were deep and often poignant," and he "attended...meetings as often as occasion would permit." His "mind at times was greatly excited" to understand the will of God. He wondered to himself: "How shall I know it to be true?" and the light guided him along a path that led to spectacular answers to all of his questions. (J.S.H. 1:8-10).

As we embrace the light, we establish a prayerful attitude. As we study matters out in our own minds preparatory to receiving answers to our prayers, we become actively, rather than passively, involved in the process of inquiry. We dust off our agency, and actually use it as it was envisioned. We move beyond control, coercion, compulsion, intimidation, and external influence to friendly persuasion and independence of action. We expand our capabilities as we exercise the gifts, resources, and reserves provided by the perfect Plan of Salvation. Spencer W. Kimball promised: "If there be eyes to see, there will be visions to inspire. If there be ears to hear, there will be revelations to experience. If there be hearts which can understand, know that the exalting truths of Christ's gospel will no longer be hidden and mysterious, and all earnest seekers may know God and his program." (C.R., 10/1966).

If we want to walk in the light, our vocal prayers will summon the angels who have been commissioned to unlock the portals to heaven. The example of Joseph Smith in the Sacred Grove teaches us how to pray with emotion, intensity and the power of concentration. As he knelt in humility and offered up the desires of his heart, when necessity required it, he exerted all his resources to call upon God. (J.S.H. 1:13-16). Later, the Lord spoke through him to those who followed his example: "Blessed art thou for what thou hast done; for thou hast inquired of me, and behold, as often as thou hast inquired thou hast received instruction of my Spirit." (D&C 6:14).

"Do you offer a few trite words and worn-out phrases, or do you talk intimately to the Lord?" asked Spencer W. Kimball. "Do you pray occasionally when you should be praying regularly, often constantly? When you pray, do you just speak, or do you also listen? Do you give thanks or merely ask for favors?" ("New Era," 3/1978).

If we want to walk in the light, we must prepare ourselves to recognize truth when it comes. As long as we stay with the Plan, "by the power of the Holy Ghost (we) may know the truth of all things." (Moroni 10:5). "Most recorded revelations in the Doctrine and Covenants were a consciousness of direction from above. This is the sort of revelation individuals often have for their own needs." (Spencer W. Kimball, "Faith Precedes the Miracle," p. 30). The light illuminates our deep impressions, gives them breadth, depth, and width, fine-tunes our perception, and kindles the sparks of recognition that allow us to make the vital distinctions between revelation and its worldly counterfeits. The Lord provided counsel to Oliver Cowdery that confirms what President Kimball taught: "Did I not speak peace to your mind concerning the matter?" He asked. "What greater witness can you have than from God?" (D&C 6:22-23). Have we not all experienced similar peace that has spoken to our minds, concerning matters of great personal importance?

When we walk in the light, we eschew implicit denial of the revelations of the Lord. (See 3 Nephi 29:6). "Many people expect that if there be revelation it will come with an awe-inspiring, earth-shaking display. For many, it is hard to accept revelations as deep, unassailable impressions settling down on the mind and heart as dew from heaven, or as the dawn dissipates the darkness of night. Expecting the spectacular, (they) may not be fully alerted to the constant flow of revealed communication" that we receive on a daily basis. (Spencer W. Kimball, "Instructor," 8/1960).

Those who walk in the light carefully cultivate their church attendance and treasure their fellowship with the saints. They see the Sacrament service as a channel of power and the ordinance as a mighty tool enabling them to approach Heavenly Father so that His promises might be fully realized. They have experienced the truth in Melvin J. Ballard's declaration that "the road to the Sacrament table is the path of safety for the Latter-day Saints."

Those who walk in the light exercise devotion to their callings. Having been set apart to do a particular work in the church, they understand that it no longer belongs to anyone else, and no-one else has a right to it. They claim ownership of the position and realize that if they don't do the job, it will not be done. Therefore, they accept positions with the intention to carry out the associated responsibilities as though their lives depended on it, as indeed they do. Their constant prayer is that after they have been "set apart," everyone within the circle of their influence will be enriched because His work was given into their hands. Therefore," said the Lord, "Let every man stand in his own office, and labor in his own calling, that the system may be kept perfect." (D&C 84:109-110).

Those who walk in the light listen to the counsel of their priesthood leaders, and read the scriptures daily. As Dallin Oaks explained: "We do not overstate the point when we say that the scriptures can be a Urim and Thummim (translation: "lights and perfections" or "revelation and truth," or "doctrine and truth") to assist each of us to receive personal revelation. Because we believe that scripture reading can help us receive revelation, we are encouraged to read the scriptures again and again." ("Ensign," 1/1995).

Those who walk in the light expand upon the counsel of Nephi, and view it in a larger context. "Wherefore, ye must press forward (with complete dedication and) steadfastness (or confidence and a firm determination) in Christ, having a perfect brightness of hope, and a love of God and of all men. (If we do this,) feasting upon the word of Christ, (or receiving strength and nourishment from the scriptures,) and endure to the end (in righteousness), behold, thus saith the Father: (We) shall have eternal life," that is the greatest gift He may bestow upon us. (2 Nephi 31:20).

Those who walk in the light emulate the righteous example of others. As Chauncey Riddle reflected: "I felt I had received some revelation before. However, I saw that random revelation was not sufficient. To be a rock, a bastion of surety, revelation must be something on which one can count and receive in every occasion of real need.

I began to seek it actively. I prayed, I fasted, and I lived the gospel as best I knew. I was faithful in my church duties. I tried to live up to every scruple which my conscience enjoined upon me. And dependable revelation did come. Intermittently, haltingly at first, then steadily, over some years it finally came to be a mighty stream of experience. I came to know that at any time of day or night, in any circumstance, for any real need, I could get help.

That help came in the form of feelings of encouragement when things seemed hopeless. It came in ideas to unravel puzzles that blocked my accomplishment. It came in priesthood blessings that were fully realized. It came in anticipation of what the General Authorities of the church would say and do in General Conference. It came in the gifts of the Spirit, as the wonders of eternity were opened to the eyes of my understanding.

That stream of spiritual experience is today for me a river of living water that nourishes my soul in every situation. It is the most important factor of my life. If it were taken away, all that I have and am would be dust and ashes. It is the basis of my love, life, understanding, hope, and progress.

My only regret is that though this river is so wonderful, I have not been able to take full advantage of it, as yet. My life does not yet conform to all that I know. But now I do know; I do not just believe." ("Sunstone," 5/1988).

Our sole objective when we walk in the light is to find out what the Lord has revealed, and then to believe, and finally to act accordingly. This is reminiscent of a statement attributed to Brigham Young: "I never count the cost of anything. I simply find out what the Lord wants me to do, and I do it."

Those who walk in the light and have grasped the principles of truth, brim over with charity as they find comfortable accommodations in the household of faith. They let virtue garnish their thoughts unceasingly. They cultivate a contented and confident companionship with the Spirit, and the doctrine of the priesthood washes over their minds as the dews from heaven. They celebrate the light, and the Plan becomes a talisman of truth that is interwoven into the coat of many colors that is the fabric of their being. Its principles become the elements of a tapestry that is everlasting, and without compulsion or coercion those who walk in the light become independent agents with the freedom to embrace their destiny and claim their eternal reward. (See D&C 121:45-46).

"Many times a day, I realize
how much my own life is built upon
the labors of my fellow men, and how earnestly I
must exert myself in order to give as much as I have
received. My peace of mind is often troubled by the
depressing sense that I have borrowed too
heavily from the work of others."
(Albert Einstein).

We Ask Thee in Humility

Author's note: As I have read over this essay, I can say with unqualified certainty that it is one of the best I have ever written. ☺

Humility is a feeling of contrition, or the sense that we cannot make progress without the sustaining influence of the Savior. It is characterized by a broken heart that has been touched by the Spirit to seek forgiveness for sins through repentance. It is typified by complete and utter dependence upon the Atonement. It is by our faith in the saving principles of the gospel that we follow this pattern: "Let him that is ignorant learn wisdom by humbling himself and calling upon the Lord his God, that his eyes may be opened that he may see, and his ears opened that he may hear." (D&C 136:32).

The exercise of humility is something that everyone can practice, no matter what their station in life may be. "And whosoever shall exalt himself shall be abased; and he that shall humble himself shall be exalted." (Matthew 23:12). Ultimately, it is "better to be of an humble spirit with the lowly, than to divide the spoil with the proud." (Proverbs 16:19).

When our faith finally convicts us of our sins, and we have come "down into the depths of humility" because our hearts have been softened by the Spirit, we reach the point where we may be "baptized (and) visited with fire and with the Holy Ghost." (3 Nephi 12:2). We develop the companion virtues of "faith, virtue, knowledge, temperance, patience, brotherly kindness, godliness, charity, (and) diligence." (D&C 4:6).

Humility is a recognizable sense of inadequacy that creates a tangible need for the tender mercies of the Lord. It was in this context that Moses exclaimed: "Now, for this cause I know that man is nothing, which thing I never had supposed." (Moses 1:10). Humility is an outgrowth of meekness, and is a conscious submission to God's will. It leads us, as it did the people of Zarahemla, to exclaim: "The Spirit of the Lord Omnipotent…has wrought a mighty change in us, or in our hearts, that we have no more disposition to do evil, but to do good continually." (Mosiah 5:2). Humility tugs at our heartstrings with resonant chords that harmonize with the words of the hymn "I Need Thee Every Hour." (Lyrics by Annie S. Hawks).

But can we really know when we are humble? Can we put our finger to its pulse to perceive its faint stirrings? Is humility such a tender trait that runs so deeply in our character that it seldom surfaces to be recognized? Can humility have its origins in both the sacred and the secular? Are both weaknesses and strengths intertwined with humility? Does our growth in spiritual stature go hand-in-hand with humility? Is losing ourselves in service an unconscious exercise in humility? Can we gain a testimony of humility by practicing the principle, or is it a characteristic that is gained by observance of other principles? Just what is an "exercise" in humility?

Is the blessing of exaltation in the Celestial Kingdom of God predicated upon humility? Peter counseled: "Humble yourselves therefore under the mighty hand of God, that he may exalt you in due time." (1 Peter 5:6). The Lord said of the saints: "For behold, I have prepared a great endowment and blessing to be poured out upon them, inasmuch as they are faithful and continue in humility before me." (D&C 105:12). James taught: "Humble yourselves in the sight of the Lord, and he shall lift you up" at the last day. (James 4:10).

Do we feel humility only when we are touched by the better angels of our nature? If we lack humility, can we righteously desire to obtain it? Is it one of those qualities, like greatness, that is thrust upon us? Is humility a tool that awakens in us the remembrance of who we are? Are we being honest with ourselves, and with God, when we pray: "We come to Thee in humility…?"

Clearly, those with humility have embraced a set of standards that runs counter to the world's expectations. The lifestyle of humble disciples may even seem silly to those who would have us believe that good guys finish last, and that you don't get what you deserve, you get what you negotiate. Those who are humble, unpretentious, self-effacing, meek, and lowly can expect to be bullied and taken advantage by the arrogant, the conceited, the egotistical, and the haughty. But as Paul explained: "God hath chosen the foolish things of the world to confound the wise; and God hath chosen the weak things of the world to confound the things which are mighty." (1 Corinthians 1:27). Those with delicate spirits should not expect, and indeed do not deserve, tangible rewards for being humble.

Daddy Warbucks, reflecting on his life in the shark-infested waters of the business world, told Annie: "You don't have to be nice to those you step on or climb over, on your way up the ladder of success, if you don't plan on coming back down again." To put it even more bluntly, from the world's perspective: "He who has the gold makes the rules." But, as Brigham Young taught: "If we go on lusting after the groveling things of this life which perish with the handling, we shall surely remain fixed with a very limited amount of knowledge and like a door upon its hinges, move to and fro from one year to another without any visible advancement or improvement." (J.D., 10:265-274). The Savior was speaking from personal experience when He articulated the celestial principle: "He that is greatest among you shall be your servant." (Matthew 23:11).

Religious history teaches us interesting lessons about humility. Lowly Israel, and not the mighty kingdoms of Assyria, Babylonia, or Egypt, remained the repository of true religion. "Christianity did not go from Rome to Galilee; it was the other way around. In our day, the routing is from Palmyra to Paris, and not the reverse." (Spencer W. Kimball, C.R., 4/1978).

The Little Town of Bethlehem, and not mighty Jerusalem, was the birthplace of the Savior. Bethlehem stands in the shadow of the 6,000 year old Holy City. Attesting to its strategic importance, Jerusalem has been completely destroyed at least twice, attacked 52 times, besieged 23 times, and captured and recaptured 44 times. Humble Bethlehem, just 6 miles down the road, has been largely ignored in the process. The cave or grotto on the outskirts of the town in which Joseph and Mary took refuge was a far cry from the 5-Star King David Hotel in Jerusalem that was booked to capacity. If only Joseph had flashed a Hilton Honors Frequent Guest card, he might have received more personalized attention!

The Savior was not the Lord of a worldly domain, but was the Prince of Peace, a monarch without a kingdom, and a man without a country, so to speak. "Foxes have holes, and birds of the air have nests; but the Son of man hath not where to lay his head." (Luke 9:58). He cared little for the profane emblems of power, because His was a royal priesthood that was not of this world. The kings of the earth, in order to validate their claims to authority, hold in their hands the orb, an emblem of power, usually made of precious metal encrusted with jewels, and consisting of a sphere with a cross on it. The orb symbolizes the universe as a harmonious whole. It hearkens back to Rome and beyond, but the Holy Roman Emperor Henry II was the first to hold it in his hand during his coronation in 1014. From the perspective of the Latter-day Restoration, we view his pomp and circumstance as a feeble attempt to usurp the supreme power and authority of "the blessed and only Potentate, the King of kings, and Lord of Lords." (1 Timothy 6:15).

Latter-day Saints are familiar with the Liahona that was passed from father to son by Lehi's descendants. It was a royal treasure, and probably the prototype of the orb. Critics of The Book of Mormon have ridiculed the Liahona, but of all the symbols of royal authority, it is the most authentic. We do not know exactly what it looked like, although Nephi described it as "a round ball of curious workmanship; and it was of fine brass. And within the ball were two spindles; and the one pointed the way whither we should go into the wilderness." (1 Nephi 16:10).

Similar religious artifacts, royal orbs, spheres of the firmament, crystal balls, and the like have survived in art, although they are stylized almost beyond recognition, and understanding of their underlying power has been completely lost. That power came from Jesus Christ, Who was the Author of Salvation, and not of best-sellers. If He wrote anything at all, it has been lost to the ages. The only tantalizing reference in the scriptures to His writing is John 8:6: "Jesus stooped down, and with his finger wrote on the ground." The gospel narratives relating to His ministry were only written years afterward.

The first Christian father to quote Matthew was Ignatius, who died around 115 A.D.. It is generally believed that the gospel according to Matthew was written before 70 A.D., and perhaps as early as 50 A.D.. Mark was not an eyewitness to the Savior's ministry; it is believed that it was Peter's recollections that guided Mark to record his gospel. His account of the Savior's ministry may be the earliest Gospel to be written, between 55 A.D. and 70 A.D.. Nor was Luke an eyewitness of the life of the Savior. He was a Gentile convert and companion to Paul, who likewise was not an eyewitness! But they both had many opportunities to interview disciples who had known Christ and could provide substance to the gospel and the Book of Acts being written by Luke. The gospel according to Luke was written around 62 A.D.. The gospel according to John was an eyewitness account of the theological aspects of the ministry of Christ that confirmed His divinity. He wrote his gospel during his banishment to the Isle of Patmos, around the end of the first century. So, the four canonical gospels were written about the Savior, but the New Testament, a narrative of the greatest story ever told, includes nothing written by the Savior Himself. There would be no lucrative book deals for Him!

We know that He was "the firstborn of every creature." (Colossians 1:15). When we view our existence from the gospel's perspective, our humility is enlarged to eternal proportions. We realize that Jesus Christ was not only the first of our Heavenly Father's children, but also the best and the brightest of His offspring. "For by him were all things created, that are in heaven, and that are in earth, visible and invisible, whether they be thrones, or dominions, or principalities, or powers: all things were created by him, and for him: And he is before all things, and by him all things consist. And he is the head of the body, the church: who is the beginning, the firstborn from the dead; that in all things he might have the preeminence." (Colossians 1:16-18). The birthright fell to Him, because He was the Firstborn. If anyone deserved to feel special, it would be Him, and yet, He was the personification of humility.

He has been likened unto a lamb without spot or blemish. The Lion of Judah is the symbol of the tribe of Judah, originating with the blessing given to Judah by Jacob. (See Genesis 49:9). Isaiah referenced lions, lambs, and a little child. He wrote that in the Millennium, "the wolf also shall dwell with the lamb, and the leopard shall lie down with the kid; and the calf and the young lion and the fatling together; and a little child shall lead them." (Isaiah 11:6).

The Lion of Judah may also represent the Lord. (See Revelation 5:5). However, most Christians prefer to think of Jesus Christ as "the Lamb of God, which taketh away the sin of the world." (John 1:29). What better example could there be of true submissiveness to the will of the Father, than of the One who said: "Father, if thou be willing, remove this cup from me: nevertheless not my will, but thine, be done." (Luke 22:42).

He was the grand architect of our salvation. We are all familiar with those who focus their worship on "elegant and spacious buildings and fine work of wood, and all manner of precious things." (Mosiah 11:8-11). We remember the Emperor Justinian, who "began a new Santa Sophia. He summoned the best architects to plan and superintend the work. Abandoning the traditional basilican form, they conceived a design whose center would be a spacious dome resting not on walls but on massive piers, and buttressed by a half dome at either end. Ten thousand workmen were engaged, and 320,000 pounds of gold were spent on the enterprise. In five years and ten months the edifice was complete, and on December 26, 537 A.D., the Emperor led a solemn inaugural procession to the resplendent cathedral. Justinian walked alone to the pulpit, and lifting up his hands, cried out: "Oh Solomon! I have vanquished you!" (Will Durant, "The Lessons of History," 4:130). News flash: Justinian has long since left the great and spacious building, headed for parts unknown.

1,463 years later, writer and director James Cameron stood before the Academy of Motion Picture Arts and Sciences and a television audience of around 40 million viewers, and with an Oscar trophy in each of his raised hands, cried out, "I'm the king of the world!" At uncomfortable moments like this, visions of the "Prince of Darkness" loom before us. (See John Milton's, "Paradise Lost"). We retreat to the sanctuary of the Savior's counsel: "Lay not up for yourselves treasures upon earth, where moth and rust doth corrupt, and where thieves break through and steal." (Matthew 6:19). We acknowledge that humility need not be incompatible with temporal successes, but realize that it cannot co-exist with the raw and ugly feelings of pride that are sometimes associated with that success. Truly, "pride goeth before destruction, and an haughty spirit before a fall." (Proverbs 16:18).

In 1964, John Lennon famously declared: "Christianity will go. It will vanish and shrink. I needn't argue with that; I will be proved right. We're more popular than Jesus now." ("London Evening Standard," 3/4/1966). The Beatles broke up 6 years later, and in 1980, Lennon went the way of all flesh to meet his Maker, "to stand with shame and awful guilt before the bar of God." (Jacob 6:9). Today, by most reports, Christianity is still alive and well. Latter-day Saints are reminded of the more popular part of the Zoramites, who were the rock stars of their day, who "were angry because of the word (of God), for it did destroy their craft," that was The Book of Mormon equivalent to heavy metal music, "therefore they would not hearken unto the words" of eternal life that would have been the key to their salvation. (Alma 35:3). The proud and the haughty, "who undertake to set themselves up as judges of truth and knowledge, are shipwrecked by the laughter of the gods." (Albert Einstein).

Sometimes there is a fine line between a humble and yet confident leader like Jesus Christ and the nattering nabobs of negativism that are so prevalent in the world, and that seek so seditiously to subtly seduce us. Their defiance provokes fear, while the Savior creates confidence. Their detractions generate resentment, while the Savior promises peace. Their distain leads to apathy, while the example of Jesus Christ breeds enthusiasm. Their denigrations shout "I," while the Lord Omnipotent softly says "We." They decry accountability and assign blame, while our Advocate goes about fixing mistakes. These doubters crave control, while the Lord Jehovah endows us with responsibility. They disregard know-how, even as our Exemplar shows how. Their disparagement reduces work to drudgery, while the Lord of the Vineyard elevates effort to excitement. Their derision drives the masses, while the Prophet of The Highest is out in front leading His army of Christian soldiers. The real measure of the Man of Holiness is that "when he had sent the multitudes away,' when there was no one left to sustain Him, "he went up into a mountain apart to pray: and when the evening was come, he was there alone." (Matthew 14:23). There was no fanfare, no public display of support, no exclusive interviews by the silver-haired news anchors of a fawning press corps, no merchandising of His celebrity status, just quiet reflection, meditation, contemplation, introspection, and a deep desire to draw near to His Father. Our prayers, both audible and inarticulate, reflect the same conviction. Though our flesh and our hearts fail, God is our strength and our portion forever. (See Psalms 73:26).

There is no evidence that Jesus ever received a gold watch or a brass plaque to commemorate His achievements. Instead, He quietly counseled: "When thou doest thine alms, do not sound a trumpet before thee, as the hypocrites do in the synagogues and in the streets, that they may have glory of men. Verily I say unto you, They have their reward." (Matthew 6:2). "And when thou prayest, thou shalt not be as the hypocrites are: for they love to pray standing in the synagogues and in the corners of the streets, that they may be seen of men." (Matthew 6:5). "Moreover when ye fast, be not as the hypocrites, of a sad countenance: for they disfigure their faces, that they may appear unto men to fast." (Matthew 6:16).

Too many of us engage in chit-chat that is nothing more than a parody of principles, a distortion of doctrine, a simulation of standards, a caricature of canon, and a façade of faith within the mirrored walls of crystal cathedrals. Too often, our most pressing concern is to be as photogenic as possible. If we want to gain a new perspective on humility, however, we might study the masterful discourse given by the Savior and recorded by Matthew, known as the Sermon on the Mount. (See Matthew 5, 6, & 7). It can be divided into sections: the Beatitudes, new laws, the Lord's Prayer, a discussion of money, and warnings. Nowhere, however, do we find evidence that He used His influence to solicit monetary contributions, established a Go-Fund-Me account, or formed a political action committee, became a media mogul, sought product endorsements, promoted merchandise, inked a book deal, or engaged in a lucrative T.V. ministry. In fact, His polar opposites are characterized by today's televangelists, of whom it has been written: "Someone needs to say this plainly: The faith healers and health-and-wealth preachers who dominate religious television are shameless frauds. Their message is not the true gospel of Jesus Christ. There is nothing spiritual or miraculous about their on-stage chicanery. It is all a devious ruse designed to take advantage of desperate people. They are not godly ministers, but greedy impostors, who corrupt the word of God for money's sake. They are not real pastors who shepherd the flock, but hirelings, whose only design is to fleece the sheep. Their love of money is glaringly obvious in what they say as well as in how they live. They claim to possess great spiritual power, but in reality they are rank materialists and enemies of everything holy." (John MacArthur, gty.org). The lesson to be learned is that we need to be careful about our motives, and to be sure we are preaching the word for the right reasons. The barometer of humility can be a measure of whether or not we are headed toward "the personality precipice" envisioned by Neal A. Maxwell. ("B.Y.U. Devotional," 4/27/1972).

When religion becomes "magical," and when the power by which the church operates is transferred from God to those who profess to be His earthly representatives, but who are instead only fiercely competing for "market share," we are having a problem with humility. When the Bible becomes a fairy tale, conveying power and knowledge without the aid of revelation, we are having a problem with humility. When priesthood acquires the status of an office that automatically bestows power and grace without any regard for the spiritual or moral qualifications of its possessor, we are having a problem with humility. These phenomena, declared Thomas Jefferson, "constitute the power and the profit of the priests. Sweep away their gossamer fabric of factitious religion" he declared, "and they would catch no more flies." ("The Writings of Thomas Jefferson," 6:192).

He wrote that "the religion builders (who, in his day, sought to lead the church without humility) have so distorted and deformed the doctrines of Jesus, so muffled them in mysticisms, fancies and falsehoods, have caricatured them into forms so inconceivable, as to shock reasonable thinkers. Happy in the prospect of a restoration of primitive Christianity, I must leave to younger persons to encounter and lop off the false branches which have been engrafted into it by the mythologists of the middle and modern ages." ("Jefferson's Complete Works," V. 7, p. 210 & 257).

Back in the day, Nathanael asked: "Can there any good thing come out of Nazareth?" (John 1:46). Others wondered: "Is not this the carpenter's son?" (Matthew 13:55). Isaiah prophesied: "He hath no form nor comeliness; and when we shall see him, there is no beauty that we should desire him." (Isaiah 53:2). There is no record that His likeness was ever captured on canvas, much less in a music video, a movie trailer, on a theater marquee, or on a boulevard billboard, and no cameo exists that would provide clues to His appearance, but if we desire to know what He looked like, humility could be the passport to our spiritual rebirth, wherein we receive the image of God in our countenances. (See Alma 5:14). With humility, we just might be able to look in the mirror, in order to catch a glimpse of a divine presence.

During His ministry, the Savior used simple and easy to understand examples to teach the doctrine of salvation, such as birds, coins, flowers, leaven, olives, pearls, sowers, talents, travelers, wind, bread and wine, candles under bushels, fig trees, loaves and fishes, mustard seeds, sheep and goats, tax gatherers and sinners, vessels of oil, and wheat and tares. His examples were familiar to his relatively unsophisticated disciples who were fishermen, husbandmen, hypocrites, lepers, tax collectors, family members, the deaf and dumb, laborers in vineyards, scribes and Pharisees, the blind and lame, the weak and infirm, and widows.

He used no Power Point or Keynote presentations to convey His message, no green screen, no C.G.I., no personal information devices, and no social media. He had no hashtag, no Twitter account, and no Facebook followers. He didn't augment His message with a boost from Industrial Light and Magic, Dolby sound, or IMAX, for that special "pop." He never composed a text message and never sent out an email blast. He never posted on Instagram, and never established a Pinterest board. And yet, through it all, He remains our Exemplar and our Spiritual Rock, Who invited us: "Come unto me, all ye that labour and are heavy laden, and I will give you rest." (Matthew 11:28). He only asks that we be "willing to mourn with those that mourn; yea, and comfort those that stand in need of comfort, and to stand as witnesses of God at all times and in all things, and in all places that (we) may be in." (Mosiah 18:9). He asks for the sacrifice of a heart broken down in humility, that can only be done individually, one faithful disciple at a time.

If we follow His example, will we, too, have humility? Only once in the New Testament, and once in The Book of Mormon, is the Savior characterized as being humble, and yet He was its personification. Paul wrote: "And being found in fashion as a man, he humbled himself, and became obedient unto death, even the death of the cross." (Philippians 2:8). Speaking from the dust, Moroni told us: "And then shall ye know that I have seen Jesus, and that he hath talked with me face to face, and that he told me in plain humility, even as a man telleth another in mine own language, concerning these things." (Ether 12:39).

Everything written about the Savior, though, suggests a profound humility that was intrinsic to His nature. John declared: "The Son can do nothing of himself, but what he seeth the Father do." (John 5:19). He urged his disciples: "Be ye, therefore, perfect, even as your Father which is in heaven is perfect." (Matthew 5:48). He taught us how to pray: "Our Father which art in heaven, Hallowed be thy name." (Matthew 6:9-10). In His agony, He declared: "Thy will be done." (Matthew 26:42). He submitted completely to the will of His Father.

If we are anxiously engaged in following His example, humility will be like a butterfly that comes and sits quietly on our shoulder. Because of Him, we can be a little more cheerful, concerned, considerate, faithful, friendly, generous, gentle, grateful, helpful, hopeful, kind, prayerful, and thoughtful. We can be facilitators, intercessors, mediators, and peacemakers. We can be more motivated to be charitable, compassionate, and thankful. We can give ourselves completely to consecration, forgiveness, quiet contemplation, reconciliation, sacrifice, service, and worship. We can devote ourselves to family, friends and neighbors, our church, community, nation and the world. We can be less inclined to be concerned about keeping up appearances, less discouraged by influences that are out of our control, less distracted by telestial toys, less focused on a temporal time table, less likely to be puffed up in pride, less pressured by our peers, less prone to criticism, less quick to anger, less susceptible to the siren song of social media, less swayed by carnal, sensual, and devilish desires, and less wrapped up in ourselves and smitten by our seeming successes.

If we are anxiously engaged, we will be a little more like Captain Moroni, of whom Mormon wrote: "Yea, verily, verily I say unto you, if all men had been, and were, and ever would be, like unto Moroni, behold, the very powers of hell would have been shaken forever; yea, the devil would never have power over the hearts of the children of men." (Alma 48:17). We will have humility, but will be so outwardly focused on the peaceable things of the Kingdom that we will scarcely notice.

We want to be
able to resoundingly declare
that we have been born of God,
and have received His image
in our countenances; that
we have experienced
a mighty change
in our hearts.

What Think Ye of Christ?

When "the Pharisees were gathered together, Jesus asked them, Saying, What think ye of Christ? Whose son is he?" Sadly, their sluggish response, "The Son of David," was tendered with little feeling or emotion. (Matthew 22:41-42). Although it was technically correct, it lacked spiritual horsepower. Its dearth of traction was obvious, its inability to generate spontaneity was palpable, its lack of energy to engage enthusiasm was noticeable, its incapacity to spark vitality was evident, and its failure to candidly acknowledge the powerful relationship that can exist between man and God was clear. Following the Savior's rebuke of their hesitancy and equivocation, none of the Pharisees were thereafter "able to answer him a word, neither durst any man from that day forth ask him any more questions." (Matthew 24:46). They had been weighed in the balances and had been found wanting, for they were spiritually bankrupt on an institutional scale. (See Daniel 5:27).

And yet, with adequate preparation, thinking about Christ could have generated the energy to lift them heavenward on a groundswell of emotion. Their example should be motivation enough for us to elevate the level of our worship to something more dynamic than the simple mechanical observance of a multiplicity of ceremonial rules, and to help us to avoid the pit into which the Pharisees fell. Thinking about the Savior should be more than a repetitive exercise to be performed only by the numbers. As the daily antidote to our tendency toward pride, selfishness, and self-reliance, it should help us to catalyze feeling, capture emotion, contour attitude, crystallize thought, congeal passion, compartmentalize action, and convey sentiments that lead to our spiritual revitalization.

Since those were, perhaps, among the most important and penetrating questions that could have been asked of anyone, at any time in history, or at any place on earth, we can be sure that the Pharisees were not the Savior's only intended respondents. He cast a much wider net. The Master, Who expounded all scripture in one, demands that you and I answer, as well, that we might also have the opportunity to squirm under the microscope of His scrutiny.

It matters little whether we identify with the Pharisees or the Sadducees, with Buddha, Confucius, Guru Nanak, Zoroaster, or with gods of wood and stone. We may concur with the monotheism of Islam or the Bahá'i, the pantheistic theology of Hinduism,

Shintoism, or Taoism, with secular humanism or irreligion, with Catholicism or Eastern Orthodoxy, with evangelicals, fundamentalists, or Protestants, or with the existential nihilism of the postmodern world. Paul observed of the Athenians, who were not so very different from us, that they were inclined to bow down before unknown gods, whom, therefore, they ignorantly worshipped. It is in the hope that this essay will help you to stand independently in your witness of the true and living God, that "him declare I unto you." (Acts 17:23, see 1 Thessalonians 1:9).

You may be a trusting Timothy or a doubting Thomas, a spiritual giant or a philosophical naturalist, of a ready wit or resoundingly dull, earnestly enlightened or frivolously facetious, casually indifferent or energetically enthusiastic, a dedicated disciple or a distracted detractor, a true believer, an agnostic, or an atheist. In a moment of despair, you may have thrown up defensive dross designed to disregard, deflect, discourage, or disparage the question: "What think ye of Christ?" If you have wandered into disbelief, you may have deferred or deterred your response to the question: "Whose son is he?" If that day has already come, or if it looms large on your horizon, you can be sure that your stammering apologies will be unceremoniously swept aside when your true feelings are finally revealed.

In every case, no matter that you are a defender of the faith or an ambassador of the adversary, all of heaven will hold its collective breath as time stands still and your fate hangs in the air as a dandelion seed caught in the doldrums of a hot summer afternoon. How you answer will define you or destroy you, for your response will delineate your dreams, as it describes your destiny and determines how, where, and with whom you will spend eternity. I hope this essay can help you to prepare for that great and dreadful day when you will be asked to stand and give your sworn deposition before God, angels, and witnesses, to be counted among the sheep or the goats, on His right hand or His left hand.

To insure that your answers might be animated with energy, to have no regrets, and to avoid the fate of the Pharisees, you have been given the Light of Christ. It proceeds from His throne as a powerful influence for good that is intended to groom you to receive the Holy Ghost. It is a gift that miraculously multiplies even as it divides within a universe populated with individuals whose actions are governed by free will. It is given, the Lord revealed, "that every man may act in doctrine and principle pertaining to futurity, according to the moral agency which I have given unto him." (D&C 101:78, see D&C 93:31).

It has been benevolently bestowed upon all of us by One Whom we can be sure "denieth none that come unto him, black and white, bond and free, male and female; and he remembereth the heathen; and all are alike unto (him), both Jew and Gentile." (2 Nephi 26:33). The Light of Christ stimulates our soul-sweat as it works on our conscience, our sense of duty, and our scruples. It provides a shield of protection against the corrosive spatter of perspiration cast off by the destroyer, who is insidiously and persistently working overtime to damage our doctrinal defenses, dull our spiritual sensitivities, diminish our charitable capacity, deplete our bountiful reservoirs of sympathy, and destroy our devotions, even as we labor with an equal but opposite intensity to deify our work on the earth.

The Light of Christ exerts a nurturing influence, as well. Although we must daily travel farther from the East, we are nevertheless oriented toward the radiant glow emanating from that distant horizon. It provides us with the regularly recurring reassurance of a religious recalibration that autocorrects with fortuitous frequency and celestial precision. It envelops us in an intuitive appreciation of where we came from, why we are here, and where we are going. As in a heavenly language that is rhythmical, melodious, soothing to our ears, and calming to our souls, when we hear the Spirit quietly whisper: "You're a stranger here," we are comforted by the realization that it is because we have "wandered from a more exalted sphere." (Eliza R. Snow). The Light of Christ examines what it means to be anxiously engaged, inspires us to plumb the depths of our commitment to the Savior, sensitizes us to the nobility of His work, expands upon the visions of immortality, and makes us more acutely aware of His glory, as it brings eternal life within our purview.

In a way, thinking about the Savior can be likened to a primer on midwifery, because one of its purposes is to facilitate the arduous process of our spiritual rebirth, by contributing to our preparation to answer with conviction the questions that were first posed to the Pharisees so long ago: "What think ye of Christ?" and "Whose son is he?" When we feel the urge to push His agenda, the Light of Christ can be our labor coach, providing us with just the right amount of encouragement to successfully deliver our witness of the Savior without being overbearing.

One exciting element of the manifestation of the Light of Christ is the constant stream of inspiration and revelation that cascades down from above. This insures that all may walk along illuminated pathways, and that no individual or institution may legitimately claim or have a monopoly on divine guidance. It exerts a leveling influence that is the great equalizer, giving each of us the same privileges to use our faculties of mind, intellect, and spirit to our best advantage, that we might discern between truth and error, no matter upon what spiritual plateau we might be currently relaxing. It permits us to listen with sensitivity and to be receptive to the cries of the downtrodden and oppressed, to see with a lucidity that allows us to be responsive to our environment, and to be benevolently blind to the shortcomings of others.

The Light of Christ provides us with a nurturing influence that makes it easier to have lips that have learned to articulate only positive expressions of speech and never speak guile, shoulders that have developed the strength to bear the burdens of those who have been battered and bruised by the vicissitudes of life and who may be faltering under the heavy weight of sorrow or sin, backs that have become sturdy enough to brace us against the fierce winds of adversity and the subtle wiles of the adversary, hearts that have become the receptacles of pure and virtuous principles upon which we may draw in times of need, bowels that are moved to compassion for those who are struggling with misfortune, hands that have become accustomed to lifting those who are in need of support, and feet that have been conditioned to speedily carry us to those who are imprisoned by poor choices, bad habits, or unfortunate circumstances.

Even now, heavenly messengers who minister by the Light of Christ are nursemaids to the nations of the earth, and use its power as a resource to reach out and caress those who are poor in spirit. Men and women of all persuasions feel that angels are watching over them. Witness countless newlyweds who are certain that their match was made in heaven before the world was. Others sense that they have been assisted by acts of providence, are the beneficiaries of divine intervention, have been touched by angels, are moved to compassion, or have been otherwise blessed to "walk in the light of the Lord." (Isaiah 2:5).

Guidance in the form of spiritual promptings and impressions are more common that many would suspect. Powerful intuitive communicators strongly influence nearly all of us to move in the direction of our dreams, toward a greater appreciation of the majesty and power of our Creator. Truly, He "is no respecter of persons" Who causes the sun to shine on the wicked, as well as on the just. (Acts 10:34). Therefore, we must venture forth out of the shadows, even beyond the direction we receive from the Light of Christ and the ministration of angels, if we want to begin to appreciate the special familiarity that the Lord enjoys with those whom He has characterized as "the children of light." (John 12:36). The more we think about Christ, the easier it is to craft with words the sensations that naturally flow to each of us as a result of the stirrings of those feelings of intimacy.

As we think about Christ, we realize how heavily we have borrowed from the towering examples of those who, over the years, have been our mystical mentors, our sensible chaperones, our spiritual guides, our surrogate Saviors, as well as our compassionate critics. They are our avatars, who have shown us the way, strengthened our testimonies, taught us humility, been there to steady and nurture us, applied the Balm of Gilead and bound up our wounds, provided both tangible and immaterial support, emboldened us with words of encouragement, and cheered us on with wise counsel. When think of this multitude of angels thinly disguised as our family, friends, and peers, we remember the words of Sir Isaac Newton, who, when pressed to reveal the great secret behind his accomplishments, simply replied: "I stood on the shoulders of giants."

If we are fortunate, we are privileged to do so, as well. As we think about our Savior, we draw upon the faith, testimony, and spiritual insight of the General Authorities and lay members of The Church of Jesus Christ of Latter-day Saints, as well as playwrights and poets, philosophers and humanitarians, authors, journalists, essayists, classicists, religious scholars of all persuasions, statesmen, sages, mystics, stoics, and the composers and lyricists with whom we are familiar. Our friends and family are often more influential than they could ever imagine. We are fortunate if we have been blessed with such wonderful traveling companions during our journey through mortality. Such gurus, guides, and governors can profoundly touch our lives with influences that help us to shape tender feelings as we think about the Savior.

In the end, however, we sometimes need to ask for the pardon of our traveling companions when they are confronted by the literal and figurative blemishes, the idiosyncratic foibles, and the objective and subjective imperfections that too often subtly work their way into our character, if we are not vigilant. Whenever we take poetic license with foundation principles, or add needless ecclesiastical embroidery to gospel truths, we beseech the indulgence, and the forgiveness, of our peers. If our passion clouds our vision or overpowers our zealous intentions, if the syntax of our speech seems tortuous, too bland, or too spicy, if our feelings are understated or if we have been given over to hyperbole, or even if we appear to drift over the line separating true doctrine from baseless speculation, we beg for the forbearance of our contemporaries, that they might take a step back and allow our expressions to simmer for a while before returning to sample anew their flavor. The reduction sauce of time may enhance the palatability of our perspective.

In any case, as the congealed distillate of our life experiences, our feelings relating to the Savior stand revealed as our innocent attempts to yoke our emotions to language. We hope that others will find them refreshing, and that they too will rely upon the Light of Christ before we consume them as food for thought.

We dream that we might feel the gentle caress of the touch of the Master Potter, as He turns our lives with the hand of time. We want Him to mold us and shape us as the Artisan of our destinies. "As the clay is in the potter's hand, so are ye in mine hand," said the Lord to His prophet. (Jeremiah 18:6). As Isaiah declared: "O Lord, thou art our father; we are the clay, and thou our potter; and we all are the work of thy hand." (Isaiah 64:8). We hope and pray that as our thoughts to turn to the Savior, we may remain pliable and impressionable to the Light of Christ.

All of us need to learn to utilize the divinely designed accouterments of the matchless and multi-talented Carpenter of Nazareth, Who will help us to construct the stages upon which will be enacted the drama of our lives. We can imagine that our efforts will be validated by appreciative applause from the audience, and by the occasional bouquets of red roses that are thrown at our feet. But it will be even more satisfying to remain as His poor understudies, and to give our best efforts to supporting roles in off-Broadway performances that count for more than mere entertainment.

His Plan does not require that we be the stars of the show. Our path of progress to perfection is a process, and not a point. We do not need top billing to fulfill our destiny. We do not seek to garner a People's Choice Award. Rather than becoming the objects of attention of an adoring paparazzi, we foresee ourselves being enveloped instead in dazzling clouds of divinely directed diamond dust that glitters with thousands of points of light, and becoming the participants in daily dramas that far surpass the pomp and circumstance of any "American Idol" production. Ours will be performances exhibiting displays of celestial energy worthy of notice from above. As fire in the sky, the air in the theater of life will be charged with an electricity that represents the inevitable merger of the universal encouragement of the Light of Christ with the pointed and providential guidance provided by the Holy Ghost. When these influences streak in tandem across the heavens, their trajectories will coalesce to trace a flaming trail that sparkles over a vast cosmic ocean of thought. Over the ebb and flow of its tide, the Spirit will create an effectual bridge of understanding that is buttressed by the cohesive influence of the mighty foundation of faith.

Our innermost longings to apprehend these visions of the eternal world are epitomized in our triumphant realization of dreams fulfilled. Our emotions are painted by words that depict our progression toward distant mileposts along the well-marked paths that lie before us. Our quest for the Holy Grail is defined as much by the obstacles we have encountered, as it is by the hurdles we have yet to face. We are molded by personal victories and by our commemoration of the achievement of our goals, but we are also refined by our frustrated plans, and shaped by our preparations to address challenges that lie just around the next bend in the road.

In the learning laboratory of life, experience is the active ingredient in a fertile matrix carefully created by God as He meticulously prepares the personalized petri dishes that are best suited to our individual circumstances. This rich culture medium becomes just the agar we need in order to nurture our metamorphosis, as we are transformed, not by maturation but by generation, into the full stature of our spirits. The infusion of a heavenly element readies us to receive with equanimity whatever might come during an incubation process that was designed to be just as challenging as it would be rewarding.

All this leads back to our basic objective, which is to keep the Savior in our thoughts, that we might encourage a daily atmosphere of reflection, maintain an eternal perspective, initiate positive change, and harmonize our behavior with His charitable example. Our determination to do so comes, in part, thanks to Moroni, whose words stir our souls as a voice whispering from out of the dust of centuries past. On one occasion, he wrote: "I speak unto you as if ye were present, and yet ye are not. But behold, Jesus Christ hath shown you unto me, and I know your doing." (Mormon 8:35).

Because we will one day be asked to give accountability reports to the Savior, we try to heed King Benjamin's ancient but apropos warning to watch ourselves judiciously, to be the meticulous guardians of our thoughts, the scrupulous custodians of our words, and the prudent caretakers of our deeds, to fastidiously observe the commandments of God, and to continue evenly in the faith. (See Mosiah 4:30). As we hesitantly inch our way through mortality, this admonition invigorates us with renewed energy, and instills in us the desire to redouble our efforts to know the Savior better.

We persist because the simple questions: "What think ye of Christ?" and "Whose son is he?" should make a difference to each of us. These inquiries demand that we dig deeply within ourselves before we tender our responses, because it is all too easy to superficially retreat into colorless and insipid verbiage as the easy way out. If we casually and carelessly steer a course away from Him with dismissive, inconsiderate, and offhand remarks, until He is conveniently out of sight and far from our minds, we can realistically expect in return nothing more than a stupor of thought. Any fleeting, albeit faux, feelings of liberation from the constraints of conscience will soon give way to an inner emptiness that cannot be satisfied with the poor imitations of the settled conviction in our minds of the peace that surpasses understanding, that could have been ours. If, in our knee-jerk reactions to the healthy opposition that stimulates our growth, we kick against the pricks, we will surely further estrange ourselves from the Spirit, until we are left with neither root nor branch. We will be tossed to and fro by every wind of doctrine, as flotsam and jetsam on the sea of life.

None of us would choose to perish because of our willful neglect of the things that matter most, or to lead marginalized lives because we had intentionally become spiritually depleted on a personal or an institutional level. We persevere because we do not want to die of spiritual starvation, doctrinal dehydration, or intellectual inhibition, while only inches away from the living bread that would have satisfied our hunger, or from the healing fountains of truth that could have slaked our thirst. We elect to think about our Savior in positive and meaningful ways that lead us to green pastures and still waters. The process draw us into the warmth of His embrace, where we are permitted to enjoy an intimacy that allows us to pause for a moment to feel the touch of His garment, before His strident call to action reawakens within us a sense of our duty that quickens the pace of the inexorable journey back to our beginnings.

Precious few "self-help" books address the issues of self-denial, meekness, and charity, or ask that we surrender to the greater good our desire for self-actualization, self-renewal, self-determination, self-fulfillment, or self-aggrandizement. Not often are we taught to concentrate our efforts on the quality of self-control that honors God's design, rather than some twisted temporal theory of emotional or spiritual well-being that lacks an upward thrust. But that is exactly what we must do. We must "let go and let God." Only then, will we catch a religious fever that elevates our testimony temperature enough to get our juices flowing with an appreciation of Who He really is. Only then, will we experience the earth shaking and mind bending theophany that we are His spiritual offspring, and will we recognize the potential of our position. The precious emanation of familiar and soothing oscillations of energy resonating from within the limitless reserves that are selflessly shared by the Holy Ghost will carry us along on rolling waves of the Spirit toward a more sure witness of the Savior's divinity. That is why we must keep Him in our thoughts.

This pulsing arpeggio ignites our souls with passion, and may have been the catalyzing influence that was missing from the pedantic model of righteous behavior that was adopted, almost by default, by the Pharisees. We want our preparation for the performance of our lives to include fast-scale runs through more than half a dozen octaves on all 88 of the glistening black and white ivory keys of experience. As we rehearse in our minds our witness that Christ is our Savior, we want to be accompanied by a celestial symphony that has been scored for every instrument. We want to expand our repertoire to include, not only inspiring artistic compositions representing every epoch of musical literature, but also our own original and signature harmonic inventions.

But most of all, in the orchestration of life, we want the Senior Recital that showcases our command of pitch, rhythm, dynamics, timbre, and texture, to be worthy of His approbation. Along the way, we want to find our way back to the Source of our inspiration, that we might one day enjoy master classes as we sit at the feet of the Maestro Who first created musicality by matching movement and form to the melody and mood of His celestial creations. We want to become reacquainted with our perfect fit. Then, when we have finally completed our dissertation on life, we hope that our composition may be recognized as our magnum opus. After we have successfully defended our thesis, we would like to be able to express our thanks at the exercises that not only celebrate our lives, but that also observe and honor our commencement. We hope to gratefully acknowledge our devotion to the one who became our doctoral advisor, who was none other than "the Christ, the son of the Living God." (Matthew 16:16).

We want to have a yearning to consecrate our lives to Him, and to throw ourselves upon an altar of faith that is of our own construction, whose foundation is buttressed by a supernal display of divine direction. We want to enjoy an unwavering confidence that drives us relentlessly forward so that we might one day squarely and unflinchingly meet His penetrating gaze with clear eyes, that His power to save might thereby be unleashed in our behalf, and that it might flow over our wounds as a healing balm.

When we look around, we want to find ourselves among those who have been born again, who are "called the children of Christ, his sons, and his daughters." (Mosiah 5:7). We want to experience the thrill of being spiritually begotten of Him, and of having our hearts changed through faith on His name. We want Him to be ever before us so that, without distraction, our thoughts might turn to Him, that we might feel His energy building within us until it lifts us to the zenith of experience where the lines distinguishing mortality from eternity blur, and we find ourselves consumed in the fire of everlasting burnings.

We want to be able to resoundingly declare that we have been born of God, and have received His image in our countenances; that we have experienced a mighty change in our hearts. (See Alma 5:14 & 26). Only then, through saving faith, will we be prepared to respond to the questions that loom before us: "What think ye of Christ?" and "Whose son is he?" As we ponder our relationship with the Savior, our proper prior preparation will prevent our poor presthood performance. It will nudge us off our complacency plateaus, away from the trendy cafés situated along the broad avenues of Idumea, and transport us as on the wings of eagles beyond the boundaries of our self-imposed limitations, right to the edge of eternity, where "forever" will finally stand revealed before us.

At that moment, as the power fueling our actions charges our spiritual batteries and energizes our sight with infinite perspective, there will be created a pulsing stream of inspiration whose flow has no temporal or spatial boundary. We will be swept up by quickening currents into the direct experience of a holy communion with God. Although the heavens will always be higher than the earth, His thoughts will somehow have become our thoughts, and His ways our ways. (See Isaiah 55:8-9). We will be caught up in His work and His glory, and finally understand that "the universe is a machine for the making of gods." (Henri Bergson, "Two Sources of Morality and Religion," p. 306).

"If I prove
a timid friend to
truth, I am afraid that I
will not survive to ve read
by those in whom these
times are ancient.
(Dante).

William Tyndale:
An Appreciation

To really appreciate the New Testament, you need to know something beforehand about William Tyndale (1494 – 1536) and the times in which he lived. In his preface to "Obedience of a Christian Man," published in Antwerp, Belgium, on October 2, 1528, he wrote: "Prepare thy mind, therefore, unto this little treatise; and read it discreetly; and judge it indifferently. And when I allege any scripture, look thou on the text whether I interpret it right: which thou shalt easily perceive by the circumstance and process of them, if thou make Christ the foundation and the ground, and build all on him, and referrest all to him; and findest also that the exposition agreeth unto the common articles of the faith and open scriptures."

It behooves all of us to brush up on our religious historical scholarship as we prepare ourselves to commemorate the 500th anniversary of the publication of his Bible, the first to be translated and printed in the English language (1526), and the prototype for the King James Version, published 85 years later (in 1611). We owe it to Tyndale to know something about his life, and about his ultimate sacrifice, his martyrdom for the cause, on October 6, 1536.

Every time we open our Bibles, we should say a silent prayer in our minds, thanking God for William Tyndale, and for men and women like him, who either inspired him or dedicated themselves to follow his example. But he would have been uncomfortable with our tributes. His was a simple faith that was expressed without ambiguity. On one occasion, he wrote: "Give to every man, therefore, his duty: tribute to whom tribute belongeth; custom to whom custom is due; fear to whom fear belongeth; honour to whom honour pertaineth. Owe nothing to any man; but to love one another. For he that loveth another fulfilleth the law. For these commandments, thou shalt not commit adultery, thou shalt not kill, thou shalt not steal, thou shalt not bear false witness, thou shalt not desire, and so forth, if there be any other commandment, are all comprehended in this saying: Love thine neighbour as thyself. Love hurteth not his neighbour. Therefore, is love the fulfiling of the law."

A bumper sticker that has enjoyed popularity for years declares: "If you can read this, thank a teacher." In fact, we should display bumper stickers that proclaim: "If you can read the Bible, thank William Tyndale!" When you finish reading this essay, I hope that you will have gained insight into the character of this great man, and will be better able to appreciate his incalculable contribution to our understanding of God through his interpretation of scripture as set forth in the English tongue, which was the language of the people.

He has brought a love of the scriptures within the grasp of untold millions. He urged: "Be strong in the Lord, and in the power of his might. Put on the armour of God that ye may stand steadfast against the crafty assaults of the devil. For we wrestle not against flesh and blood: but against rule, against power, and against worldly rulers of the darkness of this world, and against spiritual wickedness in heavenly things." The epic battle between light and darkness was constantly before his eyes, and he was ever mindful of the eternal consequences of the exercise of agency, in an age when simply engaging the principle of free will was dangerous, and particularly so when it related to ecclesiastical matters of faith, and when it was severely curtailed by what he perceived as the unrighteous dominion, and even the tyranny, of the state church.

If Tyndale seemed to rail against the establishment, he was on solid footing. At the very least, the careful list of grievances that has survived in his writings provides a vivid illustration of a mind-set forged by circumstance, and puts in perspective his dogged determination to set things right. "Who slew the prophets?" he asked. "Who slew Christ? Who slew his Apostles? Who the martyrs and all the righteous that ever were slain? The kings and the temporal sword at the request of the false prophets." There was no confusion in his mind regarding the individuals or institutions that squirmed uncomfortably in the cross-hairs of his criticism. He pulled no punches, even as he charted and negotiated very dangerous territory, for his was a stark and brutal world where to dare to disparage the church was to invite institutional opposition, ecclesiastical persecution, spiritual excommunication, and even temporal death by burning at the stake, all at the hands of secular authorities who received their sanction by the very leaders of a church whose heavenly mandate was to selflessly minister to and protect the flock.

In many ways, as we become more familiar with Tyndale, we are struck by his similarities to Joseph Smith, another martyr for the cause. Neither one was inclined to complain to God about his lot in life. On only one occasion is it recorded that Joseph ever did so. He was quickly put in his place by the Savior, Who responded to his entreaties: "My son, peace be unto thy soul; thine adversity and thine afflictions shall be but a small moment; And then, if thou endure it well, God shall exalt thee on high; thou shalt triumph over all thy foes. Thy friends do stand by thee, and they shall hail thee again with warm hearts and friendly hands. Thou art not yet as Job; thy friends do not contend against thee, neither charge thee with transgression, as they did Job." (D&C 121:7-10). It is unclear whether, at the bitter end, Tyndale was as Job, without friends upon whom he could rely, or who could provide for him even a few small comforts. We do know that after his betrayal, from his cold and dreary cell in the castle of Vilvoorde, near Brussels, where he spent the last six months of his life, he wrote: ""My overcoat and my shirts are worn out. All I ask is to be allowed to have a lamp in the evening, for it is indeed wearisome sitting alone in the dark."

Joseph Smith could have related well to one of Tyndale's observations: "Adversity also received I of the hand of God as a wholesome medicine, though it be somewhat bitter." Smith wrote from bonds in Liberty Jail: "O God, where art thou? And where is the pavilion that covereth thy hiding place? How long shall thy hand be stayed, and thine eye, yea thy pure eye, behold from the eternal heavens the wrongs of thy people and of thy servants, and thine ear be penetrated with their cries? Yea, O Lord, how long shall they suffer these wrongs and unlawful oppressions, before thine heart shall be softened toward them, and thy bowels be moved with compassion toward them?" (D&C 121:1-3).

With philosophical resignation, Tyndale confessed: "The world loveth that which is his, and hateth that which is chosen out of the world to serve God in the Spirit." Both Tyndale and Smith were molded through adversity by the hand of God to be creative and inventive vessels. Both knew by first-hand experience the workings of the Spirit, and willingly yielded themselves to its influence. Tyndale wrote: "As our strength abateth, groweth the strength of Christ in us: when we are clean emptied of our own strength, then are we full of Christ's strength."

Joseph would have concurred. In a similar vein, he wrote: "Let thy bowels also be full of charity towards all men, and to the household of faith, and let virtue garnish thy thoughts unceasingly; then shall thy confidence wax strong in the presence of God; and the doctrine of the priesthood shall distil upon thy soul as the dews from heaven. The Holy Ghost shall be thy constant companion, and thy scepter an unchanging scepter of righteousness and truth; and thy dominion shall be an everlasting dominion, and without compulsory means it shall flow unto thee forever and ever." (D&C 121:45-46).

Both were refined in the crucible of opposition, a condition that Tyndale repeatedly and eloquently described: "Lo, persecution and adversity for the truth's sake is God's scourge, and God's rod, and pertaineth unto all his children indifferently: for when he said he scourgeth every son, he maketh none exception." On another occasion, he observed: "The weakness of the flesh is the strength of the Spirit. And by flesh understand wit, wisdom, and all that is in a man before the Spirit of God come. And of like testimonies is all the scripture full." Joseph recorded the comforting words of the Savior that must have been a spiritual impression with which Tyndale was surely intimately familiar: "Thy days are known, and thy years shall not be numbered less;

therefore, fear not what man can do, for God shall be with you forever and ever." (D&C 122:9).

But what of Tyndale's legacy. As of November 2014, the full Bible, in large part based on His daring work, has blossomed into translations in no fewer than 531 languages, and 2,883 languages have at least some portion of the Bible in the vernacular. The King James Version dates from 1611, and stems directly from Tyndale's Bible. Since that time, familiar and widely used translations have included the New International Version, the New Living Translation, the New American Standard Bible, the New Revised Standard Version, and the New Jerusalem Bible.

In fact, 84% of the K.J.V. New Testament, and 76% of the K.J.V. Old Testament, is verbatim Tyndale. "In so great diversity of spirits," he asked, "how shall I know who lieth, and who sayeth truth? Whereby shall I try and judge them? Verily by God's word, which only is true. But how shall I that do, when (the Catholic Church) wilt not let me see scripture?" More than any other bold individual, he single-handedly remedied that deplorable situation. Certainly, he must have been among "the noble and great ones" that had been singled out in the pre-earth existence, to come to earth to address an entire laundry list of injustices preparatory to the restoration of the gospel in the Last Days. (Abraham 3:22).

Reading the Tyndale Bible can give us a new appreciation of the 7th Article of Faith of The Church of Jesus Christ of Latter-day Saints: "We believe the Bible to be the word of God as far as it is translated correctly." Tyndale would have been quite satisfied to use that declaration of belief as his springboard for action, for he scathingly wrote of the ecclesiastical misanthropes of his day: "O crafty jugglers and mockers with the word of God! Know ye not that scriptures sprang out of God?" He characterized church leaders, from the pope to the parish priest, as a generation of vipers. "How can ye say well," he asked, "when ye yourselves are evil?" (Matthew 12:34).

Tyndale personified He to whom Paul referred, when he taught the Athenians: "In Him we live, and move, and have our being." (Acts 17:28). He recognized the stirrings of the spirit within his breast, and knew beyond the shadow of a doubt that we are quickened and are alive because of Jesus Christ, and Him alone.

The United States Constitution (June 21, 1788) with its Bill of Rights (December 15, 1791), was ratified roughly 250 years after Tyndale's martyrdom, but it can trace its origins right back to his dogged determination to make scripture the ultimate source of knowledge that would be available to the common man. The First Amendment includes freedom of religion and freedom of speech, and reads: "Congress shall make no law respecting an establishment of religion, or prohibiting the free exercise thereof; or abridging the freedom of speech, or of the press." Even the articulation of those eternal principles was only possible because of the groundbreaking efforts of William Tyndale. In 1528, at the dawn of the Reformation in mainland Europe, he challenged the English clergy: "But how shall I (conform my life to the teachings of Jesus Christ), when ye will not let me have his testimonies, or witnesses, in a tongue which I understand? Will ye resist God? Will ye forbid him to give his Spirit unto the lay as well as unto you? Hath he not made the English tongue? Why then forbid ye him to speak in the English tongue?"

Tyndale presaged the Declaration of Independence (1776), and Thomas Paine's "The Right of Man" (1791). The Declaration asserts: "We hold these truths to be self-evident, that all men are created equal, that they are endowed by their Creator with certain unalienable rights, that among these are life, liberty and the pursuit of happiness. That to secure these rights, governments are instituted among men, deriving their just powers from the consent of the governed… And for the support of this Declaration, with a firm reliance on the protection of divine providence, we mutually pledge to each other our lives, our fortunes and our sacred honor." The framers of the Declaration cast their lot with those who would defy authority to insist upon the exercise of "the rights of man." Surely, as men of intelligence, reason, and of faith, with a sense of history, they would not have been unaware of the precedent established by William Tyndale, or of the example he set when he lay his life on the altar of sacrifice in the defense of principles of freedom that he held sacred.

Tyndale would probably have considered himself a true Catholic, for he never wavered from his faith. It was only the bishops, monks, and friars with whom he took umbrage, evidenced by his characteristic vitriolic responses to Sir Thomas More and others of the establishment who challenged his beliefs and convictions. He influenced Hugh Latimer and Nicholas Ridley, who, at Oxford (on October 16, 1555, nearly twenty years after his martyrdom,) were burned at the stake in defense of their similar beliefs, at the behest of "Bloody Mary," the Catholic queen of England. Latimer is said to have urged his companion: "Play the man, Master Ridley; we shall this day light such a candle, by God's grace, in England, as I trust shall never be put out." Nineteen years earlier, Tyndale's last words had been: "Lord, open the king of England's eyes." That prayer was answered just two short years later, when newly Protestant King and Defender of the Faith Henry VIII (by the 1534 Act of Supremacy, two years before Tyndale's martyrdom!) ordered that the Bible of Miles Coverdale be used in every parish in the land. Largely based on Tyndale's work, the Coverdale Bible was a large volume, meant to grace a pulpit, unlike Tyndale's small pocket-sized New Testament, designed to be held in the hand as a prized personal possession, to be referred to regularly. Amazingly, in 1539, just three years after his martyrdom, Tyndale's edition of the Bible became officially approved for printing and distribution in England!

Martin Luther (1483-1546) was Tyndale's German contemporary. He and the Dutch Renaissance humanist, Catholic priest, social critic, teacher, and theologian Erasmus (1466-1536) provided fuel for the fire his faith. Perhaps they gave him the courage to ask his English religious contemporaries to act on the Savior's penetrating question: "Can ye not discern the signs of the times?" (Matthew 16:3). The times were surely changing in Europe, with the initiation of the Protestant Reformation with its 95 Theses, propositions for debate concerned with the question of indulgences, written (in Latin) and posted by Luther on the door of the Schlosskirche, Wittenberg, Germany, on Oct. 31, 1517.

Tyndale's familiarity with Luther's theses and Erasmus' philosophy helped him to see things in a new light. In his mind, the persecution and accusations of heresy that followed his challenge of dogma were not crises, but instead, were wonderful opportunities. I am sure that, if he had been given a choice, he would have lived in no other time or place. He was no "Man for All Seasons," reacting involuntarily to political and ecclesiastical pressures, following the path of least resistance, or bowing to expediency. Rather, he must have been supremely confident that he had been raised up to perform a specific work at a specific time. He was as one who had been foreordained to "walk before the Lord in the land of the living." (Tyndale Bible, Psalms 116:9)

His perspective on the scriptures is, even today, refreshing and stimulating. He was a polyglot who was fluent in eight languages, and his mastery of these tongues was so powerful that it was said that when speaking any of them, one listening would be hard pressed to discern if it was his native tongue. The greater point is that he was able to see scriptural source material in German, Latin, Hebrew, and Greek with equal intimacy, and utilize that enlightened understanding as the key to knowledge. Tyndale carefully and meticulously used a number of reference works when carrying out his translations of both the New and Old Testaments. When translating the New Testament, he referred to the third edition (1522) of Erasmus' Greek New Testament. He also used Erasmus' Latin New Testament, as well as Luther's German version and the Latin Vulgate. It is believed that he refrained from using Wycliffe's manuscript Bible as a source text because he didn't want its English usage, that reflected pre-Renaissance terminology, to taint his translation as archaic. Tyndale wanted his Bible to be easily understandable in the language of the people. (See below).

John Wycliffe had been an English philosopher, theologian, reformer, seminary professor at Oxford University, and dissident within the Roman Catholic church. He is generally recognized as being the first to translate, or more likely to oversee the translation, of the Bible into Middle English, in 1382 (?), around 60 years before the invention of the printing press. All copies were handwritten manuscripts that were verbatim translations of St. Jerome's Latin Vulgate Bible, inasmuch as in the 14th century, Greek and Hebrew texts were not generally available. Wycliffe has been called the "Morning Star of the Reformation" because he at least orchestrated, and certainly presaged, the growing opposition in Europe to ecclesiastical abuses. (Interestingly, there still exist as many as 250 manuscripts, complete or partial, of Wycliffe's translation).

His unauthorized translation of the Latin Bible into English was banned by the church in 1408, and Wycliffe, who had died on New Year's Eve, 1384, was so vilified by the papacy that on October 8, 1427, over 41 years after his death, on the orders of the Council of Constantine (the same council that had ordered Jan Hus / John Huss burned at the stake in 1415) he was condemned on 260 counts of heresy, and his bones were exhumed, burned, and dumped in the River Swift. The council probably thought that by doing so, Wycliffe might be forgotten. A later chronicler observed: "They burned his bones to ashes and cast them into the Swift, a neighboring brook running hard by. Thus, the brook conveyed his ashes into the Avon, the Avon into the Severn, the Severn into the narrow seas, and then into the main ocean. And so, the ashes of Wycliffe are symbolic of his doctrine, which is now spread throughout the world."

Today, Wycliffe's translation is difficult to read. For example, he translated James 1:5-8 as: "And if ony of you nedith wisdom, axe he of God, which yyueth to alle men largeli, and vpbreidith not; and it schal be youun to hym. But axe he in feith, and doute no thing; for he that doutith, is lijk to a wawe of the see, which is moued and borun a boute of wynde. Therfor gesse not the ilke man, that he schal take ony thing of the Lord. A man dowble in soule is vnstable in alle hise weies."

On the other hand, reading that same scripture from Tyndale's translation, we can easily recognize and relate to its poetical flow, and we can thank him for the rendition that provided the scriptural impetus for the King James Translators, whose version drove Joseph Smith to the Sacred Grove nearly three centuries later: "If any that is among you lack wisdom, let him ask of God, which giveth to all men without doubleness, and casteth no man in the teeth: and it shall be given him: but let him ask in faith, and waver not. For he that doubteth is like the waves of the sea, tossed of the wind, and carried with violence. Neither let that man think that he shall receive any thing of God. A wavering minded man is unstable in all his ways." (Tyndale Bible, James 1:5-8).

It is interesting to see how the phraseology of the scriptures evolved, from even before Wycliffe, through Tyndale and on to the familiar King James Version. Consider below the textual variants in only a few of the earliest English translations of John 3:16, that is today rendered in the King James Version as: "For God so loved the world, that he gave his only begotten Son, that whosoever believeth in him should not perish, but have everlasting life."

1st Ed. King James Version (1611): "For God so loued the world, that he gaue his only begotten Sonne: that whosoeuer beleeueth in him, should not perish, but haue euerlasting life."

Rheims (1582): "For so God loued the vvorld, that he gaue his only-begotten sonne: that euery one that beleeueth in him, perish not, but may haue life euerlasting."

Geneva (1560): "For God so loueth the world, that he hath geuen his only begotten Sonne: that none that beleue in him, should peryshe, but haue euerlasting lyfe."

Great Bible (1539): "For God so loued the worlde, that he gaue his only begotten sonne, that whosoeuer beleueth in him, shulde not perisshe, but haue euerlasting lyfe."

Tyndale (1534): "For God so loveth the worlde, that he hath geven his only sonne, that none that beleve in him, shuld perisshe: but shuld have everlastinge lyfe."

Wycliff (1380): "for god loued so the world; that he gaf his oon bigetun sone, that eche man that bileueth in him perisch not: but haue euerlastynge liif,"

Anglo-Saxon Proto-English Manuscript (995 AD): "God lufode middan-eard swa, dat he seade his an-cennedan sunu, dat nan ne forweorde de on hine gely ac habbe dat ece lif."

Interestingly, even the Book of Doctrine and Covenants of The Church of Jesus Christ of Latter-day Saints (February 4, 1831) renders the verse differently: "Who so loved the world that he gave his own life, that as many as would believe might become the sons of God." (D&C 34:3).

In the twenty-first century, it is sobering to reflect upon the sacrifices of our own forefathers, who shed their blood, that they might articulate and protect the freedoms of religious expression and free speech that were purchased so long ago, at the cost of the best blood of England; that of Wycliffe, Tyndale, Latimer, Ridley, and other martyrs. To safeguard the freedom of speech that we too frequently take for granted, today we often take our cases to impartial courts, but it was not always so. Every time we open our mouths to express our opinion, every time we read a controversial book, every time we post our thoughts of social media, every time we do a Google search on an interesting topic, we have men like Tyndale and his contemporaries to thank. They gave their lives to first establish, and then to protect, and finally to preserve for all generations their desire for unhindered scholarship in the comfort of their native tongue. "If any man hear my voice and open the door, I will come in unto him and will sup with him, and he with me." (Tyndale Bible, Revelation 3:20). So that divine communication might freely flow, Tyndale opened that door by squarely addressing the question: "How can we whet God's Word our children and household, when we are violently kept from it and know it not?"

It must have been so painful for Tyndale to witness the persecution of true believers that he could not stand by as a silent witness to the martyrdom of parents who only wanted their children to become familiar with the Lord's Prayer or with the Ten Commandments. Therefore, he determined to make the scriptures within reach of even the illiterate ploughboys who dotted England's rural countryside. He wrote: "Here seest thou that it is God's gift, to suffer for Christ's sake. Happy are ye if ye suffer for the name of Christ; for the glorious Spirit of God resteth in you. Is it not an happy thing, to be sure that thou art sealed with God's Spirit to everlasting life? And, verily, thou art sure thereof, if thou suffer patiently for his sake. Tribulation maketh feeling; or it maketh us feel the goodness of God, and his help, and the working of his Spirit. Lo, Christ is never strong in us till we be weak. As our strength abateth, so groweth the strength of Christ in us. Therefore, very gladly will I rejoice in my weakness, that the strength of Christ may dwell in me." Confronted with that quality of conviction, how could the authorities ever hope to successfully compete?

On another occasion, Tyndale wrote: "Behold, God setteth before us a blessing and also a curse: a blessing, if we suffer tribulation and adversity with our Lord and Savior Christ; and an everlasting curse, if, for a little pleasure's sake, we withdraw ourselves from the chastising and nurture of God, wherewith he teacheth all his sons, and fashioneth them after his godly will, and maketh them perfect, and maketh them apt and meet vessels to receive his grace and his Spirit, that they might perceive and feel the exceeding mercy which we have in Christ, and the innumerable blessings and the unspeakable inheritance, whereto we are called and chosen, and sealed in our Savior Jesus Christ, unto whom be praise for ever." There is no indication that Tyndale ever wavered in that determination or conviction during a relentless persecution that lasted for well over a decade.

When we study his translations and writings, we sense the portent of his own martyrdom, but more significantly, we are enveloped in the fire of his words that brim over with an enthusiastic expectation of unspeakable joy. He was as Jeremiah, who wrote: "But his word was in mine heart as a burning fire shut up in my bones, and I was weary with forebearing, and I could not stop." (K.J.V. Jeremiah 20:9). Or, as Tyndale wrote in his Old Testament translation: "But the word of the Lord was a very burning fire in my heart and in my bones, which when I would have stopped, I might not." (Tyndale Bible, Jeremiah 20:9).

He made little or no distinction between the anticipation of eternal happiness in the resurrection and the realization of joy, or more properly, hope, during his sojourn through this vale of tears. His faith was firmly based on that hope, which gave him the ability to see things as they really are. Consequently, he enjoyed a confidence that was not dependent upon circumstances. "Forasmuch, then, as we must needs be baptized in tribulations, and through the Red sea, and a great and a fearful wilderness, and a land of cruel giants, into our natural country; yea, and inasmuch as it is a plain earnest that there is no other way into the kingdom of life than through persecution, and suffering of pain, and of very death, after the ensample of Christ; therefore, let us arm our souls with the comfort of the scriptures: how that God is ever ready a hand, in time of need, to help us; and how that such tyrants and persecutors are but God's scourge, and His rod to chastise us." Faced with that sense of determination, his tormenters could never gain the upper hand, for in his mind they were special friends sent from God to try him and to prove him, and to make sure that he was worthy of his hire.

He may have been something of a fatalist, but it cannot be disputed that he was somehow completely at ease with the memory of his former life and the purpose of his call, and that he never wavered in his zealous determination to fulfill a mission whose objective was clearly defined in his own mind. He persevered because he was sure of his election as a servant of the Lord Jesus Christ, and it seems that, particularly in his darkest hours, his Master had already invited him to come and "sup with Him." (Tyndale Bible, Revelation 3:20). The Savior had granted His faithful servant a peace that surpasses our understanding. "Let us receive all things of God," he encouraged, "whether it be good or bad: let us humble ourselves under his mighty hand, and submit ourselves unto his nurture and chastising, and not withdraw ourselves from his correction."

Before his martyrdom, Joseph Smith had said: "I am going like a lamb to the slaughter; but I am calm as a summer's morning; I have a conscience void of offense towards God, and towards all men. I shall die innocent, and it shall yet be said of me: he was murdered in cold blood." (D&C 135:4). The conduct of William Tyndale's life expressed a similar peace born of confident expectation. "He will not work until all be past remedy," Tyndale wrote, "and brought unto such a case, that men may see, how that his hand, his power, his mercy, his goodness and truth, hath wrought altogether. He will let no man be partaker with him of his praise and glory. His works are wonderful, and contrary unto man's works. Who ever, saving he, delivered his own Son, his only Son, his dear Son, unto the death, and that for his enemies' sake, to win his enemy, to overcome him with love, that he might see love, and love again, and of love do likewise to other men, and overcome them with well doing?" The Catholic Church in England did not stand a chance, in the face of such passionate logic, conviction, and determination.

As Will Durant wrote of early Christianity, so could it have been similarly said of William Tyndale: The evidence and memory of his ministry could have just quietly faded away, but as time passed and events unfolded, there was instead "no greater drama in human record than the sight of a few Christians, scorned and oppressed by a succession of emperors, (or popes!) bearing their trials with a fierce tenacity, multiplying quietly, building order while their enemies generated chaos, fighting the sword with the word, brutality with hope, and at last defeating the strongest state that history had known (that was, in Tyndale's mind, the Vatican state of the Holy Roman Empire). Caesar and Christ had met in the arena, and Christ had won."

Tyndale knew what he was up against, but he eagerly sought out the foe on the field of battle. For him, it was a war of words, an ideological conflict with the contestants engaged in a fight, not to the temporal death, but for spiritual life. In a sense, he may have had a tactical advantage, because he positioned himself as the protagonist, while the ecclesiastical establishment was cast as the unpopular antagonist. Tyndale was able to choose his field of battle by defining the parameters of the debate. In the arena of public opinion, he was destined to win, although the eventual outcome would be agonizingly slow in an era when the interactive communication of ideas was in its infancy.

Although he took the fight to his adversaries, the constant sparring was on the home turf with which he was ever comfortable, where he could be nourished and refreshed, and receive validation from the spiritual compost and scriptural foundations of his rhetoric. Its vigor may have added fuel to the fire, but it surely kept things lively. "So sore have our false prophets brought the people out of their wits, and have wrapped them in darkness, and have rocked them asleep in blindness and ignorance!" he exclaimed. "Now ye preach nothing but lies, and, therefore, are of the devil, the father of all lies, and of him are ye sent." His politically incorrect protestations were the 16th century equivalents of modern day "sound-bites" that would be sure to catch the attention of those who watched the "5 o-clock news," garnering the support of a people starved for the word of God, while forcing his opponents to respond as silly-sounding robots in the early Renaissance arena of public opinion.

Because of his contributions to our understanding of the nature of God, we know today to Whom we must look if we are to obtain eternal life. The word of God has become firmly entrenched in our minds, hearts, and society, and is now readily available to billions of our brothers and sisters. As Tyndale translated the Psalms, he might have identified with David, who wrote: "Quicken me, O Lord, for thy name's sake: for thy righteousness' sake bring my soul out of trouble." (Tyndale Bible, Psalms 143:11). The same could be said of his translation of Paul's epistle to the Ephesians: "God, who is rich in mercy, for his great love wherewith he loved us, even when we were dead in sins, hath quickened us together with Christ." (Tyndale Bible, Ephesians 2:4-5).

Tyndale may have thought of his own revelatory experiences, when he discovered the following quotation from Job among his source texts: "For when God doth once command a thing, there should no man be curious, to search whether it be right. In dreams and visions of the night season, when slumbering cometh upon men, that they fall a sleep in their beds, he roundeth them in the ears, he informeth them, and sheweth them plainly." (Tyndale Old Testament Job 33:14-16). The later King James Version beautifully renders these same verses: "For God speaketh once, yea twice, yet man perceiveth it not. In a dream, in a vision of the night, when deep sleep falleth upon men, in slumberings upon the bed; then he openeth the ears of men, and sealeth their instruction." (K.J.V. Job 33:14-16).

These verses are reminiscent of Joseph Smith's experiences when, during the quiet hours of the evening, he was visited numerous times by angels. Although there is no existing record that Tyndale enjoyed similar visions, we would like to believe that this gentle spiritual giant was also attended and comforted by emissaries sent from the throne of God. Tyndale must have been encouraged, as was one latter-day lyricist who was also familiar with trials, tribulations, and persecution, who wrote: "Gird up your loins, fresh courage take, our God will never us forsake!" (William Clayton). As one having authority, Tyndale declared: "A true messenger must do his message truly; and say neither more nor less than he is commanded."

As we near the 500th anniversary of the publication of those 3,000 precious copies of Tyndale's Bible, published by Peter Schoeffer in the German city of Worms, in 1526, we can once again thank him for expressions such as: "gave up the ghost," "a shining light," "my brother's keeper," "they laughed him to scorn," "be of good cheer," enter ye in at the strait gate," "blessed are the meek, "fight the good fight," "riotous living," "the powers that be," "suffer fools gladly," "wandering stars," "fallen from grace," "eye hath not seen," "that old serpent," "bottomless pit," "live and let live," "cast the first stone," "stiff-necked," "Passover," "Atonement," and "wept bitterly," to name just a few. (See Appendix Four). Today, only three copies survive from that initial printing, but his legacy lives on in countless translations of the Bible, and its ripple effect has worked its way into the English language as a whole. It has been said that, in the shaping of modern English, Tyndale has been even more influential as a wordsmith than Shakespeare.

In the words of Steven Lawton: "With his New Testament, William Tyndale became the father of the Modern English language. He shaped its syntax, grammar, and vocabulary more than any man who ever lived; more than the author Geoffrey Chaucer, the playwright William Shakespeare, or the poets Percy Shelley and John Keats. At the dawn of the sixteenth-century, the English language was crude and unrefined, lacking precision and standardization, a strange mixture of Anglo-Saxon and Norman features with an ancient Latin vocabulary. Tyndale proved to be its change agent. As he translated the Bible, giving careful thought to words, phrases, and clauses, he shaped the language at its transition point from Middle English to Early Modern English. The speech of a nation was constructed in his mind and flowed from his pen. In providing the English Bible, Tyndale became the father of Modern English." ("William Tyndale: The Father of Modern English," 2/11/2015).

Think of Winston Churchill, who delivered an address of hope to the oppressed of Europe, in January 1940: "The day will come when the joy bells will ring again throughout Europe, and when victorious nations, masters not only of their foes, but of themselves, will plan and build in justice, in tradition, and in freedom, a house of many mansions where there will be room for all." Vintage Tyndale, underlining mine. (See Tyndale's Bible, John 14:2). Or, Thomas Jefferson: "I have sworn upon the altar of god eternal hostility against every form of tyranny over the mind of man." (K.J.V. Psalms 43:4, underlining mine, see Tyndale's Old Testament, Psalms 43:4). Or, John F. Kennedy: "The rights of man come not from the generosity of the state but from the hand of God." (K.J.V. Mark 16:19, underlining mine, See Tyndale's New Testament, Mark 16:19).

We can all thank Tyndale for providing the Bible that has become our platform for provident living. In the words of John Quincy Adams: "My custom is to read four or five chapters of the Bible every morning immediately after rising. It seems to me the most suitable manner of beginning the day. It is an invaluable and inexhaustible mine of knowledge and virtue." Or, Abraham Lincoln: "I am profitably engaged in reading the Bible. Take all of this Book upon reason that you can, and the balance by faith, and you will live and die a better man." Or, Grover Cleveland: "The reception of the teachings of Christ results in the purest patriotism, in the most scrupulous fidelity to public trust, and in the best type of citizenship." Or, Ronald Reagan: "Of the many influences that have shaped the United States into a distinctive nation and people, none may be said to be more fundamental and enduring than the Bible."

Would Tyndale be encouraged by the progress that has been made during the past 500 years, to put the vernacular scriptures in the hands of the people, and to facilitate the understanding of God's word so that it is now almost universal? According to the Gideon Society, there have been somewhere in the neighborhood of six billion Bibles published since the original 3,000 copies of the Tyndale Bible were hidden in bales of cloth and smuggled by ship from the Continent into England. Three of those original copies remain. They are the Stuttgart Copy, that was only recently discovered, and that is now owned by the Wurttemberg State Library in Stuttgart, Germany. It is complete with both its title page and the original binding. A second copy is owned by the British Library. Its 706 page New Testament is pocket-sized, bound in crimson leather, and is richly illuminated. It was acquired in 1994, at a cost of one million pounds sterling (U.S. $1,420,000.00 in 2015). It would be hard to put a proper price on one of Tyndale's Bibles, but a million dollars seems like a good starting point. The only other known copy of Tyndale's New Testament, safeguarded in St. Paul's Cathedral, London, has 59 leaves missing.

When considering the life of William Tyndale, one is reminded of the words of Tom Paine, who wrote: "Tyranny, like hell, is not easily conquered; yet we have this consolation with us, that the harder the conflict, the more glorious the triumph. What we obtain too cheap, we esteem too lightly. 'Tis dearness only that gives everything its value. Heaven knows how to put a proper price upon its goods; and it would be strange, indeed, if so celestial an article as (the) freedom (of speech and of the press) should not be highly rated." ("The Political Works of Thomas Paine," p. 55).

Tyndale would have been encouraged by the spread of Protestantism, as well as by the reforms of the Catholic Counter-Reformation, beginning with the Council of Trent, that were fueled by the dissemination of information made possible by the invention of the printing press by Johannes Gutenberg, around 1440. Tyndale would have been thrilled by the progress made at the Second Vatican Council, convened on October 11, 1962, by Pope John XXIII. One of the changes implemented by that council has been the use of vernacular languages, instead of Latin, in the Mass. This process only began 430 years after Tyndale's death, so he might have judged the reform to be too little and too late. But I think he would have, nevertheless, been overjoyed to participate in a Mass conducted in a language other than Latin, and also to see that the church had finally severely restricted the practical application of indulgences. But he would still be fighting to put an end to confession, transubstantiation, and the dogma relating to purgatory and intercession by Saints.

While he would have been particularly pleased to know that, as the Reformation gained momentum, there was a Catholic Anti-Reformation, he would have been more encouraged by the later Ages of Reason and Enlightenment made possible by the Renaissance, (although he would have been dismayed by their rationality), and finally by the restoration of the gospel, that was more in line with his philosophy of direct and personal interaction with God by the people.

He would have been bewildered by the rationality of the Last Days, and particularly by the new irreligion spawned by man's unrestrained, unfocused, and undisciplined reason. But he would not have judged his sacrifices to have been wasted, or squandered on an undeserving or uncaring people. He welcomed each opportunity that God gave to him to suffer for the Savior, thinking himself particularly blessed that Jesus Christ would think so much of him that He would give him opportunities to experience his own personal Gethsemane. He was utterly consumed in Christ. The way before him was clarified by the Spirit, and as he spent the last year of his life in the darkest of dungeons, the narrow confines of his small cell must have been illuminated with an undeniable celestial light that only he could discern.

In Latter-day Saint circles, it has often been said that the Restoration could not have taken place without the groundwork that had been laid by the architects of the Reformation. But it is not often acknowledged or even recognized that the Reformation itself might have fizzled were it not for brave men like William Tyndale. "And as pertaining unto them that despise God's word, counting it as a fantasy or a dream; and to them also that for fear of a little persecution fall from it, set this before thine eyes; how God, since the beginning of the world, before a general plague, ever sent his true prophets and preachers of his word, to warn the people, and gave them time to repent. But they, for the greatest part of them, hardened their hearts, and persecuted the word that was sent to save them. And then God destroyed them utterly, and took them clean from the earth. As thou seest what followed the preaching of Noe in the old world; what followed the preaching of Lot among the Sodomites; and the preaching of Moses and Aaron among the Egyptians; and that suddenly, against all possibility of man's wit."

Tyndale may have been anti-establishment, but he was no rebel without a cause. He knew precisely what his mission was, and he was incredibly centered. In spite of a variety of temporal deprivations, his intellect and his emotional and spiritual stability remained remarkably intact. He wrestled with no inner conflict, suffered no crisis of confidence, and battled no inner demons. "So ought every preacher to preach God's word purely, and neither to add nor minish." He made no bones about the fact that he was a sinner, and freely acknowledged his utter inability to work his way into heaven. He steadfastly believed in salvation by the grace of the Lord Jesus

Christ. That commitment is evident in his translation of Ephesians: "God, who is rich in mercy, for his great love wherewith he loved us, even when we were dead in sins, hath quickened us together with Christ." (Tyndale Bible, Ephesians 2:4-5).

"Another conclusion is this," he taught, "that no person, neither any degree, may be exempt from this ordinance of God: neither can the profession of monks and friars, or any thing that the pope or bishops can lay for themselves, except them from the sword of the emperor or kings, if they break the laws. For it is written, 'Let every soul submit himself unto the authority of the higher powers.' Here is no man except; but all souls must obey. The higher powers are the temporal kings and princes; unto whom God hath given the sword, to punish whosoever sinneth. God hath not given them swords to punish one, and to let another go free, and sin unpunished."

We owe him a debt of gratitude that he picked his battles so carefully, and focused his energies on the larger issues of life. "He that avengeth himself on every trifle," he wrote, "is not meet to preach the patience of Christ, how that a man ought to forgive and to suffer all things. He that is overwhelmed with all manner riches, and doth but seek more daily, is not meet to preach poverty. He that will obey no man is not meet to preach how we ought to obey all men."

Tyndale had a grasp of the first principles and ordinances of the gospel, which are those sacraments that are necessary for salvation. Of the Savior, he wrote: "Outwardly he disguised him not; but made him like other men, and sent him into the world to bless us, and to offer himself for us a sacrifice of a sweet savor, to kill the stench of our sins, that God henceforth should smell them no more, nor think on them any more; and to make full and sufficient satisfaction, or amends, for all them that repent, believing the truth of God, and submitting themselves unto his ordinances, both for their sins that they do, have done, and shall do."

The problem, as Tyndale saw it, was that "without a promise can there be no faith. The sacraments which Christ himself ordained, which have also promises, and would save us if we knew them and believed them, them minister they in the Latin tongue." He argued that "Peter in the second of the Acts practiced his keys; and by preaching the law brought the people into the knowledge of themselves, and bound their consciences, so that they were pricked in their hearts, and said unto Peter and to the other apostles, 'What shall we do?' Then brought they forth the key of the sweet promises, saying, 'Repent, and be baptized every one of you in the name of Jesus Christ, for the remission of sins, and ye shall receive the gift of the Holy Ghost.' For the promise was made to you, and to your children, and to all that are afar, even as many as the Lord shall call. Of like ensamples is the Acts full, and Peter's epistles, and Paul's epistles, and all the scripture."

Of the first of the principles of the gospel, he wrote: "Faith cometh by hearing, and hearing cometh by the word of God. And how shall they hear without a preacher, and how shall they preach except they be sent?" He reasoned: "Faith, that loveth God's commandments, justifieth a man. If thou believe God's promises in Christ, and love his commandments, then art thou safe. If thou love the commandment, then art thou sure that thy faith is unfeigned, and that God's Spirit is in thee. Faith justifieth before God in the heart; and love springeth of faith, and compelleth us to work; and the works justify before the world, and testify what we are, and certify us that our faith is unfeigned, and that the right Spirit of God is in us."

Of the second of the principles of the gospel, he wrote: "Contrition and repentance are both one, and nothing else but a sorrowful and a mourning heart." And also: "If God make him feel in his heart that lusts and appetites are damnable, and give him power to hate and resist them; then is he free, even with the freedom wherewith Christ maketh free, and hath power to do the will of God."

Of the first of the ordinances of the gospel, he wrote: "Ask the people what they understand by their baptism or washing? And thou shalt see, that they believe how that the very plunging into the water saveth them. But of the promises they know not, nor what is signified thereby." How he wished the people could read and understand that "Christ cleansed the congregation in the fountain of water through the word."

Of forgiveness of sin without confession, or ear-shrift, to a priest, he wrote: "Believe the promise, we are sure by God's word, that he is loosed and forgiven in Christ. When a man feeleth that his heart consenteth unto the law of God, and feeleth himself meek, patient, courteous, and merciful to his neighbor, altered and fashioned like unto Christ; why should he doubt but that God hath forgiven him, and chosen him, and put his Spirit in him, though he never crome his sin into the priest's ear?"

Of the second of the ordinances of the gospel, he wrote that the 20th chapter of the gospel of John clearly explains: "Receive the Holy Ghost. Whosoever's sins ye remit, they are remitted or forgiven; and whosoever's sins ye retain, they are retained or holden. With preaching the promises, loose they as many as repent and believe. And for that John saith, 'Receive the Holy Ghost.' I say that a steadfast faith, or belief in Christ and in the promises that God hath sworn to give us for his sake, bringeth the Holy Ghost, as all the scriptures make mention." He knew that the scriptures, translated into a language that the common man could understand, would be his most formidable weapons. "And in the last of Matthew, saith he: 'All power is given me in heaven and in earth; go, therefore, and teach all nations, baptizing them in the name of the Father, and of the Son, and of the Holy Ghost; teaching them to observe whatsoever I commanded you.'"

Of the Sacrament of the Lord's Supper, he wrote somewhat wistfully: "No more doth it hurt to say that the body and blood are not in the Sacrament." On the contrary, he felt the power of the Lord's encouragement: "This do in the remembrance of me." (Tyndale Bible, 1 Corinthians 11:24). "We have a promise," he explained, "that Christ, and his body, and his blood, and all that he did and suffered, is a sacrifice, a ransom, and a full satisfaction for our sins; that God for his sake will think no more on them, if we have power to repent and believe."

Of Christ's ability to save our souls, he wrote: "Who dried up the Red sea? Who slew Goliath? Who did all those wonderful deeds which thou readest in the Bible? Who delivered the Israelites evermore from bondage, as soon as they repented and turned to God? Faith verily, and God's truth, and the trust in the promises which he had made."

He wrote of our responsibility to bring up our children in light and truth, and emphasized that it could only be done if they were taught the gospel in their native tongue: "Bring them up in the nurture and information of the Lord," he urged. "Teach them to know Christ, and set God's ordinance before them, saying, 'Son, or daughter, God hath created thee and made thee, through us thy father and mother; and at his commandment have we so long thus kindly brought thee up, and kept thee from all perils.'" He would have identified with Nephi of old, who had explained that "we talk of Christ, we rejoice in Christ, we preach of Christ, we prophesy of Christ, and we write according to our prophecies, that our children may know to what source they may look for a remission of their sins." (2 Nephi 25:26).

Because he was born again in the fiery crucible of experience, he wrote in a personal way of enduring to the end. "When all is at peace, and no man troubleth us, we think that we are patient and love our neighbors as ourselves. But let our neighbor hurt us in word or deed, and then find we it otherwise. Then fume we, and rage, and set up the bristles, and bend ourselves to take vengeance. If we loved with godly love, for Christ's kindness' sake, we should desire no vengeance; but pity him, and desire God to forgive and amend him, knowing well that no flesh can do otherwise than sin, except that God preserve him."

He alluded to being born again: "Ye are born anew, not of mortal seed, but of immortal seed, by the word of God, which liveth and lasteth ever." Of our ultimate salvation and exaltation, he wrote: "Moreover, let us arm our souls with the promises both of help and assistance, and also of the glorious reward that followeth. The tribulations of the righteous are many, and out of them all, will the Lord deliver them. The Lord keepeth all the bones of them, so that not one of them shall be bruised. The Lord shall redeem the souls of his servants."

Because of his profound understanding of the scriptures as they must have fallen from the lips of the prophets, he was able to counsel: "But as Christ biddeth us beware of the leaven of the Pharisees, so beware of their counterfeited keys, and of their false net; which are their traditions and ceremonies, their hypocrisy and false doctrine, wherewith they catch, not souls unto Christ, but authority and riches unto themselves. Let Christian kings, therefore, keep their faith and truth, and all lawful promises and bonds, not one with another only, but even with the Turk or whatsoever infidel it be. For so it is right before God; as the scriptures and ensamples of the Bible testify." Thus, he was able to see more clearly his mission to bring the people of England to the truth.

The reward of both cultural and religious evolution is the elaboration of new and reformed behavior. Tyndale's Bible will stand forever as one of the talismans of civilization, and he joins the Sumerian mathematicians, the Greek philosophers, the architects of Angkor Wat, the mystics of the East, the engineers of the Renaissance, and the framers of the Declaration of Independence, to name only a few who have been part of a cooperative effort carried out over millennia on the grand scale of a world stage, punctuated by innumerable acts and curtain calls, and who have all personified a marvelous plasticity of mind that is at the very heart of the ascent of our species.

I think of William Tyndale each time I read "Lays of Ancient Rome," by Thomas Babbington Mccaulay: "Then out spake brave Horatius, the Captain of the Gate: 'To every man upon this earth, death cometh soon or late. And how can man die better, than facing fearful odds, for the ashes of his fathers, and the temples of his gods?" (Stanza 27).

"We decided
one morning to tweak
our Communist guides, all confirmed
atheists. Once we were seated at the breakfast
table, we Americans bowed our heads in prayer. The
Soviets looked startled and uncomfortable. Later that day,
one of them approached me. "What you did this morning
was very disrespectful," he said angrily. "What do you
mean?" I asked. "No one," he said, "should ever
address God without kneeling down."
("People Goes to Russia," 1987).

Woe Unto You Hypocrites

"Woe unto you, scribes and Pharisees, hypocrites! (1st time). For ye pay tithes...and have omitted the weightier matters of the law, judgment, mercy, and faith: these ought ye to have done, and not to leave the other undone. Ye blind guides, which strain at a gnat, and swallow a camel. Woe unto you, scribes and Pharisees, hypocrites! (2nd time). For ye make clean the outside of the cup and of the platter, but within they are full of extortion and excess. Thou blind Pharisee, cleanse first that which is within the cup and platter, that the outside of them may be clean also. Woe unto you, scribes and Pharisees, hypocrites! (3rd time). For ye are like unto whited sepulchres which indeed appear beautiful outward, but are within full of dead men's bones, and of all uncleanness. Even so ye also outwardly appear righteous unto men, but within ye are full of hypocrisy and iniquity." (Matthew 23:23-28).

Jesus really disliked hypocrites! Three times in the above quoted scripture, He condemned them. In Hebrew, to repeat something three times makes it superlative, as in "good," "better," and "best." The scribes and Pharisees, of whom Jesus was so critical, were like many of us today. They paid tithing, gave to the poor, attended worship services, and went regularly to the temple. What was it, then, that caused the Lord to condemn them? The Savior simply said: "All their works they do for to be seen of men." (Matthew 23:5).

On one occasion, "as he returned into the city, he hungered. And when he saw a fig tree in the way, he came to it, and found nothing thereon, but leaves only, and said unto it, Let no fruit grow on thee henceforward for ever. And presently the fig tree withered away." (Matthew 21:18-19). The tree had leaves, and by all intents and purposes, it should have borne much fruit. But its appearance was deceiving; it was, in fact, devoid of figs. By cursing the tree, the Savior emphasized how serious a sin is hypocrisy. He was especially mindful of the Pharisees, who "loved the praise of men more than the praise of God." (John 12:43).

When Jesus triumphantly entered Jerusalem a week before the Passover, "the multitudes that went before, and that followed, cried, saying, Hosanna to the Son of David: Blessed is he that cometh in the name of the Lord; Hosanna in the highest. And when he was come into Jerusalem, all the city was moved, saying, Who is this? And the multitude said, This is Jesus the prophet of Nazareth of Galilee." (Matthew

21:9-11). But just seven days later, this same multitude demanded the death of the Savior, crying: "His blood be on us, and on our children." (Matthew 27:25). How quickly does the pendulum swing!

When Jesus came "into the temple, the chief priests and the elders of the people came unto him as he was teaching, and said, By what authority doest thou these things? and who gave thee this authority?" Faithlessly, they demanded to know by what power He conducted His ministry. The questioned His judgment, and sustained Him by the outward show of an uplifted hand, but not with their actions. "Jesus saith unto them, Did ye never read in the scriptures, The stone which the builders rejected, the same is become the head of the corner: this is the Lord's doing, and it is marvellous in our eyes?" (Matthew 21:42).

Because they summarily rejected Him, He said: "The kingdom of God shall be taken from you, and given to a nation bringing forth the fruits thereof. And whosoever shall fall on this stone shall be broken: but on whomsoever it shall fall, it will grind him to powder." (Matthew 21:43-44).

When Jesus came to Bethany, to the home of Mary and Martha, Mary took "a pound of ointment…very costly, and anointed the feet of Jesus, and wiped his feet with her hair: and the house was filled with the odour of the ointment. Then saith one of his disciples, Judas Iscariot…Why was not this ointment sold for three hundred pence, and given to the poor? This he said, not that he cared for the poor; but because he was a thief." (John 12:3-6). Sometimes, we say things because it is politically correct or expedient, or to our advantage. Likewise, sometimes we do not say things that should be said, because we fear the consequences. But as Abraham Lincoln cautioned: "To sin by silence, when words should be spoken, makes cowards of men."

Modern scribes and Pharisees omit the weightier matters of the law such as faith and mercy. They strain at a gnat, and swallow a camel. They appear to be righteous, but inside are "full of extortion and excess." (Matthew 223:25). Our sincere desire to serve and obey Jesus Christ, motivated by love and faith, brings us closer to Him, leaving no room for hypocrisy to creep into our lives.

The Words
of Mormon were written
by Mormon on The Small Plates
of Nephi about 385 A.D.. His insert was
intended to be a bridge between the body of
The Small Plates of Nephi, comprising
The First Book of Nephi through The
Book of Omni, and Mormon's own
abridgment of The Large Plates
of Nephi that starts with
The Book of Mosiah.

Words of Mormon

Even though Mormon's abridgment of The Book of Lehi, from The Large Plates of Nephi, was included with all the other records, he must have known that Joseph Smith's manuscript translation up to the Book of Mosiah would be corrupted in some way. Therefore, he went to great pains to include this transitional book on the last leaf of the record comprising the Small Plates of Nephi.

Speaking of the loss of the manuscript translation of The Book of Lehi, the Lord declared to Joseph Smith that "the works, and the designs, and the purposes of God cannot be frustrated, neither can they come to naught." (D&C 3:1). He can prepare for any exigency, inasmuch as He is omniscient. He knows all things. (See 2 Nephi 9:20). He knows the end from the beginning. (See 1 Nephi 9:6). He is the same yesterday, today, and forever. (See 1 Nephi 10:18). Past, present, and future are ever before His face. (See D&C 130:7). "With God, all things are possible." (Matthew 19:26).

Mormon taught that God the Father knows all things, "being from everlasting to everlasting." (Moroni 7:22). From our perspective, eternity spans the time from when we were unorganized intelligence, through our spiritual development as children of our Heavenly Father, on into mortality, and finally to our reunion with Him in the resurrection. Faith, hope, and charity circumscribe His absolute perfection. If we were to model our behavior after any individual, it would be Christ, Who in every quality is One with the Father. This is why Mormon taught: "In Christ there should come every good thing." (Moroni 7:22).

Mormon taught that God the Father knows all things, "being from everlasting to everlasting." (Moroni 7:22). From our perspective, eternity spans the time from when we were unorganized intelligence, through our spiritual development as children of our Heavenly Father, on into mortality, and finally to our reunion with Him in the resurrection. Faith, hope and charity define His attributes in absolute perfection. If we were to model our behavior after any individual, it would be Christ, Who in every quality is One with the Father. This is why Mormon taught: "In Christ there should come every good thing." (Moroni 7:22)

We are completely helpless to alter the progress or affect the outcome of any of God's activities. It was when Moses realized his utter dependence upon Him that he exclaimed: "Now, for this cause I know that man is nothing, which thing I never had supposed." (Moses 1:10). Our debt to God is total and complete. King Benjamin asked his people: "Can ye say aught of yourselves? I answer you, nay. Ye cannot say that ye are even as much as the dust of the earth; yet ye were created of the dust of the earth; but behold, it belongeth to him who created you." (Mosiah 2:25).

Jesus Christ counseled: "Remember that it is not the work of God that is frustrated, but the work of men." (D&C 3:3). Joseph Fielding Smith, Jr. declared: "No power on earth or hell can overthrow or defeat that which God has decreed. Every plan of the adversary will fail, for the Lord knows the secret thoughts of men, and sees the future with a vision clear and perfect, even as though it were in the past." Jacob clearly understood this, when he wrote: "Oh, how great the holiness of our God. For he knoweth all things, and there is not anything save he knows it." (2 Nephi 9:20). Else He would cease to be God, and we could not have faith in Him.

Joseph Smith explained to John Wentworth: "No unhallowed hand can stop the work from progressing. Persecutions may rage, mobs may combine, armies may assemble, calumny may defame, but the truth of God will go forth boldly, nobly, and independent, until it has penetrated every continent, visited every clime, swept every country, and sounded in every ear; till the purposes of God shall be accomplished, and the Great Jehovah shall say: The work is done." (H.C., 4:540). "The truth is, that after the thousands of attacks, and scores of books that have been published, not one criticism has survived, and thousands have borne witness that the Lord has revealed to them the truth of this marvelous work." (Joseph Fielding Smith, Jr.).

At the opening of every dispensation of the gospel, Satan has made a frontal attack against the restoration of truth. He deceived the sons and daughters of Adam and Eve in the first gospel dispensation. At the beginning of the mosaic dispensation, "Satan came tempting him saying: Moses, son of man, worship me." (Moses 1:12). In the Dispensation of the Meridian of Times, Satan attacked the Master Himself. (Luke 4:1-13). We learn from the Prophet Joseph Smith that Satan was also present and contested the opening of the Dispensation of The Fulness of Times. (See J.S.H. 1:15).

Certainly, he tried very hard to frustrate the work of the translation of the plates delivered into the hands of Joseph Smith. He knew that The Church of Jesus Christ could not be organized until the publication of The Book of Mormon. "The loss of 116 pages of manuscript translated from the first part of The Book of Mormon, that was called The Book of Lehi, must have seemed a serious blow at first, to Joseph Smith. The Prophet had reluctantly allowed these pages to pass from his custody to that of Martin Harris, who had served for a brief period as scribe in the translation of The Book of Mormon." (Superscript to D&C 3). But the Lord had provided a duplicate record, in the form of the Small Plates of Nephi.

Mormon was about to deliver to his son Moroni the record that he had been making. He had finalized his abridgment of The Large Plates of Nephi from The Book of Lehi through The Book of Mormon, chapter 7. This was a comprehensive effort that chronicled almost 1,000 years of Nephite history. Mormon had witnessed the last great battles between the Nephites and the Lamanites, and the record of his people was completed, having been abridged by him from The Large Plates of Nephi onto the Plates of Mormon.

Mormon recorded: "And it came to pass that when we had gathered in all our people in one to the land of Cumorah...I made this record out of the plates of Nephi, and hid up in the hill Cumorah all the records which had been entrusted to me by the hand of the Lord, save it were these few plates which I gave unto my son Moroni." (Mormon 6:6).

Mormon hoped that his son Moroni would be able to document the outcome of the final conflict between the Nephites and Lamanites. "And it is many hundred years after the coming of Christ that I deliver these records into the hands of my son," he wrote, "and it supposeth me that he will witness the entire destruction of my people. But may God grant that he may survive them, that he may write somewhat concerning them, and somewhat concerning Christ, that perhaps some day it may profit them." (V. 2).

Mormon continued: "And it came to pass that my people, with their wives and their children, did now behold the armies of the Lamanites marching towards them; and with that awful fear of death which fills the breasts of all the wicked, did they await to receive them." (Mormon 6:7). What a contrast this was to the description of the experience of the righteous, who also stared death in the face, but did so without flinching: "And it shall come to pass that those that die in me shall not taste of death, for it shall be sweet unto them." (D&C 42:46). "They shall never die the second death and feel the torment of the wicked, when they come face to face with eternity." (Joseph Fielding Smith, Jr.). Better than anyone, the righteous know that "death hath passed upon all men to fulfil the merciful plan of the Great Creator." (2 Nephi 9:6).

When the work of death at Cumorah had been completed, Mormon confirmed: "All my people, save it were...twenty and four who were with me, and also a few who had escaped into the south countries, and a few who had deserted over unto the Lamanites, had fallen." (Mormon 6:15). "And they that die not in me, wo unto them, for their death is bitter." (D&C 42:47). Such are unprepared to meet God. ('See Alma 48:23). "Do not procrastinate the day of your repentance until the end," pleaded Alma, "for after this day of life, which is given us to prepare for eternity, behold, if we do not improve our time while in this life, then cometh the night of darkness wherein there can be no labor performed." (Alma 34:33).

The wish of Mormon that his son Moroni might survive the conflict to record the destruction of the Nephites was granted, and his writing was preserved on The Plates of Mormon, and now comprise Mormon chapters 8 and 9, as well as the entire Book of Moroni. The Doctrine & Covenants validates the efforts of Mormon and Moroni: "And for this very purpose are these plates preserved, which contain these records - that the promises of the Lord might be fulfilled, which he made to his people." (D&C 3:19).

In the Words of Mormon, the prophet explained his intention to write an appendage to The Small Plates of Nephi, which he had only recently discovered among all the other plates in the library of the Nephite prophets. "After I had made an abridgment from the (Large) Plates of Nephi, down to the reign of this king Benjamin, of whom Amaleki spake, I searched among the records which had been delivered into my hands, and I found these plates, which contained this small account of the prophets, from Jacob down to the reign of this king Benjamin, and also many of the words of Nephi." (V. 3). Mormon also wanted to add a few historical notes, in order to bring the narrative of The Small Plates of Nephi to the precise point at which the Book of Mosiah, abridged from The Large Plates, began on the Plates of Mormon.

It has been explained that the portion of The Large Plates of Nephi concerning Nephite history to the reign of Benjamin was called The Book of Lehi. This book covered the same time period as the whole of The Small Plates of Nephi, but was probably much more detailed. (See v. 3). The Book of Mosiah, which followed The Book of Lehi on the Large Plates of Nephi, inaugurated a combined religious and secular history that continued until the time of Mormon. The entire record of The Large Plates of Nephi was then abridged onto The Plates of Mormon, and was deposited with the other records in the sanctuary at the Hill Cumorah.

It was Joseph Smith's 116 page manuscript translation of Mormon's abridgment of The Large Plates (down to the reign of King Benjamin) that was lost by Martin Harris. This required the translation of the entire record of The Small Plates of Nephi, that was a record of the same period of Nephite history ("a small account of the prophets") as that which had been lost.

When Mormon was yet a child, the body of plates of all the Nephite prophets had been deposited for safekeeping by Ammaron, who, "being constrained by the Holy Ghost, did hide up...all the sacred records which had been handed down from generation to generation." (4 Nephi 1:48). Mormon was of such spiritual stature that he was charged with the responsibility to care for these plates when only 10 years of age. "And Ammaron said unto (Mormon): I perceive that thou art a sober child, and art quick to observe. Therefore, when ye are about twenty and four years old I would that ye should....go to the land Antum, unto a hill which shall be called Shim; and there have I deposited unto the Lord all the sacred engravings concerning this people." (Mormon 1:3).

Fourteen years later, Mormon "did go to the hill Shim, and did take up all the records which Ammaron had hid up unto the Lord." (Mormon 4:23). By this time, "wickedness did prevail upon the face of the whole land." (Mormon 1:13). The entire fabric of Nephite society was unraveling, and it must have taken extraordinary powers of concentration for Mormon to focus on his responsibilities as prophet-historian.

He related that after he had made an abridgment from the (Large) Plates of Nephi, he discovered within The Small Plates of Nephi much that was pleasing to him, "because of the prophecies of the coming of Christ." (V. 4). Therefore, he chose these plates as the vehicle to finish his record. (V. 5). Following the engravings of Amaleki, Mormon wrote his last few words (The Words of Mormon) in what little space remained on the Small Plates of Nephi.

When Mormon declared: The "remainder of my record I shall take from the (Large) Plates of Nephi," he meant that, in order to write an understandable transitional narrative that would maintain flow and continuity from The Small Plates to his abridgment of the Large Plates (which had already been completed), he would need to make a brief account on The Small Plates of the life of King Benjamin, using as his reference text The Large Plates of Nephi. (V. 5).

Mormon's statement that he could not "write the hundredth part of the things of (his) people" is tantalizing to the mind. (V. 5). Jacob had said the same thing, and both Mormon and Moroni repeated this lament in various places in their abridgments. (V. 5, see Jacob 3:13, Helaman 3:14, 3 Nephi 5:8 & 26:6, & Ether 15:33).

Mormon took The Small Plates of Nephi and deposited them with the remainder of his own abridgment, called The Plates of Mormon. This was done "for a wise purpose." (V. 7). A thousand years earlier, Nephi had also been commanded by the Lord to make a duplicate record "for a wise purpose" known only to the Lord. (1 Nephi 9:5). The reason would only become apparent when, in 2,400 years, the translation by Joseph Smith of the abridgment of The Large Plates of Nephi, concerning Nephite history from Lehi down to the reign of King Benjamin, and comprising 116 pages of handwritten manuscript, would be lost by Martin Harris, to whom it had been temporarily entrusted. (See D&C 3 & 10).

In verse 8, we once again encounter the expanding circle of concern by the prophets, as faith, hope, and charity are manifested in Mormon's thoughts, words, and deeds. Remember that he had just witnessed "almost all the destruction of (his) people." (V. 1). Nevertheless, he wrote: "My prayer to God is concerning my brethren (the Lamanites), that they may once again come to the knowledge of God, yea, the redemption of Christ; that they once again be a delightsome people." (V. 8, see Moroni 7:44-48).

Nephi had reported that the Lord cursed the Lamanites "because of their iniquity. For behold, they had hardened their hearts against him, that they had become like unto a flint; wherefore, as they were white, and exceedingly fair and delightsome, that they might not be enticing unto my people the Lord God did cause a skin of blackness to come upon them." (2 Nephi 5:21). This is the only reference in the entire Book of Mormon where a definite color adjective is used to refer to this mark, or to describe the curse. All other references call it a "skin of darkness" or "a dark skin." Interestingly, in Hebrew, the terms "blackness" and "darkness" are interchangeable.

Those who repent and become the Lord's disciples are also described in the scriptures as "white, fair, and beautiful." (1 Nephi 13:15). Moroni used the terms "spotless, pure, fair, and white." (Mormon 9:6). Such individuals are cleansed by the blood of the Lamb, in a rite of purification. As Isaiah said: "Though your sins be as scarlet, they shall be as white as snow. Though they be red like crimson, they shall be as wool." (Isaiah 1:18).

When verse 8 is read with frequent reference to Mormon's masterful discourse on faith, hope, and charity, that his son Moroni thoughtfully included in his Book of Moroni, it becomes a powerful witness to his total commitment to Jesus Christ and His teachings. (Moroni 7:25-48). At every opportunity, it seems that Mormon unconsciously demonstrated the qualities of a true disciple.

In the next verse, Mormon wrote: "And now I...proceed to finish out my record, which I take from the (Large) Plates of Nephi; and I make it according to the knowledge and the understanding which God has given me." (V. 9).

When he attached these words to the last leaf of The Small Plates of Nephi, he had already completed his abridgment of The Large Plates of Nephi, and had also recorded his testimony in The Book of Mormon inclusive of chapter 7. The knowledge and understanding with which he accomplished this came by the Spirit. "And now come, saith the Lord, by the Spirit, unto the elders of his church, and let us reason together, that ye may understand." (D&C 50:10).

With the completion of the Words of Mormon, the records of the Nephite people were reconciled. After King Benjamin had received The Small Plates from Amaleki, he put them with The Large Plates, and from that point on, they were kept together by the Nephite kings and by the prophets who wrote exclusively upon The Large Plates of Nephi. But it was left to Mormon to fashion the bridge that would connect them as a part of the restoration of the gospel.

From verse 12 to the end of the Words of Mormon, we are provided with a brief summary of the reign of King Benjamin: "And now concerning this king Benjamin...", wrote Mormon. (V. 12). He knew that those who would read The Book of Mormon would not have access to the account of the whole life of King Benjamin that was contained in The Book of Lehi, for that was lost with the 116 pages of manuscript translation that was mishandled by Martin Harris.

In the Book of Omni, only 3 verses concern King Benjamin, and what Mormon had written about him in his abridgment of the Book of Mosiah was confined to the last 3 years of the king's life. Nevertheless, what we do know of Benjamin, because of Mormon's abridgment of the Book of Mosiah, is invaluable. The recorded discourse of King Benjamin, for example, is one of the greatest sermons in the scriptures, and is a practical statement of religious conduct applicable to all times. It is the Book of Mormon equivalent to the Sermon on the Mount.

Verse 13 of the Words of Mormon suggests that the Lamanites had overrun the wicked Nephites who had stayed behind in the Land of Nephi. These Lamanites had come down out of that land to battle the Nephites in the Land of Zarahemla. At that time, the young and vigorous Benjamin fought "with the strength of his own arm" wielding the Sword of Laban that was kept by the Nephite kings throughout their history.

Fortunately, the battle plan and strategy of these Nephites under the leadership of King Benjamin was once again founded in the Lord. In His strength "they did contend against their enemies" until the Lamanites were driven from the "land of their inheritance," which was Zarahemla.

The construction of verses 15-18 suggests that Mormon, anxious because there was so little room left on The Small Plates of Nephi, hastily finished his record in an uncharacteristically awkward style. One cumbersome sentence of no less than 172 words makes up these three verses: "And it came to pass that after there had been false Christs, and their mouths had been shut, and they punished according to their crimes; And after there had been false prophets, and false preachers and teachers among the people, and all these having been punished according to their crimes; and after there having been much contention and many dissensions away unto the Lamanites, behold, it came to pass that king Benjamin, with the assistance of the holy prophets who were among his people - For behold, king Benjamin was a holy man, and he did reign over his people in righteousness; and there were many holy men in the land, and they did speak the word of God with power and with authority; and they did use much sharpness because of the stiffneckedness of the people - Wherefore, with the help of these, king Benjamin, by laboring with all the might of his body and the faculty of his whole soul, and also the prophets, did once more establish peace in the land." (V. 15-18).

These verses could probably be condensed down to the following 16 word sentence, without losing its meaning: "And it came to pass that...king Benjamin...did once more establish peace in the land." In effect, Mormon wanted to say that after the Nephites in Zarahemla had dealt with false Christs, prophets, and teachers, and after desertions and defections to the Lamanites by those weak in testimony, with the help of holy men, Benjamin was able to establish peace in the land.

Mormon was an amazing individual who could see beyond the terrible suffering caused by the apostasy of his own people, and who could differentiate behavior from the intrinsic goodness of both the Nephites and the Lamanites. He truly believed that his people were "numbered among the people of the first covenant," meaning the magnificent Abrahamic Covenant, that had first been made between the Father of the Faithful and God Himself. (Mormon 7:10). To the very last, perhaps just hours before he was slain by the Lamanites, Mormon wrote: "If it so be that ye believe in Christ, and are baptized, first with water, then with fire and with the Holy Ghost, following the example of our Savior, according to that which he hath commanded us, it shall be well with you in the day of judgment. Amen." (Mormon 7:10).

Mormon's perception was clear and accurate. He could see the autobiographical thread of his people leading backward to Deity, and understood that even the most hardened soul has, within itself, "the acorn of a potential oak, the unsculptured image of a glorified personality." (Truman Madsen, "Eternal Man," p. 17).

"It is a serious thing to live in a society of possible Gods and Goddesses," wrote C.S. Lewis, "to remember that the dullest and most uninteresting person you talk to may one day be a creature which if you saw it now you would be strongly tempted to worship. ...There are no ordinary people. You have never talked to a mere mortal. It is immortals with whom we joke and work, and whom we marry, snub and exploit... Our charity must be a real and costly love. ...Next to the blessed Sacrament itself, your neighbor is the holiest object presented to your senses. If he is your Christian neighbor, he is holy in almost the same way, for in him also Christ is truly hidden and glorified."

Perhaps this is the hidden meaning in the scripture that enjoins us to "love the Lord thy God with all thy heart, and with all thy soul, and with all thy mind, and with all thy strength. This is the first commandment. And the second is like, namely this, Thou shalt love thy neighbour as thyself. There is none other commandment greater than these." (Mark 12:30-31). Mormon certainly had a great capacity to love his people. The essence of his message on faith, hope, and charity for all is reflected in these lines penned by Edwin Markham: "He drew a circle that shut me out, Heretic, rebel, a thing to flout. But Love and I had the will to win. We drew a circle that took him in."

Mormon felt genuine love for both the Nephites and the Lamanites, in the same sense as the Savior, Who, on the Cross, besought His Father, and prayed: "Father, forgive them; for they know not what they do." (Luke 23:34). He surely would have agreed with the following sentiment, articulated on a smaller scale, but nonetheless relevant: "Wouldn't it be nice if, as we tuck our children into bed after particularly stressful days, we could say something like this. "I've been watching you, and you are about the most special human being I've ever met. I'm proud to wear your name. I know we had a disagreement today, but that was behavior. It's the person I love. It's behavior I got bothered with, but not you. I love you unconditionally, not based on achievement, but based on you, and your potential. I love you very much." (Anonymous). This is charity, the pure love of Christ, and the quality that Mormon personified throughout his writings. The thoughtful student will find its expression throughout Mormon's abridgment of The Large Plates of Nephi that follows the transitional Words of Mormon, in The Book of Mormon.

"The first great principle that
ought to occupy the attention of all mankind, and
which is the mainspring of all action, is the principle of
improvement." (Brigham Young, D.B.Y., p. 87). Work is
an eternal principle. The scriptures loudly proclaim
our Father's mission statement: "This is my work
and my glory, to bring to pass the immortality
and eternal life of man." (Moses 1:39).

Work and Personal Responsibility

Our first parents were commanded to work. "In the sweat of thy face," promised God, "shalt thou eat bread." (Genesis 3:19). Israel was likewise charged: "Six days shalt thou labour." (Exodus 20:9). At the time of Christ's mortal ministry, the Church received a similar injunction: "If any provide not for his own, and specially for those of his own house, he hath denied the faith." (1 Timothy 5:8). The Latter-day Saints have a long history and tradition of labor: "Work is to be re-enthroned as the ruling principle in the lives of our church membership," declared Heber J. Grant, in the midst of the Great Depression. (C.R., 10/1936).

If we are not hard at work, life can be disastrous. Even if we are on the right road, we're going to get run over if we just sit there. Coming together can be a beginning, and keeping together is progress. But working together is success. "Keep your dish right side up," counseled Brigham Young, "so that when the shower of porridge does come, you can catch your dish full." (D.B.Y., p. 310).

Work is central to the successful implementation of the Plan of Salvation, so much so that we are warned: "The idler shall not have place in the church, except he repent and mend his ways." (D&C 75:29). "He that is idle shall not eat the bread nor wear the garments of the laborer." (D&C 42:42). Honest work is engrained in our nature, and our spare moments can be put to good use, if we recognize them as the gold dust of time.

Idleness can be devastating, because it leads to an erosion of the work ethic and feeds the monster within. Those who waste their time putting forth minimal effort or chasing petty pursuits cannot see that it is not that they have set their goals too high, and have failed to reach them after all they could have done. It is, rather, that they have settled for mediocrity, and have abandoned their dreams to an expediency that requires little expenditure of honest effort. Homogenizing expectations by lowering the bar doesn't make it easier to make forward progress, it just increases the odds of tripping and falling flat on our faces. An agenda that demeans the value of work corrodes our ability to distinguish between the "cheap thrills" that are so tantalizing and tempting, and the "lofty goals" represented by the work-ethic that is an integral part of God's Plan.

"Aha! Here we have someone paying for the sin of idleness," said Pogo the cartoon philosopher. "The hobnailed boots of indiscretion's marathon dancer tap a rowdy two-step across the terracotta of your consciousness. Reason was cast into the rumble seat of your libidinous juggernaut. Now the piper must be paid!" (Walt Kelly).

"Clean money is pay received for a full day's honest work, reasonable pay for faithful service, fair profit from the sale of goods, commodities, or service, and income received from transactions where all parties profit. Filthy lucre is money obtained through theft and robbery, gambling, sinful operations, bribery, and from exploitation." (Spencer W. Kimball, C.R., 10/1953).

The only man who ever got all his work done by Friday was Robinson Crusoe. The ability to work is a blessing from God. Those who have put their shoulder to the wheel realize that the dictionary is the only place where success comes before work. "If you develop the habit of work," said Ernest L Wilkinson, "it will be the most invigorating, satisfying, even relaxing and greatest blessing of your life. The opportunity to work is God's greatest blessing to mankind, and this means six days of each week." ("The Banyan," 1968). " Let us realize that the privilege to work is a gift, that the power to work is a blessing, and that the love of work is success." (David O. McKay, "Pathways to Happiness," p. 381.).

If we cannot work to support ourselves, we should first turn to our families for temporal assistance, and then to the Church, if necessary, remembering that its Welfare System is designed to sustain life, and not lifestyle. It is designed to get us back on our feet. One of its missions is to empower those with employment challenges. Welfare is at its best when it is the conduit through which its recipients receive the endowment of satisfaction and enjoyment in personal achievement and progress.

Welfare is tied to the Law of Inertia. The best programs are designed to get people moving so that they may maintain forward momentum. In the process, work well done is almost always accompanied by new opportunities to work even harder. In contrast, programs that are designed to help us to glide smoothly and effortlessly through life contribute to our downfall. The blessing of concentrated and sustained effort is that we move to higher planes of achievement. Positive reinforcement ingrains the virtues that accompany the work ethic, and we realize that nothing is really hard labor unless we would rather be doing something else. We move from complete oblivion to knowing how, and then to knowing why, and this can make all the difference. Teach a man to fish, and you have fed him for a lifetime.

We need to prepare ourselves before traveling the road to success, because once we've started the journey, it's almost always going to be uphill. In the process, we should "make no small plans, for they have no magic to stir (our) souls." (Daniel W.

Burnham). Providentially, the Lord has provided us with all the elements to create Zion both on earth and in heaven. All we have to do is to get to work and organize these elements into their proper frame and order.

Work without vision is drudgery, while vision without work is dreamery. But work with vision is destiny. The story is told of two men who were resting by the side of the railroad tracks. They had been pounding spikes for a new line, when a train came into view, and slowed down as it passed the work site. As it went by, the President of the line leaned out the window of his personal rail car, waved, and called out "Hello Jake!" "Hi Paul," Jake responded. As the train disappeared from view, the other worker asked, "Jake. I didn't know you were on a first name basis with the President of the railroad." Jake, replied, "Yes. Twenty five years ago, we both got our first jobs working for the Union Pacific. At that time, he went to work for the railroad, and I went to work for $1.25 an hour."

We cannot lengthen our stride while sitting down. When Spencer W. Kimball urged us to new levels of achievement, he knew that our spirituality would be intensified. Christ urged the man in bondage to go the second mile, to double his stride. "The second mile is a gift of spiritual independence that removes the veil of insensitivity to our destiny." (Richard L. Gunn, "Sensitivity and Spirit," p. 197).

Work can prepare us for that destiny. "I will prepare myself, and someday my chance will come," said Abraham Lincoln. He knew that perspiration must precede inspiration, and that "there must be effort before there is excellence." (Spencer W. Kimball, "B.Y.U. The Second Century," 10/10/1975).

"Men are that they might have joy," declared Lehi. (2 Nephi 2:25). Work is a key element in that equation, and there is a causal relationship between work and rest. All work and no play makes Jack a dull boy. "Six days is more time than we need to labor," declared Brigham Young. "One third to one fourth of (your) time that is spent to procure a living would be sufficient, if your labor were rightly directed." (D.B.Y., p. 311).

While we are at work, we would do well to remember that to possess the world's goods is not wealth, and is not the real objective of work as it was envisioned by the Plan. "The race," after all, "is not to the swift, nor the battle to the strong, neither riches to men of wisdom." (Ecclesiastes 9:11). One measure of our wealth, the fruits of our labors, is similarly found in our ability to produce conveniences and comforts from the elements. "All the power and dignity that wealth can bestow is a mere shadow, the substance is found in the bone and sinew of the toiling millions. Well-directed labor is the true power that supplies our wants. It gives regal grandeur to potentates, education and supplies to religious and political ministers, and provides the wants of the thousands of millions of earth's sons and daughters." (Brigham Young, D.B.Y., p. 308-309).

But another, far more important, measure of wealth is the satisfaction we receive from our efforts to secure for ourselves and our loved ones the blessings of heaven. Our wealth need only be enough to allow us to enjoy health, strength, and power in sufficient quantities that we might be able to share it with others. Our most prized possession should be an endowment of the Spirit, and our work should lead us to the Holy Ghost, that He might be our constant companion. When that is the case, our moral compass will point us toward righteousness and truth, are the fruits of our obedience ill be an everlasting dominion, and without compulsory means the blessings of heaven will shower down upon us.

Author's Note

As you peruse Appendix One in this volume of essays, you will notice that Volume One contains 59 essays, Volume Two 76 essays, Volume Three 71 essays, Volume Four 69 essays, and Volume Five 56 essays. These, together with the 55 essays in this volume, bring the grand total to 386. It was a push for me to complete the last essays in this final volume, but I wanted to provide enough and to spare for a full year's worth in the six-volume set. I leave for readers to do with these essays what they will. As for me, I can breathe a deep sigh of relief, and move on to other writing projects!

In all, the six volumes contain somewhere around 1,250,000 words. By comparison, there are just over 268,000 words in The Book of Mormon. (For additional perspective, see "Understanding Textual Changes in The Book of Mormon," "Ensign," 12/1983).

What makes Joseph's experience all the more remarkable, is that I only best express myself when I have pondered a topic for a while, and have taken the time to turn it over and over in my mind. Then, in a flurry of activity, I write a preliminary draft. Afterward, I let it simmer on the back burner for a few days or weeks. Finally, I return to it with fresh enthusiasm, and add finishing touches. However, sometimes I leave it alone again, hoping to come back one more time with fresh eyes and a clear mind. I make another revision or two, generally finishing with a product that contains a third again as much material as I initially had thought would be sufficient. At last, I put it to rest.

Because this is the process that works for me, more than once during the construction of these essays, I have been struck by how different was the experience of the Nephite prophets. Instead of putting pen to paper, or keystrokes to a word document, they made records on plates of ore, with no room for error or revision. (For a look into the process, see my essay entitled "Writing on Metal Plates was a Pain" in Volume Four). If each of these essays took a couple of weeks to complete following the scenario outlined above, these six volumes represent around 15 years of brain and soul sweat. Joseph, on the other hand, completed his translation of The Book of Mormon in an astonishing 65 days. (See "How long did it take Joseph Smith to translate the Book of Mormon?" "Ensign," 1/1988).

My admittedly unrealistic goal was to provide readers with enough material to tackle one essay each day, for a year. At 55 words per minute, that's only a little over an hour's worth of reading per day. My more practical suggestion would be for you to instead spend quality time reading the scriptures. For example, accept the challenge to read The Book of Mormon in a year. (See: "Taking the Challenge," "Ensign," 12/2006). You'll be far better off for having done so. But, if after doing that, you're tired of late-night T.V. or movie re-runs, crack open one of these volumes, and give one of the 386 essay a shot. You should quickly be able to find a topic that will help you fall asleep more easily, dream more pointedly, and awaken more refreshed. Enjoy!

Appendix One
List of Essays
(Volume One – Volume Six)

Volume One: Spray from The Ocean of Thought

1	A Christmas Miracle
2	A Letter To A Non-member Friend
3	A Mailbox Marked With An "X"
4	A Personal Mission Statement
5	A Perspective On Civil Liberties (Alma 50-51)
6	A Perspective On The Apostasy
7	A Recipe For Success
8	A Standard Of Excellence
9	A Testimony Of Christ
10	A Thirty-Day Spiritual Fitness Program
11	A Whirlwind Into Heaven (The Doctrine of Translation)
12	Abstinence In A Permissive World
13	Agency And Opposition
14	Alma's Discourse On Faith (Alma 32)
15	An American Gospel
16	An Elect Lady (D&C 25)
17	Apostasy
18	Are Christians Mormon?
19	Are Life And Death Mutually Exclusive?
20	Are Mormons Christians?
21	Are We Alone In The Universe?
22	Baptism: A Foundation Ordinance
23	Baptism: The Gateway To The Celestial Kingdom
24	Batteries Are Not Included
25	Be Happy Attitudes
26	Because Of The Book of Mormon
27	Become As Little Children
28	Before A Wound Can Heal
29	Being L.D.S. Is Like Being A Pumpkin
30	Being Well-Grounded
31	Benevolent Blindness
32	Book Of Mormon Hiking Song
33	Book Of Mormon Historicity
34	Born Again
35	Bosses And Leaders
36	Brevity

37	Buddy, Can You Spare A Dime?
38	Caesar (Mosiah 29)
39	Celestial Marriage And Eternal Families
40	Chastity Amid Permissiveness
41	Cherubim And A Flaming Sword Or Mercy And Justice
42	Christmas Is the Season Of The Year When
43	Christmas Thoughts
44	Church Organization And Government (D&C 20)
45	Combating Evil
46	Common Consent (D&C 26)
47	Conference (D&C 44)
48	Covenant Consciousness
49.	Conversion: An Ongoing Process
50	Dentistry In The Scriptures
51	Detecting Satan's Fingerprints
52	Diversity
53	Do Justly And Love Mercy (Micah 6:8)
54	Do We Dye Our Skins?
55	Does God Obey The Speed Limit?
56	Edward Partridge: First Bishop Of The Church (D&C 36)
57	Embrace The gospel (D&C 49)
58	Enduring To The End
59	Entropy In The Physical World

Volume Two: Ripples on a Pond

60	Eternal Progression In A Dynamic Universe
61	Everyone Wants To Go To Heaven
62	Evidences Of God
63	Faith, Hope And Charity
64	Faith Is A Principle Of Power
65	Faith, Knowledge And Education
66	Fasting: A Principle Of Perfection
67	Fayette, New York – The Last Revelation (D&C 38)
68	Focus
69	Focusing On The Important Things
70	Follow The Prophet
71	For Unto Us A Child Is Born
72	Gifts of the Spirit
73	Goal Setting
74	God, Give Us Men!
75	God Goes Green
76	Godly Qualities (D&C 4)
77	Good, Better And Best
78	Gratitude Is An Attitude
79	Happiness And Sharing The gospel
80	Having Been Commissioned Of Jesus Christ (D&C 22)
81	Higher Dimensional Realities
82	How Does God Get Things Done?
83	Huckleberries And Chokeberries
84	I Am The Light of The World (John 8:12)
85	I Have Fought A Good Fight (2 Timothy 4:7)
86	I Have Overcome The World (John 16:33)
87	I Will Obey – James Covill (D&C 39)
88	If It Seems Too Good To Be True, It Probably Is
89	Is Heaven Hotter Than Hell?
90	It's Our Book! (Mormon 3)
91	Joseph Smith History
92	Just Get Back On The Bike
93	Justice And Mercy (Alma 42)
94	Lamanites By The Waters Of Sebus (Alma 17:37)
95	Let A History Be Kept (D&C 47)

96	Let Me Be Perfectly Honest
97	Life Is A Three Act Play
98	Life Is Like A Game of Racquetball
99	Life's Greatest Questions
100	Life Support And Decisions (Life's Important Decisions)
101	Light
102	Light And Darkness
103	Look Who's Coming To Town (It isn't Santa Claus)
104	Lucifer
105	Maintaining A Positive Mental Attitude
106	Management By The Spirit
107	Marriage Is Ordained Of God
108	Missing Scripture
109	Missionary Work: Our Greatest Call
110	Moral Discipline
111	Mothers In Zion
112	Multi-tasking
113	Navigating On The Snake
114	Ninety Nine Questions Answered By The Book of Mormon
115	No Greater Call
116	Obedience Is The First Law Of Heaven
117	Obtaining The Spirit Of Revelation
118	One Hundred And One Things
119	One Lord, One Faith, One Baptism
120	Open Your Gates To The gospel (D&C 32)
121	Orson Pratt: A Son Of God (D&C 34)
122	Our Educational Responsibilities
123	Our Eternal Nature
124	Our Family Constitution
125	Our Limiting Beliefs
126	Our Talents
127	Our Weaknesses
128	Overcoming Adversity
129	Parallelism In Hebrew Poetry
130	Pioneer Day Perspectives
131	Power: The Ultimate Test of Character
132	Professors
133	Proper Prior Preparation
134	Putting Labels On Others
135	Quorum Sensing

Volume Three: Serendipitous Meanderings

136	Receiving Revelation (D&C 8)
137	Removing The Barnacles Of Life
138	Restoration Of The Aaronic Priesthood (D&C 13)
139	Revelation
140	Reverence
141	Sacramental Waters
142	Salvation by Grace
143	Satan
144	Seraphim
145	Set Apart
146	Sharper Than A Two-Edged Sword (D&C 33)
147	Signs
148	Sixty Five Ways To Express Gratitude
149	So You're Getting Married
150	Speak Kind Words To Each Other
151	Spiritual Calisthenics
152	Spiritual Identity Theft
153	Spiritual Manifestations
154	Steadying The Ark
155	Strangers In The Land Success
156	Studying The Scriptures
157	Success Strategies
158	Sydney Rigdon: Scribe To The Prophet (D&C 35)
159	Symbolism In The Scriptures
160	Symbols
161	Teaching In The Church
162	Teaching Key Doctrine
163	Technological Traps
164	Temple Work
165	Testimony
166	The 13th Article Of Faith
167	The 14th Article Of Faith
168	The Ablest Mariner
169	The Best Education Is To Be Perpetually Thrilled With Life
170	The Bible And Other Scripture
171	The Bible: Basic Information Before Leaving Earth

172	The Biggest Loser
173	The Character Of God
174	The Church In The Last Days
175	The Church Of Jesus Christ In Former Times
176	The Circle Of Knowledge
177	The Creation Of The World
178	The Desert Shall Rejoice (D&C 57)
179	The Door Swings Both Ways
180	The Dust Of The Earth
181	The Duty Of The Priest (D&C 20:46)
182	The First Revelation (D&C 2)
183	The First Revelation In Ohio (D&C 41)
184	The Heavens Were Opened
185	The Holy Ghost
186	The Hour Glass of Opportunity
187	The Isaiah Chapters In The Book Of Mormon
188	The Last Judgment
189	The Law Of The Church
190	The Little Princess
191	The Lord's Prophet
192	The Lost Manuscript
193	The Lost Ten Tribes
194	The Manifestation Of Spirits (D&C 50)
195	The Meaning Of Doctrine
196	The Millennium
197	The Mind of God
198	The Nature Of God And Our Covenants
199	The New And Everlasting Covenant (D&C 22)
200	The Order Of Revelation (D&C 28)
201	The Parable Of The Pencil
202	The Plan Of Salvation
203	The Prime Directive
204	The Prophet Joseph Smith
205	The Purpose Of Life
206	The Q Continuum

Volume Four: Presents of Mind

207	The Rapids Of Life
208	The Recipe For A Successful Church Address
209	The Sabbath
210	The Sacrament
211	The Spirit of Gathering
212	The Second Coming
213	The Secret Garden
214	The Seeds Of Apostasy (D&C 31)
215	The Signs Of The Times
216	The Spirit
217	The Spirit World
218	The Springtime Of The Year
219	The Switch Points In Our Lives
220	The Temple
221	The Testimony Of Phil Hudson
222	The Third Part
223	The Three Witnesses
224	The Thrill Of Victory / The Agony Of DeFeet
225	The Voice Of Prophetic Warning
226	The Windows Of Heaven
227	The Word Of Wisdom
228	Then The Pig Got Up And Slowly Walked Away
229	This Is A New Day
230	Those "Gold" Plates
231	Thoughts On The Atonement (Alma 7:11-13)
232	Time
233	To Err Is Human; To Forgive Is Divine
234	Touching His Garment
235	Tough Questions (Alma 5)
236	Travel At The Speed of Dark
237	True to Our Covenants
238	Twenty-Five Qualities Of High Achievers
239	Unity
240	Up / Down
241	Updates Are Ready
242	We Are Foreordained To Greatness

243	We Are His Hands
244	We Lived Before We Were Born
245	Well, That's Life
246	Were There Two Cumorahs?
247	We Talk of Christ
248	What About Cherubim?
249	What About The Mormons? (D&C 45)
250	What Did He Just Say?
251	What Falls Down, Must Go Up
252	What Goes Around Comes Around
253	What I Have Lost (James Covill) (D&C 40)
254	What I Say Unto One, I Say Unto All (D&C 19)
255	What Is A Christian?
256	What Is Happiness?
257	What Qualifies Us For The Work? (D&C 4)
258	What Think Ye of Christ? (Matthew 22:42)
259	What's In It For Me?
260	Who Is Packing Your Parachute?
261	Why Do We Laugh?
262	Why Is Happiness So Elusive?
263	Why Read The Doctrine & Covenants? (D&C 1)
264	Why Was The Book of Mormon Preserved For Our Day?
265	Wickedness Never Was Happiness
266	Without The Book of Mormon
267	Work
268	Worlds Without Number Have I Created
269	Worship In Music
270	Wresting The Scriptures
271	Writing On Metal Plates Was A Pain
272	You Took No Thought Save To Ask
273	Zion
274	Zion And The New Jerusalem (D&C 57)
275	Zion Versus Babylon

Volume Five: Mental Floss

276	Agency And Youth
277	Attributes Of God
278	Bah! Humbug!
279	Baptism And Accountability
280	Blood, Covenant, And Land Israel
281	Born Again Christians
282	A Change Of Heart
283	Choose The Harder Right
284	Choose Ye This Day
285	Christ's Church Is Restored
286	Citizenship In The Church and Kingdom
287	A Coat Of Many Colors
288	Commitment
289	Connections
290	Construction Zone: Proceed With Caution
291	Covenants
292	Dancing With The Stars
293	Diversity
294	Doctrinal Switch Points
295	Enduring To The End
296	Establishing The Word
297	Faith is Like A Screw
298	Fate
299	Father, Forgive Them
300	Finding Balance In Our Lives
301	Friendship
302	General Conference: The Super Bowl Of Spiritual Symposia
303	God Is NowHere
304	God's Tactical Flashlight
305	Heaven Can Wait
306	How Then Can I Do This Great Wickedness?
307	I Am A Child of God
308	In Defense Of The Family
309	In Defense Of The Prophet Joseph Smith
310	Joseph Smith's History
311	Joseph Smith's World

312	Jumping Out Of Our Skin
313	Keep Smiling
314	Lest We Forget
315	Light And Truth
316	Living Water
317	Lost Books Of The Bible
318	Marriage And Family Are Ordained of God
319	May The 4th Be With You
320	Our Father In Heaven Knows Us
321	Our Neighbors
322	Pennies From Heaven
323	Plan Of Salvation
324	Premortal Life
325	Preparation
326	Pride
327	Priesthood Keys
328	A Primer On Addressing Deity
329	A Primer On Personal Revelation
330	Proper Prior Planning Prevents Poor Priesthood Performance
331	Recognizing The Church Of Jesus Christ

Volume Six: Fitness Training for the Mind and Spirit

332	Reflections On Her Mission
333	Sealed For Time And For All Eternity
334	Service: Mission Reflection
335	Serving In The Temple
336	Sharing The Gospel
337	Similitudes In Hosea
338	Snowbiking Through Life
339	Strengths And Weaknesses
340	Swiss Chocolate
341	Take My Yoke Upon You
342	Teachings Of The Minor Prophets
343	Temple Blessings For All Mankind
344	The Bestowal Of Spiritual Gifts
345	The Church Has Been Restored
346	The Creation
347	The Fall
348	The Germination Of Our Faith
349	The Highways And Byways of Life
350	The Holy Ghost: Getting To Know Him
351	The Holy Grail Of Religious Doctrine
352	The Hourglass Of Life
353	The Light Of The World
354	The Lord's Patient Protection And Affordable Health Care Act
355	The Lord's Touchstone
356	The Mantle Of The Prophet
357	The Martyr's Mirror
358	The New American Bible: Uninspired Version
359	The Number Of The Disciples Was Multiplied
360	The Parable Of The Hiawatha Trail
361	The Plan Of Salvation: 15 Names
362	The Political Spotlight
363	The Power Of Proverbs
364	The Priests Of Baal in Our Lives
365	The Principle Of Agency
366	The Prophet Joseph Smith: The Third Of The Three Pillars Of Testimony

367	The Sacrament
368	The Second Mile
369	The Seven Deadly Sins
370	The Strait And Narrow Path To Discipleship
371	The Tools Of The Trade
372	The Twelve Tribes Of Israel
373	The Unknown Possibilities Of Existence
374	The Year Without Summer
375	Thoughts of Kolob
376	Thou Hast Done Wonderful Things
377	Tithing
378	Travel At The Speed of Thought
379	True Discipleship
380	Walk In The Light
381	We Ask Thee In Humility
382	What Think Ye Of Christ?
383	William Tyndale: An Appreciation
384	Wo Unto You Hypocrites
385	Words Of Mormon
386	Work And Personal Responsibility

Consummatum Est

Appendix Two
Topical Guide to the Essays
(Volumes 1 - 6)

One hundred
fifty five topics are herein
cross-referenced to the three
hundred eighty six essays within
the six volumes, in order
to facilitate matching
source material to
a particular area
of study

The topics are,
as follows:

Aaronic Priesthood
Abstinence
Achievement
Adversity
Agency
Apostasy
Articles of Faith
Atonement
Attitude
Attributes of God
Authority
Baptism
Belief
Book of Mormon
Born Again
Brevity
Character
Cherubim
Children
Christ
Christians
Christmas
Church
Church Government
Civil Liberties
Commandments
Compensation
Conversion
Courage
Covenants
Creation
Cumorah
Death
Darkness
Dentistry
Decisions
Devil
Discipline
Diversity
Doctrine
Doctrine & Covenants

Education
Emma Smith
Endurance
Environment
Eternal Progression
Evil
Example
Excellence
Faith
Family
Fasting
Feet
Focus
Forgiveness
Friendship
Gathering
Goals
Good and Evil
gospel
Grace
Gratitude
Happiness
Heaven
History
Holy Ghost
Honesty
Humility
Improvement
Isaiah
Israel
Joseph Smith
Journal
Justice
Kindness
Knowledge
Language
Last Days
Laughter
Labels
Leadership
Life

Light
Marriage
Mercy
Millennium
Mission Statement
Missionary Work
Morality
Mother
Multi-tasking
Music
Nature
Obedience
Opportunity
Opposition
Perseverance
Pioneers
Plan of Salvation
Potential
Prayer
Pre-Earth Life
Preparation
Priesthood
Professors
Prophecy
Prophet
Public Speaking
Questions
Renewal
Repentance
Restoration
Resurrection
Revelation
Reverence
Sabbath
Sacrament
Satan
Scholarship
Scripture
Second Coming
Seraphim
Service

Set apart
Signs
Spirit
Spirit World
Spiritual Fitness
Spiritual Gifts
Spirituality
Success
Symbolism
Talents
Teaching
Technology
Temple
Tenacity
Testimony
Third Part
Time
Tithing
Tolerance
Transgression
Translation
Unity
Universe
Walking in His Footsteps
Weakness
Wisdom
Wishful Thinking
Witnesses
Word of Wisdom
Words
Work
Zion

Aaronic Priesthood

- Restoration of The Aaronic Priesthood (D&C 13)
- The Duty of The Priest (D&C 20:46)

Abstinence

- Abstinence in a Permissive World

Achievement

- Heaven Can Wait
- Twenty-five Qualities of High Achievers
- We are Foreordained to Greatness

Adversity

- Construction Zone: Proceed with Caution
- Finding Balance in our Lives
- Overcoming Adversity
- Spiritual Calisthenics
- Spiritual Identity Theft
- The Highways and Byways of Life
- The Martyr's Mirror
- The Rapids of Life
- The Seven Deadly Sins
- This is a New Day
- Travel at The Speed of Dark

Agency

- Agency and Opposition
- Agency and Youth
- Choose the Harder Right
- Fate
- The Prime Directive
- The Principle of Agency
- The Q Continuum

Apostasy

- A Perspective on The Apostasy
- Apostasy
- Christ's Church is Restored
- God is NowHere
- Recognizing the Church of Jesus Christ
- The Church Has Been Restored

- The New American Bible: Uninspired Version
- The Seeds of Apostasy (D&C 31)
- William Tyndale: An Appreciation

Articles of Faith

- The 13th Article of Faith
- The 14th Article of Faith

Atonement

- Thoughts on The Atonement

Attitude

- Be Happy Attitudes
- Finding Balance in Our Lives
- I am a Child of God
- Maintaining a Positive Mental Attitude
- The Martyr's Mirror
- This is a New Day
- Twenty-five Qualities of High Achievers
- We are Foreordained to Greatness

Attributes of God

- Does God Obey The Speed Limit?
- Evidence of God
- Godly Qualities (D&C 4)
- How Does God Get Things Done?
- Our Heavenly Father Knows Us
- The Character of God
- The Tools of The Trade
- The Mind of God
- The Nature of God and Our Covenants
- Touching His Garment
- Travel at The Speed of Thought

Authority

- Steadying the Ark

Baptism

- A Change of Heart
- Baptism: A Foundation Ordinance
- Baptism and Accountability
- Baptism: The Gateway to The Celestial Kingdom

Belief

- Commitment
- Our Limiting Beliefs
- We are Foreordained to Greatness
- What Think Ye of Christ?

Book of Mormon

- Because of The Book of Mormon
- Book of Mormon Historicity
- Book of Mormon Song
- It's Our Book! (Mormon 3)
- Ninety-nine Questions Answered by The Book of Mormon
- The Lost Manuscript
- Those "Gold" Plates
- Words of Mormon
- Why Was The Book of Mormon Preserved for Our Day?
- Without The Book of Mormon
- Writing on Metal Plates Was a Pain

Born Again

- A Change of Heart
- Born Again
- Born Again Christians
- Connections
- The Hourglass of Life
- Walk in The Light

Brevity

- Brevity

Character

- A Change of Heart
- A Coat of Many Colors
- Godly Qualities (D&C 4)
- I am a Child of God
- The Lord's Touchstone
- The Martyr's Mirror
- The Seven Deadly Sins

Cherubim

- Seraphim
- What About Cherubim?

Children

- Become as Little Children
- I am a Child of God

Christ

- A Testimony of Christ
- For Unto Us a Child is Born
- I am The Light of The World (John 3:12)
- I Have Overcome The World (John 16:33)
- Look Who's Coming to Town (It Isn't Santa Claus)
- The Ablest Mariner
- The Second Coming
- Touching His Garment
- We Talk of Christ
- What Think Ye of Christ? (Matthew 22:42)

Christians

- A Coat of Many Colors
- Are Christians Mormon?
- Are Mormons Christian?
- The Martyr's Mirror
- What is a Christian?

Christmas

- A Christmas Miracle
- Bah Humbug!
- Christmas is The Season When…..
- Christmas Thoughts
- For Unto Us a Child is Born

Church

- Being L.D.S. is Like Being a Pumpkin
- Christ's Church is Restored
- Church Historian (D&C 47)
- Church Organization & Government
- Citizenship in The Church and Kingdom
- Conference
- General Conference: The SuperBowl of Spiritual Symposia
- One Lord, One Faith, One Baptism
- Recognizing the Church of Jesus Christ
- The Church Has Been Restored
- The Church in The Last Days

- The Church of Jesus Christ in Former Times
- The Lord's Patient Protection and Affordable Healthcare Act
- What About The Mormons? (D&C 45)

Church Government

- Caesar
- Common Consent
- Conference
- Edward Partridge: First Bishop of The Church (D&C 36)
- Fayette, New York: The Last Revelation (D&C 38)
- General Conference: The SuperBowl of Spiritual Symposia
- Quorum Sensing
- Sydney Rigdon: Scribe to The Prophet (D&C 35)
- The First Revelation (D&C 2)
- The First Revelation in Ohio (D&C 41)
- The Law of The Church (D&C 42)
- The Lord's Patient Protection and Affordable Healthcare Act
- The Political Spotlight
- The Three Witnesses

Civil Liberties

- A Perspective on Civil Liberties
- The Martyr's Mirror

Commandments

- What I Say Unto One, I Say Unto All (D&C 19)

Compensation

- What Goes Around Comes Around

Conversion

- Bah Humbug!
- Connections
- Conversion
- We are Foreordained to Greatness

Courage

- Choose the Harder Right
- God, Give us Men!
- May the 4th Be With You
- The Martyr's Mirror
- This is a New Day

Covenants

- Covenant Consciousness
- Covenants
- The Nature of God and Our Covenants
- The New and Everlasting Covenant (D&C 22)
- True to Our Covenants

Creation

- Are We Alone in The Universe?
- Diversity
- Higher Dimensional Realities
- The Creation
- The Creation of The World
- The Dust of The Earth
- Worlds Without Number

Cumorah

- Were There Two Cumorahs?

Death

- Are Life and Death Mutually Exclusive?
- Everyone Wants to Go to Heaven

Darkness

- Travel at The Speed of Dark

Dentistry

- Dentistry in The Scriptures

Decisions

- Choose the Harder Right
- Construction Zone: Proceed with Caution
- Finding Balance in our Lives
- Heaven Can Wait
- The Highways and Byways of Life
- The Martyr's Mirror
- The Switch Points in Our Lives

Devil

- Combating Evil
- Detecting Satan's Fingerprints
- Lucifer
- Spiritual Identity Theft
- Wickedness Never Was Happiness

Discipline

- Choose the Harder Right
- Choose Ye This Day
- Commitment
- Construction Zone: Proceed with Caution
- Finding Balance in our Lives
- May the 4th Be With You
- Moral Discipline
- Spiritual Calisthenics
- Taking My Yoke Upon You
- The Lord's Touchstone
- The Number of Disciples was Multiplied
- The Second Mile
- The Seven Deadly Sins
- The Strait and Narrow Path to Discipleship
- This is a New Day
- True Discipleship
- We are Foreordained to Greatness
- What Think Ye of Christ?

Diversity

- Diversity

Doctrine

- Teaching Key Doctrine
- The Meaning of Doctrine
- The New American Bible: Uninspired Version

Doctrine & Covenants

- Why Read The Doctrine & Covenants? (D&C 1)

Education

- A Coat of Many Colors
- Our Educational Responsibilities

- The Best Education is To Be Perpetually Thrilled with Life
- The Highways and Byways of Life

Emma Smith

- An Elect Lady

Endurance

- Endure to The End
- Enduring to The End
- I Have Fought a Good Fight (2 Timothy 4:7)
- Spiritual Calisthenics
- The Highways and Byways of Life
- The Martyr's Mirror
- The Parable of The Hiawatha Trail
- The Seven Deadly Sins
- This is a New Day

Environment

- God Goes Green

Eternal Progression

- A Coat of Many Colors
- Connections
- Entropy in The Physical World
- Eternal Progression in a Dynamic Universe
- We are Foreordained to Greatness

Evil

- Combating Evil
- Detecting Satan's Fingerprints
- Lucifer
- May the 4th Be With You
- Satan
- Spiritual Identity Theft
- The Seven Deadly Sins
- Travel at The Speed of Dark
- Wickedness Never Was Happiness
- Zion Versus Babylon

Example

- Orson Pratt: A Son of God (D&C 34)

- The Ablest Mariner
- The Lord's Touchstone
- The Martyr's Mirror
- Then The Pig Got Up and Slowly Walked Away

Excellence

- A Standard of Excellence
- Good, Better, and Best
- Experiencing the Highways and Byways of Life
- Spiritual Calisthenics
- This is a New Day
- Twenty-five Qualities of High Achievers

Faith

- Alma's Discourse on Faith
- Faith is a Principle of Power
- Faith is Like a Screw
- Faith, Hope, and Charity
- Faith, Knowledge, and Education

Family

- I am a Child of God
- In Defense of The Family
- Marriage and Family are Ordained of God
- Our Family Constitution

Fasting

- Fasting: a Principle of Perfection

Feet

- The Thrill of Victory / The Agony of DeFeet

Focus

- Being Well-Grounded
- Choose ye This Day
- Construction Zone: Proceed with Caution
- Focus
- Focusing on The Important Things
- May the 4th Be With You
- The Martyr's Mirror
- This is a New Day
- Twenty-five Qualities of High Achievers

Forgiveness

- Father, Forgive Them
- The Door Swings Both Ways
- The Martyr's Mirror
- The Secret Garden
- The Third Part
- To Err is Human, To Forgive is Divine

Friendship

- Connections
- A Letter to a Nonmember Friend
- Friendship
- Our Neighbors

Gathering

- Blood, Covenant, and Land Israel
- Covenant Consciousness
- Strangers in The Land
- The Gathering
- The Lost Ten Tribes
- The Twelve Tribes of Israel

Goals

- Goal Setting
- Spiritual Calisthenics
- This is a New Day
- Twenty-five Qualities of High Achievers

Good and Evil

- May the 4th Be With You
- Finding Balance in our Lives
- The Seven Deadly Sins
- Up/Down
- Wickedness Never Was Happiness

Gospel

- An American Gospel
- Embrace The gospel
- Establishing the Word
- Living Water
- The Lord's Patient Protection and Affordable Healthcare Act

- The New American Bible: Uninspired Version
- The New and Everlasting Covenant (D&C 22)

Grace

- Salvation by Grace
- The Martyr's Mirror
- Thou Hast Done Wonderful Things

Gratitude

- Gratitude is an Attitude
- I am a Child of God
- Pennies from Heaven
- Sixty Five Ways to Express Gratitude

Happiness

- Happiness and Sharing The gospel
- Keep Smiling
- What is Happiness?
- Why is Happiness so Elusive?
- Wickedness Never Was Happiness

Heaven

- Heaven Can Wait
- Is Heaven Hotter Than Hell?
- Up/Down

History

- Let a History be Kept (D&C 47)
- The Parable of The Pencil

Holy Ghost

- Batteries are Not Included
- Management by The Spirit
- The Holy Ghost
- The Holy Ghost: Getting to Know Him

Honesty

- Let Me Be Perfectly Honest

Humility

- Pride
- The Dust of The Earth
- The Seven Deadly Sins
- We Ask Thee in Humility
- Wo Unto You Hypocrites

Improvement

- A Coat of Many Colors
- Choose the Harder Right
- Construction Zone: Proceed with Caution
- Our Limiting Beliefs
- Spiritual Calisthenics
- The Highways and Byways of Life
- The Lord's Patient Protection and Affordable Healthcare Act
- The Seven Deadly Sins
- This is a New Day
- Twenty-five Qualities of High Achievers
- Updates are Ready
- We are Foreordained to Greatness

Isaiah

- The Isaiah Chapters in The Book of Mormon

Israel

- Blood, Covenant, and Land Israel
- Covenant Consciousness
- Strangers in The Land
- The Gathering
- The Lost Ten Tribes
- The Twelve Tribes of Israel

Joseph Smith

- In Defense of The Prophet Joseph Smith
- Joseph Smith History
- Joseph Smith's History
- Joseph Smith's World
- The Lord's Prophet
- The Mantle of The Prophet
- The Prophet Joseph Smith
- The Prophet Joseph Smith: The Third of the Three Pillars of Testimony
- The Year Without Summer

Journal

- The Parable of The Pencil

Justice

- Cherubim and a Flaming Sword
- Do Justice and Love Mercy
- Justice and Mercy (Alma 42)
- The Last Judgment
- The Third Part

Kindness

- Benevolent Blindness
- Speak Kind Words to Each Other
- The Lord's Touchstone
- The Martyr's Mirror

Knowledge

- I am a Child of God
- The Circle of Knowledge

Language

- What Did He Just Say?

Last Days

- Blood, Covenant, and Land Israel
- The Church in The Last Days
- The Twelve Tribes of Israel

Laughter

- Keep Smiling
- Why Do We Laugh?

Labels

- A Coat of Many Colors
- Blood, Covenant, and Land Israel
- Putting Labels on Others

Leadership

- Bosses and Leaders

Life

- Are Life and Death Mutually Exclusive?
- Life is Like a Game of Racquetball
- Life's Greatest Questions
- Life Support and Decisions (Life's Important Decisions)
- The Highways and Byways of Life
- The Purpose of Life
- The Seven Deadly Sins
- Well, That's Life

Light

- God's Tactical Flashlight
- Light
- Light and Darkness
- Light and Truth
- May the 4th Be With You
- The Light of the World
- Walk in the Light

Marriage

- Celestial Marriage and Eternal Families
- Marriage and Family are Ordained of God
- Marriage is Ordained of God
- Sealed for Time and All Eternity
- So You're Getting Married

Mercy

- Cherubim and a Flaming Sword
- Do Justice and Love Mercy
- Justice and Mercy (Alma 42)
- The Martyr's Mirror
- The Third Part

Millennium

- Blood, Covenant, and Land Israel
- The Millennium
- The Twelve Tribes of Israel

Mission Statement

- A Personal Mission Statement

Missionary Work

- Conversion
- Establishing the Word
- Happiness and Sharing The gospel
- Missionary Work: Our Greatest Call
- No Greater Call
- Open Your Gates To The gospel (D&C 32)
- Sharing the gospel
- Swiss Chocolate
- We Talk of Christ
- What About The Mormons? (D&C 45)
- What Qualifies Us For The Work? (D&C 4)

Morality

- Abstinence in a Permissive World
- Chastity Amid Permissiveness
- The Seven Deadly Sins

Mother

- Mothers in Zion

Multi-tasking

- Finding Balance in Our Lives
- Multi-tasking
- This is a New Day

Music

- Worship in Music

Nature

- Our Eternal Nature
- We are Foreordained to Greatness

Obedience

- Construction Zone: Proceed with Caution
- Do We Dye Our Skins?
- How Then Can I Do This Great Wickedness?
- I Have Fought a Good Fight (2 Timothy 4:7)
- I Will Obey – James Covill (D&C 39)
- Navigating on The Snake
- Obedience is The First Law of Heaven

- The Hourglass of Life
- The Seven Deadly Sins
- What's In It For Me?

Opportunity

- Heaven Can Wait
- The Hourglass of Opportunity

Opposition

- A Coat of Many Colors
- Agency and Opposition
- Huckleberries and Chokeberries
- I Have Fought a Good Fight (2 Timothy 4:7)
- Lamanites by The Waters of Sebus (Alma 17:37)
- May the 4th Be With You
- The Priests of Baal in our Lives
- Spiritual Identity Theft
- The Seven Deadly Sins
- This is a New Day
- Zion Versus Babylon

Perseverance

- Just Get Back on The Bible
- Spiritual Calisthenics
- The Highways and Byways of Life
- The Parable of The Hiawatha Trail
- This is a New Day
- Twenty-five Qualities of High Achievers
- We are Foreordained to Greatness

Pioneers

- Pioneer Day Perspectives
- The Martyr's Mirror

Plan of Salvation

- Connections
- Life is a Three-Act Play
- Life is Like a Game of Racquetball
- Life's Greatest Questions
- The Fall
- The Germination of our Faith
- The Holy Grail of Religious Doctrine

- The Lord's Patient Protection and Affordable Health Care Act
- The Plan of Salvation
- The Plan of Salvation (V. 6)
- The Plan of Salvation: 15 Names
- The Purpose of Life
- The Third Part
- The Isaiah Chapters in The Book of Mormon
- The Little Princess

Potential

- Connections
- May the 4th Be With You
- The Little Princess
- The Unknown Possibilities of Existence

Prayer

- A Primer on Deity

Pre-Earth Life

- I am a Child of God
- Life is a Three-Act Play
- Life's Greatest Questions
- Pre-mortal Life
- We Lived Before We Were Born

Preparation

- Preparation
- Proper Prior Preparation Prevents Poor Priesthood Performance
- Snowbiking Through Life
- Who is Packing Your Parachute?

Priesthood

- General Conference: The SuperBowl of Spiritual Symposia
- Having Been Commissioned of Jesus Christ (D&C 22)
- Priesthood Keys
- The Mantle of the Prophet

Professors

- Commitment
- Professors
- The Martyr's Mirror

Prophecy

- Blood, Covenant, and Land Israel
- The Voice of Prophetic Warning

Prophet

- Follow The Prophet

Public Speaking

- The Recipe for a Successful Church Address

Questions

- Tough Questions (Alma 5)

Renewal

- The Springtime of The Year

Repentance

- Before a Wound Can Heal
- Removing The Barnacles of Life
- The Biggest Loser
- The Door Swing Both Ways
- The Secret Garden
- To Err is Human, To Forgive is Divine

Restoration

- Blood, Covenant, and Land Israel
- Christ's Church is Restored
- God is NowHere
- The Church Has Been Restored
- The Desert Shall Rejoice
- The New American Bible: Uninspired Version
- The Twelve Tribes of Israel
- William Tyndale: An Appreciation

Resurrection

- What Does Down Must Go Up

Revelation

- A Primer on Personal Revelation
- Fayette, New York: The Last Revelation (D&C 38)
- Obtaining the Spirit of Revelation
- Receiving Revelation (D&C 8)
- Revelation
- The First Revelation (D&C 2)
- The Heavens Were Opened
- The Manifestation of Spirits (D&C 50)
- The New American Bible: Uninspired Version
- The Order of Revelation (D&C 28)
- Thoughts of Kolob
- You Took No Thought Save to Ask

Reverence

- Reverence

Sabbath

- The Sabbath

Sacrament

- Sacramental Waters
- The Sacrament
- The Sacrament (V. 6)

Satan

- Combating Evil
- Detecting Satan's Fingerprints
- Satan
- The Seven Deadly Sins
- Travel at The Speed of Dark
- Wickedness Never Was Happiness

Scholarship

- You Took No Thought Save to Ask

Scripture

- Blood, Covenant, and Land Israel
- Lest We Forget
- Lost Books of the Bible
- Missing Scripture

- Parallelism in Hebrew Poetry
- Sharper Than a Two-edged Sword (D&C 33)
- Similitudes in Hosea
- Studying The Scriptures
- Symbolism in The Scriptures
- Teachings of The Minor Prophets
- The Bible and Other Scripture
- The Bible: Basic Information Before Leaving Earth
- The Isaiah Chapters in The Book of Mormon
- The New American Bible: Uninspired Version
- Wresting The Scriptures
- Writing on Metal Plates Was a Pain

Second Coming

- The Second Coming

Seraphim

- Seraphim
- What About Cherubim?

Service

- The Lord's Touchstone
- We are His Hands

Set apart

- Set apart

Signs

- Blood, Covenant, and Land Israel
- Signs
- The Signs of The Times

Spirit

- Batteries are Not Included
- Jumping Out of Our Skin
- Management by The Spirit
- Spiritual Identity Theft
- Spiritual Manifestations
- The Spirit

Spirit World

- The Spirit World

Spiritual Fitness

- A Coat of Many Colors
- A Thirty-Day Spiritual Fitness Program
- Construction Zone: Proceed with Caution
- Jumping Out of Our Skin
- May the 4th Be With You
- Spiritual Calisthenics
- The Highways and Byways of Life
- The Seven Deadly Sins

Spiritual Gifts

- Gifts of The Spirit
- Pennies from Heaven
- The Bestowal of Spiritual Gifts

Spirituality

- Connections
- Spiritual Calisthenics

Success

- A Recipe for Success
- Finding Balance in Our Lives
- Success Strategies
- This is a New Day
- Twenty-five Qualities of High Achievers
- We are Foreordained to Greatness

Symbolism

- A Coat of Many Colors
- Similitudes in Hosea
- Symbols
- Symbolism in The Scriptures

Talents

- I am a Child of God
- Our Limiting Beliefs
- Our Talents

Teaching

- Teaching in The Church
- Teaching Key Doctrine

Technology

- Technological Traps

Temple

- Connections
- Sealed for Time and All Eternity
- Service in The Temple
- Temple Blessings for All Mankind
- Temple Work
- The Temple
- Tithing

Tenacity

- A Coat of Many Colors
- Choose Ye This Day
- Finding Balance in Our Lives
- I Have Fought a Good Fight (2 Timothy 4:7)
- The Highways and Byways of Life
- The Seven Deadly Sins
- Twenty-five Qualities of High Achievers
- We are Foreordained to Greatness

Testimony

- A Change of Heart
- Testimony
- The Testimony of Phil Hudson
- We Talk of Christ

Third Part

- The Third Part

Time

- Time

Tithing

- The Windows of Heaven
- Tithing

Tolerance

- Do We Dye Our Skins?

Transgression

- What I Have Lost (James Covill) (D&C 40)

Translation

- A Whirlwind into Heaven

Unity

- May the 4th Be With You
- Unity

Universe

- Are We Alone in The Universe?
- Dancing With The Stars
- Higher Dimensional Realities
- May the 4th Be With You

Walking in His Footsteps

- A Change of Heart
- The Highways and Byways of Life
- The Lord's Touchstone
- The Martyr's Mirror
- The Seven Deadly Sins
- The Thrill of Victory / The Agony of DeFeet

Weakness

- Our Weaknesses
- Spiritual Calisthenics
- Strengths and Weaknesses
- The Seven Deadly Sins
- We are Foreordained to Greatness

Wisdom

- One Hundred and One Things I've Learned
- The Word of Wisdom

Wishful Thinking

- If It Seems To Good To Be True, It Probably Is

Witnesses

- The Three Witnesses

Word of Wisdom

- The Word of Wisdom

Words

- What Did He Just Say?

Work

- Work
- Work and Personal Responsibility

Zion

- Zion
- Zion and The New Jerusalem (D&C 57)
- Zion Versus Babylon

*Frui
in via*

About the Author

Phil Hudson and Jan, his wife of 49 years, have 7 children and over 20 grandchildren. They enjoy spending time with family at their cabin nestled in the Selkirk Mountains, on the shores of Priest Lake, the crown jewel of North Idaho. Phil had a successful dental practice in Spokane, Washington for 43 years, before retiring in 2015. He has an eclectic mix of hobbies, and enjoys riding motorcycles and ATVs. In his free time, he can be found hiking, boating, cycling, snow biking, and traveling with Jan. He always finds time, however, to record his thoughts on his laptop. He understands Isaac Asimov's response when he was asked: "If you knew that you only had 10 minutes left to live, what would you do?" He answered: "I'd type faster."

Also by the Author

Essays

- Volume One: Spray from The Ocean of Thought
- Volume Two: Ripples on a Pond
- Volume Three: Serendipitous Meanderings
- Volume Four: Presents of Mind
- Volume Five: Mental Floss

Book of Mormon Commentary

- Born in The Wilderness
- Voices From the Dust
- Journey to Cumorah

Minute Musings: Spontaneous Combustions of Thought

- Volume One
- Volume Two
- Volume Three

Calendars

- In His Own Words: Discovering William Tyndale
- As I Think About the Savior
- Daily Inspiration from Scriptural Symbols

Diode Laser Soft Tissue Surgery

- Volume One
- Volume Two
- Volume Three

These, and other titles, are available from online retailers.

www.ingramcontent.com/pod-product-compliance
Lightning Source LLC
Chambersburg PA
CBHW082107280426
43661CB00090B/922